# LITERATURE AND ART
# IN THE MIDDLE AGES

# LITERATURE & ART
# IN THE MIDDLE AGES

### F. P. PICKERING

## UNIVERSITY OF MIAMI PRESS
*Coral Gables, Florida*

© F. P. Pickering 1970

Licensed edition. Original version under the title *Literatur und darstellende Kunst im Mittelalter*, © Erich Schmidt Verlag, Berlin, 1966

*Published by*
UNIVERSITY OF MIAMI PRESS

*Library of Congress catalog card no.* 79–102698

SBN 87024–152–4

*Printed in Great Britain by*
ROBERT MACLEHOSE AND CO LTD
*The University Press, Glasgow*

Again for my Wife

# CONTENTS

# LIST OF ILLUSTRATIONS

*Book cover*

Old Testament types of the Cross
Enamelled cross, by Godefroid de Claire (?), (Meuse region, twelfth century)
British Museum. (*By courtesy of the Trustees*)

*Between pages 202 and 203*

# PREFACE

THERE is a simple answer to the question why I wrote this book first in German. I was invited to do so by the general editors and the publisher of a series of handbooks covering the whole range of German studies (*Germanistik*).[1] The invitation was to show students of German literature what can be gained from a study of medieval art. I had already written a few articles on those lines. I learnt a great deal more in preparing my book, which, however, turned out to be long. Pruning and compression made it, some readers have said, difficult for students. My hope is that they will make what use of it they can in the knowledge that 'literature and art' will never be examinable.

A first draft of this English translation was completed before the German edition was fairly on the market and before any reviews had appeared. At the same time it was a revision, benefiting from numerous hints given by friends and colleagues and by the anonymous expert reader on behalf of the present publishers. In the end I was glad of the latter's insistence that I should be made to do the translation myself, little as is the pleasure it has given me at times.

No doubt many English readers would find my book more useful if in the process of translating I had lessened the weight of reference to medieval German literature and art, and to German scholarship. That would, however, have been ungracious and unscholarly. Merely to have added 'equally good' English references would have been a questionable step. (No great harm can be done in adding one to the modest number of English books on medieval themes which draw much of their evidence from German sources.) On the other hand I have been as helpful as I could with translations, whether from medieval works or modern scholarship. As for Latin quotations, I have been realistic. Where I wish to ensure that a passage is read I translate it or in some other way convey its meaning. I need hardly say that in this

[1] *Grundlagen der Germanistik*, herausgegeben von Hugo Moser, mitbegründet von Wolfgang Stammler (Erich Schmidt Verlag, Berlin): IV *Literatur und darstellende Kunst im Mittelalter* (1966).

English edition I do not assume special knowledge of medieval German literature.

It is impossible to list or classify all the further minor adjustments made to keep this translation at least as readable as the German original. Strangely, it may seem to many, this often involved writing at greater length. Complex German sentences of one's own making seem to be compact and relevant. Translating them into English one has often to spread their content, sometimes to provide links, with the inevitable result that passing thoughts intrude. Only in rare and well-signposted cases have I yielded to the temptation to elaborate my original argument.[1]

It has been brought home to me again that I have written – even in English – a difficult book. I have therefore done what I can in several revisions during the last year and a half to reduce the number of digressions and asides, to make my main arguments more readily accessible. I have made some concessions to those who prefer system to method, not however to the extent of sacrificing method. I do not provide a final bibliography of 'the subject'. There is no subject 'literature and art'. There is however an index of proper names with the help of which readers can find titles again at the point where they were relevant. There is also a table of abbreviated titles of standard works or text series and of two articles of my own to which repeated passing reference is made. Any reader seeking a comprehensive survey of work done under the general heading of themes treated in medieval literature and in art – not the purpose of this book – is recommended to consult Wolfgang Stammler's *Aufriss der deutschen Philologie,* 2nd ed. (Erich Schmidt, Berlin, 1961) III, cols. 613–98, or the article 'Literatur und bildende Kunst' by G. Bebermeyer in the *Reallexikon zur deutschen Literaturgeschichte,* ed. W. Kohlschmidt and W. Mohr, 2nd ed. (De Gruyter, Berlin, 1955) II 82–103. My aim, particularly in Chapters III and IV, was to offer as thorough an introduction as I can in areas where I think I can see interrelations between literature and art as they were seen in the Middle Ages. Elsewhere, where I have made no special investigations and have nothing new to contribute, I give guidance to the studies which others have made. Chapter I of Part Two chronicles

---

[1] It should particularly not be inferred from the simpler title that the scope of the book has been enlarged. I consider virtually only 'representational' art (*darstellende Kunst*), but the term is not sufficiently familiar – and alternatives (visual arts, for instance) present their own difficulties.

an attempt to come to terms with the basic problem of meaning where both words and pictures are involved, that is where two traditions intersect. I still have mixed feelings about submitting so frank an account to public scrutiny, and have more than once thought of cancelling the chapter, but I have allowed it to stand. In it and in my Introductory Survey I have also taken considerable risks, revealing *inter alia* the extent to which I am distrustful of organised scholarship. I also accept the fact that as a pedagogue I make embarrassingly simple statements when I think methodical exposition requires them.

My thanks are due to colleagues whose subject is art history proper, particularly – over a long period – to members of the Warburg Institute. More recently I have in addition enjoyed the enthusiastic collaboration of James Marrow, Research Fellow since October 1967 at the University of Reading. His phenomenal learning and methodical industry, both in art history and the study of medieval devotional literature, have led to the revival of my interest in some topics which had more or less exhausted me and of which I appear to take my leave (see particularly the concluding remarks to Chapter IV, the true date of which is 1966–7). Any further contributions of mine, however, will more usefully be passed on for incorporation in James Marrow's own accounts of the devotional art and literature of the Low Countries in the fifteenth century. Here I wish particularly to acknowledge his assistance in the final stages of this present work. For the rest, for typing, re-typing, and for general pilotage through the floodwaters of administration I again have to thank Mrs Marga Black, Secretary of the German Department, University of Reading. This is her fourth book in six years. I am also grateful to Frau Dr Ellinor Kahleyss, head of the Erich Schmidt publishing house in Berlin, for agreeing to what was to have been an almost immediate translation into English of the work which with exemplary patience she first saw through the press in the period 1964–6.

My thanks are due to the following, who have kindly helped me to secure photographs for reproduction in this book (see also the List of Illustrations): the Librarian, Burgerbibliothek, Bern; the Directors, Herzog Anton-Ulrich Museum, Braunschweig, Kunsthalle, Bremen, Museum of Fine Arts, Budapest; the Master and Fellows of Corpus Christi College, Cambridge; the Director, Wallraf-Richartz Museum, Cologne; the Director, Hessische Landes- und Hochschulbibliothek, Darmstadt; the Hon. Librarian, the Chester Beatty Library, Dublin;

the Librarian, Dean and Chapter Library, Durham; the Director, University Library, Erlangen; the Librarian, Chorherrenstift St Florian (St Florian bei Linz, Austria); the Librarian, Stiftsbibliothek, St Gallen (Switzerland); the Librarian, Staats- und Universitätsbibliothek, Hamburg; the Director, Kärntner Landesarchiv, Klagenfurt; the Trustees of the British Museum, the Director, Courtauld Institute of Art, the Trustees of the National Gallery, the Director, Warburg Institute, London; the Librarian, the John Rylands Library, Manchester; the Director, Bayerische Staatsbibliothek, the Librarian, University Library, Munich; the Trustees of the Pierpont Morgan Library, New York; the Warden and Fellows of All Souls College, the President and Fellows of Corpus Christi College, Oxford; Service Photographique of the Bibliothèque Nationale, Archives Photographiques of the Caisse Nationale des Monuments Historiques, Paris; the Directors of the Württembergische Landesbibliothek, Stuttgart; the Librarian, Stadtbibliothek, Trier; the Director, Mainfränkisches Museum, Würzburg; also the photographic agencies Foto Marburg, Éditions Gallimard, Giraudon, Mansell Collection, Photo Alinari.

# ABBREVIATIONS AND SHORT TITLES

*Aufriss: Deutsche Philologie im Aufriss*, ed. Wolfgang Stammler, 3 vols, 2nd ed. (Berlin, 1961).

Beckwith: John Beckwith, *Early Medieval Art, Carolingian, Ottonian, Romanesque* (World of Art Library: History of Art): Thames & Hudson (London, 1964).

'Christlicher Erzählstoff': 'Christlicher Erzählstoff bei Otfrid und im Heliand', in *Zeitschrift für deutsches Altertum*, LXXXV (1955) 262–91.

'Christusbild': 'Das gotische Christusbild. Zu den Quellen mittelalterlicher Passionsdarstellungen', in *Euphorion*, XLVII (1953) 16–37.

de Boor: Helmut de Boor and Richard Newald, *Geschichte der deutschen Literatur von den Anfängen bis zur Gegenwart*, vols I and II, 2nd to 7th eds (Munich, 1955–66).

DTM: Deutsche Texte des Mittelalters (Preussische, now Deutsche Akademie der Wissenschaften), Akademieverlag (Berlin, 1904– ).

*DVJSchr.*: *Deutsche Vierteljahrsschrift für Literaturwissenschaft und Geistesgeschichte* (Halle, 1923– ; Stuttgart, 1949– ).

EETS: Early English Text Society.

Ehrismann: Gustav Ehrismann, *Geschichte der deutschen Literatur bis zum Ausgang des Mittelalters* (Handbuch des deutschen Unterrichts), 2nd ed. in 4 vols (Munich, 1932–5).

*Geschichtsdenken*: *Geschichtsdenken und Geschichtsbild im Mittelalter. Ausgewählte Aufsätze und Arbeiten aus den Jahren 1933–59,* ed. Walther Lammers (Wege der Forschung XXI), Wissenschaftliche Buchgesellschaft (Darmstadt, 1961).

GLL: *German Life and Letters* (Oxford, 1947– ).

*Das erste Jahrtausend*: *Das erste Jahrtausend. Kultur und Kunst im werdenden Abendland an Rhein und Ruhr*, ed. Victor H. Elbern, 3 vols, volume of plates = vol. I (Düsseldorf, 1962).

*JW(C)I*: *Journal of the Warburg (and Courtauld) Institute(s)*.

L: *Dürerzeichnungen nach Lippmanns Verzeichnis*, 7 vols (Berlin, 1883– ).

Lexer: *Mittelhochdeutsches Handwörterbuch*, by Matthias Lexer, 3 vols (Leipzig, 1872–8).

*MGH*: *Monumenta Germaniæ Historica* (Hanover, 1826– ).

*MLR*: *Modern Language Review*.

*PL*: J. P. Migne, *Patrologiæ cursus completus, Series Latina* (Paris, 1844– ).

Schwietering: Julius Schwietering, *Deutsche Dichtung des Mittelalters* (Handbuch der Literaturwissenschaft), 2nd ed (Darmstadt, 1957).

*RDK*: *Reallexikon zur deutschen Kunstgeschichte*, begun by Otto Schmitt, ed. Ernst Gall and L. H. Heydenreich, in progress (Stuttgart, 1937– ).

PART ONE

# INTRODUCTORY SURVEY

*Philosopher æstheticians are admirably trained against talking
nonsense; but there is no security that they will know what they
are talking about*

R. G. COLLINGWOOD, *The Principles of Art* (1938) Introduction


## 1. A GENERAL AESTHETIC THEORY
## FOR ALL THE ARTS?

THE study of literature and the study of art are neighbouring disciplines,
but they remain separate. This is not a consequence of 'specialisation'.
It is the reflection of a difference between the works which are studied
in each case. In this Introductory Survey we shall be mainly concerned
with differences – between poets and artists, their works, and the
disciplines devoted to their study. Later, when we are comparing the
treatment of certain themes in works of literature and of representational
art in the Middle Ages, we shall not lose sight of the fact that a poem is
always a poem and a picture a picture.[1] No amount of talk about the
poet's vision or the artist's or sculptor's message can bridge the gap
except at its own level – that of talk. Before we go into any such details
it will be as well to recall why we are evidently reluctant to accept
this situation.

'Fundamentally there ought to be', we seem to persist in saying, a
branch of study devoted to all the principal arts in a given period –
poetry, song and instrumental music, architecture, the plastic and other
arts. German writers would probably extend this list to include
philosophy and even theology. We would prefer to regard the demar-
cation lines drawn by the Muses as (like themselves) mythical, the
fictions of a mentality simpler than our own, and hope some day to see
and understand all the arts as manifestations of the spirit of their age. Or
at a lower, academic level we think it should be possible to work out a
system of common *terms* for the discussion and analysis of works of
several, if not all kinds; and by abstraction and generalisation to work
our way forward to a comprehensive aesthetic theory. At the same
time we sense that such a theory could never be usefully applied, and
that any systematic approach to artists and their works is bound to fail.

[1] There are a number of hybrids about which it is too soon to talk, e.g. historiated initials, rebus pictures, etc.

3

The poets and the artists will always elude the pursuit of academics and their systems.

This does not mean that there is no way at all of examining literature and the neighbouring arts at the same time, and of writing of them as mysteriously, or perhaps inevitably harmonious expressions of the spirit of their age. I mean merely that this is not the task of any academic discipline. It can only be the work of a poet – a poet reflecting, or, as Schiller called it, thinking and writing 'sentimentally'[1] and formulating his reflections on the office of the poet and other artists, and the modes of expression available to each. Any poet-theoretician will, however, invariably use terms lacking logical precision, and they will not be acceptable to the academic. Academics translating Schiller have discovered to their discomfort how few of his key-words are fixed terms; they take colour from their surroundings and must always be referred back to their context. Whether Schiller's aesthetic theory is complete in itself is not for us to discuss here. We cannot use it, or anything like it for the purposes of scholarly enquiry. We have difficulty in following his own use of it, for instance when he assigns German and other poets to one of his categories 'naïve' or 'sentimental'. The most we can do is to seek to master his theory as a work in its own right, and admire it for its high idealism. It has not been found wanting or superseded (like Lessing's *Laocoön*), but for various reasons it has not been 'successful'. Schiller's principles established no prescriptive laws for the poets or other artists; they have not helped critics or scholars in their tasks of analysis and interpretation. For practical purposes we need something simpler and more systematic, and dissatisfaction with the separation of our disciplines remains.

## 2. THE DISCUSSION OF WORKS
## OF LITERATURE AND OF ART

A *Discursive Enquiry*

We are of course still far from an answer to our question why the notion persists that a general theory must somehow emerge, as a synthesis of our reflections on the various arts. This hope is nourished by the very activity of talking about the arts; not only when we compare

---

[1] *Über naive und sentimentalische Dichtung* (1800).

them, but even when we profess to keep to works of one kind, casting only occasional glances at the others.

The phraseology of simple response to a poem or painting is soon exhausted, trite. From the moment we decide to go on, we become discursive. We analyse and expound the poem (or the painting) in a series of more or less orderly statements. The terms we use reflect our experience and training; they already have the authority of a tradition of discussion, or we seek authority for them. We may continue to stare hard at the work, but we none the less set it somewhat to one side so that we may speak more freely of it and be reminded of other things – all from a point of view, in cautious formulations, or more rhetorically, perhaps even with passionate conviction; or to persuade or teach someone else. In the process we repeatedly cite the work, or point to it if it is a picture, or handle it. Perhaps to reassure ourselves that we still have it under proper consideration, but in the main to invoke the work's support of our disquisition on it. We make the poet or painter our witness that we understand his intention and represent him correctly – in our own 'secondary' work in neutral prose.

It is we who have meantime been at work, observing the conventions of discourse, or perhaps more accurately those of the tribunal. The work we have examined has itself been silent (statue or painting), or it has had to speak with the inflexions we think appropriate (poem). A listener may help us out or along with an apt formulation without committing himself to agreement. He is perhaps quicker to sum up and repeat to us what we have said, with a judicious correction of emphasis which we accept, with or without comment.

Not every discussion of a poem or a painting runs as smoothly, or as short a course, as these simple reminders suggest. To take only the extreme cases, it may lead to the writing of an essay which acquires an authority lasting for a decade or more; it may equally well start off an unprofitable controversy, the work itself having done little more than provoke and prolong the discussion. There is no doubt that whatever the outcome, the work has – by this attention devoted to it – become better known, and the terms and formulations used will enjoy a certain currency. They will generally have to be at least ritually repeated before they can be replaced by others. There may, if there has been dispute, be a general reluctance for a time to resume the discussion at all; it would be tedious. The work itself is for a while 'better not discussed'.

By now we have followed this line of argument far enough. The aim was to recall that there exists beside any notable work of literature or art a corpus of prose lore concerning it. In theory it should be possible to ignore it; in practice it is not. And now to look at some of the complications when medieval works are involved. (The purpose of these preliminary remarks will soon become clear.) The works of literature and of art of remoter centuries first come to our attention in the prose transposition of some authority or expert. Take for instance Wolfram von Eschenbach's grail romance, *Parzival*, some thirty thousand lines of difficult medieval German, but known – where it is known at all – to be the greatest and profoundest work in any Western language in its day (say 1200). *Parzival* is in fact accessible to new readers only by courtesy of professors of German in their lectures or handbooks, or through translations (in the conventional sense) 'with Foreword' in some kind of Everyman library. For some, but relatively few, newcomers to Wolfram there is – later – the possibility of an actual reading of the text itself, first of all the famous passages, annotated and glossed. This reading is in practice an inadequate performance overshadowed by consciousness of a weighty tradition of Wolfram interpretation. So matters remain for the majority of readers. I do not suggest for a moment that the traditional treatment of the *theme* 'Wolfram's *Parzival*' is dull or without value. I merely repeat that we encounter it first, and imply that any 'intention' which Wolfram may have had in writing his monumental work is virtually powerless in face of the coherent and persuasive, and no doubt correct statements which the experts have made concerning that intention. (They can illustrate or prove these by quotations, phalanxes of line-references, word-counts and structural diagrams.) In another context than this book one would say that the newcomer becomes acquainted with the present state of Wolfram scholarship; he becomes an informed reader. My purpose here is to suggest that he is introduced to a system of terms and formulations for the discussion of Wolfram. They may not be sacrosanct, but they are sanctioned. They are held to be appropriate.

Modern interpreters of medieval works will of course claim to be fully aware of their modes of operation. They will, however, also claim that they are being objective and that their observations are based on evidence – when they describe works, make their comparisons or discriminate. None the less they interpose essays of their own, in which formulations stand substitute for the ideas, the ideals and the moods of poets. These formulations mediate (see below). They mediate by the very fact that they are in each case designed to bring the work nearer to us today. They are therefore not medieval, nor are they modern, but historical, for at the same time as they appeal to us they refer the poet, or his treatment of his subject (or his ideal of chivalry or his religious sentiments) to the Middle Ages as they are seen by the expounder. This means in the nature of things that the literary historian, while 'keeping to literature' will often be tempted to enliven his story by direct or sidelong reference to the historical essays of experts in other fields – the other arts, historiography itself. His readers or hearers may find this interesting and illuminating, or tiresome and mistaken – instinctive reactions. In the following sections we shall consider some of the pitfalls into which we may be led by too ready an acceptance of current terms: the terms thrown up by the mere activity of talking and writing about works.

### B  *Comparison: Mediation*

The moment we begin to talk discursively about two or more works (let us think first of works of one kind) in order that we may compare and contrast them, we begin to use either mediating or discriminating terms. Let us single out comparison. Comparison involves the choice of – or makes us have recourse to – convenient middle terms. One literary genre may 'sing' or 'say' this or that; another will say that this or that was so, or happened thus. Works in different genres (ode, essay) will, however, have at least some *theme* in common, if they can be compared at all. In comparing them we then seek the middle term of 'treatment', and so avoid reference to the modality of either genre. Differences of genre or indeed of medium can, by our choice of terms, be excluded from the discussion of 'treatment of theme'. The treatment is 'of course' different – in the long poem in rhyming couplets on the one hand and in the engraving or woodcut in the other. Meantime our disquisition itself is in the same medium (language) as the poem, but in a different genre, and in a medium completely distinct from that of the engraving, when we compare, say, two treatments of the Rape of Lucrece. We translate each work into the only accessible neutral genre of the prose work 'on' the treatment, and in this genre we make our statements concerning the two treatments. We may, and inevitably do return to the poem or the picture to adduce or cite it – to recite a line or two, or to show a lantern slide. It is, however, the comparison of our *statements* which demands and gets the main attention – ours and that of our audience. The works themselves are reduced to evidence.

No terms are more suspect than those resulting from endeavours to mediate between different arts – to mediate, so to speak, between the media. Every critical reader is aware of the dangers of giving such terms even a hearing. Our instinct is to reject them; and yet we tolerate them, many of them. We are willing to be tempted. Looking a little closer now:

The discourse of the comparatist must mediate: in terms moreover which are unstable in their meaning, poised at varying referential distances from the objects compared. Having chosen them with initial concern for one of the objects to be compared, the comparatist extends their meaning metaphorically to embrace the other. Or he borrows a term from the area of a third art, often architecture or music (but rarely music in medieval studies) and extends it in two directions, so that it may be applied simultaneously in the discussion of, say, a poem *and* a mural painting. The intention in the choice of such a term is obvious, and we cannot fail to notice what is being done, but we await the outcome. From instance to instance we may be impressed (entertained, irritated) by the aptness (quaintness, effrontery) of a comparison made in this way. Generally we are disposed to be charitable. The criterion is 'acceptability'.

What we are now apparently asking is (*a*) what generalisations of the comparatists are acceptable (and acceptable to whom)?; and (*b*) what do we get in return for giving them a hearing? By the time the reader has got to the end of this book he will probably have forgotten that I asked these questions. He will see that I am myself reluctant to use the available mediating generalisations.

It is indeed by now clear that one of my main preoccupations is the terms (the words) in which we discuss works of literature and works in the other arts, if and when we choose to consider them together. The danger is that we may be trapped into accepting linguistic fictions and so stray into an 'as if' aesthetic. The best safeguard is for each of us to remain more or less strictly technical, allowing language no other function than to name or *state* things and facts as they are or occur in each art, enlivening our dryasdust accounts only by a transparently figurative use of language, as in the following example:

'Simplicity was combined with monumental size at Speyer I. As at Limburg, the only exterior ordering elements were pilaster strips with corbel friezes and arched window openings. The interior too was restrained: nave and clerestory wall on square piers, articulated by blind arcades on shaft-like engaged columns; side aisles with groin vaults; the nave unvaulted; cubic capitals throughout. Norman architecture in the Age of William the Conqueror, *while working with a somewhat different vocabulary, arrived at a language of similar clarity*, simplicity and forcefulness . . . Mont-Saint-Michel, about 1060 [the author returns immediately to his discussion of architecture] . . .[1]

The use of 'vocabulary' and 'language' in this passage on architecture does not disturb me in the least. What I should find disquieting would be a systematic comparison of the 'articulation of Speyer I' with the *syntax* of Latin prose at the time of the Norman conquest, or the *versification* and musical structure of lyrics or hymns composed at that time. This would be 'reciprocal illumination' according to the approved Wölfflin formula, but what real validity can terms have which cover both 'articulation' (already remote enough from architecture) and syntactical or verse structures?

Equally, no great risk is involved when terms appropriate to the discussion of one art are systematically used in a 'sustained figure' for the analysis of works in another medium, for instance musical terms to describe a painting. The danger lies not in patently rhetorical devices of this kind, but in the discovery or invention of neutral terms which through 'effective' use acquire the status of generalisations. A few of them we must undoubtedly allow if comparisons are to be made at all, and a synonym or two will always be acceptable; but word magic and convenient ambiguity begin when terms are devised to suppress reference to time, space, movement or materials.

Everyone is aware of the confusion surrounding the term 'form' – noun and verb. German has in addition *Gestalt* (which nowadays appears untranslated in the terminologies of several disciplines quite unrelated to the arts), with its verb *gestalten*; and this in turn, with the ubiquitous suffix *-ung* gives *Gestaltung* as a *nomen actionis*. Let us look for a moment at the latter when it has entered into further composition with *Raum*, itself meaning (*a*) 'space' and (*b*) 'an enclosed space'.

*Raumgestaltung*, literally 'space moulding', can be used (I accept the facts of current practice) to describe the activity of the narrative poet

[1] Howard Sealman, *Medieval Architecture, European Architecture 600–1200* (London and New York, 1962) sect. 28.

*and* the draughtsman, neither of whom makes any use of space, or moulds or shapes it in any real sense. Indeed one has to think hard whether there is any artist who moulds space, and comes to the conclusion that the activity is a fiction ascribable to the ambiguity of the word *Raum*, or the ingenuity of writers intent on bridging the gaps between the arts and assisting them to a reciprocal illumination.

1. *Raum* means 'space', 'a space' or what encloses a space – a hall or room. In what way then does the architect (the only artist who has a vague claim to be considered) 'mould' space? In German one can say that he forms or moulds (instead of 'builds') a 'space', which in this case is surely the building. To pretend that he takes space in his hands as a potter takes a lump of clay is scarcely acceptable. From the somewhat primitive activity of laying hands on stones or bricks the critic dissociates the architect and his men by a linguistic device, substituting a near-synonym for 'build' and introducing by metonymy 'space' for building ('contained for container'). In so doing he substitutes a linguistic fiction for a valid statement. But it is, as we said, now available to critics writing in German as a middle term for comparisons made between any pair of 'moulders'.

2. A draughtsman traces on his block the outline of an area, divides it up with further strokes and shades or washes some of the areas which result. Conventions of representation and recognition make us willing, perhaps because we are more interested in his 'figures' than in his spaces, to supplement his efforts and ignore 'contradictions' in his treatment of spatial relationships. To our reasonable satisfaction the artist has represented figures at rest or in motion in three-dimensional space, and we recognise his treatment of a subject known to us from tradition – perhaps the *Rape of Lucrece* again. We may refer to his *Raumgestaltung* as being thus or thus – perhaps even realistic, meaning illusionistic.

3. To take a special case, Wolfram von Eschenbach is said by modern interpreters to have presented a world-picture in his *Parzival*, with the court of King Arthur occupying an area in the middle distance. In the background is the realm of the kings and knights of the Grail. This is all conventional enough, and convenient. It has always been possible to speak of the narrator's imagined world, its atmosphere – perhaps, too, its foreground and background, as though the poet were a painter. Wolfram in fact does more than most narrative poets to ensure that we see his world 'in depth'. The journeys of Gahmuret, Parzival's father, in books I and II have already mapped out the Mediterranean and the

Angevin worlds before Parzival is born into the latter. Those of Parzival – from book III to the end (book XVI) – are measured by day or night journeys, to and away from reference points just this side of, or just beyond the confines of the familiar worlds of fact and of Arthurian fiction.[1] Of all these things we may write under the heading 'Wolfram's *Raumgestaltung*'.

When, however, writers begin to think of the contours of the *story* and the symmetry and proportions of the text as it is written on the parchment of the manuscripts, and when they compare the black and white colour symbolism of the prologue and the clair-obscure of man's situation generally – and Parzival's religious crisis in particular – our suspicions surely begin to be aroused. We know that we are soon to be asked to accept *Parzival* as 'late romanesque' or 'early gothic' in structure and style, and to agree that this is a fruitful 'reciprocal illumination of the arts'. Mediating terms like *Raumgestaltung* enable us, if we are willing, to see Wolfram's *Parzival* as something which merely happens to be a narrative poem. Before the reader is aware of it, the structuralist has drawn him the ideal shape of Wolfram's *Parzival*, which, as we have had it presented to us in a fair number of monographs or articles since the War, is remarkably like the ground-plan of a cathedral with nave and transepts, but no crypt or spire. When other critics, surveying the whole artistic production of the high Middle Ages, have claimed to recognise a characteristic *Formwille*, the expression of a *Seinsstruktur* (an aesthetic will expressing medieval existence in characteristic form), I have to ask, not I trust on behalf of myself alone, whether language has not taken over more or less completely.

So far I have been making reservations – perhaps those of the inveterate philologist, whose principal task is critical scrutiny of language in use, not least the language of his colleagues. But there are other virtues than caution, and for my part, so long as I am convinced that the bolder theories and structures of modern interpreters are true projections of findings and insights, or an enthusiastic cadenza rounding off a technically correct and professionally conducted piece of work with a flourish, I shall, like any reasonable contemporary, give them a careful hearing. They are evidence of our endeavours to understand the

---

[1] See articles by Marianne Wynn, 'Geography of Fact and Fiction in Wolfram von Eschenbach's *Parzival*', in *MLR* LVI (1961) 28–43, and 'Scenery and Chivalrous Journeys', in *Speculum*, XXXVI (1961) 393–423.

Middle Ages. They may (in the sense of Faust's words to his famulus Wagner)[1] throw more light on our own age than on the age they claim to illuminate, but even so. . . .

c *Essays in Synthesis*

In the last section we spoke of the mediation of discursive analysis. There is an element of mediation when even a single work is interpreted. Proceeding next to the methods of the comparatist we took *Raumgestaltung* as an example of terms strictly applicable to no known art, yet now widely used for the analysis of several arts, and for the making of comparisons. *Raumgestaltung* is neither a true abstraction nor a common denominator. It is a figment of language, a neutral, noncommittal term with possibly some positive but surely more negative features – evasion, retreat from the reality of works. Nothing more can be said with assurance about *Raumgestaltung* than that it is a compound abstract noun which has been formed and used 'successfully'. Its meaning is not stable but circles about an imagined centre. With its help we can (vaguely) visualize space-moulders at work.

The critic who elects to use this and similar terms is making use of the resources (and the resourcefulness) of language. He is entitled to do so in the execution of a secondary work. If in so doing he can convince himself of a similarity between Wolfram's narrative and the work of a contemporary artist[2] or the conceptions of an architect, he has indeed reached the point where he may propose to call *Parzival* 'late romanesque' or 'early gothic', and to find in it a characteristic spirituality. We should surely be interested in such a proposal. This particular one and several like it (suggested for other poets) have, however, failed to convince. Though we still feel there must be affinities between a massive literary composition in sixteen books and a major work of architecture, we cannot yet agree what should be the terms of the comparison. We must continue to be grateful to scholars who seek formulations which shall seem strikingly true and apt when used of Wolfram and at least illuminating when applied to the arts with which

[1] *Faust*, part I (opening scene, *Nacht*, 575 ff): Was ihr den Geist der Zeiten heisst,/Das ist im Grund der Herren eigner Geist.

[2] 'Contemporary artist'. I write at this stage as though drawing and painting present no particular problems of chronology. See section 5 (c) below, on drawing as the 'latest' of the arts and the one most likely to trail behind or stagnate.

we are less conversant. Any formulations offered must, however, command respect and not be mere neologisms of an interdisciplinary *lingua franca*.

To come back for a moment to the long narrative poem. Any discussion must be suspect which begins by translating the poem's themes into problems, perhaps under the heading 'problematics' (some languages allow this abstraction). The résumés and prose paraphrases in twentieth-century works are too often just such transpositions. The poet's quest, his *Weltanschauung*, are given a coherence of which he was unaware in his endeavours to come to terms with the world in story, in his struggle to portray men in their dignity and integrity, their perplexities in fortune and misfortune. He is deemed to have philosophised and moralised exactly thus and thus.[1]

Let us assume that, making reasonable use of the resources of language, the student of medieval literature arrives at formulations which prove acceptable. Picking up a point already made above we may say that he has interposed a work of his own creation – and *this* work he may now wish to compare with works similar in kind, but from other areas. He compares his findings, we would normally say, with those of scholars in other fields. Findings is, however, something of a misnomer. He compares his scholarly fiction with those of specialists in other fields, perhaps historiography, philosophy, or the music of the Middle Ages. These he should of course be prepared to accept as they stand. At any rate he is not entitled to substitute for them further fictions of his own. Generalisations about works of a given kind are the concern of specialists. If they are to be used in comparative studies, they must be known to be well-founded in origin. It is, for instance, not legitimate for a literary historian to write his own essays on medieval cathedrals or manuscript illustration. They would inevitably gravitate towards a median line, coincident with or parallel to his reflections on literature.

Let us, however, suppose that our literary colleague takes all necessary precautions, elects to become an exponent of *Geistesgeschichte* and risks an essay of synthesis; and that, profiting from every insight, he arrives at a coherent view of the arts of the Middle Ages. His synthesis may win

[1] The situation is worse when with an array of Migne references he is assigned a position in the history of dogma and doctrine. The secular poet operates with homelier terms, often analogous to but rarely identical with those of the philosopher or theologian. Cf. Hugo Kuhn, 'Zur Deutung der künstlerischen Form', in *Dichtung und Welt im Mittelalter* (Stuttgart, 1959) pp. 1 ff.

fairly general retrospective approval. The result may seem to justify what began as an act of faith – or temerity. Vulgarly expressed, his essay 'comes off'. But the writing of *Geistesgeschichte* – a kind of historiography claiming to deal with nothing less than man's intellectual and spiritual life as it is expressed in all the arts and sciences, not to speak of forms of devotion, ceremonies, conventional behaviour – is a perilous undertaking. Because of its broad sweep it is only tenuously in touch with the works which it claims to illuminate from a centre. It is not surprising that opinion is divided. Some still think of it as a scheme of history to which all others are tributary; some admit that, though notionally it may represent the ultimate in historiography, it is, of all schemes, the most vulnerable. The verdict of a palæographer, a librarian or a philologist on the date or provenance of a single manuscript fragment is sufficient (should be sufficient) to throw a whole chapter of *Geistesgeschichte* into disarray. Nowadays we are disinclined to trust the methods; the findings are not regarded as in any sense assured knowledge. For all that, *Geistesgeschichte* appears permanently to have enlarged the scope of scholarly writing in our various disciplines. Mindful of its Icarus flight, however, investigators now keep one foot on the ground.

We have shown ourselves sufficiently distrustful of any *intention* to bring about a 'reciprocal illumination of the arts', but admitted that such attempts may be useful in their way. It is also understandable if a modern investigator, having done what is required of him in detailed, technical and scholarly analysis, or having traced the treatment of a theme in a given period, offers something more. In either a foreword or in an epilogue to his more professional account he 'enlarges upon his subject'. Whether he is conscious of his debt or not, he is profiting from the example of the better exponents of *Geistesgeschichte*. He will, however, speak of and try to define at most the 'spirituality' of the works he has himself investigated, and not find in them examples of the spirituality formerly predicated with great assurance of their age.

We shall later have to consider what art historians say when they 'enlarge' in the manner just indicated; and to compare the more general statements which students of literature are likely to make about the Middle Ages. To anticipate, the art historian's formulations differ in many respects from ours. The reason for this is that he starts from works different in kind, produced in different conditions. He sees the

Middle Ages differently. Not from the viewpoint of the knight and the *ministerialis*, the itinerant minstrel or the goliard. The recluse and the ascetic are known to him only by hearsay. He sees the Middle Ages rather from the viewpoint of the prince-bishop or the abbot. We will fill in some of the details later. Much more urgently therefore than the 'reciprocal illumination of the arts' which Wölfflin sought (and himself may have found)[1], we need an exchange of information and materials – a reciprocal supplementation of our subjects. That is not yet our theme. We are still in pursuit of the differences between the works with which our studies are concerned. Let us turn now from our methods, first to the works themselves. These are there for us to read or to see, but in what sense are they 'there'?

## 3. WORKS OF LITERATURE AND OF ART

### A  *The Works*

Consider first the medieval work of art. We said it is 'there'. More professionally it is 'extant', to be seen or ignored in art gallery, museum or cathedral treasury; or it is *quasi* present in a facsimile edition or art book as a good reproduction. Generally we know nothing about the discussions which took place when the work was being planned and executed, and nothing about the views of masters and connoisseurs when the work was first finished and displayed.

We are better informed in the case of literary works. Modern scholars have reconstructed more than one 'feud' for us; for instance between the lyric poets Reinmar von Hagenau and Walther von der Vogelweide at the end of the twelfth century. Slightly later there was (it is still generally held) a feud between the two great narrative poets, Wolfram von Eschenbach and Gottfried von Strassburg, in which neither named his opponent.[2] The historian believes he can trace the exchanges in some detail, almost round by round. Knowledge of them

---

[1] Readers unfamiliar with *Geistesgeschichte* as it was expounded by minor practitioners in the thirties will wonder why I make all this fuss; and perhaps E. R. Curtius' strictures (some of which I reproduce incidentally, below, pp. 61 ff) are better known than I have allowed for.

[2] P. Ganz has recently questioned our belief in this feud in 'Polemisiert Gottfried gegen Wolfram?', in *Beiträge zur Geschichte der deutschen Sprache und Literatur*, LXXXVIII (1966) 68 ff.

has led to intensified study and understanding of texts, their allusions and their inflexions. Then there is a famous review of 'the contemporary state of German literature' – a longish passage in Gottfried's *Tristan*[1] in possible emulation of which other reviews were written. There are also eulogies and 'occasional' laments. From all these sources we learn a good deal about criteria, *the terms in which* literary works were discussed and assessed in their own day.

To repeat: we do not know what medieval connoisseurs of *art* thought about individual works. We infer that the artist was held to be good and that the commissioner of his work was satisfied with what he got. His descendants or successors in office thought the work to be worth keeping, but we cannot know in what words its value and quality were assessed and expressed (a little more on this aspect, p. 45).

The medieval artist has not addressed himself to us, except vaguely as 'posterity'. Any specific message he had would be to 'remember the artist and pray for his soul'. No doubt he hoped in his less strictly devout hour that posterity would remember him when it praised famous men – for his skill, and possibly discuss his work as experts had done in his day; but there is nothing in his work which *requires* us to speak, and the artist has not spoken at all. This is now our new point of departure.

The work of art is, for the sake of argument, the picture of a Minnesänger in the so-called 'Manesse' manuscript; or it is an ivory plaque depicting the life of Mary. These are, in the sense of our opening remark, before us. If it is suggested that the same can be said of a lyric *poem* of the same Minnesänger in the same manuscript, or of the *text* of the life of Mary – that these are also there and accessible, it must immediately be pointed out that the apparent similarity of the cases rests on the ambivalence of terms. Conventionally we may read a picture or recognise a poem at sight; but of Walther's poems in the Manesse manuscript only the letters of the script are before us in approximately the same sense as the famous picture of the poet (sitting on his rock and propping his chin (plate 9a). The letters of the text await their reader. Under the picture there is a *titulus* which we read, but the manner of reading changes when we begin to interpret the rebus

[1] See A. T. Hatto's translation, Penguin Classics (L 98), pp. 105 ff. (=lines 4619–4817).

image masquerading as a coat of arms for Walther 'von der Vogelweide' (bird-cage image). The picture of Walther himself we do not read at all; we examine it, and muse or speculate (the *titulus* tells us it is Walther). We look at the ivory plaque too, and are tempted to run our fingers over it. The subject represented is, however, not given away in any inscription, and we can – *or* we cannot – recognise it. Recognition is here not a reading process, or any 'spelling out' of the content. One cannot convince any person able to read that the poems 'Über allen Gipfeln ist Ruh' and 'Ein Fichtenbaum steht einsam' are the same poem. By contrast, the student of medieval art who does not know the apocryphal motif of the Annunciation to Mary at the Well would unfailingly recognise Christ and the Samaritan Woman (plate 15a) in any pictorial representation of the scene. He might feel unhappy about certain details, but it is on the whole more likely that he would 'explain these away' than that he would recognise another subject, perhaps an Old Testament scene. We cannot read pictures as we read words.

Let us admit that we do finally take in the content (or a content) of a pictorial representation, or the purpose for which an evidently useful object (a reliquiary, a censer) was or 'will have been' intended, and to this kind of recognition we shall eventually want to refer as a kind of reading. The picture is meantime there before us, from the moment we notice it until we turn away from it. Has the picture changed in the meantime? Not to be too subtle, the picture is still there, itself unchanged.

The poem, however, even if we know it by heart, is only by a convention of language 'present' in mind at a given moment. It is only *as* one reads a poem attentively or listens carefully to a reading that it is in any real sense present. Anything else is recollection of the occasions when it was read or discussed. None the less one may learn and know the poem and be prepared on some kind of demand to repeat its words, or offer an interpretation, however inadequate, with quotations. Pictures cannot be learnt (*as* pictures) or known in this way. The so-called photographic memory is somewhat freakish and of dubious value. We need (or more accurately, we would not elect to dispense with) some kind of aid to memory – a reproduction, a tracing, a rough sketch. It is almost inevitably a shock to encounter again a picture of which one had no more dependable record than a vivid recollection of 'what it looked like'. The remembered picture is almost inevitably a falsification for which we are ourselves in part responsible. One can return to a poem to learn it 'properly'. The picture more or less defeats us.[1]

In short, the work of the artist can affect us only when we are looking at it attentively. One has to read or re-read a poem before it can begin to have its effect. If we may again dispense with refinements: any formula which seeks to eliminate this distinction must have recourse to metaphors. We shall have to use some in the end, but in the end we shall also (more or less) have justified the metaphors we use. That will take some time.

### B  The Makers of the Works: Authors, Artists

We now approach our topics from the other end, making our starting-point the poets and the artists. This is going to sound for a time, like much that has been said so far, rudimentary.

If we are to avoid metaphors, the beggars of all questions, we can say of both – poet and artist – only: (1) they contrived to 'make' the works they have left us; (2) they elected to leave their works 'thus'; (3) their works affect us. Let us not be in a hurry to say more about the works, and wary of the assertion that poet and artist 'expressed' – themselves or something – in their works. If this is all too primitive, we can speak of an 'achievement', by which at this stage I mean that they finished their works and that we recognize in them merit or value. But now we must differentiate in the sense that each is to be credited with a special achievement. The difference between the two reflects a difference of ability or talent, not merely of materials. We are, most of us, denied first-hand experience of such achievement, and beyond a certain stage the skills involved cannot be taught or learnt. There are however varying degrees of giftedness down to aptitude and only potential talent.

---

[1] About ten years ago, when I became interested in Goethe's use of images from the emblem books (see 'Der zierlichen Bilder Verknüpfung – Goethes *Alexis und Dora*, 1796', in *Euphorion*, LII (1958) 341–55), I made a note to look into his poem 'An Schwager Kronos'. I was convinced that the imagery of that poem was not determined solely by a coach journey of which Goethe writes as the occasion; but also by Alciati's emblem *Stultitia – In temerarios* (a picture of Phaeton in a chariot drawn by the sun-steeds). Alciati offered, as I proceeded to remember, both the image and (generally) the theme. After an interval of several months I had to disbelieve my own notes and the page reference (p. 68). I still think the emblem *In temerarios* has to be considered as I had proposed, but this experience of confrontation with a remembered picture put me off the subject completely.

Mythologies, philosophies, proverbial wisdom and even the idioms of our languages assure us that these various skills and talents are gifts of the gods or the Muses, or of the Holy Spirit, or genius, or Nature. There seems to be no valid reason to quarrel with tradition in these matters. These are simple truths to which we have to return to confess them afresh. At the same time there are well-established disciplines of criticism and history-writing associated with the works of the poets and the artists which have actually come down to us.

About the *poet* and the way in which his work comes into being literary theory and our histories of literature seem to have set down the valid generalisations, and provided a full documentation. For all that, poems exist in and as the poet's own *words*, which are ineffective until they are spoken. At that point we stop. We need nothing more elaborate.

What then of the *artist* and his special skill or ability? Let us note at once that the person who 'cannot draw', or in whose *hands* the mass of clay refuses to be shaped, will never become an artist, *pace* Goethe's Werther (who said that he had never been a greater artist than in those moments when he could not bring pencil to paper, and that he would persist in his efforts as a plastic artist, even though the result might have to be so many pies – *Werther*, letters of 10 May and 24 July). Unskilled hands can never produce a work of art – even by accident, for skill can only truly exist in association with an intention or purpose. It is not possible to define the skill of an artist or his intention with any precision in words. Not because these things are absolutely beyond human understanding, but more simply because of the inadequacy of our linguistic equipment. Our verb systems lack tense-forms corresponding to the stages in the execution of a work of art; their time-scale cannot be bent and twisted to follow the alternating and interacting pressures and resistances, assertions and yieldings of hand and matter, or to chronicle the emergence of a shape – and the artist's final recognition and 'confession' of this as his work. To describe the intention of even the master of a given medium, our armoury of modal auxiliaries is inadequate.

We occasionally write of the poet's struggle to give final shape to his unmalleable or stubborn or recalcitrant material, but that is, of course, a shower of metaphors. How consciously do we use them? These all associate the poet too closely with the plastic artist, or tend to identify the skill of each with that of the archetypal moulders, whether

Prometheus or the Christian God (or the Trinity) of Genesis; they all ignore completely the poet's medium, words.

To come back to the makers of the works. They were gifted in a particular way, a way so particular to them or to their kind that history knows of few men who were richly endowed with more than one gift. The graphic or the plastic artist's gift resides in his hands, and the more absorbed he is in the exercise of it, the more profound is his silence. He does not talk (or even think in words) when he is at work, nor does his work talk when he has finished it. The poet may work in silence, but his poem talks, or we make it talk on his behalf. Not to become too involved at this point, the poet cannot deny us his words. Above all let us not forget the hands of the artist and the tongue of the poet in our eagerness to ascribe everything to the mind, the heart or the spirit. It is to cope with these – and 'inspiration' – that earlier ages invented their myths, most of which still have the truth of myths. The space between – for pseudo-myth and quasi-history – can with profit be left blank.

We spoke a moment ago of the artist's intention in relation to his skill and his final achievement. One could at this point write about the intention, 'message' and so on of the medieval artist. That would, however, be a somewhat academic and wasteful exercise, for in the Middle Ages we have to make considerable allowances for the wishes of sponsors and commissioners of practically any work of art. We are not yet ready to deal with the question of sponsors.

### c Scholars and Branches of Scholarship

We turn again to the study of medieval works. If we are consistent we shall surmise that scholars who write about literature will write a language proper to the discussion of works of literature, and that art historians will use words with strict reference to the works which are assigned to them. That was our starting point, which we now hurry past to note that, in so far as these branches of study write *history* they will write literary history *or* the history of art. It will always seem that it should be possible to harmonise these in a higher historiography – and there we are back at 'should be'. This possibility can no longer delay us, for there are whole libraries of literary and of art history. These cannot be spirited away or assigned to basements to make room for something of which they are the hypothetical derivates.

## 4. INTERIM QUESTIONS

At this point I feel that the reader is entitled to know whether we are ever going to consider medieval man in more general terms, and whether the spirit of the Middle Ages will be a subject of discussion at all. Suppose 'spirit of the Middle Ages' smacks too much of *Geistesgeschichte*, is nothing to be said about the style or styles of the arts in, say, the ninth to the fourteenth and fifteenth centuries? – or of individual poets or artists? These are all justifiable questions, but if there must be an immediate answer, it has, I am afraid, to be 'no' to the lot. Like the majority of my readers, I am still engrossed in the study of medieval works, with many more to read and see and much more to learn. Further, I am old-fashioned enough to believe that style is not something a poet has in common with his age, but something that he still has when we have explained everything else that can be found out about his work. Of this *preliminary* work a great deal still remains to be done. I see this book as a study in that sense, on lines hitherto somewhat neglected.

As for medieval man, whose mind or spirit may at one stage be equally expressed in the miniatures of an evangeliary prepared for the Emperor Otto III *and* in the more or less contemporary German poem we call the *Ezzolied*, at another stage both in the architectural design of a certain cathedral and in Wolfram's *Parzival* – well and good, let there be 'medieval man', but in the same sense as statistical man of the modern world. This book is not about medieval man.

To return to our real topics. We had broached the subject of style, not in general, but in the narrower context of the separateness of our various studies. We now have to ask, not what is medieval or twelfth-century style, but how does each subject arrive at its conceptions and definitions of such styles? We have in other words to consider why literary and art historians have not found common criteria for the characterisation, or terms for the designation of styles as they encounter them. That means, I am afraid, more interim questions. It will take a fair time yet to show why this state of affairs is entirely as it should be, and not regrettable.

## 5. MEDIEVAL STYLE: LITERATURE

A  *Why Pictures? A Digression on Illustrated Histories of Literature*

So far we have assumed literature and the study of literature to be familiar territory, while art and the study of art are relatively strange. As I now settle down to the task of contrasting various ways of characterising and designating style, I introduce a complicating factor with what may seem a tedious question, namely: to what extent are our conceptions already influenced by familiarity with reproductions of works of art, and: do our statements about the style of medieval poetry owe some of their colour to recollection of miniatures and illuminations? Momentary embarrassment is caused no doubt by my apparent contradiction of the title on the cover of this book, which surely implies that students of literature should know more about medieval art. We shall find in the end that there is no real contradiction here.

A brief analysis of the situation (which I have to make with reference mainly to German studies) will help to clarify matters, particularly if I may restate my question in a really provocative form. Why do we enjoy reading illustrated histories of literature and 'miss the pictures' when none are provided? A provisional answer might be that we want to see the 'relevant' or contemporary pictures, otherwise literary history is bound to present the Middle Ages in too sombre colours. This is an interesting answer and point of view, but what picture is it that literary history should show us, whether by design or incidentally? Of the Middle Ages as a whole, or of medieval poetry?[1] Or can it be that pictures compensate for some inadequacy in our attempts to do justice to the *style* of medieval poetry by more orthodox and professional means? We now have a cluster of heterogeneous questions. For a time we shall steer a varying course, but we shall find some answers and learn a certain amount on the way.

It is a simple fact of experience that the richly illustrated volumes

---

[1] Poetry: *Dichtung* in German covers all imaginative literature including prose narrative, and extends even to the didactic and expository genres, while *Literatur*, particularly in medieval studies, may cover translations and adaptations, at a pinch glosses and commentaries. It will be enough to remember that I shall occasionally use 'poetry' to include at any rate verse romance.

of the *Handbuch der Literaturwissenschaft*[1] show us a Middle Ages infinitely more picturesque and colourful than other histories of Germanic and German literature in the Middle Ages. Distinguished scholars wrote these volumes and were directly involved in the choice of the illustrations. They clearly seized an opportunity of illustrating – what? What is the intention of the many illustrations which are not reproductions of literary manuscripts, but of ships, armour, castles, stained-glass windows, copes, pluvials, chalices, etc.? For some purposes we prefer these volumes. What are those purposes? We do not stop to define them, I think. By contrast, the sombrest image of the Middle Ages is provided by some of the soundest of our literary histories, for instance Ehrismann's,[2] which is not illustrated.

At this point I find it useful to recall an older work of 1897, *Vogt und Koch*. It is no longer quotable, I understand, on medieval German literature. In this handbook Friedrich Vogt offers, beside an account of literature, an outline of history proper which is only slightly tailored to the needs of the literary historian. It includes a history of the Germanic tribes, their conversion, their culture and something about their arts and crafts, and continues with this broad sweep down to the end of the Middle Ages. A work on this scale is probably impossible nowadays. (No scholar could afford the time to inform himself so fully.) In Vogt's work the illustrations need no special justification, for he takes the trouble to provide his pictures with appropriate commentary, assigning them to an archæological, historical or art-historical context. Since Vogt's day, however, we have had the phase of *Geistesgeschichte*, and in Julius Schwietering's much more recent volume on German poetry in the Middle Ages[3] the survey of all aspects of civilisation gives way to something else. Schwietering deals with German literature in the Middle Ages and those trends in the intellectual and religious life of Germany and Austria which on his reading find expression in poetry.

[1] Ed. Oskar Walzel (Akademische Verlagsanstalt, Potsdam) in which Andreas Heusler, *Die altgermanische Dichtung* (1929) and Julius Schwietering, *Deutsche Dichtung des Mittelalters*, 2nd ed. (Bad Homburg, 1957). With these may be compared (in the *Handbuch der Kulturgeschichte*, ed. Heinz Kindermann, Akademische Verlagsanstalt, Potsdam) Hans Naumann, *Deutsche Kultur im Zeitalter des Rittertums* (1938) and Hermann Gumbel, *Deutsche Kultur vom Zeitalter der Mystik bis zur Gegenreformation* (1936). The picture repertories for *Literaturgeschichte* and *Kulturgeschichte* are not markedly different in kind, but perhaps in number.

[2] Gustav Ehrismann, *Geschichte der deutschen Literatur bis zum Ausgang des Mittelalters* (Handbuch des deutschen Unterrichts) 4 vols (Munich, 1932–5).

[3] See previous page, footnote.

Perhaps as a corrective. He has no nostalgia for the pagan, heroic past. The pictures illustrate *his* history of literature, and its bias. This can up to a certain point be justified. Medieval piety was indeed the inspiration not only of the vernacular poetry which he discusses with great insight, but also of the very miniatures and the works of sculpture he reproduces. I stress, however, 'also' and I shall later consider some implications. Now a further word about Ehrismann (above) and the most recent handbook of Helmut de Boor.[1] These offer no pictures.

These two works do not in any sense claim to treat the Middle Ages. They are histories of German literature, literature taken in the widest sense. Some scholars will find the exclusion of pictures artificial. It isolates literature from the related art of illustration in a way in which the Middle Ages did not isolate the two. The suggestion that in these circumstances we should read all these histories of literature leaves us exactly where we were with our question (why pictures?), which has now acquired the variant: why no pictures? We cannot yet come to a decision. There are various kinds of evidence for us to consider.

First we must look again at the works of medieval literature and consider in what shape and form we now encounter them, and contrast with this their real appearance as books in the Middle Ages. Perhaps I should also recall why (or one of the reasons why) we are making this long detour: the question of 'style' and its definition. Let us again take the most familiar of all examples as our starting-point. That is medieval German Minnesang and the one hundred and thirty-seven Minnesänger portraits, many of them so familiar to every student of German literature (and every educated German), as *both* are found in the so-called Manesse Manuscript – and then immediately narrow down our enquiry to Walther von der Vogelweide. We know that a full century divides Walther's *Spruch* in the so-called 'Reichston' (1197) beginning *ich saz ûf eime steine*, and the related picture of the poet indeed seated upon a rock in the role of thinker as he enacts it in the poem (plate 9a). We gather that he is reflecting on the plight of the Empire during the Interregnum. The missing century cannot be overlooked. It extends from the heyday of chivalry and Minnesang at the courts to the emergence of a patriciate in the civic centres. By the end of that century Walther belonged to a receding golden age of German poetry. The picture so familiar to us (the Manesse picture) was

[1] Helmut de Boor (and Richard Newald), *Geschichte der deutschen Literatur . . .* in 7 vols, still incomplete, I and II, 2nd to 7th eds (Munich, 1955–66).

therefore not known to either Walther or his audience. He and they knew an antecedent image of the thinker or sorrowing minstrel, and this image Walther's song recalled. We have therefore, strictly, no less than three images to think of. There is the prototype image of minstrel (bard, court poet)[1] and Walther's re-creation of this in words: the two are not quite identical. Then there is the Manesse picture. To the layman the Manesse picture is Walther ('idealisation, not really a portrait'). But even the specialist student of Middle High German literature cannot but think of the Manesse picture as he reads *ich saz ûf eime steine*. We accept this state of affairs. The image is a welcome respite from the after-images of close study of the poem – the appearance of the page in our learned editions, the array of symbols for the rhyme-scheme and versification of the 'Reichston'. Perhaps I do our studies a disservice in these last reflections, but it remains true that we cannot but have the Manesse 'Walther' in mind (which neither he nor his contemporaries knew) when we reflect on the *style* of Walther's courtly poetry.

And now, for me at any rate, a difficulty. How many people ever saw the pictures commissioned by (let us call him) Rüdiger Manesse of Zürich?[2] I find it disquieting that our image of the Middle Ages (and indeed of medieval art) is largely conditioned by familiarity with works which in their day were seen by only a few privileged people, pretty certainly by few of our vernacular poets. Most of these splendid works were received by those who had commissioned them with pomp and ceremony, and then for centuries screened from public view. We must try to decide from case to case, not on the basis of a first verdict. Let us forget the Manesse manuscript and its portraits. It is too late in date to provide us with real guidance on these matters. Consider instead the evangeliaries, psalters and collections of pericopal readings with their often full-page illuminations, decorated initials and miniatures which art historians judge to be masterpieces of Carolingian, Ottonian or later art (it requires no effort of persuasion to convince us that they are).

[1] See pp. 92 ff for a fuller discussion of seated figures generally, minstrels, seers, etc.

[2] 'The Heidelberg [Manesse] and the Weingarten MSS of medieval German lyrics were designed to afford their owners the satisfaction of knowing that they had in their possession a most authentic record of the songs and music of the courts and the nobility. Their very format and the richness of appointment precluded their use.' (My translation.) Ewald Jammers, *Ausgewählte Melodien des Minnesangs*, Altdeutsche Textbibliothek, Ergänzungsreihe I (Tübingen, 1965) pp. 1 ff.

These were not in their day 'works of art', pure and simple. They were offerings dedicated to the Christian God in his church, testimonies of faith and thanksgiving. The miniatures and illuminations were meant to illustrate (make illustrious) God's own word, itself faithfully traced by the gifted scribe's hand. The books were not presentation copies, but dedicated works. After the dedication they were for a time on high feast days of the Church opened with due ceremony at the lesson and, as it were, read from (but in fact barely scanned, the texts were known by heart), and then restored to the treasury and its custodian. They were no doubt soon kept there and replaced by less splendid service books. In the art historian's monograph and in more general handbooks on the art of the medieval Church, pictures from the most famous manuscripts are offered to us with the introductions and the commentaries they may justly claim, that is with proper reference to the occasion for which they were commissioned or acquired.[1]

In the handbook of medieval German (or any vernacular) literature, reproductions from such manuscripts do all too much honour to their surroundings. Recall what we ourselves say of vernacular works. In so far as they deal with Christian themes they are 'fairly popular in their expression of piety and belief'; they were 'probably intended for the edification of educated laymen'. Why then do we adduce masterpieces of ecclesiastical art, and allow them to seem to illustrate the poems we have to discuss? The vernacular works are by comparison mere votive offerings. Is the juxtaposition intended to help us to see the style of the poems? Or have we already assumed that our *Ezzolied*, for instance, 'will be Ottonian' (like the evangeliaries)? No magic formula of 'medieval gradualism' will bridge the gap, and no allusion to the widow's mite will help us to recognise genuine piety in the poems, possible ostentation in the sumptuous evangeliary. The lesson is surely that at a time when artists produced works of superb quality for high dignitaries of Church and state, monks and clergy were accommodating the Christian faith, its stories and its teaching, to a still humble range of genres in the vernacular. The miniatures and illuminated initials reproduced in our histories of literature have, in short, little to do with the matter in hand.

---

[1] The organizers of great occasions must as part of their office know of work in progress and be ready to bespeak it, so enhancing its importance in any case, no doubt often influencing the quality of the work – and forestalling objections to ostentation or display.

In dealing with the Middle Ages we have to accept the fact that the best artistic talent was drawn to the centres of wealth and power. We have no cause to distinguish arts fine and applied, or to think that any genuine art went a-begging. The good Bishop Günther of Bamberg, of whose generosity the first verse of our *Ezzolied* sings, will not have been in doubt about the value and artistic excellence of the considerable treasures of his cathedral. He will *also* have recognised the solid worth and talents of the composer(s) of the *Ezzolied* with which we in German studies are primarily concerned. As for the minstrels with their repertory of heroic songs, we learn elsewhere that they kept him entertained. There is a time for most things, the Preacher tells us; Günther of Bamberg was interested in many. Not every day was a high festival of the Church requiring his appearance in full regalia. According to the day and the circumstances (the status of his guests, for instance) the cathedral treasures, the German verses of his canons regular and the tales told by the minstrels will have seemed each in their own way meritorious. We shall not go far wrong if we take the *Ezzolied* as we have it – whether in a more austere earlier version or in a later redaction. It is a German poem (of between say 25 and 35 stanzas) celebrating the miraculous history of the Christian world from the Creation to the Resurrection. (The later redaction makes simple but effective use of the new science of typology.) It has its own colours and style or styles which we are better equipped to judge when we are *not* invited to seek and see parallels in contemporary masterpieces of ecclesiastical art. The *Ezzolied* was probably fully worthy of the occasion (about 1060) for which it was written, but it is perhaps significant that we cannot name it with assurance. The art treasures, however, are of a different order of importance. They are associated with the year 1021 when Bamberg became a bishopric and received the finest 'works of art' which an Emperor could acquire so that they should be dedicated on that occasion.

As for illustrations which accompany works of vernacular literature in the manuscripts themselves, these we should surely regard as part of a 'tradition' which is our concern in literary studies. Wolfgang Stammler's survey of illustrated 'epic' manuscripts (as he called them) startled us all, I think, into a realisation of just how many manuscripts of this kind there are.[1] Our handbooks of literary history have hitherto

---

[1] 'Bebilderte Epenhandschriften', in *Wort und Bild* (Berlin 1962), pp. 136–60, revised in *RDK* IV cols 810–57, with 24 plates. The detailed review by Hella

scarcely referred to these illustrations. Only little is gained if we simply list them, however, but how are we to do more – to *discuss* them, when the art of the miniaturist is clearly a matter for specialists?

The pictures in question are naturally not the work of our poets, and in scarcely any case will a poet have seen the pictures his work attracted. They were, in the main, produced at a time when medieval German literature had gone into its quick decline after the Blütezeit. It was the time of the *epigonoi*, latter-day emulators of the masters – of Minnesang and court romance. Were the artists also latter-day emulators? The answer is a good deal more complicated than that.

Further (a thing we find it difficult to grasp at first, if our training has been in literature only), the pictures were in many cases drawn by artists who had *not read* the works they were commissioned to illustrate. They did not study the works first, decide what episodes warranted illustration and then produce what would meet the case. It is not possible to offer a formula to cover all instances, but we have to think generally rather of consultations in which the artist's pictures – in an album or on sheets – for, say Genesis, the life of Mary or the Alexander story, are considered. Someone involved (see below) 'finds the places', spaces are left for the artist's pictures as agreed, in a Genesis, life of Mary, etc. Additional pictures may be requested; suitable patterns will be sought and adapted. If the appropriate series is not already available, it has to be evolved with the help of models from elsewhere, which may be an entirely different area within European tradition. Here is an example.

The illustrations in the Cassel manuscript of Wolfram von Eschenbach's *Willehalm* are, according to one art historian, 'an example of English influence on Rhenish book illustration in the fourteenth century'.[1] That in itself sounds remarkable. English, Rhenish – what has that to do with *Willehalm*? Further, iconographically and stylistically the pictures are not derived from any series devised for illustrating romances or *chansons de geste* at all, but from psalters. To understand this assertion one needs to know that the Book of Psalms, illustrated,

---

Frühmorgen-Voss in *Beiträge zur Geschichte der deutschen Sprache und Literatur*, LXXXVII (1965) 461–7, is fairly strictly critical of Stammler's chapter and recommends the *RDK* revision.

[1] Robert Freyhan, *Die Illustrationen zum Casseler Willehalm-Codex. Ein Beispiel des englischen Einflusses in der rheinischen Malerei des XIV. Jahrhunderts* (Frankfurt a. M., 1927), see also below, pp. 41 ff. Freyhan's thesis is naturally not unchallenged.

provided Europe with its richest repository of drawing patterns. The *Willehalm* artist (*c.* 1330) found in *English* psalter work, moreover, the drawing-style he elected to emulate. The discussions and consultations did not involve the poet (Wolfram, he was dead) or his continuator – but, it is to be assumed, the commissioner of the artist's work, the scribes, the artist for whose pictures the proper spaces had to be left.[1] Landgraf Heinrich II of Hessen knew or learnt that German book-illustration was at a low ebb, hence the foreign models, probably proposed by the artist. Considerations such as these may make it seem not our concern after all to attend to pictures – even when they accompany 'our' works. Such a conclusion would, however, be wrong, I think. If we claim to be interested in literature only, it is still a fact of literary history, or at least of the history of literary taste, that one connoisseur or book-lover wished to have *Willehalm* in this form. There is a connection between the poem and the pictures, which he himself established. We need not look upon this as a matter of over-riding importance, or consider the connection to be vital for our understanding of *Willehalm*. It is, however, a closer link than in a modern bibliophile edition of Goethe's *Reineke Fuchs* or *Hermann und Dorothea* 'with engravings' (of X or Y).[2] We should at very least take cognisance of the fact that the *Willehalm* pictures and many others have already made history (art history) and been described and assessed. Should the commissioner of the manuscript, to judge by the quality of the pictures, have done our work inadequate justice, or more than justice, that would in itself be a fact worthy of note. But who is to tell us about the quality of pictures if they have *not* hitherto attracted the attention of the art historian? He will always oblige with an opinion, but we should prefer to have a full and authoritative statement from him. (Our own reflections now change course.)

Literary historians and art historians have long been out of step in their work on illustrated medieval manuscripts, and there have been some rather startling cases of what we should now call lack of com-munication. The situation has improved in the last decade or two, but the fact remains that when we are being professional we speak very

[1] Who *did* read the text to decide where the selected pictures were to go? Each case will be individual and there is little point in setting down all the possibilities. They include the already illustrated immediate source with the pictures in place.

[2] One can, I agree, argue the opposite view: the 'fine edition' is something of a problem.

different languages and mainly about different things. Not the least of the difficulties of communication is the ignorance students of literature may show of atelier traditions, and of possibilities and probabilities in the development of these. We saw just now that the illustration of *Willehalm* constitutes a distinct event in the history of German book-illustration, and in the history of German style – in art. It is, however, totally unrelated to the events of literary history as we tell it. What then do we discuss when we sit down with the art historian over the Cassel *Willehalm*? In the circumstances not, I should hope, medieval style in art and in literature.

To take a second example. Art historians are interested in the many important treatments of the *Tristan* story, particularly perhaps the numerous illustrations of Gottfried von Strassburg's *Tristan* as we have it in a Munich manuscript of about 1230–50.[1] This is, however, the very manuscript which we reject! – in which Gottfried's romance is re-edited and approximated in its diction to the more 'classical' norm of Hartmann von Aue. Of the several artists involved one is said to be a master of his craft. How shall we (who shall) co-ordinate these various pieces of heterogeneous history in a single statement, or in a couple of parallel statements? As yet, we cannot. The pictures belong to art history – some are bold, progressive; the text belongs to literary history in which it represents, we think, a retrogression, or 'not Gottfried'.

In these two cases (*Willehalm* and *Tristan* manuscripts) the art historian and the literary historian each have a story which the other may hear with interest. It is doubtful, however, whether there is much that either can do with the other's story beyond noting it.

For the rest there seem to be considerable areas where the two disciplines have little material in common. There are, for instance, in the later Middle Ages works of art of considerable distinction – paintings, frescoes, tapestries – which illustrate scenes from late romances which we cannot be troubled to read, and we must leave it at that.[2] On the other hand art historians spend a great deal of time over the illustration and illumination of texts (down to single initials) which can

[1] In Fr Ranke's *Tristan und Isold* (Bücher des Mittelalters, 1925) there are useful shorter analyses of the principal Tristan illustrations ('Zu unseren Bildern', 276 ff).

[2] It required the omniscience of Wolfgang Stammler and his delight in solving conundrums even to identify the subjects for the art student, *Wort und Bild* (Berlin, 1962) pp. 71 ff, 'Aus ritterlicher Dichtung'.

quite literally not concern us directly as literary historians: the Gospels, the Psalms and the Liturgy in Latin, or canon tables and calendars.

We have now reached a point where we could declare that the study of pictures presents too many difficulties. We could, therefore, either leave them out of account, since they give us no direct help, or merely 'show' them. Despite the evident dependence of artists on texts for their subject matter, art history does not run a parallel course; it does not illustrate literary history. Is that really the end of the matter? Some scholars clearly think that it is, and an important point in their favour may be that illustrations are rarely associated with what the editors of texts consider to be the best manuscripts, nearest to the poet's words.[1]

I incline to the view that if we do not set our expectations too high, and if we approach pictures with no preconceived ideas of what they should be able to tell us, we shall not be wasting our time. One must, however, be prepared for the consequences of the corrollary (to having no preconceived ideas). What we learn from pictures may provide the substance of little more than an isolated footnote to the history of literature. It may pose questions to which we have no answer. Only occasionally shall we find grounds for re-opening discussion of this or that topic. A few concluding examples follow. Of these I take the late example first because we have just now observed that literary historians do not read service books. Any illustrations which these contain might *a priori* seem too remote for our consideration. That is not necessarily the case.

There are most impressive pictures illustrating service books – a Missal and a *Liber viaticus* – which were owned by Johannes von Neumarkt (*c.* 1310–80). We have not paid much attention to them in German studies. The art historians have. As they rightly say, Johannes was Bishop of Olmütz from 1364. *Our* Johannes von Neumarkt is the same man, not as bishop but as head of the Imperial chancelry (from 1353) when Charles IV's capital was in Prague. We know him as the cultivator of an elegant rhetorical and rhythmical German prose style, and a leading figure in a revival of intellectual life which Konrad Burdach urged us to recognise as a 'Bohemian Renaissance'. But even

---

[1] To deal with this point properly one would have to open up the whole subject of critical editions, stemmata etc. It should suffice here to recall that it is, technically, virtually impossible for an artist to have read the text with which his pictures are now associated in a bound manuscript volume. His textual source, if he was using a text at all, was at least one, possibly more steps nearer the archetype. The possibilities are nearly endless.

this Johannes we know almost solely because Burdach's endeavours seem to us to provide the background, not to Prague as one of the most spectacularly beautiful cities in Europe north of the Alps but to a remarkable short prose work in German of about 1400, the *Ackermann aus Böhmen*.[1] It cannot but seem a far cry from the *Ackermann* to the pictures of the service books of Johannes von Neumarkt, but is it? This is not the place to pursue the matter in detail, but in explanation of the remarkable pictures an art historian writes: 'Between Prague and Avignon there was, one might say, a continuous to and fro. Charles IV himself went to Avignon twice ... books were purchased there ... single books and whole libraries. It is scarcely surprising in view of these contacts, that certain atelier traditions in the art of miniature painting found their way back [to Prague].'[2] This is surely an example to add to the outside influences of which so much is made in *Ackermann* studies. From this I draw no other moral than that we might understand the temper of the *Ackermann aus Böhmen* better if we stood back and looked around, *inter alia* at Bishop Johannes' service books and their illustrations. The latter are, incidentally, to the art historian 'late Gothic'.

It is unkind to recall what pictures we do occasionally reproduce, merely because their subject is our Dialogue of Death and the Ploughman. They are often miserable woodcuts. We must accept the fact that the great works of medieval German literature did not attract the artists which we think they deserved. That seems to me to invite – beside resignation – speculation why the vernacular works which *were* favoured by the artists (there are a few notable examples) came so to be favoured. The explanation can evidently not be a general one.

Take first Priest Wernher's 'Three Lays of the Virgin' – which are in fact a life of Mary.[3] The work was composed around 1172, the illustrations (in a Berlin manuscript missing since the War) are dated about

---

[1] For an account of the work itself and the background see M. O'C. Walshe *Medieval German Literature, A Survey* (London, 1962) ch. 6. References there to editions (Walshe's own, London 1951, ranks high among them). A good English translation by K. Maurer, *Death and the Ploughman* (London, 1947).

[2] *Die Illuminatoren des Johann von Neumarkt*, by Max Dvořák, Jahrbuch der kunsthistorischen Sammlungen des allerhöchsten Kaiserhauses, XXII 2 (Vienna, 1901) 81. See also *Czechoslovakia, Romanesque and Gothic illuminated MSS* (New York Graphic Society, 1959) – a handsome folio volume.

[3] Text: ed. Julius Feifalik (Vienna, 1860) or Carl Wesle (Altdeutsche Textbibliothek, XXVI, 2nd ed. by Hans Fromm, Tübingen, 1969). Facsimiles of the 85 pen drawings of the Berlin MS (mgo 109) in Herman Degering's modernisation, *Des Priesters Wernher drei Lieder von der Magd* (Berlin, [1925]).

forty years later. The first surprise for students of German is that the art historian seems to have formed his high opinion of the pictures without reading a word of Priest Wernher, but that point has already been covered. The apparent oversight is justifiable in this case as follows. The life of the Virgin had by 1200 been an artists' subject for several, say seven, centuries (since the mosaics of S. Maria Maggiore in Rome). There is no reason to think that an artist would modify his pictures for the sake of a vernacular poem on the subject. The ultimate *narrative* source of the pictorial tradition in ecclesiastical art is the apocryphal New Testament, in all essentials the book we call *Pseudo-Matthew*.[1] All that the art historian needs to know is that Priest Wernher's source is also *Pseudo-Matthew*. Only a picture falling quite outside the norm would (might) make him read Priest Wernher. That still leaves us with the main question unanswered. It has, I think, to be answered obliquely. *Pseudo-Matthew* itself was by the end of the twelfth century absolutely and finally proscribed as apocryphal. Endeavours to suppress this and other apocryphal books north (as well as south) of the Alps had been made since the days of Charles the Great. A vernacular adaptation for the edification of the laity (there were to be many in the next two centuries) may have provided ecclesiastical artists with a welcome opportunity of associating the full range of their pictures with the story of Mary and the Infancy of Christ in book form. (Later they were to rely mainly on pious tradition – which they helped to sustain.) This attempt at an explanation may not satisfy everyone, but I hope it will be found better than to assume that the pictures belong exclusively to the world of art. The main historical fact is the persistence of the *Pseudo-Matthew* tradition: it is of *this* that the pictures and the Lays are evidence.

Is it, to take another case, purely of art-historical interest that

[1] It is impractical to complicate this account by references to the *Protevangelion* On Pseudo-Matthew (*Liber de Ortu Beatæ Mariæ et Infantia Salvatoris*) see first M. R. James, *The Apocryphal New Testament* (Oxford, 1924) pp. 70 ff, or Ante-Nicene Christian Library, XVI (Edinburgh, 1870), pp. 16 ff. See K. Tischendorf, *Evangelia Apocrypha* (1876, Ps. Matthew 51–112), reprint Olms, Hildesheim, 1966. Edgar Hennecke, *Neutestamentliche Apokryphen*, I, *Evangelien*, 3rd completely rev. ed. by Wm Schneemelcher (Tübingen, 1959) gives up-to-date reports on all research into the numerous 'gospels' which were finally excluded from the canon. We shall repeatedly have to refer to pictorial and narrative traditions which go back to *Pseudo-Matthew* or to the so-called *Gospel of Nicodemus* (*Acts of Pilate*, M. R. James 94–146 or Ante-Nicene Christian Library XVI, 125 ff). See above, Annunciation at the Well (p. 17) and Subject Index.

Heinrich von Veldeke's *Eneit* (*c.* 1175–90) comes down to us in a handsomely illustrated manuscript of about 1200?[1] Is the explanation merely that as an adaptation (of an adaptation) of Virgil, Heinrich von Veldeke's work was privileged? We are so preoccupied establishing the position of the *Eneit* in German literature, and in characterising the poet's treatment of Amor and the gods in twelfth-century terms that we have not found time to consider the status of a vernacular Virgil as such. The quality of the illustrations may be an indication.

Questions of this kind, asked and answered by a student of literature, may lead, as I said, to the writing of here and there a footnote, but from my final example here (and the main chapters of this book) it will be seen that there are several points at which more fundamental discussions with the art historian can be opened or re-opened. The subject cannot be style. The only ground we can make common is that of content – the iconography of the pictures, the visualisation of subjects by the poets. To pick up a previous point, we can redirect the art historian's attention to pictures which had ceased to interest him, by making informed contributions to a reviewed interpretation of the subject-matter of the pictures.

We have had a recent valuable monograph on the so-called 'Millstatt Genesis', a copiously illustrated copy of our 'Old German Genesis'.[2] The illustrations of the Millstatt manuscript are, it now appears, poor in quality and provincial in style. (Their iconographic interest has never been in dispute.) They were probably produced in the Salzburg area (about 1200), perhaps in Millstatt itself. These are all useful things for us to know reliably. The monograph had, however, in a manner of speaking to be provoked, firstly by a literary historian who tried to write the required art-historical notes for us (not very successfully), then by an attempt of my own to explain pictures which fall outside the general canon of Genesis illustration or are otherwise irregular.[3] My

---

[1] The Berlin *Eneit* scores a lion's share of the illustrations in both Schwietering's and Hans Naumann's handbooks (titles above, p. 23 n. 1). In this English edition I retain the references to Schwietering (*Eneit*, illus. 75–80), which is readily accessible to students of German.

[2] Hella Voss, *Studien zur illustrierten Millstätter Genesis*, Münchener Texte und Untersuchungen zur deutschen Literatur des Mittelalters, IV (Munich, 1962).

[3] My contributions are 'Zu den Bildern der altdeutschen Genesis; Die Ikonographie der *trinitas creator*', I and II, in *Zeitschrift für deutsche Philologie*, LXXV (1956) 23 ff and LXXXIII (1964) 99 ff – the latter a reply to Hella Voss.

I add here an incidental note for students of German. We conventionally call the older of the versions of the Old German Genesis the 'Wiener Genesis'. There

starting-point was one of the problem pictures on which Otto Pächt consulted me, and a renewed examination of the German text with reference to the remaining pictures. The present situation is a little confused, but at any rate the highly improbable titles assigned to some of the pictures in the past can be ignored. Omitting details, what is at issue here is that there is an important tradition of Genesis illustration in the Middle Ages, which the art historians associate directly with the biblical Genesis and a certain amount of patristic commentary. There is, however, also a tradition of Genesis narrative enlarging the story – particularly adding a Fall of the Angels. The pictorial tradition is believed to be Eastern (Syrian, Byzantine). The main narrative tradition and the relevant exegesis is Western: we can follow it from the sixth-century poet Avitus at the latest,[1] down via Old Saxon and Anglo-Saxon poems to the Old German Genesis – and indeed Milton. The two lines of development intersect in important illustrated manuscripts, notably in the 'Cædmon Genesis' and in 'Millstatt'. The art historians have paid little attention to the narrative tradition which was no less the teaching of the Church than the subtleties of exegesis. At that point we must drop the subject here. To repeat: the art historian does not want to hear our views on the style, date and provenance of pictures. He will listen to us if we can help him to determine what they represent. We are now at the end of our digression. The aim of the provocative and perhaps factitious question about illustrated histories of literature was to show how many risks we take when we merely display pictures – to be effective or to enhance the appeal of a handbook. Now a truce to all these reservations. We shall always in the end recognise in medieval works features which conform to our conceptions of medieval style. Let us therefore by all means plead our reading of the evidence and seek to convince others. I myself would think it best to leave pictures out of account until we have come to more final terms with the style or styles of the literary works which are our primary concern. If we wish to introduce pictures to relieve tedium, or perhaps to

---

is a far better known 'Wiener Genesis' of the art historians: a magnificently illustrated Syriac MS of the sixth century. It is edited by Hartel-Wichoff (Vienna, 1895). More handy is *The Vienna Genesis*, ed. Emmy Wellesz (Faber Library of Illustrated Manuscripts: London, 1960).

[1] For quick orientation, see F. J. E. Raby, *A History of Christian-Latin Poetry*, 2nd ed. (Oxford, 1953) pp. 77 ff. For some further remarks on Genesis pictures (not relevant in this Introductory Survey), see Subject Index s.v. Genesis and *Trinitas Creator*.

compensate for something vivid and colourful which has not been transmitted to us (the courtly setting, music and pageantry of Minnesang, for instance) let us say so clearly.

### B  *Architecture as the Norm?*

So far I have restricted remarks to illustration, to pictures (indeed the smallest of these, miniatures) associated with literary tradition. The only references to architecture have been made in passing, and the context did not favour anything more. We now need a more detailed statement, and begin with the question whether it would not be both simple and practical to accept the architectural norm as something given and seek analogies in graphic art and literary works? The historical sequence of styles in architecture has been worked out mainly with reference to rounded and pointed arches: romanesque, late romanesque, early gothic, and so on. It would seem a sensible way out of some of our difficulties, but on the other hand we know this has been tried and found unsatisfactory. I dispense with a rehearsal of the allocations of poets and works to romanesque, gothic and even 'medieval baroque'[1] and consider instead what may be wrong in the choice of architecture as the norm, first for the periodisation and stylistic determination of literature. Then, more briefly in a separate section, we look at the implications for drawing and painting.

We clearly cannot dismiss the most monumental of the arts out of hand as irrelevant, but we can ask as a fundamental question whether the transition from rounded arch to pointed is more 'important' than less easily signalised phenomena in literature and language itself. Is it more important than the change from alliterating long lines to rhyming couplets in the Germanic languages, or from assonating *laisses* to rhymed verse in Old French? Or (much later) than the emergence of a more strictly syntactical structure of complex sentences after 'classical' periods in which parataxis was almost normal? However that may be, the style sequence in architecture has been recognised and designated. The romanesque and gothic styles have been more or less successfully characterised. Should it not be possible to find similar styles in the poetry of the Middle Ages? Why have the attempts to do so not convinced? We are first of all inhibited in our endeavours by a number of important medieval writings which treat at great length the

[1] Wolfgang Stammler gives a brief survey in *Aufriss*, III, cols 696–8.

symbolism of the liturgical ceremonies within the church, the apparel and the 'offices' of the officiating priests, furnishings of the altar and so on. The church as a building is taken in these works as given. We know these works and their authors, Beleth, Durandus and their predecessors writing under the title De Officiis, either directly or through summaries and generous extracts in our handbooks of Christian symbolism.[1] We cannot ignore them. But if modern scholars (Sauer on church architecture, Jungmann or Franz on the Mass)[2] find anything in them which they themselves would call romanesque or early gothic, it is the kind of piety or religiosity to which these medieval authorities bear witness. The appearance of the church as a building is something which the modern reader seeks in the text, if he must! That is to say that Durandus mentions steps because he is going to talk about the Gradual, and from his point of view that is why the steps are there, to have a meaning in the context of the Church's devotional ritual.[3] We may, if we wish, note 'steps' and from this and similar details (portico, nave, windows) build a church of generally romanesque or gothic appearance. The authors themselves probably visualised a vaguely contemporary cathedral in so far as their sources allowed (they were writing in a tradition). We incline to help them out because we are passionately interested in architectural styles. We are not generally interested in liturgy; that is another study.[4]

How then do we proceed, if we add (as we must) what Durandus says to what we know from our own more technical architectural studies? We recall round or pointed arches and what these typify for us (Durandus is no help); we recall the functions and symbolical meanings

[1] J. J. M. Timmers, Symboliek en iconographie der christelijke Kunst (Romen's Compendia, Roermond-Massiek, 1947) pp. 617–71.
[2] Jos. Sauer, Symbolik des Kirchengebäudes (etc.) (Freiburg i. Br. 1902); Jos. A. Jungmann, Missarum Solemnia, 2nd and subsequent eds. (1949– ; Engl. abridgment, 1951); Adolph Franz, Die Messe im deutschen Mittelalter (Freiburg, 1902; reprint Darmstadt, 1963).
[3] Oxford Dict. of the Christian Church (1957) under 'Gradual' (after Jungmann, Eng. ed. pp. 421 ff).
[4] Though the criticism is not particularly relevant at this point, there is a perhaps compensatory tendency, when medieval symbolism (not style) is the subject, to take everything that Durandus says on absolute trust, forgetting that like all compilers of handbooks he has extended his method of symbolical interpretation to include much that is fortuitous or trivial. Given that so many features of the church as a building and of the office as a commemorative ritual are significant, the temptation is great to interpret all realia and every movement according to a few set principles.

of all the internal dispositions, the words of the liturgy, the moods of the various festivals (Durandus, hymns and sermons are relevant) – the changing colours of the altar cloths. We may not forget the nameless architect and the generations of masons who worked beside the rising walls of the nave.[1] There are perhaps drawings which show that the towers were planned to be higher. All these things are in some way relevant. Making full use of the resources of language we now undertake our essay on the romanesque or the gothic style in architecture and the spirituality which inspired both it *and* (if architecture is to be the norm) contemporary works of secular literature. My purpose is not to make light of such an essay before it is written but to ask what round and pointed arches, or the proportions of a façade have to do with the stanza we call after the poet Der Kürenberger for instance, or with the 'Stollen' and 'Abgesang' (*pedes* and *cauda*) of classical Minnesang, or the structure of the story in *Nibelungenlied* or *Kudrun*, *Iwein* or *Parzival*. If we have assumed that the signature of an age must be traceable in all its works, where shall we look for the characteristic ductus? What curve corresponds to enjambement, what kind of interval in a line of pillars is hiatus? Are end-stopped couplets the equivalent of the round arch? The temptation is, of course, not to press such comparisons, which can readily be ridiculed, but to write a passage of fine prose on the chivalric doctrine of 'measure' (Middle High German *mâze*) and claim this as the counterpart of the rounded arch of romanesque, and so to characterise the visionaries and mystics among the poets that the pointed arch, the soaring vault and the spire or tower clamour to be compared. That is where the trouble begins. The first Mystics are too early and we become involved in sophistries.

The urge to seek sanctuary in the medieval cathedral seems to be irresistible to many scholars. It is there that they can best reflect on the orderliness of the medieval world: where it itself sought to come to terms with its Maker in a coherent statement of faith. Outside, in the world of the poets, the artists, and in the workshops of the architects we may surely think of their more immediate intentions and aspirations. The architect himself aimed at enclosing a space with walls, glazed windows and a weather-proof roof, to a design that should be worthy of his craft and show his ingenuity. Outside the cathedral with him, we

---

[1] There is a recent comprehensive monograph on medieval German architects and building supervisors, Kurt Gerstenberg, *Die deutschen Baumeisterbildnisse des Mittelalters*, Deutscher Verlag für Kunstwissenschaft (Berlin, 1966).

can make allowances for virtues which are not so easily accommodated within a uniformly Christian ethic – a pride of craft and a tempered arrogance, a spirit of emulation and a desire for fame. The humility of Christian teaching is not expected of artists in their works but in their prefatory formulas of dedication and final prayers of thanksgiving. Fear of failure and humiliation is always a more effective spur to high endeavour than a meek and humble mind.

Walther von der Vogelweide's poems on the crisis of the Interregnum have to be translated and translated again before we can bring them into any kind of conformity with a contemporary cathedral. Wolfram von Eschenbach endeavoured to invest a 'Welsh' tale with a message for Christian knighthood transcending both that of his predecessor (Chrétien de Troyes) and the teaching of the Church. To see in these works a style the ideal image of which is presented by the interior or the façade of a cathedral as we interpret them is to do violence to the evidence as it lies before us. I myself think that we are not called upon in our various branches of scholarship to attempt such forceful essays of synthesis. For this reason there will be little enough in the remainder of this book about architecture – unless the poets elect to describe some ideal edifice, whether a Temple of Love or the Temple of the Holy Grail. (See Chapter II, section 1.)

There was a fair amount of polemic in some of the things I have been saying and I cannot be entirely conciliatory even at the end of this section. There will, of course, always be wide areas of agreement. We all recognise in medieval works of every kind severe and restrained or relaxed and free 'styles', displays of sentiment and pathos, or detachment, or virtuosity. Some scholars will continue to regard it as their most pressing task to deal adequately with these – the less tangible features of medieval works, their mood, their temper, and to associate these meaningfully with forms and structures, all under the heading of 'style'. I welcome such essays at any level of sophistication and abstraction which I can follow linguistically – as works in their own right. What disturbs me is the claim made, generally not by but on behalf of the author, that such works of higher stylistic interpretation mark out a field for further organised scholarship, with the implication that an obeisance is required of anyone proposing to work within hailing distance. In these areas there is no current 'state of knowledge' and there can be no planned research to advance it. Essays of stylistic interpretation which take architecture as the norm must always go back to the round and the pointed arch and say in words what, for the duration of the essay, these are to be accepted as meaning.

### c '*Gothic*'

In a short and self-contained section I refer now to some special difficulties of chronology which arise from the media in which writers and the various kinds of artists work, and the time which they require to complete their works. There is also an evidently related and complicating question, whether skills and styles have in historical fact developed at roughly similar, or very different rates in the various arts – and in the various countries of Europe. It is, as I know, possible if one merely speculates on these matters, to labour under serious misconceptions, and it will be as well if I begin with that point.

Until quite recently I used myself to think that if parallels to the structure and style of German courtly romances (about 1190–1230) are to be sought anywhere, then surely in contemporary drawing and painting *or* in roughly contemporary *designs* for cathedrals (which in practice means in the cathedrals completed getting on for a hundred years later). This belief sustained my refusal to use period or style designations taken from architecture, as was fashionable in the thirties. (My rejection of the architectural norm is, however, more fundamental than this – see above.) In respect of the romances and the cathedrals, I still think this is reasonable. What I had not allowed for is the art-historical fact that architecture may develop at a pace which keeps it close behind the graphic arts which it may overtake, should they ever stagnate. It is then something of a shock to learn that in Germany the period of the greatest flourishing of literature (Minnesang, *Nibelungenlied* and the court romances) is one of relative stagnation in the art of the book illustrator – followed by the thirteenth century in which Germany fails to produce a Gothic.[1] Or: Gothic art in Germany is so late, and by comparison with the art (in book-illustration) of France, Spain and England so inferior in quality that we have no proper basis for the comparison of anything in German literature which we might wish to call gothic. It is convenient and proper that I

---

[1] Only at one point in this introduction did it seem necessary to give warning of these reservations, p. 12 n. 2.

should allow this to be said more fully by other writers, specialists in art history.

We turn first to the authority who dealt with the illustrations of the Cassel *Willehalm* – and the influence of English models on Rhenish book-illustration in the fourteenth century. He seeks to account for the lack of suitable German work which, had it been of European standard, would by that time have been 'gothic'.

It is not until the middle of the thirteenth century that we find the gothic style in *miniature painting* fully developed – in France. The evolution of the gothic in painting is therefore *slower* and lags behind [developments in] architecture and sculpture by almost half a century . . .

Architecture and [sculpture] . . . had long since succeeded in throwing off the overpowering influence of the mature art of Antiquity which had lain so heavily on the young barbarian nations. . . . By the twelfth century the architects and sculptors had learnt to think afresh in terms of their materials. They were no longer dependent on classical models.

In *painting*, however, *the latest of the arts* in the field, the artist receives no guidance at all from his materials, as to how he should use them. By comparison with the stratified mass of walls and the inescapable weight of stone, lines and colours are infinitely variable. Medieval painting was defenceless in face of the art of Antiquity.

The use made by *early* medieval book illustrators of the graphic conventions of late Antiquity must be regarded as one of the most fruitful and productive of all misunderstandings which history records . . . but it is precisely in these early centuries that the ways of the nations divide. The Anglo-Saxons and the Romance peoples, particularly Spain and France, do not abandon themselves permanently to the attractions of antique art; their antique phase is an *episode only* . . .

In Germany the influence of Antiquity on Carolingian painting is *no episode* . . . and indeed the works of Ottonian book illustrators develop the Carolingian style to a perfection achieved by no other nation at that time. But the Ottonian style shows few native primitive features and engenders no taste: the maturity of representational skill is without native roots: it derives solely from [and remains] an *artistic* tradition.

Stereotype formulæ then linger on and on, for the better part of two centuries – unable to suggest any new conceptions to the sculptors.

German painters were never again, like their fellows elsewhere, to see their conceptions translated into stone.[1]

It seemed to me proper to give this passage a certain prominence in this book which, I may recall, was originally written for the benefit of students of German literature. It seeks to explain in reasonable terms what one may encounter elsewhere stated with a frankness that seems excessive. For instance: 'The Gothic movement, which produced such a remarkable development in the art of illumination in England, France and Flanders during the thirteenth century left Germany almost untouched.'[2] It states openly what has otherwise to be read between the lines in German handbooks dealing with the later Middle Ages.[3] Everyone agrees that Ottonian book-illustration is one of the glories of the Christian Middle Ages. It would be helpful to all concerned with German studies – perhaps particularly literature – if it could be more regularly stated that this pre-eminence of German art about A.D. 1000 was not only not sustained: it was followed by a long period of stagnation. If the reciprocal illumination of the arts is a valid working principle, we should have to ask whether German literature from 1250 to 1450 is not also one long stagnation – again by comparison with what was happening elsewhere. We know that that would be a grave injustice to several movements, writers and works. The moral of all this is that we should be very sparing in our use of the period or style designation 'gothic' in literary studies.

[1] From the Introduction to Robert Freyhan's monograph on the Cassel *Willehalm*, title above, p. 28, n. 1. My abridged translation, italics and explanatory parentheses.

[2] J. A. Herbert, *Illuminated Manuscripts* (London, 1911) pp. 207 ff.

[3] One has to infer the low ebb of German book-illustration from the despondency of Albert Boeckler's introduction to *Deutsche Buchmalerei der Gotik* (Die Blauen Bücher, 1959). He says that the pictures of the famous Manesse manuscript of Minnesang are 'more independent' than some of the examples he has had to discuss. He notes a 'Kraft und Grösse im Formalen wie im Darstellerischen', which is a way of saying that by comparison with what gothic book-illustration could be, the Manesse pictures are rather large. They are in fact enlarged miniatures, and often crude. Their unique value to the literary historian is another matter. See Ewald Jammers, *Das königliche Liederbuch des deutschen Minnesangs* [=Manesse MS] (Heidelberg, 1965).

Finally, for disparaging references to the Gothic as something un-German (romanesque art is German), premature and unnecessary even in architecture, see Hans Naumann, *Deutsche Kultur im Zeitalter des Rittertums* (1938) (see above, p. 23 n. 1), passim. Such views could be expressed in print in 1938. They have not been entirely abandoned since then.

D *The Determination of Style in Medieval Literature*

We have now come to the end of our interim questions. I recall that the intention is still to establish how the two studies of art and literature characterise the style of the works they examine. Common to both is that they must make use of language. Further, their approach must be by the way of professional technical analysis. There is no short cut to evaluation and appraisal. Let us take first an example from literary study.

Hartmann von Aue's narrative poem *Gregorius* will serve. Access to a work such as this is not blocked by insuperable obstacles. It offers us plenty of problems none the less, perhaps first of all the question of the literary genre involved ('narrative poem' is a stop-gap designation). Readers who would not generally consider genre as a matter to be settled before we can begin to speak of style, will, I hope, recognise a problem of some kind here. This is the situation. A Swabian author of the late twelfth century, Hartmann von Aue, trained as a cleric but remaining a layman, proposes, as he writes in his prologue, to tell his lay public 'the truth'. (That had evidently not been his primary intention in earlier works.) The truth he has in mind is, we infer, the Church's teaching on the efficacy of penance and the inexhaustible mercy of God. This is a task which Hartmann as a layman is not in any authoritative way entitled to undertake. He thereupon illustrates this true teaching by narrating at length the chivalrous adventures and incredible sins – including incest – of his fictitious hero Gregorius. Seventeen years of bitter penance spent chained to a sea-girt rock come to an end when emissaries from Rome find their way to 'the good sinner'. Divine Providence has made it known that he is to become Pope.

Hartmann's Pope Gregorius is not known to us from the annals of the Church. He was known to Hartmann through an Old French *Vie du Pape Grégoire*.[1] To call this sophisticated fiction a 'courtly legend' as is customary in German studies, is to evade many issues, but we can see an end to all this. It is scarcely possible that we have totally misinterpreted Hartmann's intentions and the nature of his work. On the major problem of the genre involved, and then on all more detailed questions of technique within the genre we shall reach a measure of

---

[1] Thomas Mann knew the much shorter version of the story from the *Gesta Romanorum* (*Der Erwählte*, 1951).

agreement, for it must surely finally be possible to do approximate justice in words to a work fashioned in words. Analysis and description are an appropriate next stage. For this Hartmann gives us some further guidance in his prologue. Moreover Gottfried von Strassburg (in his 'literary review') used terms when discussing Hartmann which we must and can adapt and supplement: to characterise Hartmann's diction, his rhyme and verse technique, *inter alia* in *Gregorius*, all preliminaries to a definition of his style both in this work and generally. Some of the terms are clearly contemporary technical terms. Picking up 'verwære' (literally 'colourist', but Gottfried uses it rather of the narrative poet's shaping of his story), we consider the part played by school rhetoric in the elaboration of characteristic scenes and in exchanges of dialogue, or in the author's motivation of his story. We are enjoined by Gottfried further to note a 'fair consonance of word and meaning'. This we try to do. If we think that 'der âventiure meine' (again Gottfried, and of Hartmann) is in some way analogous to biblical *historia* and its *interpretatio* (as every trained writer had practised this), we may compare story and gloss in the relevant passages of *Gregorius*. If this all seems still too analytical and dryasdust to serve as (or in) an essay on Hartmann's style, we are free to draw on our picture of Hartmann as we know him through his works. Finally we can, and shall generally want to make good all the shortcomings of stage-by-stage analysis by *reciting* his work. Insights gained in close study of the text give us the confidence to do this. Hartmann again has an audience, possibly as appreciative as any he ever had. The recitation may be an approximation (academic mannerisms, excessively weighted dips, more-than-Swiss diphthongs), but the style of the poet is again effective and calls us back to the task of characterising it satisfactorily in words.

## 6. THE DETERMINATION OF STYLE IN MEDIEVAL ART

In his endeavours to characterise the style of a medieval work of art the modern scholar has a significantly more difficult task.[1] The reader is by now, I assume, out ahead of me. He was asking himself as he read the last section what is to be said at each stage in the case of the work of

---

[1] E. R. Curtius expressed the opposite view, see below, pp. 61 ff.

art. The most important difference is obviously that it cannot be recited. It can only be displayed. The expert can do no more than tell us in his own words what he sees. The work provides him with no terms to adopt and modernise, paraphrase or simply quote. He must seek elsewhere. In the average case we have no testimony of the work's reception. In favourable circumstances the artist's contemporaries may have listed it in an inventory. The best we may hope for is a chronicle entry stating that the materials used were precious, the finest that were to be had, or that the brethren were amazed that human hand could fashion a work of such exquisite workmanship.[1] There is nothing to be compared with Hartmann's prologue or Gottfried's review, though some inferences are possible, perhaps from a dedication (generally pictorial again) or the circumstances of custodianship. The student of art[2] must make his own surmises and seek to substantiate them with 'considerations' of some credibility to us now. None the less–despite all these handicaps – he is expected to express an opinion on the quality, and to characterise the *style* of the work. Indeed he must *cite* the style as a criterion in his endeavours to determine the work's date and provenance.

How then does the art historian arrive at his formulations? Naturally, the study of art has like any other branch of scholarship its approved terms and a well-tried phraseology for all objective descriptions. There are periodic accretions for the answering of 'the questions asked nowadays', that is reflecting developments in the study of art. For certain purposes, for instance the preparation of inventories, a routine of description is virtually prescribed. It inevitably requires the style of an investigated work to be *named*. We shall, however, prefer to observe the art historian when he is engrossed in a work and preparing to write monographically about it. We pass the most important points in quick review. He can naturally say very little about his work until he has recognised its purpose or its subject, or until he believes he has recognised these. Almost at once he thinks in terms of possible models or immediate sources. This is mainly a technical enquiry, again involving a good deal of rather laborious systematic description and

[1] Said, for example, of the works of the monk Tuotilo in the Chronicles of the Monastery of St Gall, see *Geschichtsschreiber der deutschen Vorzeit*, cvi (the *Casus S. Galli* of Ekkehard IV) (Cologne-Graz, 1958) 57 ff. Reproductions of Tuotilo's ivories: Schwietering, illus. 11, Beckwith, illus. 65–67.

[2] *Kunstwissenschaftler:* I abandon the unequal struggle and generally call him an art historian from here onwards.

corresponding in many ways to our treatment of medieval manuscripts . as a preliminary to the edition of a text. Such preparatory work is naturally indispensable. The specialist will, however, still name the style, perhaps 'Ottonian'. When in literary studies we say 'Ottonian' we mean *Ruodlieb*, *Waltharius*, and Hrotsvitha's 'dramas' and her *Gesta Ottonis*. This is purely a period designation. We do not *recognise* an Ottonian style in literature at all. The art historian thinks of the illuminated manuscripts of the Ottonian era in which he has learnt to recognise a characteristic period style, and derivatives and regional variants of it.

The important point is that the art historian recognises his styles at sight.[1] He will also give his assessment of works ('brilliant', 'derivative', 'provincial') without lengthy preliminary analysis – almost intuitively, using 'flair'. After a detailed study he will no doubt always be prepared to modify what was his initial verdict. He may conclude that as second-rank works go, the one he has considered is more meritorious or important than he at first thought. This all seems to the student of literature to happen at a somewhat bewildering *speed*. The bulk of the material adduced does not alter this impression, nor the size and weight of the resultant volume, for after the purely technical descriptions, problems and their solutions are stated briefly. There is nothing in the scholarly investigation of literature which can really be compared with this.[2]

The brevity of the art historian's statements when he is substantiating his judgments is not to be ascribed to any deficiency of scholarly method, but to the nature of the works he considers. His discourse is

[1] Roughly as we recognise without reading a word – by a characteristic appearance or by 'features' – for instance the text of the *Nibelungenlied*, a page of Edda stanzas, a Middle High German *leich*; or Heusler's versification patterns, the genealogical tree of an Arthurian romance, the lay-out of Verner's Law or a cartographical representation of the High German sound shift in the Rhineland.

[2] If this sounds unconvincing, that will be because the reader has forgotten the relatively primitive level at which this argument is being conducted. It is the level at which our disciplines diverge. I illustrate with a simple example. With a 'see plate *x*' the art historian can put a work of art before us. He gives a brief instruction, 'see'. It is effective. We follow it. This work he may then compare with another in one or two short sentences. If we in our study of medieval poetry are instructed to 'see also Walther's *Nemt vrouwe disen kranz*', or worse, 'see Walther 74, 20', we do not as a rule read this poem. The instruction to compare has been ineffective. If a scholar must insist that we see the poem, he prints it and takes us through it again, and that gives us the truer measure of the pace at which the literary historian can effect a comparison.

brief, laconic even; it must lead to a verdict. Arrived at quickly, it reflects a schooled skill which he cannot allow to rust (he must 'live with' his pictures). When writing for fellow experts the art historian assumes equally their fairly clear-cut assent, dissent. The skill displayed in his exchanges with them is to a considerable extent 'specific' and more akin to that of the musicologist than that of the student of language and literature.

There is a specific skill – an affinity with subject, 'flair' – involved in the study of literature too, and many individuals are gifted with it. It has, however, to assert itself nowadays as it may in a field in which other approaches of a more evidently 'scientific' kind predominate, and it must be confessed that these provide the data for the solution of many problems of literature, perhaps particularly matters of style. These methods exploit the fact that in literature words occur in sequence, and can be examined in turn with reference to their context, classified in glossaries and concordances. Versification and the rhythms of prose can be analysed and reduced to formulæ. Methodical, or critical and discriminating use can be made of these new instruments. Similar procedures are notionally possible in the analysis of works of art. The units used, have, however, anything but the reassuring substantiality of words (as the elements of diction) or symbols for lifts and dips (as the constituents of the bar or foot of verse). It is a somewhat unnerving experience, for instance, to read an art historian's analysis of drapery folds. But now we must cut short this argument. The art historian's analysis of works is in fact mainly retrospective – a methodical description in words of a ductus, mannerisms, features of style which he himself has already *seen* as characteristic. It is conventional for him to present his analysis first, his conclusions last.

What we are next concerned to discover is how and when, and with what justification the art historian, having completed his technical analysis, begins to mediate in his discourse and to talk about other things than for instance the painterly qualities of a painting. At what point does he seek to establish connections with other than artistic forms of expression? An external criterion is his own recourse to the term 'expression' instead of 'portrayal' or 'representation'. He may of course say outright at a certain point under a new heading that he will now 'interpret' the work he has described.

Interpretation, when the art historian writes, is accomplished as the second of two distinct stages of translation. First comes, as we saw, his translation of images into technical descriptions – with some reference to the images as the work of artists. *Then*, but only to a limited extent *thence* follows the second translation into plain language. The principal problem for us is to know the origin of the terms and the phraseology used at this second stage. They are not technical. They are not technicalities reduced to simple words and phrases either. They strike us indeed as being strangely high-flown and philosophical wherever we encounter them. This lofty diction is found again when the art historian dispenses with all technicalities from the outset, in the Forewords he writes for handy series of art-books for the general reader such as *Die Blauen Bücher*,[1] half a dozen pages of text to introduce fifty to a hundred pictures. Why has this to be so? Before we go on we must recapitulate. The art historian writes at levels which are different not merely in being more technical (for specialists) and less technical. The levels also show that he changes his role to become an interpreter. The language he uses to interpret is different in kind and in origin.

Rather than continue in this strain I now quote a short passage from a major monograph on a phase of European art, in which the author is beginning to drop his technicalities in order to interpret. I think one may safely say that the passage is in plain language, which for all its high-flown diction and subtleties of phrasing any attentive Arts man can follow as *sense*, but which only the specialist in art history is qualified to examine as *scholarship*. (I count on the indulgence of the distinguished author.)

Perhaps of somewhat earlier origin is another manuscript which was certainly produced in Aachen – a Missal now in the Laurentiana in Florence. It must be conceded that the sensitively modelled and generous folds of the draperies, and the bold dramatic postures of the figures in the Crucifixion scenes can only with difficulty be compared with the more conventional courtly elegance of the pictures of kings – their costumes altogether more taut and closely fitting to the body. It would seem that here, as almost wherever in the XIII century a pure Gothic style is emerging, the trend is away from a generous painterly and plastic moulding, towards a conscious reduction and hardening of

[1] On more than one occasion I have asked whether it is fair to quote scholars from their introductions written for the general public. The answer is reassuring, and indeed such an introduction may be the scholar's most recent statement on his subject, his authoritative monographs being both out of print and of a size to discourage second editions.

forms, towards a style in which the dominant tendency is to present clearly defined contours. For all that there can be no mistaking the artistic provenance. There is (in both cases) a similarity – of technical command, and in the use of colours, and in the details: the same small and delicate heads which turn with such engaging ease and form so remarkable a contrast with the elongated figures, the effect of which is distinctly monumental.[1]

Before the literary historian says to himself that in an inspired *quart d'heure* he could probably have produced a similar passage of fine writing (as it would have been, if he had written it), he would do well to work his way through the one hundred folio pages of print devoted to purely technical description and analysis which accompany this essay of synthesis. The question for the critical reader is not, I think, whether this paragraph is valid in its arguments, but whether it is professional in origin. Nor is it the mere proximity of businesslike technicalities in other chapters which is reassuring, but the evident interdependence of analysis and interpretation. One scholar in two different roles wrote both.[2]

Here, as we approach the end of our general introduction, we may

[1] 'Vielleicht etwas früher entstanden ist eine andere gesicherte Aachener Handschrift – ein Missale der Laurentiana in Florenz. Allerdings läßt sich die weich modellierte, großartige Gewanddrapierung und der pathetisch-kühne Schwung der Figuren der Kreuzigung nur schwer vergleichen mit der höfischen und konventionellen Eleganz der viel strafferen und knapper dem Körper anliegenden Kleidung der Königsbilder. Es scheint, daß hier – wie fast überall im XIII. Jahrhundert auf dem Weg zur reinen Gotik – die Entwicklung von einer reichen und malerisch-plastischen Fülle der Gestaltung zu einer bewußten Reduzierung und Verhärtung und zu einer immer mehr von der klaren Übersicht der Contur beherrschten Stiltendenz strebt. Trotzdem aber zeigt sich deutlich die gleiche künstlerische Herkunft: sowohl in derselben technischen und farbigen Behandlung, als auch im Einzelnen in den kleinen zierlichen und leicht spielerisch gedrehten Köpfen, die in merkwürdigem Kontrast zu den überlang gestreckten, monumental wirkenden Gestalten stehen.'

[2] The literary historian will probably read carefully the title of the work from which I have taken this extract: Hanns Swarzenski, *Die lateinischen illuminierten Handschriften des 13. Jahrhunderts in den Ländern an Rhein, Main und Donau.* Deutscher Verein für Kunstwissenschaft (Berlin, 1936) p. 17. The illuminations considered occur only in Latin manuscripts. Miniatures in manuscripts of German vernacular poetry of the period are not included in the survey, I assume because they are not good enough. And would this geographical framework make sense in our thirteenth-century literary studies? (Compare this statement on 'emergent Gothic' with the views in the excerpt from Freyhan, pp. 41 ff.)

(without risk, I think) consider an imagined typical case of the art historian's monograph on an illuminated manuscript. There is a good deal, even in the purely technical chapters of such a monograph which may claim the interest of the non-specialist, though not written for him. He may, with the help of the analyses provided, succeed in seeing the differences in 'style' (from the outset, style) between the hands of the various artists involved in the many miniatures. He notes how these may be characterised in words. Next, simple identification of the subjects having afforded him an initial satisfaction, he will find in the descriptions of the miniatures a number of terms which he will contrive to understand in context. They are mainly designations of representational units. Some turn out to be standard 'abbreviations' or common conventions (a male or female figure tipping an urn: source of river, etc.). Of a large range of unfamiliar objects, items of regalia, and of stereotype gestures (indicative of prayer, salutation, admonition, questioning) the specialist writes with assurance. One may pause to ask why, when modern monographs are generally lavishly furnished with reproductions it is still found necessary to describe even *familiar* scenes and subject-matters in much the same detail. This is clearly not merely a habit inherited from older repertories like A. Bartsch's *Le Peintre Graveur*,[1] which offered exhaustive descriptions, but very few illustrative prints. The descriptions are still indispensable. Readers must know what investigators have recognised in the pictures they have examined – perhaps particularly whether there is still something, person or object, to which no name can be given with confidence. A work of representational art has not been finally interpreted if possibly significant elements are unaccounted for, or bear a patently provisional gloss.[2] Even the reader who is only aesthetically interested in pictures can learn a great deal here.

Next, the investigator will give an account of perhaps dozens of parallels and possible patterns (pictorial sources). This is done to establish or corroborate an iconographical interpretation (identification of subjects treated), or to determine the 'school' to which the pictures belong, or from which they derive. The non-specialist may ask somewhat anxiously how the art historian knows where to look for

[1] 21 vols (Vienna 1803–21), reprint Würzburg 1920–3).
[2] The interim gloss may in extreme cases have to yield to another which changes the identity of the whole picture, cf p. 88 n.1. This is analogous to the 'crucial reading' in text interpretation.

parallels and sources.[1] And then, are the 'schools' to be taken literally (school = atelier), or are they the working hypotheses of an orderly branch of study? Fairly clearly sometimes the one, often the other. At any rate each school is recognised by a style. So much one can gather fairly quickly, though it is not yet clear to what extent style may include relatively concrete conventions or mannerisms of representation, decoration and simple space-filling, to what extent it is the less easily described 'ductus' of the master's hand, imitated and emulated by his pupils.

Sooner or later the investigator must attempt to *evaluate* the drawings. Before he can do this he must have been able to clarify the full content, not merely the pictures, of his manuscript. He will have given any *texts* at least the short shrift of identification: if they are not 'standard' he will have read them in detail. As he now proceeds, he will begin to think more closely of the commissioner of the work, a sponsoring institution or the occasion. (There may be relevant details in the manuscript itself.) This is the point where the investigator's language begins to change in character, tone and direction. For instance: he has so far *named* the colours used by the artist; any epithets he used characterised colours. As he begins to evaluate and 'place' the work, the epithets change. If the manuscript is a book of devotional readings for a monastic community, adjectives applicable to the monastic life begin to suggest themselves. The writer has in mind 'contemplative'; he writes of 'subdued, simple colours', 'a modest range of colours', perhaps even of a 'restricted palette'. He may, however, be treating a more costly and splendidly illuminated manuscript. His references in that case to fine parchment (finest vellum) and splendid purples and the gold are apt and appropriate enough in a description, but they none the less prepare the way for the account there will have to be of the symbolism of regalia, insignia, or the vestments in the frontispiece portrait of a king or high dignitary of the Church. And so the investigation, having begun with details which only the specialist is able to provide, merges into an essay on the 'spirituality' expressed in 'symbolism' and in various kinds of

[1] The technical organisation of archives is more difficult in art studies, and it is almost impossible to know that a search has been completed. Are students of art as likely as we are (or less or more likely) to make far-fetched or improper comparisons? It would seem that ideas of propriety are less strict where only images are involved. Roughly anything pictorial is available for adaptation, to be and to mean something else in a new context.

idealisation. For this task the art historian draws fairly extensively on his further knowledge. As he brings together the threads, touching again on provenance and sponsor, he may find the work typical of a century, of a dynasty, of a diocese, of a group of monasteries. Unlike assignment to an atelier or school this is not art history proper, but art put into its historical context.

Let us now consider the art historian's further knowledge (see above), with reference still to the manuscript we had in mind. If the manuscript is of the eleventh century (for example), its background is now the eleventh century as the art historian knows it: a general knowledge strongly coloured by a special familiarity with the major art-historical events of that century. These are events different in kind from those of literary history, and are not those of year-by-year political history either. The student of art is accustomed to see eleventh-century history in the image of eleventh-century art: emperors, kings, princes, archbishops, abbots. To these homage is being offered or they do homage; they proffer or receive gifts, or tokens of authority. They wear imperial or royal robes and insignia, or the ecclesiastic's apparel. He sees them – virtually always and only – at some moment deemed memorable and worthy of pictorial commemoration. The art historian also knows the century in the image of smaller monks (but not yet of tiny laymen) kneeling at their prayers. The rulers are shown in their authority and dignity, the faithful in their humility. Man in his anguish, in revolt or in hell-bent enjoyment of life is scarcely known from the world of art. No reliable inferences are possible from the Church's representations of the judged and the damned – perhaps however from the gaze of the accuser, the plight of the Man of Sorrows. But by the time medieval art begins to make the Man of Sorrows a frequent devotional image, literature has moved on to the dirges of the Flagellants and other extreme expressions of asceticism and self-abasement which art again elects not to illustrate. In one area only the art historian seems to score. For the background of everyday in its better and happier, not inordinately idealised colours there are those hundreds of smaller and smallest images in the margins of medieval manuscripts, which followers of other historical disciplines will wish to share (see below).

There is then the further reading which the art historian undertakes with the special intention of elucidating the pictures before him. For this he has his convenient 'source books', but he will of course also read beyond them. What medieval masters of theology have said about Christian dogma, however, and what medieval Church and State theory offers, can only confirm an ordered society singing God's praise, at its prayers, doing homage. Meanwhile the great teachers declare a harmonious universe and a hierarchy of the sciences for its proper understanding. When the art historian 'interprets' he can, therefore, for good reason never sound anything but solemn and high-minded, reverent and wise. In the nature of things he must quote, paraphrase or at least allude to biblical texts, the liturgy, hymns of praise and thanksgiving, or rehearse theories of state, 'mirrors' of princes, of knighthood – for these are the things that art illustrates.

The same sources were also known, but often only at second or third hand to secular poets in the Middle Ages. They echoed them, often in the vernacular, as they had apprehended them, and in such reduction and simplification we know them: in religious, political and didactic poetry. But the poets also wrote of other things: of great heroes and their deeds of long ago which happened within a simpler scheme of history than that of the universal Church, and of simpler matters, and of their doubts and questionings. Of these other things they had on the whole more to say, and said it better. And so it is that in our own writing about literature we are rarely called upon to emulate the diction of the art historian. Perhaps when we treat the figure of Christ in the Old Saxon *Heliand* of the first half of the ninth century (Christian story and teaching in alliterating long lines present a challenge to us); or when we recall Otfrid of Weissenburg's eulogy of the Franks (about 860) or Walther von der Vogelweide's celebration of the Easter Day glory of court ceremonies; or when we remember the death of Roland or of Rüdeger (*Nibelungenlied*). There is, however, an important difference. The poets themselves require of us a diction which will do justice to their own. The art historian uses the diction of his pictures' *sources*. These are works which by their authority stand higher in the hierarchy of European verbal tradition than any vernacular poetry.

We may therefore say, summing up, that the art historian describes medieval drawings and paintings in terms of his own. But to interpret them he has recourse to written sources having the status of authorities. And so a circle is closed. For directly or indirectly the medieval artist uses these same sources and illustrates the subjects with which they deal. Moreover the 'spirituality' which we may discover in medieval works of art and find expressed in their style is to a considerable extent prescribed.[1]

It will, I hope, be agreed that we are still talking about our declared subject, namely how it comes about that literary historians and art historians cannot – it begins to seem that they should not – write the same language, even when they write about medieval style. In one respect, however, we have allowed the argument to drift somewhat. We wanted to consider the art historian when he is at work on a *typical* illuminated manuscript. He began to speak of style, we observed, even when he was dealing with the recognition of 'hands'. Concentrating on the origins of his 'interpretations' we allowed the dozens of miniatures he may have been considering to merge into two or three typical cases probably all devotional images of some kind – a *Majestas Domini*, the picture of an Evangelist, an Annunciation, or an enthroned emperor. Pictures of this kind would indeed send the art historian in search of written sources, authoritative texts.

We should also observe the art historian when he is dealing with simpler 'historical' pictures. These tell (rather than celebrate) sacred history – the Flight into Egypt, the Miracles of Healing, the Washing of the Feet of the Disciples. Such pictures are to be associated with the biblical word in its first, literal and 'historical' meaning. If the devotional image expresses the thoughts of the Church in the hour of prayer or praise, the historical picture states the facts of Christian story, with no further commentary than would be used in a simple sermon. It makes correspondingly fewer demands on the modern interpreter, who quotes a few Gospel verses with possibly a sentence from a standard medieval commentary (the *Glossa Ordinaria* or the *Historia Scholastica*). If he detects an intrusion of more popular piety he may recall the words of a late hymn or even a Passion Play or religious folk-song.

Many illustrated manuscripts contain a third category of pictures, neither devotional nor historical in the sense just mentioned. These are the tiny, often minuscule marginals to which reference was made a moment ago, where medieval man comes nearer to giving us a picture of his real world and saying something on his own account. (It is not surprising that we prefer to see these pictures reproduced full-size or

[1] This still leaves plenty for the art historian to do. For instance, to determine the aptness and the adequacy of the expression, and in any case the artist's use of his sources is twofold. As one trained in a 'school' with its approved models he uses them indirectly. If he is an artist of any consequence he also knows them as texts.

enlarged.) Here the medieval artist was not drawing from patterns or according to prescription.[1] The professional art historian (therefore?) writes *less* about them, if his special field is not medieval costume or armour, or a theme like 'the seasons in medieval art'. For him as for us the pictures are 'delightful', and anybody can see their style, whether he can write about it in a useful way or not. In content they are in fact of more direct interest to the historian, who collects them assiduously. He can interpret them from his knowledge of rites and customs, sumptuary laws, the feudal system, medieval economic history and so on. There is a tacit assumption that these drawings are more or less 'realistic'. The quality of the draughtsmanship is open to discussion.

A special word now on the many portraits of high dignitaries of Church or state to which the art historian must devote a good deal of attention. Our typical manuscript perhaps has one as frontispiece. They 'idealise' their subject, it is said, and the portraits are 'stylised'. It is, however, not by simple contemplation, or by the application of purely aesthetic principles that the art historian arrives at such a verdict. (Some imperial portraits are in fact pretty barbaric.) The art historian has to consider rather in what way these images *are* portraits and *what* it is they portray: the extent for instance to which a medieval imperial portrait is intended to convey 'Cæsar' or 'a David';[2] and in the light of medieval interpretations of 'Roman' and *augustus*, he must decide how these Roman and august qualities, necessarily alluded to, are shown. Did the Western world, which in so many fields cultivated a Byzantine style (style again!) see a Frankish or Saxon ruler as the equal or superior of the East Roman Emperor? What is the meaning in political terms of the homage of the lands (Gallia, Francia), and to 'whom' is the homage offered? (cf. plate 14a). To an anointed secular ruler and *defensor fidei*, or to a 'vicar of Christ'? On these difficult and possibly never finally soluble problems the art historian will not write without a due consultation of authorities, here mainly the historians.[3] It would be a reckless undertaking to attempt to distinguish neatly between the style and the meaning of any such image. The art historian knows better

[1] This will be contradicted. The onus is, however, on the art historian to prove the negative case, that medieval artists could not draw from life.

[2] Schwietering, illus. 14, Beckwith, illus. 47–49, 60, 84 and passim. A fuller discussion of Caesar – David, pp. 102, 129 ff.

[3] On medieval historiography, see *Geschichtsdenken und Geschichtsbild im Mittelalter*, a selection of essays of the period 1933 to 1959 which appeared in 1961 (full title, p. xxi).

than to try. The literary historian should show at least equal restraint. He may, however, with profit look again at some of his own texts – Carolingian poets on the subject of Charles the Great and his immediate successors, or Otfrid of Weissenburg on Louis the German. I shall be citing Otfrid on many occasions in this book. Here I restrict my remarks to the hint that his reference to 'surrounding nations owing tribute and doing homage to the King of the Franks'[1] may reflect such an imperial portrait image rather than the narrative of Frankish history.

There is, I think, no need for a final recapitulation of the many and diverse arguments into which we have been so far led by the title of this section. The aim was to disperse any general conception of 'medieval style in art'. A special concern was the skills and the kinds of knowledge which the art historian brings to bear on pictures so that he may elucidate them fully. We said that style is something he is dealing with at every stage, but almost incidentally. It is not a preoccupation. The art historian has more pressing matters to engage him. Some readers may indeed have decided that art history sounds more reward-ing than the study of literature! That was not even incidentally the impression I intended to convey, but I do admit to an intention. I wanted us, in watching the art historian at work, to become aware of a difference in approach to many matters with which we too are con-cerned. The very fact of seeing other methods applied invites reflection whether our own methods are adequate. (The art historian will be surprised to hear that he may exercise a stabilising influence in a neighbouring discipline!) The questions of media and their scope, genres and their proper content seem to gain in importance. Medieval poets and artists could fairly evidently not say, represent or 'express' whatever they liked, when and as they liked. One senses that, in art as in literature, conventions of which we have been insufficiently aware may govern the choice of genre. There may be corresponding upper and lower limits to the commentary which it is legitimate for us to make on medieval works, but of that more later and as cases arise.

Here it is more appropriate to point quite simply to the art historian's material, his pictures, their content. There is in fact, I think, no study

---

[1] *Evangelienbuch*, 1 i 75 ff. This reference, like others to Old High German and Old Saxon literature is sufficient for specialists. There are no translations con-veniently accessible.

which can so quickly and effectively supplement our knowledge of the Middle Ages. Medieval art immediately requires us to take tradition since late Antiquity into account. Literature does not. Art does not, however, offer everything, as we have already seen. No single study can deal adequately with the Middle Ages, but few are more inadequate than 'literature only'. The vernacular literatures of medieval Europe are late and their scope is narrow. The various 'Renaissances', Carolingian, Ottonian and that of the twelfth century are past history before the 'classical periods' are fairly under way in the various European countries. The scope of 'pure' literature in Latin is restricted. In short, all our subjects require supplementation. Medieval art offers beside aesthetic rewards different in kind from those of literature a wealth of material which as medievalists we may not neglect, and a study from which our own may benefit.[1]

## 7. THE COMMISSIONED WORK OF ART

We have not lost the thread of our main argument. What I wanted to recommend as a necessary first supplementation of our literary studies is the art of the Middle Ages. The suggestion is now that instead of (if it must be instead of) the laborious reading of more poets (in the remaining vernaculars and in Latin) and of theologians and schoolmen, all of forbidding aspect and bulk, we should turn to the medieval world as the artists represented it in illuminated and illustrated manuscripts – for the sake of the compensatory colours and elegant forms and, as it may often seem, evidence of greater skill and more adequate expression. It is a world which those same theologians and thinkers had interpreted

[1] Here again I have tried to generalise my remarks to lessen the dependence of this introductory survey on the course of German literature. In point of fact German studies, properly presented, offer a better introduction to the Middle Ages than French or English, in that Old High German literature antedates Old French by a century and a half (more if one includes Ulfila) and is almost in its entirety associable with Charles the Great's educational programme. In the eighth and ninth centuries there are monks and clerics busily glossing Virgil, Prudentius, Juvencus and the rest on the Reichenau, at St Gall and in Fulda. Apart from simple translations of the basic texts of the new faith we have the New Testament story on book-epic scale (*Heliand*). In the eleventh and twelfth centuries there are the *Ruodlieb* and the *Waltharius*, the work of German speakers, and early works of historiography (the *Annolied* and the *Kaiserchronik*). These enable us to offer a pretty comprehensive picture of the Carolingian and later ages.

for their fellow men, but which the artists represented in images, not in words. But of course we must be able to understand the artist's 'language' (almost to the same extent as Latin an international language), and their symbolic conventions. It is the language of lively spirits, who, though themselves neither deaf nor dumb, elected to seize upon and mould their world with their hands in a likeness which is now an image. It is a language to which we can gain access as we can to a medieval vernacular – by an appropriate study.

We have now reached the point where we can indeed speak of the 'language' of the medieval artist and of our 'reading' of his work. So far we had hesitated to take this step, substituting warnings of the pitfalls concealed for the unwary beneath metaphors. We shall now try to justify the step and indeed the metaphor, as we take up the remark that medieval artists were neither deaf nor dumb. They worked in silence, but they talked about their work.[1]

We have at various points referred in passing to the commissioner of works of art in the Middle Ages. We first came across him when we were considering the artist's intention and his achievement. We should sometimes (more frequently than we do) recall that in the 'work of art' there are – whether we can see them or not – still elements of the work commissioned; and that these correspond to special wishes and intentions of the commissioner, or they met his criticisms when the work was in progress. Discussions form the background to probably every significant work that has come down to us. Or, to put it another way, the surprised patron accepting a piece of work that is not at all what he ordered, and keeping his silence merely to avoid appearing not to understand modern art, does not fit easily into the picture we have of life in the Middle Ages. But let us not exaggerate. One cannot help thinking that the visionary power of some of the medieval masters must have sorely tested the integrity of sponsors of their work. This is a thought that strikes me whenever I look at certain notable treatments of standard themes, for instance the picture of the Evangelist Luke[2] in

[1] Students of art and of aesthetics seem generally to make heavy weather in their resolve to assume that artists do not talk even *about* their work. To make such an admission would no doubt complicate the definition of symbols. The available symbols have, I assume, always been the subject of intelligent discussion between artist and public.

[2] Beckwith chooses the Evangelist Matthew from the same manuscript, illus. 91. See Konrad Hoffmann, 'Die Evangelistenbilder des Münchener Otto-Evangeliars', in *Zeitschrift des deutschen Vereins für Kunstwissenschaft*, XX (1966)

an evangeliary (Gospel Lectionary) presented to Otto III about the year 1000. Even when one has made every allowance for the fact that we see far more 'Lukes' in a single year's reading of art books than the medieval artist saw in his life-time, and are therefore conceivably more startled by departures from the norm, one must wonder (or, to be safe, I wonder) how the commissioner of that particular image came to terms with it – *unless* he had been progressively persuaded while the work was being discussed, and had involved himself with comments and suggestions. It may be fanciful to set down such thoughts, but I think it demands a greater effort of imagination to see the unprepared recipient, startled and alarmed, but then joyfully accepting, etc.

We have, however, in each case only the finished work, and yet the work began as words – about 'the kind of thing required'. Taking care not to write the text of imagined medieval conversations, let us look briefly at the points which would have to be covered in reasonably average cases. The artist is commissioned by a magnate or patron, with a paymaster of some kind in attendance. He is informed of the permissible scale of expenditure in terms of the materials available or to be obtained, and with reference to spaces to be filled. The work is to be a fresco, or it is a series of illustrations to be matched with a text (in a co-ordinated operation), or a frontispiece portrait for a dedication volume, other artists possibly having been engaged for the remainder. The treatment of the subject is still a matter for discussion. Most students of literature are surprised (the point has been mentioned, but can be repeated) that the medieval artist could present examples of his work (or his school's work) for inspection, in the form of a book or a sheet of patterns. A preliminary draft doubtless meets the case if the commission is in any way out of the ordinary. All the more frequently commissioned subjects are in the book (a notional book if the scriptorium is otherwise organised): the four Evangelists, an Adam and Eve, one or two saints or prophets not finally identified by their standard (or local standard) attributes, a David as musician, some pictorial series (life of Joseph, life of Mary, Miracles of Healing), a *Te Igitur* initial for a missal, a *Beatus* initial for a psalter. The commissioner may know of other patterns. He may prefer something on the lines of the work his

---

17–46, for a review of possible interpretations, including the author's own. It is always a sobering experience to return to works written by art historians for art historians.

institution has on loan for the copying of the text. For a particular community (a monastic establishment) or for a special occasion certain variations in the conventional treatment of the subject or theme may be requested or are obviously necessary. And the symbols which the artist would propose to use are, or inevitably become, the subject of discussion. Their meanings will be more or less discreetly rehearsed. The commissioned artist must ensure that his sponsor is 'briefed'. As we do not wish to drift into pure anecdote at this stage, I merely mention such further complicating factors as character and personality of the contracting parties, and the possibly only vestigial survival in these conditions of the Christian virtue of humility. Sooner or later all discussion (or talk) ceases, and we have the finished work. In what does the achievement of the artist consist? And how shall we recognise the involvement of the sponsor? Can we know whether the sponsor was satisfied with the artist's 'best'? Or, again, the artist may have done his work under some constraint. Art historians have in fact recognised a freedom of line and treatment in pattern books, which are not to be found in duly executed works. This may not be all. For example: with some reservations, and without convincing all colleagues I have suggested that the dozens of spaces left empty in the Vienna Manuscript of our Old German *Genesis* represent a lapsed contract.[1] There are hundreds of these empty spaces in medieval manuscripts where pictures were to have been inserted. The conventional explanation that the artist did not live to complete his work may occasionally coincide with the facts, but there are so many other more likely explanations – from the exhaustion of funds and the impossibility of securing appropriate patterns when required, to simple failure to co-ordinate the work of scribes and artists. The possibility of an artist being sacked, breach of contract, and premature death of a sponsor must all be envisaged as

[1] The artist refused, I think, to go on working as his commission would have required him. There was an unforeseen difficulty. He had already drawn a Holy Trinity for this volume, before the Genesis poem, as an overture to it. Now he was expected to copy an entirely different Trinity present at the animation of Adam. The artist of the other extant manuscript (Millstatt) had not so committed himself by an earlier drawing: he drew the problematical one, went on and completed his commission.

Schwietering, illus. 37–39, shows some pictures from these two manuscripts. The Vienna artist drew 37 but 'drew the line at' 38 (our plate 16a). He did not draw 39 or any of the later Genesis scenes. Modify Schwietering's rubric to 38: not 'Creation' but 'Animation' of Adam. See pp. 312 ff for further references to Old German Genesis illustrations.

possibilities – but not necessarily written about. It was not always the sponsor who created the difficulties, nor will the artist who discouraged innovations always have been merely conservative, despite his appeals to 'good practice'.

By now I have uttered sufficient warnings against an easy-going or purely aesthetic approach to medieval illustrative art, and, I hope, contrived to present the warnings together with information or guidance. We may, of course, prefer to ignore the warnings and see medieval pictures simply as testimonies of man's genius, and feel something akin to the excitement they caused in their time. But for the *words in which* to do justice to medieval artists, we shall – most of us – for a long time have to depend on the expert. A dilettante may wax lyrical and will not always be wrong in his judgments, but he is not a reliable guide to himself or others. We shall find eloquence enough, if that is what we insist on, coupled with mastery of subject in the work of the expert. Experts are entitled to mediate and communicate – *inter alia* – their enthusiasm. So most of us think. No less a scholar than Ernst Robert Curtius, however, thought otherwise. We must pause for a moment to consider what his objections were and how he expressed them.

## 8. E. R. CURTIUS ON ART HISTORY

Ernst Robert Curtius's strictures on the art historians are to be found in the opening chapter of his most influential work, which, it will be remembered, is about European *literature* in the *Latin* Middle Ages.[1] The attack is therefore something incidental to his main argument; anyone not an art historian might miss it, and indeed most of us had other things to think about after a first reading of Curtius.[2] It will be evident from what I have been saying in recent sections of this book

[1] *Europäische Literatur und lateinisches Mittelalter* (Bern, 1948, 1954), English translation, *European Literature and the Latin Middle Ages*, by W. R. Trask (London, 1953). I thought it simpler to translate the excerpts (below) afresh, rather more freely than Trask to whom I supply page references.
[2] In 'On coming to terms with Curtius', in *GLL* XI (1958) 335–45, I sought to establish how much of Curtius's theory of the *topos* could be accepted by medievalists concerned with central Christian traditions, or owing a particular duty to German literature.

that I cannot be in serious disagreement with Curtius's main thesis. The Middle Ages are in Latin and are European; we learn a great deal more from literature than from other arts; we interpret literature with greater assurance. But in undertaking to write on 'literature and art', I am clearly in what was one of Curtius's many lines of fire, for not only did he apparently think that literary historians have nothing to learn from art: he also said rather outspokenly that they have no business to be reading the art historians at all. Re-reading the passages in question – not as part of the onslaught on misguided literary historians but as attacks on the art historians themselves – one may feel some misgivings. Admittedly Curtius's remarks are directed in the main against followers of Wölfflin, but they are still there in the second edition and are presumably meant to be taken seriously. Apart from italicising a few phrases (some I endorse, but equally others), I postpone comment.

On page 21 of the second German edition Curtius reviews what he calls the 'non-philological' schools of literary studies which pompously claim to represent a 'science of literature':

One branch of *Literaturwissenschaft* 'philosophises'; it scrutinises literature for its treatment of metaphysical and ethical problems, for instance Death or Love. It claims to be *Geistesgeschichte*. . . . Another branch seeks to associate its enquiries with those of the *art historian, and operates with the highly questionable principle* of a 'reciprocal illumination of the arts'; it befogs the issues by the dilettantism of its efforts. It then proceeds to apply the art-historical sequence of period-styles in its literary studies. [cf Trask, p. 11]

In these various ways the Middle Ages are split up into the areas of the *specialised disciplines*, which have no contact with one another. There is no single discipline devoted to the study of the Middle Ages as such. [Curtius, 2nd ed., p. 23]

[Whoever follows Curtius] will learn that European literature is an 'intelligible field of study' [Toynbee] which is lost to view if one divides it up. He will realise that European *literature has an autonomous structure* which is essentially different from that of the representational arts, primarily because *literature is the vehicle of thoughts, as art is not*. But literature also has other patterns of movement, growth and continuity than those of art. Literature enjoys a freedom which art is denied. In literature the past lives again in time present, or can be made to do so. A new translation of Homer renews Homer in the present and Rudolf Alexander Schröder's Homer is a different Homer from Voss's . . . [Curtius, pp. 24–5; cf Trask, pp. 13–14]

We need a technique to decipher the message of medieval literature. That technique is 'philology'. Since literary studies deal with texts, they are helpless without 'philology'. No intuition or insight into the essential nature of literature can make good the inadequacies of literary studies pursued without philology. *The study of art is easier. It operates with pictures* – and lantern slides. *There is nothing there which cannot be understood.* To understand Pindar's poems requires great intellectual effort, the Parthenon frieze makes no such demands. – *The study of pictures is effortless by comparison with the study of books.* [cf Trask, p. 15]

I said I would offer these extracts without comment. To avoid misunderstandings, I must say that I do not by any means reject everything that Curtius says, but I think it relevant to ask who it is who is proposing to split up medieval studies into watertight compartments, and what freedom of movement is to be allowed to other medievalists who do not wish to ignore art? Despite Curtius's references to the ease with which pictures may be interpreted we will go on. It may be that some of the thoughts they are able to provoke will not come amiss when we return to our philology.

## 9. METHODS OF STUDY

At the end of this very long introductory section it must be fairly clear what general lines I shall suggest for the comparative study of literature and art in the Middle Ages. Naturally we must first restrict attention to representational art with which alone comparisons are possible, and begin with subjects and motifs (themes) which are already familiar to us from literature. These can be pursued across the departmental frontier. As a secondary, but I think necessary task one must gain some idea of the internal economy of the neighbouring discipline – as it is, not as it is presented at the level of 'subsidiary subject'. The first piece of advice could be followed by reading the chapters in this book dealing with Fortune or the Crucifixion, but the latter chapter will probably be found too difficult as an introduction. Either of them should bring home the general point that when we have looked at the pictorial representation of subjects, we may have to go back to our texts and reconsider them. There are things there which we have evidently not understood completely, or perhaps misinterpreted.

The questions already discussed in this Introductory Survey, I should probably remark, were of course not my own starting-point – far from it. These things only began to seem important, and fall into the shape I have given them, when I undertook to write an introductory handbook, the inevitable consequence of which was a retrospective discovery of the principles underlying my own approach, which is not entirely conventional. If there is any particular reason for this, it is, I think, because I am (in both the English and in the continental sense of the term) by training a philologist. My own starting-point – many years ago – was certain problems of text editing which have in the event become the substance of Chapter IV. The solution of these textual problems was originally an end in itself. My interest in words developed into an interest in images, but of course only a certain range of these – what the students of linguistics would call my 'register'. There must be plenty of other more obvious or more attractive starting points.

Supposing one has heard or read the customary introduction to Pfaffe Lamprecht's version of the Alexander story, the *Alexanderlied* (about 1140–50), or knows the Alexander sections in the *Annolied* (about 1085), an obvious point to break into the parallel art-historical story is the 'Alexander' article in the *Reallexikon zur deutschen Kunstgeschichte* (*RDK*) written, significantly, by Wolfgang Stammler, the literary historian who did probably more than anyone else to establish the idea that supplementation – not 'reciprocal illumination' – is the necessary formula; or another article (Stammler again) involving Alexander, under 'Aristotle and Phyllis' (Aristotle was Alexander's tutor). One quickly learns that in medieval manuscripts and elsewhere many of the more striking scenes in Alexander's 'fabulous' career were repeatedly drawn by medieval artists, and from an early date there was a pictorial tradition which could be transmitted without Alexander texts.[1] One also sees why the episode 'Aristotle and Phyllis' could become detached and develop new associations, but – a point I want to

---

[1] See Name Index under Ross, D. J. A. His *Alexander Historiatus* (Warburg Institute Survey I, 1963) is a fundamental reference work for art-historical research.

make as quickly as I can – this is a field which has been well and truly ploughed, and is *assumed known* to all medievalists (perhaps a good reason for making a start here). There seems nothing more to be said by anyone who has not been at work for years on Alexander, but even so one will have learnt something about method, and formed an acquaintance with the *RDK*. Let us move on! In order fully to understand the short article in the same reference work on the 'Adulterers' Bridge' ('Ehebrecherfalle') by E. L. Ettlinger, one has to read a treatment of the same subject by Hans Sachs,[1] a poem I had never seen, I must confess. One learns something about Hans Sachs' principles of composition. One thing may lead to another. In this case to a detailed checking of dates, to establish which editions of prints Hans Sachs in fact used. Editors have not always identified the *pictorial source* of Hans Sachs' poems correctly.[2]

It soon becomes depressingly clear that there are hundreds of subjects and motifs which have already been treated (with reference to both literature and representational art) and filed away; and that the art historians have been anything but idle in their own search for *literary sources*. One learns to look upon the *RDK*[3] as a useful reference work for the student of literature.

Gradually one will become accustomed to seeing the titles of certain major works, always quoted when a given *theme* is mentioned (e.g. the Legend of the Three Living and the Three Dead), or whenever works in a given *medium* are involved (e.g. ivories, tapestries). Even that is useful – in suggesting that the whole field is well mapped out. Then, in our most recent encyclopædic handbook of German studies, Wolfgang Stammler's *Aufriss der deutschen Philologie*, a chapter by Stammler himself (III 613 ff) gives a comprehensive review of virtually all the themes and motifs which occur both in medieval literature and in medieval art. Stammler calls his report a reconnaissance flight. There had previously not been such a survey written specially for the German medievalist. The inexhaustible collector's zeal of this one scholar (to

---

[1] *Die Ehbrechrebruck. In dem langen Ton Müglings*, Hans Sachs edition of Paul Merker (Leipzig, 1911, 1923) I 140, with a full-page reproduction of a contemporary print.

[2] Mary Beare 'Observations on some illustrated broadsheets of Hans Sachs', in *GLL* XVI (1963) 174 ff.

[3] So far A–E, and tending now to have longer articles, and therefore progressing slowly.

whom medieval art was a companion study only) should not cause dismay. Having got the lie of the land one knows where one *would* seek further information, the case arising. But the case has not yet arisen. There is no point at all in looking here or anywhere else for subjects which have not been treated. Subjects for investigation present themselves as problems we ourselves run into. But one has by consulting Stammler grasped that there is scarcely a topic which occurs only in literature and not in art too (though often only as *illustrations* to the literary works themselves).

Art history one will have to do on the side – an essential minimum, *without* becoming involved in art history as a subsidiary subject, for our reading must be critical. By critical I mean asking the whole time, not 'is this important in art history', but 'do I need it, can I use it, does what the art historian says convince me with my different range of knowledge?' What will most likely happen is that – in time! – we find we want to say something about a topic or motif which has excited our interest and presents a problem of interpretation. Searching for information on our topic in a widened range of works, and approaching it with less anxious concern for our main studies, we may find ourselves referred backwards and forwards, not knowing on which side of the subject barrier we shall finish. Artists and poets think and thought sometimes in words, sometimes in images, but associatively, and so do scholars, for all their methods.

There is always a possibility of reciprocal illumination, not only of the arts, but of those who study them. Yet it will always be wise if the student of literature bears clearly in mind what it is he knows. In the art-historical institute he is, as he pursues his specific inquiry, moving on a very narrow path leading through tracts of unfamiliar territory, the extent of which he can at most sense. The remark he makes about literary motifs, in earshot, as it were, of the art historian, may excite interest. It may be something the art historian was not aware of, and which for some reason his reference works do not mention, or mention with reference to a long-superseded state of knowledge in literary studies.[1] In the exchange of views on a picture which the art historian has extracted from his photographic archives, we are free of course to venture the opinion that it is 'beautiful'. Of far greater interest is some

---

[1] Pending the re-opening of discussions on the Grail Temple in Albrecht von Scharfenberg's *Der jüngere Titurel*, for instance, the art historian's knowledge of this work is of about 1890–1920 vintage, see p. 147.

contribution of ours to the interpretation of its narrative or other *content*. This was always Wolfgang Stammler's approach.[1]

To come back to the observation 'not as a subsidiary subject'. Art history as a subsidiary subject is *not* what we need for comparative studies, which will only occasionally bring us into contact with the great masters and the main events. I have already (repeatedly) indicated how, and how alone the student of literature can do anything on his own account in the province of the art historian. We took the case of our reading his major monograph, to see what and how he writes for fellow specialists, *inter alia* about style. Students however and many others prefer to hear the art historian when he lectures – with lantern slides. Let us then suppose we are at his lecture, rather than reading his book, to hear how pictures are described in words, and analysed. How is the style characterised and the quality assessed? For *such* an exercise – critical examination of words in use – we have had an appropriate training. But the method of the art historian is as still mainly an unfamiliar pattern of behaviour with some gestures evidently determined by the subjects observed and analysed. Between the object displayed and the words used there is a relationship which remains something of a 'mystery'. Except, of course, when iconographical matters are being discussed: we can understand and see that a picture represents the Rape of Lucrece, Hercules at the Cross Roads, the four Seasons, the Evangelist Mark (with his Lion). The rest of what is said 'makes sense' or as yet does not. But it *can* be said – and said thus. At lectures on art, particularly medieval art, I find myself observing any faces within range whenever the lecturer begins to 'enlarge on his subject', particularly when he is speaking about style, influence, dependence, source, model. I do this to confirm that as in my case attention is divided – but between what is being shown and what is being said. By comparison with what happens at a lecture on poetry,

---

[1] From the Introduction to his *Wort und Bild* of 1962 one gathers that it used to be more difficult than nowadays to interest students of art in mundane problems of iconography. I add a brief personal note at this point. My acquaintance with Wolfgang Stammler began relatively recently, in 1953, in correspondence. I visited him twice in his retirement in the Spessart and was there again in February 1966 to receive from Frau Dr Elisabeth Roth a simple cardboard box labelled 'Fortuna', filled with Stammler's copious gleanings from texts and pictures, which he had continued to make until the last months of his life. There is a moving 'Nachruf' to Stammler by Kurt Ruh in the *Zeitschrift für deutsche Philologie*, LXXXV (1966) 1–6.

the audience listens with an almost complete critical detachment; for two reasons, I think. Firstly because the picture discussed stays there, for everyone to see, supporting the lecturer in his disquisition on it, or silently contradicting him. The interpreter is pleading an interpretation with the image as witness, as evidence. Or pictures are being compared on two screens. The lecturer sees and speaks of similarities while the audience silently approves or disapproves of the comparison. Even the note-takers begin to attend; there is nothing else that they *can* do except write 'he compared'. Secondly, the lecture-room is free from echoes. The picture shown a moment ago has gone, and cannot be brought back like the recently recited poem, by the repitition of a couplet or an appropriately inflected allusion. There is no accumulation of allusions. The speaker cannot advance on the crest of his own rhetoric. Generally each new picture eliminates its predecessor. The consequence of all this is that one leaves – with what? Let us leave aside what the lecture may have done for our appreciation of art. I think the main impression is that one has a long way to go before one could oneself venture to talk about pictures with any assurance, and would feel it to be plagiarism if one caught oneself speaking in a similar way or repeating the judgments and opinions of the expert. For the student of language and literature there is only one honest approach and that is uncommitted, unprejudiced observation of the expert at work on his subject, and critical attention to his use of language as he applies it to his subject. Of a miniature, of an ivory plaque, of a gold background he says – this or that. On *these* things one can reflect, as also on the iconographical interpretation which was more easily followed. Premature attempts to join in the professional discussion will obviously be dangerous, if only because it is evident that the experts do not always agree – even on some points of vital importance, where nothing more complicated is involved than *seeing* resemblances and differences. It serves as sufficient warning if one has ever heard one expert ask another why it is that a third 'simply cannot see' what, according to them (or the speaker only) is obvious. There is so little in art history which can be pressed beyond this point.[1] The student of art must have judgment, be known to have it and be seen to have it. He

---

[1] Perhaps things are not so very different in the study of literature at a certain level: the level at which nothing further can be said than that X must be completely insensitive.

must show his pictures when he talks about them. What he says is under constant critical scrutiny.

In time we shall have got our bearings, and feel confident enough to look at more or less anything the art historian has written and listen to whatever he says. Respect for the scholar in his field must not degenerate into mute piety, and there are easier ways of looking at pictures than always over someone else's shoulder. In any case the art historian welcomes our interest in his materials, for we come to them with a range of knowledge that does not coincide with his, and have eyes too; if they are blinkered, it may be that nothing of relevance to both of us is shut out. He is genuinely interested in what we see in his pictures.

We may discover that he in his turn has seen things we have only read about – and that he has followed them into our area. He has something to show us in our texts. For instance, Wolfram's Grail as an object; or at any rate the kind of object Wolfram may have had in mind when he wrote the words about the Grail that we puzzle over. We need not agree that Wolfram was thinking of a portable altar, but the philologist who visualises a portable altar *without* the evidence the art historian can put (several times over) before him, is asking for trouble.[1] Further, the art historian has occasionally had to come across the frontier and do some spade work on his own account; not merely read out texts but consider how we have edited them. In his discussion of the iconography of the St Albans Psalter[2] (a work of the beginning of the twelfth century from St Albans and now in St Godehard, Hildesheim), Otto Pächt had to look again at the textual history of the *Chanson de S. Alexis*, one of the earliest works written in French, before he could return to his own problem which was the drawings of the so-called Alexis-Master.

The various incursions we make across the frontiers leave the score more or less even. In the end both sides get something out of it. One example now in a little more detail. The art historian reads neither the Anglo-Saxon Genesis, nor the Old Saxon *Heliand* nor Otfrid of Weissenburg's *Evangelienbuch*. He cannot. At the same time he is anything but well provided with texts of any kind from this period

[1] See A. A. Barb, '*Mensa Sacra*. The Round Table and the Holy Grail', in *JWCI* xix (1956) 40–67, with some 50 illustrations of round tables, altars, patenas and symbolical wheel images. Schwietering offers a small selection of portable altars (illus. 83–85), but I think they are the wrong shape.

[2] *The St Albans Psalter (Albani Psalter)*, by Otto Pächt, C. R. Dodwell, Francis Wormald, Studies of the Warburg Institute, xxv (London, 1960) ch. 9.

(ninth century). Texts offering Christian narrative in paraphrase should be of interest to him, since these may (almost necessarily must) reflect contemporary Christian art. He cannot read these works without our help. On the other hand the student of Germanic dialects cannot translate some of the most important passages without the help of the art historian. Put another way: we cannot translate ninth-century texts in which biblical scenes are portrayed, unless we know what a ninth-century poet had about him in the way of Christian art, to help him to see sacred history. We need to know the repertory of the contemporary ecclesiastical artist; and of this the art historian's knowledge is incomplete. Any scholar therefore who relies on his understanding of Anglo-Saxon, Old Saxon and Old High German alone – who measures time by tenses and space by adverbs – will end with scenes and actions which are fictions of his own imagination and *wrong*; with pictures of the Crucifixion, of the Descent from the Cross and the Entombment which the art historian knows to be 'impossible in the ninth century'. An essay on the Crucifixion in the *Heliand* written some decades ago by an Old Saxon scholar remained without a word of comment from the art historians – rightly so. It was ultimately based on a completely wrong translation of an Old Saxon word, apparently meaning 'ropes' but in fact translating *vincula* (*crucis*), which are not ropes but a metaphor for nails. In this sacred context *vincula* always means nails and *funes* are ropes.[1]

At the beginning of this section we were asking about methods for the student trained in the study of literature. I have tried to answer conscientiously the questions I have raised. I am writing primarily for students of German literature to whom the *Nibelungenlied*, Minnesang, the works of Hartmann, Gottfried and Wolfram will always remain the great events of medieval history. These works he must of course first learn to understand in the light of the commentaries provided by the discipline of German studies. He will, I hope, find it reasonable for

[1] In my long chapter on the Crucifixion in art and literature (Chapter IV, pp. 223 ff) I have not been able to deal with the Crucifixion as it is treated by individual poets in their Christian narrative. My article 'Christlicher Erzählstoff bei Otfrid und im *Heliand*' (see p. xxi) does keep to specific texts, but it is too detailed to be helpful to anyone not a specialist in medieval German. I have exploited it for various sections in this book, but it may be useful to state here the method employed. Starting with the Annunciation and the Birth of Christ in each of these ninth-century poems I worked out an 'iconographical' analysis with constant cross-reference to (*a*) the Apocryphal New Testament, (*b*) the repertory of Christian art in the ninth to fifteenth centuries.

others who have had a longish apprenticeship to neglect these works for a time, to make explorations in neighbouring fields. He has my assurance that one returns to them with no decrease of affection, and yet sees them afresh in another light and with other colours. The following chapters will show (if not immediately) that some of our traditional interpretations of works of medieval German literature may have to be modified.

# PART TWO

# WORD, IMAGE, TRADITION, SELECTED STUDIES

# I

## IMAGE AND MEANING: A SEMANTIC
## ENQUIRY

THE emphasis in the long Introductory Survey was almost exclusively
on the differences between works of literature and works of art (and
the studies devoted to them). In a series of chapters we shall now be
concentrating attention, not on similarities (the term is simply not
applicable), but on connections between the two. They may be of more
than one kind, but there is only one area in which we recognise
connections at once and with assurance, namely that of *content*, what is
said in words, what is represented as image.

In later chapters we shall want to refer to the content, or details in
the contents of finished works. In such cases content is a 'subject' which
the poet or artist has treated; it probably has a recognised title. In this
more basic chapter we shall stop far short of that point. The largest unit
of statement or representation to be discussed in any detail is the 'motif'
or its graphic equivalent; that is, a notion expressed in words, or an
image of modest complexity, either of which may enter more or less
ready-made into the fabric of a larger composition. The smallest unit
will be the single word (or name) on the one hand, the 'simple image'
on the other. There is no point in trying to define these terms here and
now: we should be begging our questions. These various smaller units
have the elements of a content or a meaning in themselves, but they
mean something precise only in a context, where they have in fact been
used with the intention that they shall have that meaning. As for
context, I shall restrict it as soon as possible to Western European, and
generally to Christian tradition. Drawing these strands together, this is
to be a semantic enquiry, in which we shall be concerned with our own
*recognition* of contents on the one hand (relatively simple in the case of
literary works, more difficult in the case of pictures), and the proprieties
of interpretation on the other. In the case of pictures we shall have to
ask both how we know what they represent, and what we may say

about pictorial representations once we have 'put a name to them'.[1]

Now connections again. We generally recognise *connections*, whether between works of literature or between works of art, as something distinct from fortuitous resemblances. We are not slow to declare chance similarities to be without significance, irrelevant, misleading, best dismissed; until perhaps some fact of which we had not been aware, or had been inclined to disregard, shows them in a different light. This may make them significant after all, and we then 'change our mind about them'. They become connections. This is all common experience. It is extremely difficult to trace the operation of similar processes of adjustment in past centuries. They may for all that be reflected in the works which have come down to us. Not least among our difficulties is that of leaving a medieval picture without its gloss. We tend to *seek* connections and allusions in the light of our own knowledge which we supplement, assisted by instruments such as bibliographies, concordances, motif-indexes and picture archives, acquaintance with which the Middle Ages were largely spared. It is also difficult to disregard what medieval works mean to us as a purely aesthetic experience, even when we know that this prompts anachronistic assertions. Let us, however, assume that we can learn to see medieval works in roughly medieval perspective.

If we are not mistaken, that is to say, if the connections we see between medieval works (let us think only of works of one kind) are not an illusion, then in each case the artist or the poet involved must have seen a corresponding possibility and opportunity of establishing a connection. He alluded to or quoted an existing work with which he wished his agreement to be seen, or to which he wanted to offer some kind of homage, or (more simply) which he found it expedient to adapt or imitate. From the moment he began to write or draw he was, conversely, at pains to avoid what might seem to be a quotation or an allusion: what would seem to be a cliché or a current mannerism. And now (the point of these preliminaries): *recognition* – whether in literature or in art – is prompted by the simplest and often the most primitive of signals or 'bearers of meaning'; not by anything so complicated as trains of thought or ideas, nothing so organised as complete sentences. We can usefully disregard the primitive signals; not however the

[1] In these introductory remarks I have tried to frame my generalisations about pictures to cover both ecclesiastical and secular art. They necessarily apply primarily to the former.

simple ones. Associations which offer themselves to poets and artists through simple signals, particularly during intervals in composition, may have to be discarded after being entertained for a time; *or* they may be exploited. In the process the poet or artist consciously and sub-consciously associates his work with works of its kind. He contributes to the tradition in which he works. He may appear to us to be a considerable innovator. Various branches of scholarship make it their business to establish the position of individual works within the tradition to which they belong: by the study of connections, relationships, affinities. Let us proceed from that point.

In all our historical disciplines we record, beside the general flow of events, 'epoch-making' developments. Whatever our study, these seem generally to be ushered in and accompanied by massive 'borrowings' – a term used to cover all kinds of adaptations of foreign models. The history of language offers countless examples of borrowings, generally in the wake of a major event in political, religious or social history, conquest, mission, conversion etc. The adaptation-by-translation of the vocabulary and formulaic phraseology of the Christian religion (together with the Church's rituals and ceremonies) transformed the languages of the communities turning to the new faith. There were consequent semantic changes in the stock of native words, and endless shiftings within word-fields as new concepts were accommodated. As for literary history, the lore and the stories (and the forms of presentation) of other peoples and civilisations came each in their turn 'as a revelation' to the peoples of Western or continental Europe which received them: *matière de Rome, de Troie, de Bretagne*. They were seized upon and developed in a first flourishing or renaissance of the vernacular literatures of Europe. Native tradition was concurrently refurbished to match the standards evolved in the process of imitating foreign models. Some of the original native lore is known to us in fact only in the relatively late sophistication of emulators, *Beowulf*, for instance, or the *Nibelungenlied*.

If in the last paragraph we seem to have stretched the term recognition somewhat to include the discovery and opening up of new 'sources', we can as we turn to art say more simply that early Christian artists recognised in the repertory of late Antiquity the models they required for the illustration of Old and New Testament story, and even for the pictorial representation of tenets of the new faith, primarily belief in a resurrection and an after-life. The image of the Winged

Victory provided a suitable likeness for the messengers of the Christian God. Prometheus fashioning men became the God of Genesis. The available picture of Orpheus served for a time as David the Psalmist. Christ as he is represented on sarcophagi and the walls of catacombs is not in origin a New Testament figure at all, but the Good Shepherd (beardless, wearing a short tunic, carrying a lamb on his shoulders) of Antique art. The early Church appropriated even 'key' images of other mystery religions, for the Madonna and Child, for instance, as is almost too well known, and also for the Nativity of the Saviour. This (as a nativity in a *cave*) can be traced back iconographically via the apocryphal New Testament Gospels to an actual cave sacred to the cult of Mithra. In all these various circumstances of borrowing and adaptation in the field of art, images which have hitherto had one meaning in an 'original' context acquire a new scriptural meaning. The old meaning is at once wrong and is soon anathema to the teachers (with some delay to the taught) of the new faith. It is not even rehearsed in a catalogue of things anathematised.[1] In contrast with this 'semantic leap' to be observed in the case of images, change in the meaning of words, and in the contents of which words are the bearers, is generally more gradual and less suddenly final.

Particularly the remarks in the last paragraph might suggest that as our next step we should review some of the more important word-image case histories – in sacred or secular tradition – as these have been treated in many important monographs, and abstract from them whatever general principles we may observe, and think to be useful and applicable elsewhere. I have, however, already stated that I want to focus attention first on the processes by which associations are formed and connections seen (and evidently were formed and seen in the Middle Ages). As for basic semantic principles, they are better taken as we know them from the study of language (I give reasons for this below) and brought to bear upon images. I have chosen this more primitive approach for two reasons. First because processes of association, simple as they may seem when described, cannot be taken for granted; if for no other reason, because we all tend today to see connections between images, and texts and images, which the medieval observer cannot seriously have entertained. (We draw on post-Renaissance and post-Reformation knowledge and belief, and form wrong associations.)

[1] Heretical beliefs expressed in words were and are still rehearsed, together with the names of those responsible for them.

Secondly, associations are formed (see above) with the help of units which are far less than works, less than subjects, and for which we have no terms in our ordinary vocabulary. Further, there are generally several contexts in which these various signs can occur. Our task is to discover these, but these only, and scarcely in any circumstances to *invent* or postulate others ('there must have been pictures in which . . .' is not an admissible assertion). This is another way of saying that to interpret a medieval picture we must adduce only medieval texts, preferably the text or texts which the image was evolved to illustrate. We must refuse to see connections which merely 'strike us' as possible. Our aim is not to propose possibilities but to find proprieties of interpretation, and having found them to recognise them (acknowledge them).

This involves us in the consideration of a few texts with which we were not previously familiar or had overlooked (intervening centuries having ceased to assert their importance); more often with the reconsideration in medieval terms of texts which we now understand otherwise. For instance biblical texts. The important thing to know is not 'who really wrote it', or what the Hebrew or the Greek was, or whether it is in Mark rather than Luke, but whether it has an important place in the Liturgy. To what position in its commemorative ritual had the Church assigned it? It is its meaning there which we shall find relevant when we seek the proper interpretation of works of ecclesiastical art, and that meaning may have to be taken into account when we look at certain secular pictures which resemble them. The connection between the liturgical (biblical) word and a Christian image may be authoritative; it may even be official.

With that we come to the end of the introductory remarks I have to make. If the tone has at times seemed excessively dogmatic, there is little I can say in excuse beyond the fact that this chapter is something of an experiment. I shall remind readers of this, and point out in what ways the experiment falls short of the objectivity expected of a scientific enquiry.

*Basic Semantic Principles*

There is no generally accepted doctrine of semantics even among philologists, who make some useful initial assumptions which the 'pure' semantics of linguistic science cannot allow. (In this book I go further. I consider 'meaning' only within the context of tradition in literature and in art. But first the preliminaries.) We have some general working principles and a few well-tried formulæ to which we have reduced the more important patterns of change in the meaning of words. We use a round dozen of terms from rhetoric to characterise retrospectively changes which we recognise as having taken place, but generally speaking we do not find any 'laws' worth formulating. 'Crane' for instance, the name of the bird, seems virtually from the outset to have been an apt designation of the builder's lifting-gear (see the dictionaries under *crane*,[2] *grue*,[2] *Kran*, where we are referred to *crane*[1], *grue*[1] and *Kranich*). This is, since we need so to be reminded, a case of 'obscured metaphor'. Well and good, we see no particular point in listing all the instances, because we know that at the same time, within limits, every word has its own history. We have the principle of the 'obscured metaphor', and perhaps a score or so more, equally useful principles.

We shall not go far wrong if we assume that, just as every word has its history, so has each image. We shall falsify that history whenever we isolate it, but none the less, even an inadequate account of a word – its forms and meanings, numbered 1, 2, 3, with dates of first occurrences and *loci* – is useful to us, and we have dictionaries, generally alphabetically arranged. I propose to ask (experimentally) how far we shall get if we attempt to treat images roughly as we treat words, in order to establish basic meanings (if that is possible) and understand the developments which images have undergone. We shall naturally encounter difficulties. There will in fact be no results of the kind that might find their way into handbooks. Though the attempt must therefore in a way fail, there are so many evident parallels with word-history that we must venture out and pursue them for a time. I will not list in advance the parallels I see, but single out one to show the way. The starting-point of a change of meaning, whether of word or image, may be either an involuntary failure or a more arbitrary refusal to recognise (see and acknowledge) an accepted, conventional relationship between sign and meaning. That is: misunderstanding, misinterpretation, misuse – which may result in a permanent change. Other parallels will be pointed out as we progress. For the rest, in word-history, based as it is on evidence infinitely more massive, continuous and susceptible of interpretation than anything that the world of art has to offer, we can establish with fair precision where, when, and at least surmise why the meaning of words changed, singly or in groups. (I refer here to changes of a more modest order than 'epoch-making', see above.) To have a rough framework of reference for our discussion of images, I will therefore rehearse quickly what we normally say about semantic change in the case of words. We will keep to nouns, and not treat names as though they were a very special category; it is mainly from the study of nouns that we get our working principles.

# 1. THE WORD

Of plants and animals, tools and gears of all kinds, illnesses, states of mind, ideas and concepts (the list is endless), we can name or designate with confidence only those with which experience and training have brought us into close contact. The training may have been specialised, comprehensive and systematic, in 'a subject'; but even so the point is never reached at which we infallibly recognise and name every relevant 'object' put before us, in accordance with an accepted norm 'correctly'. I do not mean that we never catch up with the expanding universes of specialist jargons, or that there comes a point where we call a truce to discrimination and use a term which serves. I mean that we mistake an object (let us keep to objects) and give it the name of another, calling a 'gasket' for instance what is a 'template'. We are 'under a misapprehension'. And now a leap into other areas. The situation is the same with the principal figures in mythologies and legends, and with the characters in works of literature; also with the fundamental principles and the symbols of the discrete economies of thought and scientific systems; with the phraseology and terms used by the trade and professional or social groups, and more or less secret societies and sects. Names, designations, signs and symbols are recognised in their accepted meaning and used 'again', virtually unchanged. Or they are mistaken, wrongly understood, but used, with or without further consequences. A mistaken use may be tolerated (silently corrected by those who hear it). Or a speaker is discreetly or otherwise put right (in practice often wrongly corrected). Or the 'true' name or designation is constantly and repeatedly alluded to through figures (of metaphor, irony, euphemism). A figurative designation may 'take on', survive for a time as a quotation and then be discarded; or it ceases to be a quotation and enters common use (cf obscured metaphor). In mistaken designations, oblique and allusive references and varieties of wilful (witty, malicious, etc.) sense-inversion, philologists see the starting-point of perhaps most changes of meaning. All these tendencies are at work against a shifting background of historical flow and developing institutions, interrupted from time to time by momentous events and upheavals. Before we leave words, here are two brief supplementary observations.

In order to be able to write at all about changes of meaning, we have, generally, to concentrate attention on one word (or thing) at a time. Even studies devoted to 'word clusters' or 'word fields' have to do this first and last (we cannot read synoptic tables synoptically). Next: by 'signs' and 'symbols' (above) I did not mean at this stage anything profound or mysterious. At the same time, bearing in mind that we shall not be concerned with everyday situations, but with literary and artistic traditions, I should perhaps indicate as relevant: posture, gesture, intonation, eloquent silences, which may (in dialogue, or in drama on the stage) be clear in the meaning they convey. In the corresponding *images* the lack of a dimension and of movement may cause us to mistake these, even though they are generally both exaggerated and stylised in compensation. We may take 'homage' to be 'supplication', 'intercession' to be 'accusation', 'he teaches' to be 'he announces'.


## 2. THE MOTIF

We shall only rarely be concerned in this book with isolated words. We shall be considering established and developing verbal traditions in which all of us who have to deal in any way with 'writings' recognise recurrent units of the most varied kinds and magnitudes: subjects, motifs, *topoi*, elements of a philosophy, items of dogma. We observe them by and in their recurrence. They prompt reflection, which may lead to enquiry, assessment, re-assessment. We are all, according to our lights, virtually continuously engaged in this. Nothing transmitted in words – not even dogma – is stable in its meaning. The median unit on which we focus attention is, to get back to the subject, the motif. It is at this point sufficient for us to note that in so far as there is a scientific approach to the subject-matter of literature, it has recognised the motif as the working unit, and equipped itself with its motif-indexes. To repeat and continue: the starting point of our reflections on literary tradition is a *schooled*, but for all that *intuitive* recognition of similarities, common features and connections. With no further definitions at this stage, I turn now to the case of images.

## 3. THE IMAGE

In the case of images the situation is more complicated in that the draughtsman's strokes are not letters. There can be no technically infallible 'reading' of images. Recognition of the artist's meaning is consequently more difficult, not only for us moderns who happen to be interested in medieval works. Often a medieval artist mistakes the subject-matter of his pictorial model, or merely some element in it. In his endeavour to reproduce his source, he further obscures an originally intended meaning. A *new* content may then be seen by a successor, who draws what he recognises with conviction, and the original image has totally changed its identity; its meaning is then problematic. The resultant tradition (notionally three pictures) presents us with a riddle, the solution of which may be clear enough if all three pieces of evidence can be assembled. Otherwise there is a risk that we will rationalise the evidence we have, supplying an explanation which may be a pure fiction. We must hope not to encounter the third picture in isolation. A good deal more could be said at this point where by an interpretation we mean no more than the simple identification of content. The difficulties may, as I have indicated, be attributable to the circumstances in which identification is called for. A picture may have become detached from its context, the syntax of which alone reliably determined its meaning. There have always been excisers of pictures, among them occasionally their custodians. Modern scholars, it might be argued, continue this process with their endless re-shufflings of reproductions to illustrate their special theses about schools, periods, styles, or to illustrate a special history, of costume, of armour. In experience one meets an alarming proportion of the medieval pictures one ever knows, *first* in such detachment from their proper setting.

So far we have been thinking of more or less involuntary 'misreadings' and have assumed that mistaken identifications will soon be corrected. That is of course far from being the situation, but we shall be wise to move on! I touch now upon the case of more wilful re-interpretation. This can perhaps better be illustrated by reference to a well-known picture of later date. For instance the copper-engraving of about

1503 in which Albrecht Dürer offered his image of Nemesis: he himself called it 'Nemesis' (Plate 7a). He had copies with him on the Netherlands journey, and his diary refers to gifts he made of 'Nemesis'. This did not prevent his contemporaries from seeing in this picture a 'Fortune'. The picture *was* thereafter, to all intents and purposes, Fortune – a familiar concept. Nemesis is by comparison an unfamiliar, difficult or unwelcome idea. The picture is still widely quoted as *Das grosse Glück*, and scholars who know it *is* a Nemesis generally identify and legitimate their interest by referring to it as the 'so-called *Grosses Glück*'. If 'fortune' is the topic, the first, often the only picture which springs to mind today is Dürer's. Dürer's successors modelled their Fortunes on his Nemesis, *not* on his Fortunes, of which there are at least three.[1] Such wilful 'mistaking' no less than involuntarily wrong identification of an image may lead to a change of meaning. The mistake may prove irreversible. The more normal case, however, is analogous rather to the semantic 'drift' of words, where accumulated associations produce a precarious state of balance and ambiguity. The centre of gravity then finally shifts, and what had been an association becomes the 'real meaning' of the image. There are still further possibilities. One which will occupy us at several points in this study is that, in the Middle Ages as nowadays, artists occasionally intended their images to be and remain ambivalent; not merely rich in associations and provocative of thought, but poised at a nexus of associations. It is the medieval equivalent, I suppose, of a 'conceit', demanding a certain detachment and wit for a successful interpretation; why not? Or again: an artist consciously modified a traditional iconography in its outline so that it should patently allude to another *image*. In this way he also linked his picture with a wider range of *verbal* tradition. I do not attach any importance to the observation, but I should say this is analogous to our 'extended metaphor' or sustained simile. This too we must surely consider to be a development (extension) of the meaning of an image. Finally (finally among the points I wish to raise now) an artist will always try to vary and modify. Avoidance of the familiar is to be found in 'original composition' of every kind, perhaps even in what appears to be the characteristic *ductus* of an artist's hand.

From case to case one would need, if this line is to be pursued, to determine whether there has been a mere shift of meaning (e.g. Nemesis with Fortune associations becomes Fortune), roughly the

[1] A further note on Dürer's *Nemesis* in Appendix A, p. 122.

equivalent of metonymy; whether a given image has been enlivened by allusions (profound, witty); *or* whether there has been a complete and final change of meaning. In the latter case we may be faced here and there with, as it were, homonyms. It is worth noting as a characteristic of late medieval art that more and more attributes, often supported by a good deal of text in longer and wider scrolls, are needed to *identify* images, *and* to insist at the same time on the wide range of their allusive references to other images. These considerations all make it seem more difficult to envisage a comprehensive lexicon of images.

## 4. A LEXICON OF IMAGES?

This may seem to be slow progress, but I hope that our attention to semantic principles is leading and will lead to some useful interim insights. We have now reached the point where we may ask how far we should get in any endeavour to register systematically the images used in medieval art, together with their meanings. We shall soon find ourselves in insuperable logical and practical difficulties – why? The available and often quite massive compendia used by the art historians are only to a very limited extent arranged 'according to pictures'. There will be reasons for this which we are now, somewhat laboriously, rediscovering. If one disregards a certain number of graphic conventions customarily dismissed as decorative (or 'space-filling'), and a few enciphered compositions of the type 'device', 'coat of arms', there would seem to be very few medieval units or complexes which occur, let us say, only *in* or only *as* pictures: for instance 'mandorla' (an almond-shaped glory), 'nimbus' – on the one hand; the *Majestas Domini* and the 'Throne of Grace' among compositions.[1]

These two, the *Majestas* and the 'Throne of Grace', are, I should in the end say, 'pure' images, or purely images. They are known to have written sources, but these in their turn were visionaries' fictions. The

[1] *Majestas Domini:* Christ (or God) enthroned in a mandorla, supported by the symbols of the four Evangelists, e.g. Beckwith, illus. 43, 65, 76 and our own plate 23a. 'Throne of Grace': God the Father holds on outstretched hands the Cross with the crucified Son; the Holy Spirit in the form of a dove hovers above (as a rule above the head of the Crucified, occasionally with wing tips so disposed as to recall 'proceeding from the Father and the Son', see plate 17a). See Appendix B, pp. 127 ff.

*Majestas Domini* is modelled on the vision of Ezekiel.[1] Rupert of Deutz (d. 1129) was suggested by Stammler[2] as the source of what proved to be the finally acceptable image of the Trinity which we call a 'Throne of Grace'. The genre 'imaginary picture' is always trouble-some, for the pictures invented by authors are rarely susceptible of full translation into pictorial terms.[3] We may, however, as pragmatists state that the names 'Majestas Domini' and 'Throne of Grace' (*Thrône de grâce*, *Gnadenstuhl*) are technical terms used by specialists, or at any rate connoisseurs. They have no general currency. The images them-selves on the other hand are known (whether really understood or not) to everyone. It will always be proper to draw attention to the vision of Ezekiel ('scripture') as the source of the *Majestas*, but not to Rupert of Deutz (in any case conceivably a wrong attribution). In both cases the images have acquired a precedence over their written sources.[4] These two images would therefore certainly deserve important entries in our lexicon. But how will one classify them *as* pictures without immediate recourse to words or names? Let us, however, not worry too much about the technical difficulties. There are ways of classifying things according to profile.

Otherwise it seems that there are few head-words in the art his-torian's existing compendia over articles devoted strictly to images and *their* meanings. A few familiar animal names, perhaps, like lamb, lion and names of simpler realia. Here one may indeed read about the meanings of say, *Lamb*[1] to *Lamb*[5], and discover the *loci* where these occur. We need no special information on how artists in the Middle Ages drew lambs and lions (though one may be puzzled by some of their lions). As soon as we get to the less familiar animals (elephant, crocodile), and more particularly to exotic or fabulous beings like the biblical Leviathan, the stranger animals of the *Physiologus* and the bestiaries themselves – phoenix, gryphon – the sign or symbol seems less stable than the meaning, and the two have to be described and registered in parallel. Most of the animal entries differ from the pattern which was appropriate in the case of 'Lamb'; they are nearer to the case presented by 'Phoenix'. It is the name which is used as

[1] Ezek. i 5 ff.
[2] *Aufriss*, III 626.
[3] See Beryl Smalley, *English Friars and Antiquity* (Oxford, 1960) pp. 112, 118, 134. The *Ackermann aus Böhmen* (see pp. 31 ff, 178 ff) describes in chapter 16 a 'Triumph of Death fresco in Rome' which continues to baffle commentators.
[4] More on Ezekiel in Appendix B, p. 127.

head-word, and what follows is concerned not with the meaning of the image, but rather with that of the name or word, so that for meanings we might just as well start with names and words in Cruden's *Bible Concordance* or Isidore of Seville's *Etymologies*. For the rest the articles tell us how medieval artists customarily drew the particular object, animal or person, and where the image occurs in terms of places (portals, freizes, manuscripts). They also go systematically through the media and crafts down to needlework in which we may find examples. That is why the compendia are called iconographical handbooks (the counterparts of the older iconologies). In short, the art historian does not need to invent any new lexica and grammars based on meanings rather than signs and symbols, as various kinds of linguists have done. The reference works he already has, and evidently the only ones he can compile and use, are already arranged according to content, mainly by means of the names of things or persons, or titles of themes, and conventional names for motifs (Dame Fortune, Battle of the Virtues and Vices, Dance of Death). There seems to be no more natural way to sort out pictures.

By a lexical entry we understood hitherto (to return for a moment to words), a head-word, rubrics indicating *period* (Anglo-Saxon, Old High German, *etc.*) and area, the *forms* occurring in texts and the *meanings* established by contextual study. Within a reasonably circumscribed period and geographical area the forms are relatively stable. The meanings within the period, always several of them, can be classified as 'proper' and 'figurative'. These are clearly interrelated and susceptible of logical arrangement, often too of a simple historical elucidation. The meanings of pictures, however, seem to be virtually identical with the meaning, not so much of the things they represent as of the names of these in a context of almost exclusively verbal tradition. In the following list the principal and dominant associations, except in the case of more homely realia at the end, are verbal: Adam, Trinity, Host, chalice; Parzival, Grail; Emperor, Bishop, Peasant; Throne; seat, lamp. To attach meanings to these as images is, therefore, the business of the beholder, who must bring to bear on them, not a general familiarity with medieval art, but a detailed knowledge of medieval verbal tradition.

Anyone proposing to study medieval pictures may therefore experience difficulties, because the handbooks of iconography assume that he will know under what words, names or titles to 'look up' the pictures he encounters. Even with a fair knowledge of the subjects treated by medieval artists, and a considerable amount of training in this very business of interpreting pictures, he will still inevitably have to forget as rapidly as possible his initial identification of many a seemingly simple picture. And so we pass quickly to the situation where even the expert art historians are not sure how they should 'read' a picture. Though this is common knowledge, it has to be said that the normal procedure is a provisional and experimental rationalisation of the whole content it appears to present. This is done at first without prejudice, and tested in many ways. Up to a point this is analogous to our tentative approach to a passage in a foreign language, in which unknown elements or an unfamiliar construction are allotted a meaning or function. In the end one 'gets out' a meaning. (Then someone with better knowledge declares the interpretation to be right or wrong.) But in scrutinising a picture we are not directly seeking the meaning of the signs we see, or merely seeking a good and coherent sense, but we are looking for a sense *which we already know*. If the sense we arrive at is good and coherent but unfamiliar, it will in all likelihood be a fiction suggested by a number of associable marks and signs. It may be necessary to leave the picture with its provisional interpretation, which, if quoted, will remain linked with a name ('according to X', etc.) Then, as likely as not, a 'parallel' will turn up which will facilitate identification of the text actually illustrated, whereupon all parts of the picture fall into place.[1] In some cases, however, the artists 'did not know what they were drawing'. They were following an atelier tradition 'blindly' (better: unquestioningly). The compendia of the art historian, therefore, to sum up this argument, are not primarily concerned with meanings (they assume them known, but state them for convenience); their aim is to register and seek to account for conventions of representation.

At this point it may be objected that there are so many pictorial conventions with which one has been familiar since childhood, and there is so much in medieval pictures that is 'realistic anyway' – why take all this trouble over what are obvious procedures of interpretation?

---

[1] I am glad at this point to be able to refer to a study by Dr Adelheid Heimann, 'Jeremiah and his Girdle', in *JWCI* xxv (1962) 1–8, in which the interpretation of four reliefs on the West Front of Notre Dame in Paris turns on the identification of an object in one of them (bow? serpent?). Once established as Jeremiah's *girdle* all previous attempts at interpretation collapse, but the handbooks will in their professional *Schadenfreude* ensure that they are not forgotten!

We know the human figure in a fair range of conventional postures; there are attributes like crowns, haloes, wings, shields, which quickly limit the possibilities of identification; a general knowledge of Bible stories, legends, myths, romances and so on should suffice. 'The odd bits will fall into place'. For safety's sake one will not make such distinctions between familiar and unfamiliar lore. The way in which Germanic or Celtic artists represented human figures must surely demand more of us than that we be reminded of match-stick men or mummies; and a bearded patriarch, balancing a small but snarling *dragon* on top of a fluted *column* complete with acanthus capital is not to every eye (certainly not to mine) Moses with the Brazen Serpent (see plate 22b). He may have his tablets, and it is true that 'it can only be Moses'. That does not solve the column and the dragon.[1] In such cases one can indeed speak of 'foreign' conventions of representation. Some special training of the eye and mind is evidently needed if we are to become familiar with them, and a good deal more reading in written sources if we are to find their *rationale*. Here and there we shall indeed feel that something in the nature of an etymological entry would be useful too, to explain the 'roots' of some of these traditions. And since we have mentioned columns, why must Peter's cock so often be put on top of one to do his crowing (plate 18b)? Is the column a pedestal – no more?[2] It begins to look as though our notional lexicon of 'images with their meanings' might present insuperable difficulties of organisation, and as though the entries, if they are to include 'etymologies', would be of such complexity as to be virtually incomprehensible.[3]

One then needs to add that medieval artists often misinterpreted heir models, or glossed and rationalised what they did not completely understand. Not only does that complicate the task of any would-be lexicographer, who must of course register these cases; it reminds us of the temptations he would be exposed to himself. The tyranny of the alphabet, or of whatever system of classification was used, would force him to attempt the solution of problems which only monographic

---

[1] Chartres Cathedral, *c.* 1215; fuller discussion, pp. 260 ff.

[2] More on this subject, pp. 134 ff.

[3] I prepared experimentally, but decided not to print a 'lexical' word-image entry 'Dragon' (*draco*[1], *draco*[2]), with cross-references to the synonym-antonym 'Serpent' (*serpens*[1] *serpens*[3] – NB *serpens*[2] is a musical instrument and irrelevant). Even restricted to three *loci* (the Chartres Moses, the Meuse Valley Brazen Serpent and a hymn by Prudentius, to all of which reference will be found on pp. 260 ff), the entry was scarcely intelligible.

treatment of motifs can deal with. We have to conclude that although a lexicon making representational units its starting point is conceivable, its logical foundations would be questionable; it would scarcely be practicable.

In the course of these deliberations we have become aware of various circumstances which may lead to a misunderstanding of the subject of medieval pictures. Of the pictures which seem, on the face of things, to be clear and unambiguous in their meaning, some may in fact deceive us. Many apparently simple objects stand, we know, for abstract ideas. How are we to know that we have recognised them all – correctly? Here dilettante *over-interpretation* is, however, almost as dangerous as simple ignorance of conventions. The very existence of medieval lists or glossaries of numbers, colours, names of flowers, precious stones, ascribing to each item often a very specific deeper, symbolic meaning – a kind of *catechetic lore* of symbolism – should make us cautious. Firstly, all lists and compendia are suspect. They are the work of compilers who, bringing up the rear, are never prepared to leave well alone.[1] Secondly, whatever is subordinate in a work of representational art, as colours, numbers or numerical relationships and embellishments surely of necessity are, can only modify the meaning of a picture or determine its mood.[2]

There are some pictures, again, though no doubt few in number, which I think may stand substitute for ideas or situations which could not (and even today cannot) be drawn. The semantic problems raised by this phenomenon (if it can ever be reliably documented, which I doubt) are considerable. It seems to involve the off-loading of a literary motif on to an image which was not devised to, and cannot properly illustrate it. We can only be made aware of image substitution of this kind by a non-coincidence of verbal and pictorial traditions which arouses our suspicions.[3]

Before these digressions on lexicography, in which most of what I have said may appear pretty obvious to the art historian, I referred to the drawing which is *intended* to be ambiguous or ambivalent. Medieval

[1] Cf. the remarks on medieval works on church symbolism, p. 37. By catechetic lore I mean lore which is kept alive by schedules of questions ('what is the meaning of green?')
[2] This will be hotly contested. I come back to the subject towards the end of this book, pp. 346 ff.
[3] Possible examples are cited in Appendix A, pp. 122 f.

artists made greater use of this device than is generally realised. I am not thinking now of complicated 'problem pictures' of the kind that Dürer was to leave us,[1] but of compositions in which the observer is given something to think about: a statement that could not equally well have been made in words.[2] Such conceits remind one of the pun, to which the medieval mind was in any case more attached than we are. The Church Fathers had set an example in punning, which with them was more akin to our etymological fancies than to our mere word-play. The pun was used as an instrument of proof, not merely of the rightness of names, but also of the origins of things; it also clearly confirmed an argument sustained by other means.[3] The whole science of etymology (the findings of which may become parts of theology, Christology and Mariology) is based in the Middle Ages to a very considerable extent on what we should consider to be the pun.

## 5. THE EXEMPLAR (DRAWING PATTERN)

Towards the end of the last section the simple image was beginning to be displaced in our argument by a larger representational unit, the subject of which had the complexity of a motif, for instance Dame Fortune. The material found in the photographic archives of an art-historical institute is arranged largely according to motifs. (The motif is something we recognise intuitively and work with, not something we stop – unless we want to stop for ever – to define.) Can we then, having failed with simple images – roughly the equivalent of words and names – consider the feasibility of a compendium of pictorial patterns or exemplars, so that we may see what motifs are in their pictorial outline similar, and therefore associable by recognition? Since associative thinking begins with the recognition of 'images in approximate register' (I think the expression may be new, but I hope it will be immediately understood), would such a compilation not at

[1] Some of Dürer's 'problems' arise from his illustrating out-of-the-way texts and leaving us to find the key by rationalisation, or re-identification of his sources.

[2] Illustrations of this principle have been relegated to Appendix B, see particularly the treatment of 'Peters Keys' pp. 130 ff.

[3] See Willy Sanders, 'Grundzüge und Wandlungen der Etymologie' in *Wirkendes Wort*, XVII (1967) 361–84, a most useful survey of the history of etymology; on the use made by the Church Fathers, 367 ff.

least remind us of possible and conceivably proper associations in a medieval context? That would, by reminding us of possibilities, curb our tendency to 'cast around' for similarities, prevent us from making prejudiced comparisons and postulating relationships which a medieval beholder might have rejected as irrelevant. But we are here again involved in a circularity of argument, as we were when talking about a lexicon of simple images. The very idea that certain exemplars may have governed associative thinking presupposes a whole series of judgments we have ourselves passed on the meaning of images in the medieval artist's repertory. Before resigning, I propose to take the case of a possible exemplar and annotate it as fully as possible in the light of medieval tradition generally. The vicious circle may turn out in the end to be a spiral.

### The Seated Figure

In a longish section I propose now to examine the many seated figures which one may encounter in medieval contexts, whether they occur in the Church's annual commemoration of sacred history (in the Liturgy) or belong to an imperial past or a heroic age, and whether they are portrayed by artists or evoked in the words of poets. This is, for good or ill, a record of my own attempts over the years to associate these various figures *and* to discriminate between them from a medieval viewpoint. Towards the end I refer to an attempt made by a colleague in art history to survey a larger gallery of seated figures from a vantage-point in Renaissance art.[1] So that readers may know at once the range of the two completely independent investigations taken together, I mention now that the art historian's concern was to 'place' Dürer's *Melancholia*. Mine is to deal with a group of medieval images including David the Psalmist, the Man of Sorrows, and some secular figures of whom the Minstrel may stand as representative. The fundamental difference in method between the two investigations is that I have sought to distinguish between 'official' or authoritative interpretations and 'occasional' meanings. That on the one hand. On the other I have not written as an art historian with the solution of particular problems in mind, but conducted an experiment.

[1] See p. 113 (below) and Appendix A, p. 123. I retain here what were my own references to Dürer's *Melancholia*.

My starting point is a relatively simple pictorial formula which, as I describe it, will leap to mind, but refuse to be unambiguously identified: *a male figure with bowed head, seated on a rock or mound*. Who is this? A thinker (philosopher), a visionary, a *vates* or poet pondering or sorrowing (Walther von der Vogelweide, for instance)? Or is it the Psalmist David, or Christ, or Charles the Great, or King Rother in the Middle High German poem with that name? Because of the uncertainty about the rock (or mound – or heap) let us add Job. I should want to add Jeremiah to this group of seated figures, speaking the words of his threnody 'Is it nothing to you, all ye that pass by?' (*O vos omnes qui transitis per viam . . . est dolor sicut dolor meus?*). Others will think of pictures of the evangelists, others again of certain portraits of emperors which I should now prefer to exclude, not because of any pedantic insistence on rocks, but because 'with bowed head' is intended to exclude them. To avoid misunderstandings it will be well if I state again that these seated figures are in various ways associated in my mind now. Other seated figures seem to me to be derivatives (or completions) of a very similar, but for all that different exemplar. In each instance I have naturally a number of reservations to make, and I admit to some misgivings about the extension of the list to include some of my variants. I concede also that there is an arbitrary element of 'not wanting' others. And finally there is the point to be made that these seated figures have become associated in my mind without any assistance from modern compendia or as a result of specific researches; the figures have associated themselves in this way during some twenty years of my remembering, being reminded, noting, forgetting, overlooking, and then finally reflecting and applying to them what judgment I can muster.[1]

This was roughly the list of seated figures which I thought associable in a medieval context (I give my rationalisations later) when some eight years ago a colleague in German studies took me to Stuttgart to examine one particular picture in the Stuttgart Psalter. He wanted me to see the picture of *Anima* on folio 55: a female figure seated on a green mound or hill, her chin cupped in or thrust into her hand (see plate 9c). My colleague expected me to recognise with him 'Walther von der

---

[1] For convenience I have introduced a number of sub-headings (absent in the German edition) in the remainder of this section. Some have greater justification as groupings than others. It was not possible to give the first heterogeneous group of seated figures (*Anima*, Walther, Ezekiel) a heading.

Vogelweide' (see plate 9a), and was somewhat shocked at the completeness of my rejection of the suggestion. Since then I have on several
occasions shown *Anima* to colleagues in German studies, and *always* the
response has been 'Walther von der Vogelweide!'.[1] The immediate
recognition, coupled with delight at the striking similarity shuts out
any other possible parallels. That is just the point, that the other
parallels must be known. It is only when I object that *Anima* shows a
female figure, that Dürer's *Melancholia* (particularly as that picture is
recalled) is able to suggest itself for comparison. Reflecting now on
*Melancholia* and *Anima*, the 'sadness' of both figures may prompt
'Tristitia' as a middle term, which is more correct than one at first
realises. (The *Anima* picture illustrates *quare tristis es – anima mea*.)[2] If
schooled associative thinking then reminds one that *tristitia* was widely
current in the Middle Ages as a synonym of *acedia* (sloth), thoughts of
Walther von der Vogelweide have probably already been pushed far
into the background, and it is perhaps a matter for speculation whether
one should have thought of Walther at all. One asks in a self-accusatory
way whether one should have been so spell-bound by that energetic
plunging of the chin into the cupped hand.[3] The reader will not have to
read much further before he sees why I myself cannot associate *Anima*
and *Walther*; not because I see no resemblances in outline, but because
I have, I think once and for all, seen in 'David the Psalmist and Lawgiver' the nearest parallel to, and, I am convinced, the pattern for the
*Walther* in the Manesse manuscript. So (for me) Anima – a female
figure – is excluded. She and Melancholia belong to a very similar but
distinguishable group of seated female figures. A line has to be drawn.
I draw it to exclude Anima; to the reader this must at present seem
arbitrary.

Some time after I myself had come to terms with most of the
problems presented by the seated figure with bowed head, I realised
that Julius Schwietering in his *Deutsche Dichtung des Mittelalters* had

[1] It is only a slight exaggeration to say that this experience (*Anima* in the context of
German studies) is one of two or three which convinced me of the necessity of
attempting the semantic essay which became this chapter. There are fundamental
problems of recognition here which cannot be solved by making or using
indexes or 'complete' pictorial archives.

[2] Psalm (*Vulg.*) xlii, (A.V.) xliii 4–5. A further note in Appendix A, p. 124.

[3] In terms of our introductory remarks, this gesture is a representational unit
which lies at a nexus of associations. We tend today to see it as something identifying individual images.

devoted a page or so of text to a comparison of the Manesse *Walther* with a French relief carving of the prophet Ezekiel (Amiens cathedral, c. 1225–35, see plate 9d).[1] Moreover he had reproduced each image in his handbook, which is one of our standard works. This gave food for thought in various directions, not least to account for my own failure to remember that this comparison had been made at all.[2] Next, to wonder whether Schwietering knew the *Anima* picture. I think it unlikely; or perhaps his own discovery of the Ezekiel relief obliterated any memory of it. To him Walther was 'like Ezekiel'.

The Ezekiel picture is, I think, not an appropriate comparison. For Schwietering the 'Old Testament Seer' is the role in which Walther saw himself, as an inspired interpreter of the events of this world. For Schwietering the 'exemplar' involved is, he says, the image normally designated 'the Author', an inheritance from the art of Antiquity. But as I had excluded 'the Evangelist' I had automatically excluded 'the Author' too, a seated figure no doubt, but (generally) with head or eyes raised toward the source of his inspiration. Looking at Schwietering's two illustrations (our plates 9a and 9d) one *may* indeed find the likeness at first striking, but is it not again this energetic plunging of the chin into the hand which establishes the connection? I cannot see in the Ezekiel anything but the 'Dreamer and his Dream', complete with the wheels of the dream. The wheels establish the identity of the image. Walther has a scroll and a sword. If a seer at all, he has wide-open eyes. He is (provisionally) a sorrowing poet or minstrel. The picture is, as we know, intimately linked with the text of Walther's *first* poem in the so-called *Reichston*, which is not a vision. Only the second and third poems in the *Reichston* are visionary. The visions are not apocalyptic. It will be understood, I trust, that I am not seeking to prove Schwietering 'wrong'. I simply state that for me the associations of the Walther image are to be sought elsewhere, and this conviction profoundly affects my interpretation of the picture's origin, and the artist's (or his patron's) intentions, about which I shall have more to say below. This aside on Walther and Ezekiel is a further illustration of the point that the interpretation of medieval pictures will always depend on the interpreter's own sense of relevance, and on his ability and perhaps on his readiness to recall parallels.

[1] This chapter was by that time ready in typescript for the German edition. Schwietering, text 247 ff, illus. 105.
[2] I have since been able to discover that few of my colleagues remember it.

Now that we have been reminded, by my narration of recent ex-
periences, of the dangers and delights of associative thinking about
pictures (consciousness of the dangers does little to diminish enthusiasm),
let us try to pick up the argument I had begun about a postulated
'exemplar' or 'typical' image. I now begin to make some of the
reservations of which I spoke. They will result in a certain dispersal of
the crowding versions and their segregation in sub-groups, or if we are
still thinking of the lexical entry which might accommodate them all,
we are preparing to enumerate our sub-headings. We shall from now
on be able (keeping chronologies in mind) to deal with verbal and
pictorial evidence in any sequence. We have got the main working
principles established. With units of the modest dimensions of the
exemplar and the motif, cross-reference from texts to images and back
will be swift. That leaves us free to concentrate on the *relevance* of the
'connections' we propose to see.

### Charles the Great, King Rother

From my list of seated figures I now take two who are more or less 'of
a kind', Charles the Great and King Rother. They will not occupy us
for long. My starting point here is not the work of artists, but verses
from the *Chanson de Roland* (soon after 1100) and its German adaptation
(about 1170); and from the Middle High German *König Rother* (about
1150), all *epic* works, in which there is a recurrent 'vignette', slightly
varied according to the stage reached in the story and the characters
involved. I take *Rother* first. Unmistakably the epic tempo is relaxed
in *Rother*, so that we may see the king in his sorrow, mourning for the
absence (as he believes, the loss) of his men:

> Rother vf eime steine saz;
> Wie trvrich ime sin herze was!
> Dre tage vnde drie nacht,
> daz er so niemanne nicht ne sprach.   (422 ff)

Rother sat there upon a rock and great sorrow was in his heart; for
three days and three nights he spoke no word to any man.

The posture is the gesture of sadness. It is therefore superfluous to
compare Rother's 'sorrow in his heart' with *tristis anima mea* in the
Psalm. We shall in any case in a moment have the example of the
heathen, Marsile, who sits thus and says that there is sorrow in his heart.

Students of German are inevitably reminded by these lines from the *Rother*, of Walther von der Vogelweide's much more methodical description of his adoption of roughly this same – clearly traditional – posture:

> Ich saz ûf eime steine
> und dahte bein mit beine,
> dar ûf satzt ich den ellenbogen:
> ich hete in mîne hant gesmogen
> daz kinne und ein mîn wange.

I sat upon a rock and crossed leg over leg; my elbow on my knee, I had sunk my chin and one cheek in my hand (and gave anxious thought to life in this world, and how one should live it, *etc.*).

Such details as Walther gives would indeed be strange in an epic context; the pace would be far too slow. Then *Charles the Great.* At three or four points in the *Chanson de Roland*[1] Charles is shown for a brief moment assuming this same posture when he is to take counsel with himself, or he has assembled his barons to hear theirs. The briefer references to his sitting in council must surely have summoned up virtually the same image as the (only slightly) longer, complete evocations. But the scene must first be set! When Charles has important matters to deliberate he goes and seats himself, not on a rock, but on an imperial folding chair in an orchard (*verger*). ('Having heard mass and matins . . .')

> Li empereres s'en vait desuz un pin,
> Ses baruns mandet pur sun cunseill fenir[2]

The emperor goes beneath a pine and summons his barons to take counsel with them.

Charles communicates King Marsile of Saragosse's offer of peace. Roland delcares that no trust may be placed in the Paynim and the war should continue. Thereupon:

> Li emperere en tint sun chef enbrunc
> Si duist sa barbe, afaitad sun gernun,
> Ni ben ne mal ne respunt sun nevuld.
> Franceis se taisent ne mais que Guenelun.[3]

---

[1] Lines 139 ff, 771, and less certainly 3816.    [2] 168 ff.    [3] 214 ff.

Charles remained seated with head bowed, stroked his beard and his moustaches, and will not say whether he likes or dislikes his nephew's advice; the Franks are silent, but for Ganelon . . .

This latter image, it is important to note, is not always acceptable to the German revisor of the *Chanson de Roland* for *his* ideal portrait of Charles taking counsel. The work of a Regensburg cleric whom we call Pfaffe Konrad, the German 'Roland' makes Charles a more devout defender of Christendom, and more clearly a mirror for crusading Emperors.[1] The author seizes the opportunity, before the story gets fully under way, of showing Charles prostrate in prayer (throughout the night and until morning) seeking the direct counsel of God. With this one may contrast the simple (but by no means merely formulaic) 'having heard mass and matins' in the *Chanson* (above). Rather remarkably the older image of the King in council is evoked, as in the *Chanson*, but with an unmistakable added emphasis, and at slightly greater length than is strictly necessary, for the heathen king, Marsile, as though it is being assigned to him:

> Der kuninc wart gewar,
> dâ ein oleboum den scate bar.
> Dar unter gesaz er eine
> ûf einem marmilstaine.
> Er dâchte in manigen ende.
> Zesamene slûger die hende.
> Er hîz vur sich chomen
> sechs wîse herzogen,
> dar zû sechs grâven
> die sînes râtes phlâgen.
> Er sprach: 'Min herce ist bevangen [etc.] . . .' (397 ff.)

The king saw there an olive tree and the shade it bore. There he took his seat upon a marble rock, alone, and thought long and deeply. He clapped his hands and summoned six wise dukes to appear before him, and in addition six counts, who were his counsellors. He said: my heart is troubled. . .

Our German handbooks inform us of a 'changed picture' of Charles in the German adaptation of the *Chanson de Roland*. This is a literary

---

[1] A brief characterisation of the German adaptation of the *Chanson de Roland*, Appendix A, p. 12/.

historian's metaphor. In a much more literal sense we have just compared two pictures: of Charles the Christian ruler, King of France, in the *Chanson*, and of Charles the Christian Emperor prostrate before his God in the German adaptation.[1] Whether our studies will want to see 'the German picture of Charles' in more visual terms in future, I do not know. The assertion that Pfaffe Konrad saw Charles' rule and his campaigns in the perspective of Augustinian Christian history (as 'Heilsgeschichte') I consider to be an exaggeration, and to show a somewhat *simpliste* interpretation of the *Chanson*'s nostaligia for *douce France*; but clearly there is a new 'image' (almost a Byzantine *proskynesis*) for Charles, the old one being assigned to the heathen, who fills it well.

Finally one should perhaps mention that Charles' tugging of his beard remains as the image of the Emperor in his wrath, even in the German version, for instance when he pronounces sentence on Marsile: *Der kaiser erzurnte harte/mit ûf gevangem barte*[2] (The king was filled with wrath, his beard clutched in his hand), and this is a picture which an artist of the end of the twelfth century included in his gallery of scenes for the Heidelberg manuscript of this work.[3]

### Job, the Man of Sorrows, David the Psalmist

We shall have very little more to say about the Rother and Charles images. There is a more compact group of variants of what I take to be basically the same exemplar. Before discussing it, here is a final word on the examples from epic poetry. The *Rother* is relatively popular, filled with adventure; it is not primarily a devout work. The 'Roland' is totally Christian in its deeper meaning and final message, more so, some will think, in the French original version than in the German adaptation (in which the message gives way to Christian propaganda). Roland, the title hero, was wild, we know, but his story culminates in

[1] Lines 47–66, too long to quote, see editions.
[2] Lines 8771–2.
[3] The quotations: *König Rother* adapted from the edition of Frings-Kuhnt (1912); *Das altfranzösische Rolandslied*, ed. Hilka-Rohlfs (Sammlung romanischer Übungstexte 3–4: 1953⁴). The *Rolandslied* of Pfaffe Konrad, ed. Fr Maurer in Deutsche Literatur in Entwicklungsreihen (Geistliche Dichtung des Mittelalters, v: 1940).
Line drawings (39 of them) after the illustrations of the Heidelberg manuscript in Wilh. Grimm's edition of 1838; some reproductions in Schwietering (illus. 58–62), but not of the subjects discussed above.

his withdrawal and isolation on the mount. The treatment, again particularly in the French version, is a long and sustained, distant and reverent allusion to the Agony, as one would know even without Pfaffe Konrad's addition of the detail that Roland retired the length of a bow-shot ('stone's throw' in Luke). For all that, the ambit of the examples we shall now consider in much greater detail is totally different. Crossing a line we pass into the other economy of history – Christian history, indeed 'Heilsgeschichte'. These are, by comparison with the instances we have been examining, static images. The first two follow, we know, scenes of some turbulence, but are generally isolated from them.

1. The seated male figure is naked (in loin cloth) and characterised as a leper. This is *Job on his dunghill*; at the same time it is Job as a 'type' of the *Man of Sorrows* (*quasi leprosus*, Isai. liii 4), 'the rejected of men'.[1]

2. The seated male figure, naked, wears a crown of thorns. This is Christ as the *Man of Sorrows and Accuser*, speaking the words of Jeremiah in the threnody: *O vos omnes* (Lamentations i 12, and the Liturgy of Holy Week); or silent, cf Lament. iii 28: *sedebit solitarius et tacebit*.

3.(*a*) A seated or enthroned figure, with crown, with or without harp: *David* (*King, Judge, Psalmist*), and - a secular adaptation – (*b*) Walther von der Vogelweide(?).

We now have to ask whether anything is gained if we postulate that these three images with their variants *are* connected one with another. Or to put it another way, whether consciousness of an exemplar here helps us to a truer interpretation? I think it is of little help if at each occurrence of any one of these images we remind ourselves of all the others and their various further associations, for one or other of these parallels will generally be irrelevant. On the other hand, associable images do in fact determine in large measure the course of devout reflections (meditations), and we are concerned here with a number of devotional images. We must accordingly be prepared to *judge* the scope of the allusions intended when any of these images occurs. We cannot avoid some circularity of argument here. Our judgment will itself

---

[1] On the significance of Job and Isaiah liii, see pp. 108 f, 274 n. 2, 298 etc.

reflect our sense of proprieties. This should therefore be as far as possible a schooled sense.

On proprieties: a note before we proceed. The modern interpreter's task is made more difficult in that medieval poets and artists were often incompletely informed of dogma, Christology, many matters; and the knowledge they had was sometimes dangerously enlivened by zeal or wit (in German studies we think of Wolfram von Eschenbach). One will naturally always hesitate to impute ignorance and irreverence to medieval writers and artists. At the same time we know that certain things were not in the Christian canon. One rather startling example:

Two men, seated at the foot of the Cross, hold a sheet in which there is an upright chalice. A mistaken inference from the image of the men dicing for possession of Christ's tunic. The chalice to receive Christ's blood has taken the place of the dice-box.[1]

This gross solecism occurs in one of the most lavishly appointed illustrated books of the Middle Ages, an Evangeliary presented by the Emperor Henry III to the Cathedral of Speyer.

Let us before beginning a detailed discussion of the seated figures we have singled out, put our exemplar under some pressure. I have not tried to conceal some marked differences between the individual images we are considering. Do these differences *merely* identify each of the images within the group, or does one or other of them – because of the differences – belong not here, but elsewhere? The exclusion of female figures (not Anima or Tristitia) was – proper or arbitrary? In a moment, even though we have considered Charles the Great and King Rother, we shall exclude 'the ruler on his throne' (Caesar). Are we, by our exclusions and inclusions, working towards a modern investigator's fiction, or are we dealing with a valid medieval conception? Are we involved in an As-if postulate, that is, something we must have if we are to progress in a direction which we sense to be correct? Should we do better to let our exemplar go, as being merely the Christian variant of an image common to all peoples and civilisations? I concede that this is what our exemplar was in origin, but our enquiry is semantic, not etymological. And so we continue. So far I have done little more than cite examples. From now on I shall argue more discursively, with

---

[1] Albert Boeckler, *Das goldene Evangelienbuch Heinrichs III.*, Deutscher Verein für Kunstwissenschaft (Berlin, 1933) XXIII, illus. 91.

more persistent reference to verbal traditions, themselves rich in imagery and allusiveness; but they are traditions of some authority, which *must* be adduced, which we are *not* free to quote, or not, as we please.

First, a résumé. We have in mind as an exemplar or prototypical image (a Christian image) a male figure seated on a mound or a rock. When we were considering it as it seemed to be evoked by the poets of the two 'Rolands' (the *Chanson* and the German adaptation) and *Rother*, the rock on which a king might sit to grieve or take serious thought seemed to be interchangeable with a stone *seat* perhaps, or a more sophisticated folding seat.

From this image of the seated king, sorrowing or meditating, to the picture of Job in his suffering, and to the Man of Sorrows and to Jeremiah, may seem to be a series of substantial semantic leaps. Despite the near coincidence of outlines we find as yet no inner relationship. Until on further reflection (with hieratic images before us we reflect) the picture of David – *one* picture of David – asserts itself. As soon as *this* David begins to associate itself we are called upon to make a decision. Is David another picture again, or is he like Caesar, *or* does he belong to our group? As is evident from my enumeration (above) of the cases to be considered, David is 'in', Caesar 'out', and seated figures of whom one can say only that they are enthroned do not belong here. What then are we going to do about the medieval *topos* of the medieval King, Caesar *and* successor to (Solomon and) David? Charles the Great was called David. Our exemplar is now in balance between rejection and acceptance. Here therefore a digression on Caesar and David and a final discrimination, against Caesar.

### David and Caesar

We must first call to mind the *typical* medieval portrait of the *imperator*. (If we want to identify it properly, we must not approach it, as we have been doing, from the flank.) The official court artists saw and drew Caesar (if we take Ottonian art for convenience as the norm) full face, with ruler's gestures, holding his insignia, and with the lands offering him homage (see plate 14a).[1] These, particularly the insignia, are the bearers of meaning, and not a Christian 'mien'. The interpretation is to be sought first in a Christian-allegorical doctrine of vestments and

[1] Also Beckwith, illus. 84, 85.

insignia which was developed through the centuries (on divergent lines) in Germany, France and England. And here indeed colour symbolism is significant. The colours are not artists' conventions or fancies but 'official'. The typical imperial portrait does *not* show a David, Christian though the standard interpretation of the insignia may be, and numerous as may be the allusions to Old Testament tabernacle, thrones, swords, breastplates, not to speak of that occasional reminder of earthly vanity which so impresses the modern beholder, the bag of dust.[1]

There are, however, also the poets to be considered. They blur the distinction between Caesar and David. They are able to do so with impunity. A poem is not committed to one image. Homage to Caesar (called Caesar) and celebration of his victories *as* Caesar may open a poem with fulsome praise. The poet has, however, only to say 'but he is also a Christian king and defender of the faith', and the image changes. The king is now 'a David'. Charles the Great was called David, and two plaques in the so richly symbolical imperial crown show David as King, and Solomon as lawgiver.[2] There are consequently allusions in the works of the poets in two directions, successive allusions; that is beyond the ingenuity of the representational artist. He would need to draw two images; generally he was asked for the one, 'Caesar'.

For a few pages now we shall be discussing David, the David of medieval art and literature. Of the numerous pictures of David we may leave more or less out of account the 'historical' pictures (and picture series) devoted to his 'life and deeds', except to remember that he was to rue (and atone for) some of his deeds in exemplary fashion. (Medieval royal Davids were not enjoined to emulate him in adultery and manslaughter.) We are clearly not concerned either in our present argument with David dancing, surrounded by musicians, though this too is a devotional, rather than an historical image, associated particularly with the final psalms of the Psalter.[3] What we need is the most typical of all David images, generally a profile or half-profile, never, I

---

[1] See Percy Ernst Schramm, 'Über die Herrschaftszeichen des Mittelalters, *Münchener Jahrbuch der bildenden Kunst*, 3rd series, 1 (1950) 43 ff; also *Die deutschen Kaiser und Könige in Bildern ihrer Zeit*, 1 Bis zur Mitte des 12. Jahrhunderts (Leipzig, 1928) and *Kaiser, Rom und Renovatio* 1 (Leipzig, 1929). See also further details in Appendix B, p. 129.

[2] Beckwith, illus. 100.

[3] Examples in Schwietering, plate 1; Beckwith, illus. 25, 47, 64.

think, a full-face portrait. This is David 'King and Psalmist', see plate 10a. He is enthroned, it is true; his head is crowned, but it is bent forward as he strikes his harp. This is the familiar, unmistakable image which medieval art virtually reserved as the proper illustration of his Psalter as a whole, of its first page, of its first word, *Beatus*: 'Blessed is the man that walketh not in the counsel of the ungodly.' This is the image the poets had in mind and to which they turned when they said of the king, whom they had already addressed as 'Caesar', that he was a David, see plate 10b. This *topos* meant that like David the king was a valiant warrior and a *defensor fidei*; but also like David, he was in time past sorely tested and chastised by God. David had sung of his trials: *Domine, probasti me.*[1] This last comparison includes what can only in this way be hinted at in panegyric. Like David the king is a contrite *sinner*, to whom God's grace will not be denied. Like David, in short, he is (may he be) *beatus*.

In the Old High German *Ludwigslied* (c. 880) it is not stated that Louis III himself was ever a sinner. The trials his country suffered from the Norsemen's raids were sent 'to punish the Franks for their sins'. God had made himself Louis' guardian (*magaczogo*). None the less at an appointed time in his early youth 'God determined to test his capacity for suffering'.[2] An explicit comparison with David seems called for at this point, but the subject (victory over the Normans at Saucourt) is altogether too martial, and there is no occasion for any apostrophising of Louis at the end of the lay. The portrayal of a Christian king as the saviour of his erring kingdom, and the lack of any reference to the Church at all are alike remarkable. The poet exploited his chances. He let the comparison with David as a sinner rest at an unmistakable though oblique reference to the words of the Psalm (and the Liturgy): *Domine probasti me.*

Twenty years or so earlier, Otfrid of Weissenburg had dedicated his verse paraphrase of the Gospels to Louis the German (see Chapter III) For twelve long-lines and more, with continuing echoes to the end of his dedication the poet speaks of the trials and testing – *manago arabeit, manag leid* – which the king in his time had to suffer.[3]

To Christian poets therefore David was the prototype of Christian

[1] 'O Lord, thou hast searched me and known me', Ps. cxxxviii/cxxxix and *Introit* of the Easter Sunday office.

[2] koron uuolda sin god, / Ob her arbeidi / So iung tholon mahti, *Ludwigslied*, lines 9–10.

[3] *Evangelienbuch*, I 37–49.

rulers. He was, however, also to the Christian world at large, with St Peter and the Magdalen, a prototype of the humbled and penitent sinner whom God had admitted to his grace. Of the sinner-saints there was only David who was royal, who had been annointed, and to whom poets could appropriately and discreetly draw the attention of kings. It was the only way in which without *lèse-majesté* kings could be told that they were sinners too. David's example indeed was one of grievous sin and exemplary suffering and penance. So his Psalms and his story told. Charles the Bald's Psalter had on one ivory plaque of the front outer cover a portrayal of David's crimes of murder and adultery.[1] On another plaque he had before him the image of David's apotheosis, derived from the Easter Psalm.[2] For all these reasons we shall, I think, want to include this image of David, known to have suffered so direly but remembered as a recipient of grace, among the finished forms of our exemplar. The real justification will come in further evidence to be added in a moment.

### David and Walther von der Vogelweide

Now I come to a consideration of our variant 3(b) with its provisional interrogation mark. How shall we associate Walther von der Vogel-weide? With difficulty, of course, and only with some assistance from David in his role as *court musician*, the dispeller of turbulent spirits and *peacemaker*. One could predicate the same of Walther, but I do not pretend that such a mediating paraphrase proves anything or convinces anyone. The aim is not to spirit away the difficulties and obstacles.

An interim thought for students of German: why do I not pick up at this point the very similar picture of Heinrich von Veldeke on folio 30 r in the same Manesse Manuscript, or Reinmar von Zweter (folio 323 r), both singers, represented as seated, legs crossed, chin in hand? It is simply a matter of discrimination, deciding 'where one picture stops and another starts'. We had given Walther a provisional numbering 3 b(?) in order to be able to consider him at all in conjunction with David. Were our subject 'Minnesänger' he would be Minnesänger 1, and Heinrich von Veldeke would be his nearest neighbour. The distinction must be maintained. Walther, moreover, draws his own picture in his poem. The allocation of a similar image to Veldeke is the

---

[1] Bibl. Nat. MS lat. 1152; see Beckwith, illus. 37.
[2] On Psalm lvi/lvii see pp. 288 ff. See plate 19a.

artist's work; he assigns identifying birds and flowers from Veldeke's poems. The birds and flowers do not so much decorate the picture as show Heinrich von Veldeke in his most characteristic setting. The Reinmar picture is more easily dismissed.

Now distinctions again. The image evoked by Walther von der Vogelweide in his poem (*Ich saz ûf eime steine*, etc.) is strictly speaking not that of the minstrel or poet, but of the Thinker. None the less Walther sang his song, we presume to musical accompaniment. His audience saw the minstrel, and as a Minnesänger – by his repute as a singer – Walther lived on in still accurate memory for a century. Then the collectors began their work; none too soon, as the problems of editing the songs themselves show clearly enough. (I must simplify a little here. The story of the song-books, Weingarten, smaller Heidelberg, large Heidelberg *etc.*, is too complicated for effective communication in a few lines of print.) Let us say that finally in Zürich, possibly on behalf of himself and others, Rüdiger Manesse had the ideal image of Walther drawn and painted as a largish miniature for the monumental anthology which we call after him, see plate 9a. What does it show, the Thinker or the Minnesänger? I think we must conclude that it is the Minnesänger in the guise of David: David the court Musician, David the *Lawgiver* (or Judge) and Peacemaker. All of these are present in the image and in the poem. The main and final justification of this reading is the wealth of reference to the first Psalm in Walther's own poem. The poem echoes the theme: 'blessed is the man whose feet move along the path of righteousness and forsake the ways of the ungodly.' There must be justice, says Walther, if ever peace is to return to the highways, and if ever man is to know *gotes hulde*, roughly 'beatitude'. (The question the 'Thinker' of the poem asks is 'how one should live in this world') It would not have been appropriate to show David-Walther enthroned or crowned; but he sits on a rock, festively clad, with a head-covering not unlike a crown in outline. But the *sword* assigned to Walther, which leans against the rock – whence this mighty sword which stands in no discernable relation to Walther's modest enfeoffment in his later years? It is, I think, the sword of David the Lawgiver. It occurs in some *Beatus* pictures, not many.[1] Assigned to

[1] The *Beatus* image nearest in outline (also near in date) to the Manesse Walther is to be found in the Windmill Psalter, East Anglian, late thirteenth century, see plate 9b. Closer scrutiny of this seated figure which by all the rules should be a David, reveals in fact a Solomon (see the soldier, the two mothers and the disputed child to the right).

Walther it is a reference to 'Walther who sang of the rule of law'. It is also, perhaps, part of a hyperbolical reference (with the 'crown') to a 'King of Bards' in contemporary German estimation. Common to Walther and the *Beatus* David are also the gesture of sorrow. (Compare David's lament for the death of Saul and Jonathan, plate 11b.)

The fact that towards the end of the thirteenth century a *Beatus* image could be used to suggest, as we just now surmised, 'king of the bards' indicates perhaps the advent of the Mastersingers. In the earlier Middle Ages David had been first of all a king (also *propheta* and *egregius psalmista*). He is now coming to be regarded, it seems, as a singer first, and he was soon to become the patron of the Mastersingers and the Welsh bards: a King of Minstrels. David's *harp*, hitherto a sign, not merely of the musician but of the ruler (perhaps even a 'cosmic ruler', see below), is degenerating into a 'noblest of instruments'; and deeper (Orphic) meanings of its music yield to an almost romantically conceived 'power of song' (as we find it finally in a famous Danish ballad).[1] It may have been noticed at what pains I have been *not* to say that Walther plays a harp in the Manesse portrait. I have, I admit, had to teach myself to remember this; but I can always find colleagues ready to correct me.[2]

A last reflection before we abandon the comparison of David and Walther as having been pressed far enough. The *Beatus* David is about to strike the strings of his harp. Would that permit any inferences concerning medieval ideas on the poet's or musician's 'inspiration' generally? I think a sense of propriety would have prevented that. I shall show later that medieval ideas on David's harp, and on his apparent invocation of the Muse (in medieval terms, of the Holy Spirit) in the words 'Arise my harp' (*exsurge cithara*), are otherwise orientated, towards a vast complex of Crucifixion and Resurrection associations. The Christian place of these words is moreover the Easter Liturgy.[3]

[1] Meanwhile the Orphic tradition sustained by the learned world becomes associated with Davidic lore, see D. P. Walker, 'Orpheus the Theologian and Renaissance Platonists', in *JWCI* xvi (1953) 100 ff.

[2] One of them did so within minutes of examining the picture with me in some detail; another was certain that there is a harp 'in one corner at the bottom'. (This seems to be a reminiscence of the bars of the birdcage in the rebus coat of arms at the *top* of the picture.) All this, it should be noticed, when the words of the song say the poet had thrust his chin and one cheek into his hand and set his elbow on his knee. Further notes on David in medieval art in Appendix A, pp. 124 ff.

[3] Compare the section on the harp of David in Chapter IV, pp. 285 ff.

*David, Job, Jeremiah, the Man of Sorrows*

We continue with David whose 'final' picture, the *Beatus*, we have just now considered in greater detail. Another picture of David dancing (see above) we can no more than mention in this enquiry. That leaves the David of *De profundis* and the Passion psalms, a 'type' (with Job, Jeremiah and Isaiah's 'Servant') of the Christ of the Passion. In his songs from the depths, from banishment, from the midst of his assailants, David prefigures equally the sorrows and tribulations of Christendom in its persecution, beset by its enemies. Sorrow and banishment have their songs and their music too:

> . . . wo findestu tieffer, kleglicher, jemerlicher wort, von Trawrig-keit, dann die Klagepsalmen haben? . . . Also auch, wo sie von furcht vnd hoffnung reden, brauchen sie solcher wort, das dir kein Maler so kûndte die Furcht oder Hoffnung abmalen, vnd kein Cicero oder Redekûndiger also vurbilden.[1]

> Where will you find deeper, more sorrowful, more anguished words and words of mourning than in the psalms of lamentation. . . . In those places where they give voice to fear and to hope they use words which paint – as never any artist could – fear and hope, and no Cicero or rhetorician could ever so represent them either.

Some doubts still remain to be dispelled, I should think, before we assign the David of *De profundis* equally to the group Job, Jeremiah and the Man of Sorrows. It will be objected that iconographically David with his crown, on his throne, about to strike his harp, is most definitely not to be associated with the other three in their wretchedness. But our disinclination to associate them rests on what *we* see in the images, and what we remember of the Old Testament figures they represent.

The Middle Ages had a great deal more to say about these figures, some of it no longer familiar today even as Christian lore, and which may, when we renew acquaintance with it, not at once seem apt and appropriate. Some of this forgotten lore links David with the other members of the group through their *music-making*. All of them make music. I will readily excuse any reader who at this point thinks I have fallen victim to an *idée fixe*, and that I see and hear harps everywhere.

---

[1] Luther's preface to the Psalter, 1545, quoted from the Weimar edition X, i, 103.

The solution is much simpler. I take my lead from medieval texts (most of them sacred and liturgical) which repeatedly associate harp, song and suffering in the special context of *prefiguration*, foreshadowing the Passion of Christ. For a time I used to be mystified by the way in which medieval exegetes, when circumstances required them to refer in one word to the lot of Job in his suffering, called him a *harpist* (*citharista*). Where does one read in the story of Job that he made music on the harp and (though this is a much more recent complication) whence the tradition, evidently since forgotten, that not David but Job is the patron of musicians? The source of Job's harp-playing (and of the cognomen *citharista*) is Job xxx 31: 'my harp also is turned to mourning. etc., *versa est in luctum cithara mea et organum meum in vocem flentium* (with some support from Job xxx 9, see below), and of course the Church Fathers' commentaries on these words. Continuing: why is it so often said of the man exposed to the mockery and ridicule of his enemies – of Job, Jeremiah and of Christ himself – that he was their 'song' (*cantilena, psalmus*)? And finally, though a full discussion belongs to Chapter IV, why was Christ's Crucifixion and Death on the Cross compared with a *harp* (his Resurrection with a psaltery) and its music? We have here a compact group or cluster of music commonplaces and a wealth of correlations. Before we turn to the Man of Sorrows let us recall the words of two of these who prefigured Christ in this role, Job and Jeremiah:

*Nunc in eorum canticum versus sum, et factus sum eis in proverbium.*
Luther: nu bin ich jr Seitenspiel worden, vnd mus jr Merlin sein (1545).
A.V.: and now am I their *song*; yea, I am their byword.
(Job xxx 9)

*Factus sum in derisum omni populo meo, canticum eorum tota die.*
Luther: Ich bin ein Spot alle meinem Volk, und täglich ihr Liedlein.
A.V.: I was a derision to all my people, and their *song* all the day.
(Lament. iii 14)

. . . *ego sum psalmus eorum,* etc.
Luther: Schaue doch, sie gehen nieder, oder stehen auf, so singen sie von mir ein Liedlein.
A.V.: Behold their sitting down, and their rising up; I am their *music*.
(Lament. iii 63)

These *canticum* (*psalmus*) verses do not mean the same thing as the designation of Job as a *citharista*, of course; it is the bystanders who make the music when Job is 'their song', but there is reciprocal reference; and in the apocryphal Legend of Job[1] the musicians stand about Job their patron, as he sits on his dunghill, see plate 12. But we are not concerned here with legendary accretions to Job's story (his patronage for instance) and rationalisations of his role. We leave it that music-making is a nexus of associations, and note that there are involved: harp, song, suffering and prefiguration.

When today we think of a possible association of 'harp' and 'sorrow' we recall (perhaps with the help of a rather more familiar *cantilena*) the harp hanging on the willow tree of Psalm cxxxvi/cxxxvii, and the Babylonian Captivity. 'By the rivers of Babylon, there we sat down; yea, we wept, when we remembered Zion. We hanged our harps upon the willows in the midst thereof.' Are we justified in being reminded of these harps? One discovers with something of a shock that this association is completely inadmissible. But when we have come to the end of Chapter IV in this book, on the Crucifixion, and are more familiar with the 'harp on the tree of the Cross' (and the psaltery, a symbol of the Resurrection), shall we not want to insist that there is an unmistakable parallel here? The Church Fathers were of quite different opinion. They saw no connection – that should suffice! But modern readers, as I know, are reluctant to abandon their flashes of insight. First, the Vulgate does not say 'harps' but *organa*, the associations of which are not by any means all musical, but more often with *viscera* and 'this mortal frame'. Secondly, the willow is a *barren* tree, which surely settles the matter. *Salix est lignum infructuosum, et dicitur quod si quis ex illa accipiat potionem aut manducet, filios non facit. Organum enim, hominis corpus est.*[2]

### The Christian meaning of 'Sessio'

That the 'types' prefiguring Christ as the Man of Sorrows should be visualised as seated figures was inevitable. The image was 'given' in their story in most cases. The story of Job says he sat on his dunghill. Jeremiah too, sat outside the city and wept. The prefatory words in editions of the Vulgate indicating the contents of *Lamentations* say 'the

[1] A fuller account is given on pp. 344 ff.
[2] Bruno of Würzburg (*after* Jerome) on Psalm cxxxvi 2, *PL* 142, 492–3.

prophet sits weeping and laments'. He bewails at once 'the City which sits in solitude' (*quomodo sedet sola civitas*). Later there are the words: 'He sitteth alone and keepeth silence' (*sedebit solitarius et tacebit*).[1] This conforms to the prototypical image of the *outcast* sitting by the wayside, the mockery of passers-by. For all later outcasts and all who grieve, the words of Jeremiah seem fore-ordained: 'Is it nothing to you, all ye that pass by? behold and see if there be any sorrow like unto my sorrow' (*O vos omnes qui transitis per viam, attendite, et videte, si est dolor sicut dolor meus!*).[2] The real context of these words is, however, from early Christian centuries not merely (and no longer really) the Old Testament, but the Liturgy of Holy Week, into which the text of Lamentations is taken bodily, and the cry *O vos omnes* is repeated and varied (*attendite universi populi*) in antiphons.

From Old Testament types, mainly Job, Jeremiah and Isaiah's Servant, as these were recalled in the Liturgy, late medieval artists evolved their *second* image of the Man of Sorrows,[3] a seated figure distinct from the more familiar standing figure pointing to his wounds, distinct too from the *Ecce homo*. It was at least in intention a devotional image, not a historical picture at all. There was, however, no way in which the Church could prevent historical interpretations, for Christ had said in his final teaching that 'all things (*omnia de me*) should be fulfilled',[4] and the moment of fulfilment of many prophecies had been declared by the Evangelists. Towards the end of the Middle Ages there was a growing concern to determine the moment of fulfilment of all prophecies of the Passion. Solutions both unambiguous in themselves and not conflicting with one another were not readily found. Isaiah's prophecy that the Servant should appear 'like a leper' for instance, was with more or less common accord determined as referring to the appearance of Christ after the Flagellation, where the other prophecy – that every part of his body from his head to the sole of his foot should be afflicted – was also fulfilled. This prophecy was fulfilled before Pilate's pronouncement *Ecce homo*, when Christ was again clad. The artists have a separate image for the *Ecce homo*. But when did Christ sit alone and silent as Jeremiah prophesied? When was he silent in the midst of his persecutors, like a lamb before the shearers? (This is generally referred to the Mocking: *prophetiza nobis*.) Where did he sit, speaking, as in the Liturgy, *O vos omnes qui transitis per viam?* And how

[1] Lament. iii 28.  
[2] Lament. i 12.  
[3] On the Man of Sorrows, see Appendix A, pp. 126 f.  
[4] Luke xxiv 44.

were all these *historical* scenes, as they were now held to be, still to be distinguished from the *Ecce homo*? To what moment do the words of the *Dies Iræ* refer?

> Quærens me sedisti lassus:
> Redemisti crucem passus. . . .

Where, 'seeking me (a sinner)', did Jesus sit, wearied from his journeyings, *lassus*? It is partly from these words of the *Dies Iræ* and partly from *O vos omnes* in the Liturgy that the picture of Christ with crown of thorns, his hands bound, seated on a rock or stone is evolved. It is more familiar from German art, where it is called 'Christus in der Rast', more popularly 'Jesus auf dem kalten Stein',[1] and also referred to as 'Christ awaiting Crucifixion', which is of course the final 'historisation', see plate 14b, a French example. But the artists, even the most 'popular' among them, were necessarily under the surveillance of the Church and seem to have endeavoured on the whole not to specify the time or place of this scene unambiguously, and indeed the crown of thorns and the bound hands (sometimes holding a scourge of the Flagellation) are together intended to withdraw the image from any momentary historical setting. At that it remains. Later poets, tract-writers and the compilers of Passion plays were bound to try to solve these various problems of time, place, sequence, which the artists could leave open. This is not the place to record their solutions.

The starting point for a consideration of the deeper meaning, as opposed to the 'epic place' of Christ's *sessio* are the words of Psalm cxxxviii/cxxxix, verses 1 and 2. As *Psalmus* to the Introit of Easter Sunday these words are of course of absolute authority. They celebrate the glorious Resurrection, and just as vividly recall the Passion.

*Domine, probasti me, et cognovisti me: tu cognovisti sessionem meam, et ressurrectionem meam* (Versus: *Gloria Patri*) – 'O Lord thou hast searched me and known me. Thou knowest my down-setting and mine uprising'.

---

[1] A piece of statuary (sixteenth century) now in a woodland setting in Dingden, Kreis Borken, formerly in Marienfrede, has the title 'Use krumme leve Herr' in which 'krumm' (bended, twisted) harks back to the biblical *incurvatus sum* or *vermis sum*, see pp. 117, 297 ff. See Georg Wagner, *Volksfromme Kreuzverehrung in Westfalen* (Schriften der volkskundlichen Kommission des Landschaftsverbandes Westfalen-Lippe, II (Münster, 1960) 80 and fig. 96.

Distasteful as some readers may find it, the word 'session' – not commonly thought of as a sacred word – has in this context to be heard as the antithesis of 'resurrection'. The word *sessio* is thus annotated by St Augustine in his commentary on this Psalm: *humiliavit semetipsum factus obediens usque ad mortem, mortem autem crucis.*[1] Thus *sessio* is the posture of humility and obedience, of the man sorely tried. Late medieval artists interpret the obedient waiting as a waiting for the completion and erection of the Cross; indeed some (including Dürer) do not hesitate to show Christ seated *on* the Cross, awaiting the purely mechanical boring of the holes.[2] This posture of humility was however also associated with accusation and *reproach*. Christ will reproach and accuse. The seated figure is consequently an image with many associations.[3]

What began as a series of reflections on a possible 'exemplar' has, as one sees, become a lengthy illustration of the observation made near the beginning of this Chapter, that associative thinking is set in motion and sustained by images which are seen, or which fall into 'approximate register'. For all that I have restricted our reflections to lines of association which seem to have been significant in the Middle Ages; and as we came nearer to sacred images we considered virtually only the biblical word in liturgical contexts.

Theoretically it should now be possible to formulate our lexical entry for the exemplar 'seated figure', covering at the least the cases we have discussed in detail, and commenting on exclusions. 'Seated figure' would require in fact a massive entry, with many subsections. If after all this my exemplar seems to some readers merely to have served a purpose, providing a point of departure and return, I would still press that it was repeatedly drawn in its own right, necessarily, as a stage before the elaboration of any of the variants, and more simply as an obviously important drawing exercise, leaving identifying details to be added. Under what name may this seated figure have gone through the ateliers and scriptoria? Every artist had to learn to start, let us call it a 'sessio' or 'Job' or 'David', and know how to finish with practically any of the specific images we have considered.

It is useful and agreeable for me to conclude this section as I began it with a reference to related investigations by Günter Bandmann whose

---

[1] *Enarrationes in Psalmos*, in PL 37, 1671.
[2] See Chapter IV, 8.
[3] On Dante's use of O *vos omnes*, see Appendix A, p. 126.

interests centre in the Renaissance and have as their starting point Albrecht Dürer's *Melancholia*.[1] Bandmann includes in his far more comprehensive survey dozens of images which I did not myself know (mainly post-medieval). I do not think that I should have written very differently on the semantic problems discussed here, had I known them. For the purposes of these reflections I have limited myself to those pictures which in my general medieval reading have proved to be memorable. I have tried to apply semantic principles in conditions as like as I can make them to those of 'image learning' in the Middle Ages and as we experience them still. We do not learn the meaning of images in real life, any more than we learn the meaning of words or the sense of a poem, by looking things up in reference works, but in the process of a more general 'schooling'.

## 6. THE EXEMPLAR AND THE MOTIF

The dividing line between our notional exemplar and its 'completions' on the one hand (above), and the single motif with its varying iconographies on the other is not easy to draw. Any neat theoretical discrimination one would like to offer comes to grief in practice, over pictures of uncertain content and interpretation. Roughly, an exemplar becomes a motif when the latter is identified by context. What follows is offered as a series of remarks and observations under a heading, no more.

Despite variations in iconography we shall hope always to be able to *identify* pictorial representations of motifs, for instance from familiar Christian story: the Fall (Adam and Eve), Noah's Ark, Joseph in flight from Potiphar's Wife, etc. Having once established the identity of a less frequently represented scene, we will normally cease entertaining what were interim surmises, and any thoughts which they provoked become irrelevant. In the case of secular art too, we shall want to identify each patently 'historical' scene, and dismiss associations which the image by its mere outline or configuration at first suggested. But there are many difficulties here, some of which concern mere identification, which must precede any fuller interpretation. To what extent does a familiar image change its identity when we encounter it fitted (sometimes *tant bien que mal*) into a strange setting? Does it allude at all

[1] See Appendix A, p. 123.

to its former self? To illustrate with a harmless example (not all are as easily dismissed), does Moses threatened by serpents approaching him (serpent-like) in the desert *become* Laocoön merely by being transferred to the appropriate position in book II of an illustrated Virgil (with an indication of a shore and due attention paid to the number and age of supporting figures)? No general answer is possible, except to say that art historians are somewhat reluctant to accept contextual and 'occasional' meanings, and tend still to think of the descent of images as the true key. To the art historian such a Laocoön is still 'really Moses'. Students of language would say he is Laocoön. (We do not interpret texts with etymological dictionaries.) There is a late medieval Leander who drowns while swimming in what appears to be a Burgundian canal, but we recognise the motif and see no other subject.

So far we considered (mainly) 'historical' scenes. Hieratic images (devotional pictures), and ideas pictorially represented invite meditation or reflection which is inevitably fairly freely associative, even though each image is intended to suggest specific trains of thought. The only point I wish to make here is that medieval artists did not leave things to chance. They knew that some pictorial compositions were vulnerable if left without titles of some kind, to start meditations on the right lines. Towards the end of the Middle Ages this tendency runs to seed. As allegories and moralisations become more and more long-winded and garrulous, pictorial representations are provided with indicators of every kind. The resultant 'page-full' may be a complete hybrid, calling for and getting if it is lucky the attention of the scholar interested in traditions in their final dissolution. Such a composition was in its day meant to identify the motif (or an agglommeration of motifs) absolutely.

Still under the general heading of this chapter and the sub-heading which has brought us to the relationship of exemplars and motifs, there are some further considerations. Certain motifs in Christian art are familiar to us only in an iconography which already includes a 'typological' adjustment; that is, in which pictorial reference from Old Testament prophecy to New Testament fulfilment is facilitated by dispositional 'rhyming'.[1] An image is given a profile which will recall its ideal antecedent (the 'type') or *vice versa*. Eve and Adam are set to the left and the right of the Tree of Knowledge in order that the Redemption (the Crucified between Church and Synagogue and again

[1] On typology, see Chapter IV, 6.

between Mary and John) may be foreshadowed. Daniel stands between (or amidst) his lions to prefigure Christ assailed by his enemies, for the pattern of whose behaviour the lions of this prophetic figure itself (and the 'encircling' *canes* and the *vituli* of Psalm xxi/xxii) are in large part responsible. The bundle carried by Isaac, and the pieces of wood carried by the widow (see p. 258) have, occasionally in the one case and almost inevitably in the second, the shape of the cross which Christ 'was to' bear, see plate 28. Analogous to this typologising in ecclesiastical art is the 'accommodation' practised by secular artists. About 'accommodation' in general I shall have a little more to say in Chapter III (pp. 192ff). Here I can refer only to the *possible* application of the principle in illustrations of King Arthur banqueting with his knights at the Round Table. The allusion to the Last Supper is at first sight 'obvious'. On reflection it may seem to have been unavoidable. On still further reflection the artists may have taken every conceivable precaution *not* so to allude. Each point of view can be argued; I now favour the third. We can more readily accept the sidelong allusions from secular heroes and their feats to saints, and indeed fights with dragons as such have an almost Irish quality; anyone can join in, St George, St Victor, Siegfried and others. Where is the line to be drawn between shared iconography and significant allusion in these cases? If one then takes into account the continuous proliferation of iconographical solutions, one can see no real end to the possibilities of interpretation – and of over-interpretation.

If we now recall, ruefully, the idea of a lexicon of images, it will be to dismiss it once and for all, for practically every *imaginable* image seems to be there in the artist's repertory. It is as though every pun, palindrome and spoonerism had been drawn at some time. The remarkable thing is that we still contrive to understand so many of the artists' more wayward iconographies. In all these circumstances it is evident that we risk adding to confusion if we rush to rationalise the content of medieval pictures. If as students of medieval literature we are to profit more in future from the study of works of medieval art, we must distrust *all* first reactions to pictures, and unschooled reminiscences until we have established *what* pictures medieval art had in its repertory, *where* they are to be found in context, and what they mean *there*. That implies that we must first remind ourselves firmly where words, names, ideas and motifs have their place in textual tradition, for it is to these contextual meanings that medieval pictures refer for their meanings. In studying works of secular literature we consider such reference to context essential. We are strangely lax in the case of images, perhaps particularly Christian images.

Sheep, Lamb, Lion, Serpent are, as any biblical concordance in its preamble states, names having several meanings 'in the Bible'. In their various biblical contexts they each bear a traditional, that is an authoritative gloss, the gloss of the Church. It is therefore no more in order for us to assemble the sheep and lambs into droves than it is to play fast and loose with homonyms and synonyms in the study of literature. The Bible recognises several important *lions*: for example: the Lion of Judah in the blessing spoken over Jacob.[1] In the vision of Daniel we find the lion invoked by medieval historiographers,[2] in the vision of Ezekiel the later symbol of the Evangelist Mark.[3] Then there are the totally different lions in Daniel's den, see above. In the way of *serpents* we have the serpent in Eden, which was only identified with Satan by reference to Wisdom ii 24 ('birth of Envy'). The venomous serpents in the desert and the brazen serpent of salvation raised on that occasion 'as a standard' (*pro signo*) by Moses are not to be confused with the Satan. All these *serpentes* could be called *dracones* in rhetorical paraphrase and in hymns, and mean either Christ or the Devil, according to antithetical patterns within the statement made. We mentioned the 'dragon' raised by Moses, the Chartres statue (above). Below there will be several references to the biblical 'worm' or *vermis* of the Passion Psalm xxi/xxii, which in turn may be brought into meaningful association with serpent and dragon. But should anyone want in his enthusiasm to recall the worm of Isaiah lxvi 24 which 'should not die' (*vermis eorum non morietur*), that is a totally different worm (of conscience). We need to be able to recall the contexts from which these words take their meaning, and carefully to note the patristic glosses they carried. These become associations which have authority. Others which we declare that we can see ourselves have no authority, and are for safety's sake better classed as wrong.

Our task as philologists is to entertain only those associations and affiliations which we can validate by reference to medieval texts. Only in that way shall we interpret meanings correctly, recognise changes of meaning, and at the same time remain aware of the *stability* of traditions. This is all the more difficult to achieve when enthusiasm for medieval literature and art (particularly art) is now so wide-spread, and so much is 'generally known'. Our knowledge, correct though it may be, is

[1] Genesis xlix 9.    [2] See pp. 129, 175.    [3] See p. 128.

often not well organised. *Or* it is over-organised, and information is too readily available. If it is deficient, it can nowadays be too quickly supplemented. This often leads to facile over-interpretation, perhaps particularly in the area of typology. The modern interpreter may simply not notice that he has passed quite outside the range of one nexus of associations into another. Perhaps our handbooks are responsible. A couple of examples. The ordinary educated reader seems to me to know more about fish and anchor symbolism than he needs, to understand Western artistic tradition. And of forms of the Cross, particularly about the *Tau* cross, he knows too much rather than too little. There is always a risk that he will try to bring his knowledge to bear prematurely and irrelevantly, and remain unaware of features at least equally significant in the medieval works he is considering. For instance the Tau-cross appears, (*a*) in medieval pictures showing the blood of the lamb on the 'lintel and two side posts';[1] there is nothing about a 'Tau' in the text; (*b*) as a T-initial in the *Te igitur* of the Canon of the Mass; (*c*) as Moses' staff on which he holds aloft the brazen serpent. This staff with the serpent may again serve as initial of the *Te igitur*, the brazen serpent draped over the horizontal of the T; (*d*) occasionally the Cross of the Crucifixion is a Tau-cross, in which case the INRI tablet may complete the *crux immissa*; or two Tau-crosses may appear, to indicate 'ordinary' crucifixions for the thieves[2]; (*e*) the Tau-cross is treated in handbooks under 'Cross', where all the known crosses, including Peter's and Andrew's, palm-tree crosses and the many decorated variants are systematically listed. Of all these sources of Tau-cross lore, the last seems to be by far the most familiar. The contexts in which the Tau-cross occurs, which are part and parcel of its meaning, are not effectively noted when 'read up' in compendia. My apologies for the tone of this paragraph.

It is clear that in our search for general semantic principles we must always lean heavily on Christian art; that is only reasonable in view of the overwhelming preponderance of Christian over secular art in the Middle Ages. In any case the leading artists had been trained by, and served the Church, and secular art inevitably took its lead from ecclesiastical art. But here are a few notes on secular iconography, necessarily followed across the frontier into the Renaissance to provide reasonably familiar examples.

[1] Exod. xii 7, 21 ff.          [2] Cf Isidore *Etym.* bk. V xvii 34.

We can only identify secular motifs with confidence when we have *studied* the typical images and some of their variants. By comparison with the images of ecclesiastical art, secular images have little if any authority, and we are under no comparable obligation to know them. Context may be important here too, but it is not of the same decisive significance as in the art of the Christian Church. The Wheel of Fortune, the Wheel of Life and other 'wheels with figures', including the Zodiac, have to be familiar, before we can distinguish between them with certainty. *Occasio* (opportunity), *chronos* and *Kronos* became associated and confused in tradition; we need to have seen this demonstrated in a special treatment of this very problem.[1] *Philosophia*, *Grammatica* and the *Artes* have to be 'learnt', so that each figure in this gallery can be identified (but they are in fact generally labelled). *The Vices and Virtues* have been the subject of many studies. *Frau Welt's* pictorial career is erratic, and she is difficult to identify by the time she has accumulated all her associations. The *Legend of the Three Living and the Three Dead* calls for no particular effort of identification, provided one knows of the subject and encounters it in isolation; the inclusion of its six, sometimes seven figures (the seventh being the Preacher in his wayside pulpit) in a larger composition (a *Triumph of Death*, Campo Santo) is less immediately obvious. It is not, despite the skeletons, a 'Dance of Death', nor is the *Triumph of Death* 'the same subject'. A single Death lurking behind a knight or a fair lady is not, unless the artist says so, a 'Dance of Death', for the tradition up to about 1500 insisted on an actual dance. Here we are involved in problems not merely of identification, but of art history, and at the same time of classification and nomenclature. Whereas we may know (as historians) that a given pictorial motif goes back to a specific text, the successful picture may be one which has shed this dependence. Add to this that it is the natural tendency of artists not to adhere slavishly to set patterns, but to experiment with, and in time exhaust the possibilities of variation on a theme, and to enliven their treatment with allusions. A complication in the case of secular iconography is the appearance of familiar images in the proximity of others whose meaning has become obscured. Not every pictorial formula was successful; examples of unsuccessful ones may survive to tease us. For instance some wheels with figures are neither wheels of Fortune, nor any other known wheel. The monu-

[1] E. Panofsky, *Studies in Iconology*, etc. (1939; Harper Torch Books 1962) pp. 69–91.

mental wheel window of St Étienne, Beauvais, of about 1160 is, I think, *not* a wheel of Fortune, but represents some forgotten theme.[1] And then (later examples): how will one distinguish Fortune and Occasio in the late fifteenth and sixteenth centuries when Fortune has acquired Opportunity's or Time's 'forelock'? Or 'Fortune in Love' and a *Venus marina*, when Fortune may sail the seas as a naked goddess? Sometimes a last remaining attribute is peculiar to a figure which has otherwise wasted itself in allusions. Occasio is no longer identified by her hair streaming in the wind (away from the pursuer's hand), but by the shorn nape of her neck, or by a knife or pair of shears, which, as far as I know, were never surrendered to any other personification. Much depends on whether an artist decides merely to *identify* or fully to describe his subject. In the latter case he will be generous, and festoon it with attributes. Fortune's craft may be a dolphin, or a ball (shared with others), or a horizontal wheel (vortex, whirlpool, which is hers) but not, I believe, a sea shell: that belongs to Venus.[2] The context may have to be invoked to decide the issue; the artist had in any case taken it into account.

These circumstances reinforce the warning against swift and intuitive identifications of images. It is better to go in search of or wait for parallels, but even then caution is needed because of the sheer number of motifs which the poets and artists treated. Medieval contaminations, misreadings, facile glossings, leave us with records which, by their very strangeness, tend to demand disproportionate attention, while works orthodox in their formula yet distinguished in execution are 'no problem'. We shall be wise not to add hypothetical bridging or linking forms to complete what we see as lines of development. It is only by habitual caution that we shall train ourselves to recognise the bold innovation and the semantic leap.

But at the end of this long disquisition, it must be confessed that there can be no really dependable methods of work in these areas, and scarcely any final results are to be expected. To the best of my ability I have interpreted a number of important and interrelated medieval images. Much would therefore seem to depend on how reliable and representative my own knowledge of medieval tradition may be. Other medievalists would, I am sure, write a different story under some of my headings, and using the same material they would have interpreted it somewhat differently. It is also likely that in a few years' time

[1] See p. 218.    [2] See Chapter III, p. 219.

I may have to adjust some of my present ideas, for instance about the seated figure. There are many realisations of the exemplar with which my acquaintance is recent. There is no means of forecasting whether I shall some day find them more important than those which prompted me to write these pages.

# APPENDIX

To section A of this Appendix are assigned notes which could conveniently be deferred. Section B (corresponding to a *Nachtrag* in the German edition, pp. 86–91) contains supplementary material and brief treatments of minor themes.

## A

*p.* 84. (On Dürer's *Nemesis*, plate 7a.) I should interpret that contemporaries focused attention on the allusion from Nemesis to Fortune. A female figure standing on a sphere is, around 1500, almost inevitably Fortune. It takes a massive weight of attributes to impose on this image another identity, but in the *Nemesis* they are there, and to anyone who has seen a few score of medieval and Renaissance Fortunes, Dürer's image is at least untypical, or indeed clearly not Fortune. Taking the attributes into account, as we must (the goblet, and above all the heavy bridle), the meaning is, I think, that the nemesis attendant upon *indulgence* (*intemperantia* symbolised by the goblet) will overtake the offender as surely as will his fortune: to impose its bridle, curb and subdue him. 'Fate', 'destiny' are (or can be) in German, *Verhängnis*; a suspended sword is *verhängt*. This element of literalism is undoubtedly (in some ways unfortunately: I refer to *mit verhängtem Zügel*) present in Dürer's image. I do not offer this as the only 'correct' interpretation. I merely suggest that an interpretation is suspect which ignores the attributes or explains them away. They *can* be explained away in two easy moves. (*a*) Fortune is often represented with a *cornucopia*, and this may be replaced in Renaissance art by the overflowing goblet; (*b*) in *medieval* Fortunes there is often a bridle: Providence bridles Fortune. This leaves an awkward gap in the logic of Dürer's image so understood. A recent idealistic interpretation associated Dürer's *Nemesis*, 'really Fortune', with Renaissance optimism. The authors ignore the preliminary studies for the female figure. She began as a vulgar whore and is at least sensual in the finished work.

*p.* 90. (Image substitution.) Twice in reviews of essays by Wolfgang Stammler I drew attention to this possibility – his monograph *Frau Welt* (Fribourg, 1959); the chapter 'Mann im Brunnen', in *Wort und Bild* (Berlin, 1962).

'Dame World' is, according to medieval German poets, 'fair *without* but foul *within*' (*ûzen schœne, innen vûl*). I suggested that the artists' somewhat belated response in the statue of a woman (Worms cathedral, fourteenth century), fair to look upon from the *front*, but repulsive and decayed, swarmed over by snakes and vile toads *behind*, was a consequence of the impossibility of drawing 'inside' and 'outside', except perhaps in a diagram, see plate 23b and c. Some critics seem to think that in pointing out this factor, I was denying Stammler's derivation of the substitute iconography from the picture of 'the Prince of this World' (Mundus, the tempter of the Foolish Virgins, Strassburg, thirteenth century); I thought I was confirming it, adding that even 'before' and 'behind' can only be represented in a more or less freestanding statue.

'The Man in the *Well*' (of the Barlaam and Josaphat legend). This motif appears in medieval pictures as the 'Man in the *Tree*', possibly because of the impracticability of depicting the by no means simple sequence of events in the well. The substitute image 'Man in the Tree' is an adaptation of the 'Tree of Jesse' design. (The *story* is then adjusted to match to new image.) A further example may be surmised in a Fortune allegory to which I refer later, where not the impossibility but the impropriety of attempting *faber fortunæ suæ* (Fortune is a woman) demands a substitute image, see p. 199 n. 2.

*p.* 92. (Seated figures, *Melancholia*, etc.) The reference is to Günter Bandmann, *Melancholie und Musik, Ikonographische Studien.* Wissenschaftliche Abhandlung der Arbeitsgemeinschaft für Forschung des Landes Nordrhein-Westfalen, XII (Cologne and Opladen, 1960). Professor Bandmann, now professor of art history at the University of Tübingen, has given me helpful advice on a number of problems during the last few years, but conversations, exchanges of offprints and correspondence did not reveal that I was following tracks he had already trodden in pursuit of music makers (often seated figures). Had I known his monograph, my own ideas would doubtless have evaporated, a thought which is of considerable relevance in itself, in the discussion of how one comes to terms with pictures. It is impossible for me to summarise Bandmann's findings here, and it would not help if I were to show how different, occasionally, are the trains of thought set in motion by the various seated figures we have both discussed. Bandmann's is a scholarly enquiry aiming at completeness. I restrict attention to medieval images within recall, with perhaps greater insistence on their relative authority, in an essay on the semantics of images.

*p. 93. Anima* occurs on fo. 55 of the Stuttgart Psalter, see Ernst de Wald, *The Stuttgart Psalter* (*Württembergische Landesbibliothek, Stuttgart*), (Princeton Univ. 1930) I, plates (the Commentary has not appeared). It illustrates Psalm xlii/xliii, mainly verses 4–5. Of the psalters of the Middle Ages none is more persistent than Stuttgart in its endeavour to illustrate the Psalmist's prophecies of the Passion of Christ. In the *Anima* picture (see plate 9c) however, the artist follows the formula of the Utrecht Psalter and offers 'literalist' images. Thus (*a*) verse 4ff. *Confitebor tibi in cythara, deus, deus meus*: on the *left* a musician in tunic, striking his *cithara* with plectrum; (*b*) *quare tristis es anima mea? et quare conturbas me?*: Anima on her mound takes up the *right* half of the same picture. Both figures are shown against a background which we should now say indicates a distant horizon. This may reflect verse 3, *emitte lucem tuam*. The mound (a hill indeed) on which Anima sits is clearly the 'sacred mountain' of *adduxerunt me in montem sanctum tuum*.

*p. 98.* Assessment of medieval German adaptations of French sources (the 'Roland' is the first case) tends to be a matter for specialists, except where by common assent German writers furnished the 'classical' medieval form of a tale and excelled their French predecessors. Wolfram's *Parzival*, Gottfried's *Tristan* are examples of this. As for the *Chanson de Roland*, it is obvious that neither the poetry nor the ideals of the French national epic could be simply transplanted. It is none the less a fact of literary history that there *is* a German version of the *Chanson* of about 1170. If one accepts that there were only two ideas in the *Chanson* which made sense in Bavaria at that time – namely that Charles the Great's campaigns in Spain were conducted by him as Emperor and defender of the Christian faith against the heathen, and that his paladins earned (in the German version sought) the martyrdom of the *miles christianus* – the 'Rolandslied' will be found to have very considerable qualities, first as a re-interpretation of history, but as a narrative too. Konrad shows considerable skill, zest for the crusader's ideals and a lively concern for the glory of his martyr heroes. Some further remarks, in context, below.

*pp.* 105 ff. (The devotional image of David.)

(*a*) A widely reproduced image of David occurs in a Greek psalter of the tenth century (Paris, Bibl. Nat., MS gr. 139, fo. 1). It shows David in a bucolic landscape. The drawing model is Apollo or Orpheus. David is seated on a rock beside a female figure (Melodia); he plays his lyre amidst animals and other beings (personifications: Echo and Jerusalem). See *The Bible in Art, Old Testament* (Phaidon, 1956), opp. plate 168.

(*b*) The article on David in *RDK* III col. 1083 ff, by R. L. Wyss, is encyclopaedic in scope and necessarily gives up a good deal of space to 'historical' life of David pictures and picture cycles.

(*c*) Quite massive is Hugo Steger's *David Rex et Propheta, König David als vorbildliche Verkörperung des Herrschers und Dichters im Mittelalter*, Erlanger Beiträge etc. VI (Nuremberg, 1961), with 36 plates. This is naturally an important work on David, with which, however, I remain on uneasy terms. I have failed to see any trace of Germanic tradition in the medieval David, whether of the *skop* or of Wodan. The author's statistical methods and tabulations are scientific but inappropriate. The reader will, however, prefer to hear the art historian's view. Günter Bandmann writes as follows in a lengthy review in *Zeitschrift für Volkskunde*, III–IV (1962) pp. 260 ff (translated from p. 264):

While Germanic antiquity with all its traditions . . . is surveyed and brought to bear on the subject . . . classical Antiquity and its repertory of images which lie ready to hand are ignored. . . . There is no reference to Apollo at all as a classical 'type' of the medieval David. . . . Even more than Apollo, Orpheus (to whom no reference is made either) corresponds in many ways to David: both are seers, both are cosmic rulers, thanks to the power of their music; both are represented as enthroned, holding a *lyra*, surrounded by cosmological symbols. And indeed the oldest representations of David are of this type [see (*a*) above, the Greek psalter]. David is at the very least as much a Christian reflection of Orpheus as he is a reflection of the Germanic *skop*, and if on one occasion a source does indeed call him a *skop*, that will be an allusion to David's services as musician at the court of Saul, not to his later role as universal ruler.

We can, I think, cancel Bandmann's concessions in respect of the word *skop* which is no more than a gloss. It is more important for us to recall our own topic, the *Beatus*-David. In commentary on Bandmann I would note that David is not a cosmic ruler in his own person, nor is he, I think, the Christian Orpheus except in the tradition of art (i.e. as an image). In verbal tradition the cosmic ruler is Christ whom David prefigures, and through whom Christ (or God) speaks as through other

prophets. The divine musician is God, the harp is Christ, see pp. 293 ff.
On David's harp, *lyra* etc., a word of guidance on p. 285 n. 1.
*p.* III. On the Man of Sorrows in late medieval German art, see Gert
von der Osten, *Der Schmerzensmann, Typengeschichte eines Andachts-
Bildwerkes von 1300–1600*, Forschungen zur deutschen Kunstgeschichte,
VII (Berlin, 1935). The author interprets even the seated Christ, which
he rightly classes as a secondary form of the Man of Sorrows, as Christ
the Accuser. This is certainly a possible interpretation of the words of
reproach *O vos omnes* with which this image comes to be firmly linked.
It also accords well with the words of the *Dies Iræ*:

> Recordare Jesu pie
> Quod sum causa tuæ viæ,
> Ne me perdas illa die.
> Quærens me *sedisti lassus*:
> Redemisti crucem passus.

But Christ the Accuser is more generally seen in the image of the
Man of Sorrows, Type 1: Jesus *standing*, points to the wound in his side
and fixes sinful man with his gaze. (On the origins of the image, see von
der Osten.) This gesture of accusation is described in a narrative context
in the Old High German *Muspilli* poem (see p. 156).

In a coloured pen-drawing of about 1510 which he sent to his doctor
(L 130) Dürer points, it will be remembered, to a yellow patch: '. . . do
ist mir we' (that's where it hurts). This contains an unmistakable
allusion to the Man of Sorrows (Type 1), see plate 13b. In a silver-point
drawing of 1522 (L 131) Dürer treated the Man of Sorrows (Type 2):
Christ seated, naked, holding the instruments of the Flagellation. This
is held at the same time to be a self-portrait, see plate 13a and Wilhelm
Waetzoldt, *Albrecht Dürer* (1950) Figs. 10 and 16.

*p.* 113. From later poetry one can quote probably many allusions to
Job, Jeremiah, the Man of Sorrows. However many are found, the
most disturbing will remain Dante, *Vita Nuova* (ch. 7): *O voi, che per
la via d'Amor passate, | attendete, e guardate | s'egli è dolore alcun, quanto il
mio, grave*, which is on any reckoning blasphemous, but see p. 204 n.1.
Franz Werfel has a poem 'Wounded Stork' beginning:

> War jemals eine Trauer so wie die?
> Schwieg Trauer-Totenstarre jemals so? Nie, nie
> Hockt Hiob, Aussatz bergend unterm Schurz,
> Mit solchem Schweigen neben Schutt und Sturz.

The remainder of the poem disperses the Christian allusion. A less serious treatment of the outcast by the wayside is offered *in extenso* on pp. 203 ff. It is from a sermon on the fate of Belisarius, by the Austrian hot-gospeller Abraham a Santa Clara, seventeenth century. Its position in this book is determined by the preponderant references to Fortune.

# B

*Majestas Domini* and the Symbols of the Four Evangelists

Both of these, the devotional image which we call a *Majestas Domini* and the symbols of the four Evangelists were mentioned above (p. 86), but only in passing. We should certainly have lost the thread of the argument if we had stopped to deal with these subjects in any detail, particularly if we had treated them in their interrelation. Here are a few supplementary notes, of which the first must be on Ezekiel and his vision.

The correspondence between the Vision (Ezek. i 4–28, in fact the whole chapter) and Revelation iv 4–8, which seems to the modern reader 'striking', was to the Middle Ages clearly a case of Old Testament prophecy and its New Testament confirmation. Further, it is a simple fact of experience that of the whole of this tradition (Ezekiel and St John) we really remember only the summary, that is: the *image* which medieval exegesis and ecclesiastical art singled out from the confusion of the descriptions, the transfigured God upon his throne supported by the four 'animals', see plate 23a. The Church, in short, made communicable sense of what might have remained excessively obscure.

The Christian Middle Ages elected in the end to see the Four Evangelists in these four symbols. One should, however, note that this is a somewhat popular solution by comparison with a gloss assigning each symbol to an 'operation' of Christ. In the context 'the majesty of the Lord' this learned interpretation is perhaps more satisfactory. Timmers quotes in his iconographical guide (288 ff.) the following lines from Adam of St Victor (*d.* 1177), which reduce the doctrine of Christ's four operations to a mnemonic:

> *Natus* homo *declaratur,*
> Vitulus *sacrificatur,*
> Leo *mortem depredatur,*
> *Sed ascendit* aquila.

The four images are to be associated therefore with Incarnation, Crucifixion, Descent into Hell and Resurrection.

It must, however, have been difficult to sustain this as the correct interpretation when the same four figures were also paired with the four Evangelists in Christian art, virtually from the outset, for instance in Ravenna in the fifth–sixth centuries (San Vitale), and thereafter in every illustrated Evangeliary.

Turning to the Evangelists who acquired one each of Ezekiel's symbolical figures, we note that there was at first some uncertainty about the correct pairings. St Augustine wanted Matthew to have the lion, but St Jerome had assigned it to Mark who still has it. As for the rationalisations, such as they are, it was held that 'the man' belonged to Matthew because of his evident authority on the *genealogy* of Christ. The lion was finally Mark's because he records the *words* of the Baptist, prophetic of Christ, 'a voice crying in the wilderness.' There was an obvious affinity between the flight of the eagle and the ethereal *logos* doctrine of St John. That leaves Luke. Luke acquires the *vitulus*, not, I think, because of 'sacrifice'. The explanation is surely that popular piety here outstripped official teaching. This pairing was mate in one move. There is no answer to the popular association of the *vitulus* with the animals in the Nativity scene as official Christian art depicted it. The theologians could not endorse this solution openly, for as everyone knows, Luke, the only canonical source for the Nativity, does not mention the ox and the ass beside the manger. But even the earliest monuments of Christian art show the ox and the ass. They are present only in the Apocryphal New Testament, *Pseudo-Matthew*, chapter 14: 'Mary went forth from out of the cave, and entering the stable, placed the child in the stall, and the ox and the ass adored Him. Then was fulfilled that which was said by Isaiah the prophet, saying: The ox knoweth his owner, and the ass his master's crib [Is. i 3].' The text adduces Habac. iii 2 also: 'between two animals thou art made manifest.' [As is well known, 'two animals' is a misrendering of the Hebrew in Septuagint and in Jerome's *Vulgate*, see any O.T. commentary.] Let us forget the rationalisations of the Fathers and of the less learned devout. The pairings enter into the canon of Christian art.

The 'four faces' of each animal in the vision of Ezekiel are reduced to one face each by the author of Revelation; henceforward they have one face each. The group of four in Ezekiel's vision, like that in Daniel's (Dan. vii: the lion with the eagle's wings, the bear, the leopard and 'the fourth beast') are believed to have their origin in the monumental sculptures of Mesopotamia. The origin of *these* need not concern us, nor need we do more than mention the four fixed signs of the Zodiac: Taurus, Leo, Scorpio and Aquarius (roughly *vitulus, leo, aquila, homo*). There are, I believe, other parallels in occult systems. We may well be more interested in *later* developments. To the Vision of Ezekiel Western tradition owes the *Majestas Domini* in representational art. As for Daniel's vision, medieval artists drew that too, but much greater importance attaches to the use made of it in prognostic historiography. (See Chapter III, passim, and Martin Noth, 'Geschichtsverständnis der alttestamentlichen Apokalyptik', 1954, = *Geschichtsdenken*, pp. 30ff.)

*Caesar and David* (cf pp. 102 ff.)

Wolfram von den Steinen found himself confronted in his essay 'Der Mensch in der ottonischen Weltordnung', *DVJSchr.* xxxviii (1964) 1 ff (16 illustrations) with the problem of 'Caesar or David?' in medieval Emperor portraits. He treated it with reference to what he took to be the personal dilemma of Emperor Otto III. While agreeing with him in this one case, I keep to my own more general interpretation of David-likeness (as the only possible allusion to the 'sinfulness of Kings'). I quote with gratitude from von den Steinen's analysis of two juxtaposed pictures in the *Bamberg Apocalypse* (Cod. Bibl. 140 of *c.* 1001–1002).

*Fo. 59 v.* (upper picture): between Peter and Paul, who set the imperial crown on his head, *Otto III, enthroned*; (lower picture): the 'lands' offer their homage.

*Fo. 60 r.* Pictures of the Virtues. (Upper picture): *Obedience* (right) and *Chastity* (left) tread the corresponding vices underfoot; (lower picture): *Rue* and *Patience*. Between these two figures, 'A young king in royal robes. Historically the reference may be to David, but the picture was none the less painted for Otto III, then aged 20. . . . What has often seemed to reflect an inner disharmony and the immaturity of youth (namely Otto's undoubted imperial pride and his abject self-abasement) seems to be pictorially represented here in the two juxtaposed pictures.'

It seems to me, if I may draw the threads together, that these two images form a 'mirror', exhorting Otto to imitation of Caesar, *imperator* (59 v), and of David, *defensor fidei*, patient in his chastisement (60 r). He may himself have selected and influenced this treatment, or at least have given his approval of it. His case leads naturally to a further consideration of an even more ambivalent image of Caesar, and of other images.

### Ambivalent Images

(*a*) *Cæsar imperator* and *Majestas Domini*. In the article just quoted Wolfram von den Steinen deals *inter alia* with 'the most striking and disquieting imperial image produced by the Middle Ages, the dedicatory portrait in an Evangeliary of Aachen Cathedral' (loc. cit. p. 859 n 10, figs. 4 and 5). This often reproduced and much discussed picture is the work of a cleric, Liuthar, who represented the Emperor (probably Otto II) in an image closely resembling that reserved for the *Majestas Domini*. The question has often been asked whether the result is Christ in the guise of Emperor, or Emperor in the role of Christ. The text accompanying (opposite) the image was first looked at more closely, I gather, by Wilhelm Messerer in 1959, surely rather late in the day. The image evidently corresponds to a simple dedicatory prayer: 'may God invest the heart of the Emperor with this book,' and literally the symbolised Evangelists do hold a broad scroll in such a way as to indicate that their four gospels together cover or bedeck the Emperor's heart. Of this remarkable picture many things could be said, among which one must include the banality of the wish expressed in words. Before looking upon this picture as evidence of Ottonian conceptions of kingship, I should myself like to know who Liuthar was. Provisionally I propose to look upon it as a clerical conceit which may have caused Otto some embarrassment. See Beckwith, illus. 87, with the more orthodox interpretation, p. 106.

(*b*) In this note on Peter's Keys I ask (with reference to my remarks on intentionally ambivalent pictures, pp. 90 ff.) what it was that certain medieval artists actually drew, and how they themselves explained what they drew, *instead of* Peter's keys. Most of the artists naturally drew 'real' keys (examples in abundance); and the bishop's golden keys of office attested from the fourth and fifth centuries were unmistakably keys. In this note we are concerned with other, allegorical or symbolical keys. (Anything resembling them in real life would arouse suspicion.)

The starting-point of any consideration is naturally Peter's power to 'bind and loose' (Matthew xvi 18–19): *Tu es Petrus . . . et tibi dabo claves regni cœlorum* (whence the 'real' keys of the Church's image of Peter): *Et quodcumque ligaveris super terram, erit ligatum et in cœlis; et quodcumque solveris super terram, erit solutum et in cœlis.* The second part of the promise to Peter concerns his two *potestates*, conferred together with the keys. Our question is: how does the artist deal with *potestates* – if at all? There is no doubt that many artists let it rest at 'keys'; the keys then symbolise the *potestates*, as well as enabling Peter to open and lock doors as occasion may require. But this is not by any means the artist's only response to the challenge. Meantime the commentators and the poets could think of other symbols. They associated the *potestates* with the *balance* of the judge (admitting to Heaven on weighed merits) and the *rudder* of the pilot of the ship which was the Church. From Timmers (*Symboliek* etc. 2172) I again quote lines of Adam of St Victor:

> Claves duæ Petro dantur:
> Clavis una, qua librantur
> Meritorum pondera.

> . . . fit remus cœli clavis
> . . . Petri navis
> præsens est Ecclesia.

To the artist a *potestas* normally implies a staff or rod of office, and Peter is already provided with a cross-staff. Two *potestates* would mean two staffs. Is it conceivable that the artists have attempted to allude through his staff or staffs, to *keys, balance, rudder* and *cross*? I think so; and also to the name PETRUS given to him on the same occasion. They endeavour to show the 'tradition' (handing over) of *all* these things, the most important being perhaps his name. I am led to these suggestions by my simple inability to see some of the 'keys' to which the art historian's titles draw my attention. There are also contradictions. Of one and the same picture of Peter one may read that he is holding his staff, or his keys or his monogram. (The monogram has certainly been recognised by many.) As far as I can see nobody has so far seen a rudder or a balance.

Beginning with the premise that it would be strange if medieval artists had failed to consider approved alternatives to the *realia* of Peter's investiture, one may see these other things behind or through the signs which superficially might be keys. We are at any rate not entitled to say that these things were not seen in, or read into the completed pictures. To follow this argument reference to the pictures is essential. It is also important that in contexts like this we should recognise letters both as letters and as shapes. Thus **T** is a 'balance' in its simplest, symbolic form; a medieval rudder has the form of **P** (inverted **d**). The cross-staff belonging to Peter (see Jos. Braun, *Tracht und Attribute der Heiligen in der deutschen Kunst*, Stuttgart 1943, PETRUS, col. 594 ff) has three transverse bars. It may, says Braun, end at the top in *a crook*. We need to note therefore that in medieval lettering an **R** (a crook – more or less) finishing with a slight flourish may incorporate **us** as an abbreviation. In reading details of this kind into pictures, any stroke may be *read twice*, i.e. **R** may contain **P**, and a **T** may be read in the upright and one transverse of the cross-staff.

(i) In the so-called Gero-Codex (of the Hessische Landes- und Hoch-schulbibliothek, Cod. 1948),[1] assigned to the Reichenau School and dated about 969, there is a dedicatory picture showing the presentation of the Codex itself to St Peter, see Adolf Schmidt, *Die Miniaturen des Gerocodex* (Leipzig 1924) plate XI and our plate 17b.

Peter, enthroned, holds in his left hand two thin staffs the upper ends of which show above his shoulder against an empty background. No eye can fail to read the staffs as *initials* before asking what they are supposed to represent. Using the verticals twice each one reads **ꟼETR**, the verticals of **P** (reversed) and **R** being lengthened inordinately so that Peter can hold them, and ending in an **us** flourish: **PETRUS**. The completions of **E** and **T** are in the cross-staff. What Peter holds as his sign of office is therefore two staffs (*potestates*) and his name PETRUS. The medieval eye would, once it had been shown the way, also recognise the shepherd's crook or the rudder in the **R**, and the balance in the **T**. But this is principally the monogram.

(ii) A picture of Peter in MS XXIa, no. 37, of the Niedersächsisches Landesmuseum, Hanover. The manuscript is an Evangeliary, possibly from Bremen of the second half of the eleventh century, representing

---

[1] The Library's new Catalogue of Liturgical MSS. (Einzenhöfer-Knaus, Wiesbaden, 1968, p. 108) quotes the following interpretation from my first ed.

in its illustrations (I quote) 'a final anæmic phase of Ottonian art'. The editors of *Das erste Jahrtausend* (illus. 410–11) where I first encountered this image speak of 'the handing-over of the keys to St Peter'. The complete picture comprises two full-page drawings. Christ (on the right page) hands over to the Prince of the Apostles (left-hand page) his 'keys'. This was my starting-point. To anyone coming fresh to this picture Christ is handing over what one can only call ꓶR, the verticals again lengthened to allow Peter to hold these as staffs of office. The ꓶ is not an **E**; there is no sign of **T**. I think that in this final stage of Ottonian art the convention of showing Peter's monogram cannot always have been understood. One accepts unusually inadequate 'keys'.

(iii) A 'Peter' in the dedicatory picture of Emperor Henry II's Lectionary (Munich Staatsbibl. clm 4452 of about 1002–1014), (Von den Steinen, loc. cit. illus. 1).

St Peter on the left leads Henry towards Christ who is enthroned in the centre of the picture. Wolfram von den Steinen writes that St Peter 'shows his monogram', and indeed one could not wish for a clearer **E** with three bars; of the letter turned left-about one cannot say with assurance whether it is a **P** (ꟼ) with a decorative **us** abbreviation, or an **R** (ꓤ) with a slight flourish or a crook. The **T** seems to be absent, and so there is no balance; a rudder *could* be pointed to. Who is to say that nobody saw this in the eleventh century? Solution: monogram.

(iv) In the Munich MS clm 4453 (Von den Steinen, illus. 11, our plate 18a) there is a direct illustration of Matthew xvi: *Tu es Petrus*. Christ 'assigns' to Peter his name – **PTR**.

(v) See Van der Meer and Mohrmann, *Atlas of the Early Christian World*, illustr. (531? and) 533. The monogram convention was evidently used from about 400.

On the whole there was nothing that could convincingly be called a rudder or a balance in these various pictures, but awareness of the possibilities has made us critical of some 'keys'.

(c) By now it is clear that there are medieval conventions of representation which have to be learnt. Equally, if we are to know what *is* represented, we may not be timid. So far we have refused to see a 'brazen serpent' when the artist had sculpted a dragon, and keys when the artist had not drawn keys. I think we may say that our stubbornness was rewarded.

In this subsection (*c*) I now come to the case of an allusive relationship between images of similar outline where the artists seem to be ahead of the authors from the beginning and to stay there. They create a cluster of images which seem to cry out for treatment in words, and yet it comes to nothing. This is a problem which I have lived with for years, and I have still nothing of real substance to communicate. I offer none the less some notes on Peter's Cock on the Column. This image is, to me, but one variant (of getting on for a dozen) of an exemplar. As an image it is, I think, pre-Christian, but it comes to be associated from an early date with Peter's Denial. On one of the earliest Christian monuments (Van der Meer and Mohrmann, *Atlas of the Early Christian World*, illus. 173 and 175, a sarcophagus in the Museo Lateranense, our plate 18b) Peter stands beside a handsome column on which the cock crows its accusation. Peter stares at it in horror or remorse. The editors of the *Atlas* print most appropriately beside this image the text of the hymn *Ad Gallicantum* (*Aeterne rerum conditor*), the first Christian 'Dawn Song'. Next: This column *as* a column establishes an important and relevant allusion to Christ's Flagellation (see p. 230). On fo. 80 v of the so-called *Codex Egberti* (see plate 20a and pp. 338 ff.), the cock is not perched on its own column, but on a tiny round roof immediately above the column of the Flagellation. In drawings of the scene and the properties for later Passion plays the column of the Flagellation, Peter's column and the column for the raising of the Brazen Serpent by Moses (as a standard, see p. 260) are reduced to two in number. Two sufficed for any one typological lesson, and yet all three are linked by a host of meaningful and authoritative associations in the general context of the Passion of Christ (see Heinz Kindermann, *Theatergeschichte Europas*, I (1957) illus. 264 and 267, stage plans for the Lucerne and Villingen plays). Once conscious of this exemplar (the 'bird', or winged or rampant creature on the column) one is less surprised to encounter an otherwise startlingly unusual picture on folio 50 r of the same *Codex Egberti* (and on fo. 51 of the *Golden Evangeliary of Echternach*): a Peacock on a column, from whose beak water streams into a tall water-tower, see plate 22a. This represents the Pool of Siloah, more precisely labelled 'Aqueductus Siloah'. Further, lamps consisting of a standard or column and a bird-shaped vessel, often in scenes of the Last Supper, remind one again. But for all the wealth of associations I can discover no written work which has made these associations themselves a subject. In the scriptoria this basic drawing was repeatedly required for a number of important contexts. What kind of discussions did it provoke? And what was the drawing called? Incidentally, any modern reader who is sure he could never confuse those various birds and animals on columns has not seen a medieval Phoenix, or the full range of Christian and pre-Christian images of roughly this outline.

(*d*) As I hinted under (*c*) we shall have to assume that some ambiguous images may prove to have been idle conceits, leading us to nothing of any consequence for the interpretation of medieval works. For all that they will inevitably arouse and occasionally reward our interest. The chalice which in more 'allegorical' Crucifixions receives the blood of Christ often appears not at his side (held by Ecclesia) but near Christ's feet. It establishes there an association with the *fons pietatis*. Occasionally the chalice is so placed and shaped that it coincides in outline with the footrest which it then necessarily displaces (Albert Boeckler, *Das goldene Evangelienbuch Heinrichs III.* (1933), illus. 211 and 215; *Das erste Jahrtausend*, illus. 386). I mention this as the kind of thing one simply notes. In the fountain to which the chalice (so placed) alludes, sinful souls can be washed clean, and with this fountain Mary Magdalene is particularly intimately associated by the words of the *Dies Iræ* (stanzas 8, 13). These things are worthy of note in themselves. They also provide the only explanation I can find of Mary Magdalene in the role of the Samaritan Woman. This association must be old; it is 'attractive'. It appears so late that I think there must be a serious objection to it (what is the objection, and how could it be sustained in days when the Magdalen was the 'woman taken in adultery?). In a Danish folk-ballad of the seventeenth century (Sven Grundtvig, *Danmarks Gamle Folkeviser*, (1856) II 532 ff) one hears:

> Der stod en Quinde at óse Vand;
> – IEsus, HErren min! –
> Og der kom Iesus gangendes frem.
> Magdalena bad alt til vor HErre.

There stood a woman drawing water, Jesus my Lord, and there came Jesus passing by, and Magdalene prayed to our Lord.

It is interesting to see how in the various versions of the ballad the Samaritan woman's pitcher and Magdalene's unguent jar are brought under a common image. The points of contact here are many and various. I mention them without attempting any rationalisation of the stages by which the associations were made:

(i) The 'allegorical' chalice which receives Christ's blood refers, when at his feet, not to the sacrament but to the *fons pietatis* (an idea capable of endless elaboration).

(ii) Here at this fountain or well Mary Magdalene *or* the Samaritan Woman may draw water and be cleansed of sin. Mary bears a jar, the Samaritan woman a pitcher.

(iii) Christ's *sessio*. Christ sat beside the well *fatigued* by his journey (*fatigatus ex itinere* in the story of the Samaritan Woman, John iv 6). Christ's sojourn on earth, his Incarnation and his Passion are a *sessio* (see St Augustine, above, p. 113), of which sinful man is reminded by the words of the *Dies Iræ*. In stanzas 8 and 13, the *fons*, the *sessio*, the fatigue of Christ, man's sinfulness and Christ's Crucifixion are all associated in one vivid and meaningful statement with the Magdalen: *quærens me sedisti lassus*, etc.

(iv) The Magdalen and the Samaritan woman are further linked by a *race* to announce the truth. This is a more popular association but, again, an 'attractive' idea. St John says that the Magdalen ran. He does *not* say that the Samaritan woman ran; 'she left her pitcher and went away into the town' (*reliquit ergo hydriam suam . . . et abiit in civitatem*). This is rectified by the commentators who in their allegorising paraphrases say 'she *hastened* to abandon her sinful life', and from such a gloss Otfrid of Weissenburg takes his cue and recovers 'history' from allegory. His Samaritan woman 'threw away' her pitcher and 'hastened' (surely 'ran') into the town (*Evangelienbuch*, II 14, 85–6):

> So slíumo siu gihorta thaz, firuuarf sie sário thaz fáz,
> ílta in thia búrg in zen liutin, ságeta thiz al ín.

Otfrid generally handles sacred story with circumspection and careful regard for canonical texts. Did he merely enliven this episode with an innocent exaggeration, or see a connection with the Magdalen?

(v) It is a development of a different order when in representations of Christ's baptism the dove of the Holy Spirit is replaced by a winged phial, poised above Christ's head (*Hortus Deliciarum*, ed. Straub-Keller, xxviii *bis*, supplement fo. 100), or if the dove bears a phial. These iconographies represent baptism as the annointing of Christ as High-Priest (*rex et sacerdos*), Schwietering, plate v, top right.

# II

## FOUR ESSAYS OF FURTHER
## INTRODUCTION[1]

### 1. MEDIEVAL DESCRIPTIONS OF
### CHURCH INTERIORS

THE first passage to be considered here comes from the 'Gandersheim Rhymed Chronicle' of about 1216, the work of a Priest Eberhard who was deacon and notary of the monastery of Gandersheim.[2] Under the heading *Prologus, De fundatione Gandersemensis ecclesiæ* he in fact writes less about the actual founding of the monastery church than about the merit of those responsible for foundations generally, while the Chronicle itself which follows is concerned to win adherents for the monastery's rights against those of the Bishop of Hildesheim. It is, in short, not a work to claim much attention from students of literature. For all that, the first twenty lines of the Prologue amount to a brief description of a church interior to which I think we shall find few parallels. If one were to ask a student of medieval German literature whether there are any such descriptions he would, I think, say that he knew of none as such, but that there is of course the very interesting passage in Gottfried von Strassburg's *Tristan* describing (and allegorising the description of) the 'Lovers' Cave'; and then there is the lengthy account of the Grail Temple in the so-called *Jüngerer Titurel* of about 1270 which 'has always interested the art historians'. He will himself certainly have read

---

[1] I still call these four sections 'essays' as in the German edition, meaning that for students of German they treat aspects only of familiar problems. Readers whose knowledge of the Middle Ages is otherwise based may welcome these rapid excursions into less familiar territory and annotate the general remarks from their own reading.

[2] *Die Gandersheimer Reimchronik des Priesters Eberhard*, ed. Ludwig Wolff, Altdeutsche Textbibliothek, xxv (1927). In his history of medieval German literature, De Boor writes (III i 200 ff): 'sincerity and a deep attachment to the monastery of his native Gandersheim determine the tone and style of the work; the author addresses himself as in a sermon to his audience which he seeks to persuade and edify.' Further bibliography, ibid. p. 218.

the first of these as a piece of literature. The second remains something of a curiosity (see below).

And now Priest Eberhard. Twenty lines of medieval German verse are not going to revolutionise our ideas, but I think they require our attention. Was one, I wonder, prepared for what the author has to say of the beauty of the interior of his church? Of the walls draped with tapestries, of the frescoes (but the text is not absolutely clear about these), the brilliant blue, silver and gold, and of the precious stones? Would we have foreseen that the description of a church interior would so soon turn to the clouds of incense, the light of the candles and the ringing of the bells, and merge into an evocation of the divine service itself? I over-interpret slightly; the passage warrants it.

> Sint dat sek erhof de hilge kristenheit,
> der ummefank is worden lank unde breit:
> dat is von godes hülpen geschein.
> so men mach wol hören unde sein,
> schöne godeshus sint seder vele gestichtet,
> mit schöner zirheit harde wol berichtet,
> mit teppeden unde ok mit ummehangen
> alle wende vil schone befangen,
> mit mesterliken sinnen wol gemolt.
> lazur, sülver unde ok dat golt
> geven darinne harde wünnechliken schin.
> unde so se an der werlde dürest sin,
> dat se dar heten vil eddele steine:
> de sint darinne ok mit eren gemeine.
> mirre unde wirok rüket ok darinne;
> to gode erheven sek dar des minschen sinne.
> kerzen unde lampen darinne lüchten.
> darinne schal men sin mit geistliken tüchten,
> darinne höret men lesen unde singen
> unde ok de klocken to godes eren klingen.  (1–20)

Holy Christendom has spread far and wide since the days of its origin. That happened with God's help. One sees and one hears it reported that since then many fair Houses of God have been founded and decorated most beautifully, their walls furnished all about with tapestries and hangings and richly painted with masterly skill. Lapis lazuli, silver and gold shine in joyous brilliance and the rarest stones to be found, which we call precious stones; they too are there to bestow their glory. Myrrh and incense burn there, and the hearts of men soar aloft to God. Candles and lamps shine. There should be reverent attention there to the reading, the singing and the ringing of the bells to the honour of God.[1]

There is no further description of the church as a building. Eberhard goes on to say that the man who builds 'fair houses of prayer in which, early and late, honour and service are offered to God our Lord' shall be counted among the blessed, of whom David sang *Beati qui in domo tua, domine, habitant* (etc.).[2] Otherwise, interestingly enough, the only further references are to privileges, additions to the furnishings of the church at Gandersheim ('two fine pieces of work, called fore-altars', *twei düre werk, voraltare genant*, i.e. frontals or antependia),[3] a new chapel built 'with careful workmanship', and of course relics.[4]

After presenting this short excerpt I should like to refer again to the misgivings I expressed above at premature comparisons between the style of medieval churches and the styles of medieval poetry. It is surely a point of relevance that a medieval author who reflects on the beauty of his church has particularly the service in mind. For Priest Eberhard there are neither round arches nor any other kind of arches. If anything in the picture he draws is 'romanesque' it is the service itself offered by the faithful, assembled to hear and pray in a worthy setting.

The student of medieval German literature will, despite many differences, inevitably have been reminded by this passage from the Chronicle, of the one he already knew: Gottfried von Strassburg's description of the Lovers' Cave in the *Tristan*, a *quasi* sacral retreat of those dedicated to Love's service. He will also recall their 'winged' devotions, soaring to the lanterned dome of the temple cut in the living rock. But no serious comparison can be made between Gottfried's easy mastery of the routines of allegorisation to which he accommodates his description of the Cave, and Eberhard's more genuine expression of admiration and awe when he thinks of his own church. It is the artless-ness of his account which surprises us. Perhaps we are too accustomed

---

[1] There is no word for 'interior' in the text, but six times 'therein'; and no word for 'space' or 'hall'.
[2] Psalm lxxxiii (A.V. lxxxiv).
[3] Line 1816.
[4] See De Boor (p. 201) for a summary of the further content of the Chronicle, roughly the historical legitimation of the case against the Bishop of Hildesheim.

to tutored *descriptio* as we find it in the works of Hartmann, Gottfried and other writers of the 'Blütezeit'.

If there are more medieval descriptions of this 'impressionistic' kind than I can recall, they will doubtless help to bridge the gap which separates the Chronicle and the only further, extreme case known to me, namely a sequence of St Hildegard of Bingen on the subject of St Maximin. She 'describes' the service offered to God in the church dedicated to the saint. In the German edition of this book I capitulated at this point; I offered this mere indication of the contents of Hildegard's poem, and as quickly as possible referred readers to two Latin-German editions. Here I have decided to present the text itself, but with some words of introduction gratefully borrowed from a distinguished editor and translator of Hildegard's verses, Paul von Winterfeld. It is an altogether startling evocation of the interior of a church, seen, according to the opening line, by a dove which peers in through a window-grille. It concludes with a picture of 'the priest at the altar whose soul rises on clouds of incense to the Throne of God, there to intercede in his prayers for those who are his, before Him who is the eternal Light'. Between these two statements in relatively plain language there is a flood of images which puts the modern mind under some strain (or, as Paul von Winterfeld says, 'with which mortal lips contend in vain'). What we can do, none the less (von Winterfeld continues), is to state the origins of the images which in the mind of the visionary enter into fruitful correlations, each in its turn engendering the next. I pass on to the reader in my Notes those sources which von Winterfeld established, with some additions. As a preface to the poem I quote what I take to be the source of the dominant image. It is the one we need in order to gain an initial access to the poem.

The offering of a righteous man anoints the altar, and its pleasing odour rises before the Most High. The sacrifice of a righteous man is acceptable, and the memory of it will not be forgotten. Glorify the Lord generously and do not stint the first-fruits of your hands. (*Oblatio justi impinguat altare, et odor suavitatis est in conspectu Altissimi. Sacrificium justi acceptum est, et memoriam ejus non obliviscetur Dominus. Bono animo gloriam redde Deo, et non minuas primitias manuum tuarum.*)[1]

[1] Ecclesiasticus (R.V.) xxxv 6 (*Vulgate*, verse 8). Abel's sacrifice, see Gen. iv 4.

(Sequentia de Sancto Maximino)[1]

1(a)  Columba aspexit per cancellos fenestræ;
       ubi ante faciem eius
       sudando sudavit balsamum
       de lucido Maximino.

(b)    Calor solis exarsit
       et in tenebras resplenduit;
       unde gemma surrexit
       in ædificatione
       templi purissimi cordis benivoli.

2(a)   Iste turris excelsa
       de ligno Libani et cypresso facta;
       jacinto et sardio ornata est
       urbs præcellens artes aliorum artificum.

(b)    Ipse velox cervus
       cucurrit ad fontem purissimæ aquæ,
       fluentis de fortissimo lapide,
       qui dulcia aromata irrigavit.

3(a)   O pigmentarii,
       qui estis in suavissima viriditate hortorum regis,
       ascendentes in altum,
       quando sanctum sacrificium,
           In arietibus perfecistis,

(b)    Inter vos fulget hic artifex paries templi,
       qui desideravit alas aquilæ,
       osculando nutricem sapientiam
       in gloriosa fecunditate ecclesiæ.

4(a)   O Maximine, mons et vallis es,
       et in utroque alta ædificatio appares,
       ubi capricornus cum elephante exivit
       et sapientia in deliciis fuit.

---

[1] Text based on Paul von Winterfeld, *Deutsche Dichter des lateinischen Mittelalters* (Munich, 1922) Latin text pp. 438 ff, German translation p. 195; compared: Horst Kusch, *Einführung in das lateinische Mittelalter*, 1 *Dichtung* (Berlin, 1957), Latin and German pp. 378–9 (=Dreves-Blume, *Analecta Hymnica* vol. l 489).

(b)        Tu es fortis et suavis in cærimoniis
           et in choruscatione altaris,
           ascendens ut fumus aromatum
           ad columnam laudis,


5          Ubi intercedis pro populo,
           qui tendit ad speculam lucis,
           cui laus est in altis.


1(a). The Dove peered through the bars of the window; there before her eyes balsam dripped from the radiant figure of Maximin.

1(b). The hot sun blazed and shone into the darkness out of which the jewel opened to raise the pure temple of his pious heart.

2(a). He is a lofty tower of Lebanon wood and cypress; a city adorned with hyacinth and sardonix, excelling the handiwork of all other artificers.

2(b). A swift hart, he sped to the fountain of purest waters flowing from the hardest rock, which scattered a spray of sweet fragrance.

3(a). You gatherers of spices who dwell amidst the soft verdure of the King's gardens, and ascend to the heights, now that with rams, you have made your holy sacrifice,

3(b). He, the artificer and the pillar of the temple, shines forth in your midst, for he sought for himself the eagle's wings and with a kiss claimed Wisdom as his nurse in the glory of the fecund Church.

4(a). O Maximin, thou art mountain and valley and standest revealed as a lofty edifice raised in each, from which the antelope and the elephant went forth together and in which Wisdom was held the highest delight.

4(b). Thou art strong and gentle in thy rites and at thy gleaming altar, whence thou risest, like a cloud of fragrant incense to the column of praise,

5. where thou intercedest for thy faithful who strive toward that beacon of light, to which be praise in the highest.


## NOTES

The imagery of the sequence owes rather more to Ecclesiasticus (Sirach) than Winterfeld recognised, somewhat less than he thought to the Song of Songs. In Ecclesus. particularly the 'Praise of Wisdom'

(xxiv) should be compared, likewise 'the priest at the altar' (xxxv, already quoted above) and the 'art of the perfumer' (*opus pigmentarii,* xlix 1). From the Song of Songs are derived the 'dove at the lattice window' and the 'gardens of the king' (Cant. i 14, ii 9; v 1, vi 1, etc; *pigmentarii* v 13). 'The hart at the spring' is from Psalm xli 2, the 'light shining in the darkness' from John i 5 and ii Cor. iv 6. The lore of stones and beasts was familiar to Hildegard as a 'scientific' writer.

1(*a*) Compare Ecclesus. xxxv and xxiv 20: 'as choice myrrh I spread abroad a pleasant odour' (*balsamum aromatizans odorem dedi*).

1(*b*) *gemma* is both 'bud' and 'gem'; intense heat is required for the making of gems (*in partibus, ubi nimius ardor solis est, pretiosi lapides et gemmæ oriuntur,* Hildegard, *Physica,* PL CXCVII 1247).

2(*a*) 'I grew tall like a cedar in Lebanon, and like a cypress on the heights of Herman' (Ecclesus. xxiv 13/17 and Cant. iv 8). On the Heavenly Jerusalem: Ecclesus. xxiv 15 and Revel. xxi 10 ff. On 'artificers': Cant. vi 1.

2(*b*) Psalms xli and lxxxi 16; also Deut. xxxii 13.

3(*a*) *pigmentarii*: Ecclesus. xlix (*Memoria Josiæ in compositionem odoris facta opus pigmentarii*) and Cant. v 13 (*areolæ aromatum consitæ a pigmentariis*). These figures refer to 'the other saints'. *in arietibus*: Levit. xxiii 18.

3(*b*) I do not find a *nutrix sapientia* but suspect that the *sapientia* of Luke vii 37 and the *nutrix gallina* of Matth. xxiii 37 contribute. For the 'fecund Church' compare Ecclesus. xxiv 16: *in plenitudine sanctorum detentio mea* and Luke vii 35.

4(*a*) is difficult. The following passages should perhaps be considered: Deut. xi 10–11 (description of the land of Canaan), Ecclesus. xxiv 7–11 and 13. The animals remain something of a mystery. Hildegard's *Physica* has elephant lore, but nothing relevant here. Isidore on the capricorn (ibex, *Etym.* XII i 16) is not helpful beyond specifying 'high places' as its dwelling. There is little to help in *Physiologus.*

4(*b*) Ecclesus. xxiv 7: *Ego in altissimis habitavi et thronus meus in columna nubis.*

This is of course a highly 'visionary' poem (hymn). As one becomes more familiar with its content (perhaps after renewing acquaintance with the 'Eulogy of Wisdom' in Ecclesiasticus and the parallels in the Canticle) one sees that the real subject is nevertheless not very different from that of Eberhard's lines. Both are evocations of the divine service. In the one case (Eberhard) we have a tempered but sincere expression of awe and wonder. The other, an ecstatic, but for all that well composed hymn draws on a generous range of ideas and images perhaps personal to this one visionary poetess. In both works we witness a progressive 'Raumgestaltung'[1] as the action of the divine service unfolds. A *Majestas Domini* as such is not mentioned in either poem. Such an image would seem to dominate the scene evoked.[2]

But now to round off this short section, the purpose of which was to take account of a text (in the end two texts) not hitherto considered in discussions of architectural descriptions in medieval literature. By comparison with the extremes of imaginative reference which Hildegard contrived to reduce to an ordered composition, Eberhard's lines seem sober and factual indeed; they are the more welcome for that. They are also a welcome alternative to the dryly analytical and systematic rationalisations of Belethus, Durandus and other medieval theorists who have something to say of the 'significance' of every detail in the ceremony of the Mass, and of every piece of church furniture.

We may now, after this slight enlargement of the scope of our enquiry, return briefly to the two texts which have hitherto seemed to be the most important medieval descriptions of buildings, at any rate from the point of view of German studies. First the passage in Gottfried's *Tristan*, his description of the 'Minnegrotte' to which hero and heroine retire for a period of idyllic banishment from the court of King Mark. It is an ancient temple, Gottfried tells us, built and frequented by 'giants' in the days of Corineus (about whom there is plenty of information in Geoffrey of Monmouth). Readers will want to see Gottfried's full text of which there is now an excellent English translation,[3] but we may recall the main features briefly: the rock-crystal bed, in the centre of the circular sanctuary which has flawless walls and a lanterned dome above with three windows. Outside there is a pleasance, the whole area being enclosed by wild forest. The retreat is accessible only to true lovers. Gottfried then tells us at length what all these various features 'mean'. It is perhaps of interest to note that in an essay of 1925 to which

---

[1] See pp. 9 ff.

[2] In dealing with Eberhard, above, I spoke of what appeared to be an artless technique owing little to the rhetoric of the schools, and had already entertained the possibility that he was writing in a more popular rhetorical tradition. Paul von Winterfeld speaks of Hildegard's 'lyrical' treatment of her subject: 'rarely does one encounter in sequences in honour of saints so purely lyrical a treatment of subject; normally . . . something in the nature of a ballad with a lyrical framework (which may be the reason why the secular ballad exploited the sequence, etc.)'.

[3] By A. T. Hatto, Penguin Classics L 98 (1960), ch. 26.

we are inevitably referred, Friedrich Ranke said of 'this remarkable allegorical passage' that it had up till then 'been the subject of very little attention'.[1] Nowadays the passage gets possibly an excessive amount of attention at a fairly rudimentary level, and undergraduates can expound it as based on the conventions of the allegorists of ecclesiastical buildings. Then a few years ago Friedrich Ohly[2] more or less swept aside Ranke's essay as being quite inadequate to our present needs. This is indeed true. That Gottfried was using a convention of interpretation evolved by theologians to explain the *rationale* of ecclesiastical buildings is now so obvious that it is almost embarrassing to have to say so. The task ahead is (or could be) to determine Gottfried's position among allegorists, and to find not merely 'other examples' of allegorised buildings but close parallels, either to the Minnegrotte as a structure or to Gottfried's method. Ohly drew attention to Hildegard of Bingen; not, however, to the sequence which we have just examined, but to the Fourth Vision in Book Two of her *Scivias*. This is a vision of the Temple of the Holy Spirit. This may indeed have been known to Gottfried. Of other allegorical works considered by Ohly, the long tract *De tripartito Tabernaculo* by Adamus Scotus of Whithorn (d. 1180), though in many ways fascinating, seems to me far less relevant, and in scale, scope and organisation an entirely different kind of work.[3] First of all the Holy Tabernacle is, as a building, 'given' in Scripture. The building provides the 'topical' framework for a whole encyclopaedia of historical and other knowledge, sacred and profane, which the author 'places', paying of course due attention to the primary claims of the Tabernacle to be elucidated. Gottfried's Lovers' Cave is by comparison a construction of his own devising, combining features of Solomon's bed-chamber, a Temple of Venus and Hildegard's Temple of the Holy Spirit. (There are also some details which show Gottfried's providential concern for the allegory which is to follow, the choice of woods and metals for the single door and its fittings, for instance.) No doubt we shall in future know more about Gottfried's position among the allegorists, but we should not forget that there is an admixture of mock-

---

[1] 'Die Allegorie der Minnegrotte in Gottfrieds Tristan', in *Schriften der Königsberger gelehrten Gesellschaft* (1925), pp. 21–39.

[2] In an important public lecture which he informs me he is now finally revising for publication. Professor Ohly (of Münster) has meantime written profound interpretations of Goethe's allegories, e.g. the Pedagogical Province in *Wilhelm Meister* ('Goethes Ehrfurchten' etc., in *Euphorion* lv, 1961, 113 ff and 405 ff).

[3] *PL* CXCVIII; 609–796.

solemnity and irreverence in Gottfried's Minnegrotte episode, and that his 'accommodation' of the routines of allegory is *inter alia* a display of virtuosity and wit.

Finally there is the Temple of the Holy Grail in the so-called *Jüngerer Titurel*, a work of the late thirteenth century in the fashionable 'obscure style' which only a few specialists in Middle High German literature contrive to read each generation. It is an enormous amplification (about three times the length of the *Nibelungenlied*) of the story of the Grail, now finally carried forward to Prester John. Within this work there is a passage of one hundred and twelve stanzas devoted to a systematic description (with what purport to be measurements) of the Temple of the Grail. It would, I am sure, be most welcome to art historians if I would now tell them what is the state of thinking in German studies about this work, particularly whether they can safely continue to refer in their teaching to the 'famous passage' on the Grail Temple and draw attention to the text which Julius von Schlosser made conveniently accessible to art historians as long ago as 1896. The situation today seems to be such that caution is called for on every side. One may, I think, quite safely continue to refer to the existence of the famous passage, but it would be folly to seek to put details of the text to any use. It will take only a few lines of print to indicate the difficulties.

As a preliminary it may be remarked that the *Jüngerer Titurel* was believed during the century or so after its composition to be the work of Wolfram von Eschenbach,[1] a considerable factor in ensuring the work's popularity. There are over forty manuscripts. This means that the problem of editing the *Jüngerer Titurel* is forever insoluble; there can never be more than tentative editions. This in its turn means that we shall never have a text of the Grail Temple passage of which we can say with assurance that it represents in detail the poet's ideal edifice. It is of dubious value to know that there were redactions which increased the number of chapels and multiplied the dimensions. As for our understanding of the text, the scholars who have examined it recently cannot agree, for instance whether the author had a western church in mind or a Persian edifice symbolising the cosmos in its structure, or, if we keep to western models, whether he was idealising the Gothic he had seen, or projecting what it might achieve; or again

[1] The author was Albrecht von Scharfenberg. The date of the *Jüngerer Titurel* (over 6000 stanzas) is generally given as 'about 1270'.

whether the source of his inspiration was the work of architects or of goldsmiths.

At this point we can draw the threads together by contrasting an early view of the Grail Temple description and that which the art historians have got safely into their handbooks. Sulpiz Boisserée of Cologne, an early enthusiast in the cause of the Gothic and a friend of Goethe, wrote an article in 1835 declaring the Grail Temple stanzas to be 'the most important of all passages in medieval literature dealing with works of architecture'. He offered the best text he could put together and three drawings of the Temple as he had reconstructed it. As is only natural, he found a Gothic solution. Julius von Schlosser preferred to comment otherwise when in his source book of 1896 he made the text, meantime edited by the philologist Friedrich Zarncke in 1876, available to art historians. He spoke of the 'completely fantastic description of the Grail Temple' and of the 'mystic power of the new Gothic style to fire the imagination of the German Middle Ages'. The tendency now is to argue that the architectural description is not an end in itself but the vehicle for something else, whether the Mystic's view of the universe or that of the more methodical cosmographer – which accords well enough with von Schlosser's formulation. And so, at the end of this review of passages of literature dealing in one way or another with buildings, the twenty lines from Priest Eberhard's Chronicle may appear to be a most welcome addition. They bring us back to buildings actually seen.[1]

## 2. PICTORIAL TAPESTRIES (TRISTAN AND ISOLDE)

In addition to discussing problems of interpretation raised by some notable Tristan tapestries,[2] I shall endeavour here, as occasion offers, to

[1] The account I have given of the *Jüngerer Titurel* leans heavily on the long introduction to vol. 1 of Werner Wolf's edition for the Deutsche Texte des Mittelalters, XLV (Akademie-Verlag, Berlin, 1955) which I reviewed in *MLR* LII (1957) 128–30. The view seems meantime to gain ground that Wolf's over twenty-five years of editorial labour have resulted in an edition which is 'wrong'. It seems that there are only two alternatives for the editors of late medieval works transmitted in a number of manuscripts; either a critical edition which will be 'wrong', or a more or less diplomatic edition of two or three manuscripts (parallel texts) which will be 'not an edition at all'. There are recent examples of each.

Julius von Schlosser's *Quellenbuch* is more fully discussed below, pp. (308), 312 ff.

[2] For convenience I use the forms 'Tristan' and 'Isolde'.

deal with certain aspects of 'recognition' which had to be excluded from Chapter I (where we considered motifs and exemplars rather than subjects). It will be as well if we dispose of one of the problems immediately. Namely, why is it that we students of literature, who on the face of things should recognise pictures of episodes from myth, fable and romance, are in fact slow and inept? At a superficial level the explanation is simple. There are too many pictures; pictures are not our business. We try to 'read' the pictures, casting around for the subjects they might represent. (The catalogue then corrects us.) The art historian is quicker. He has several advantages. Not only are pictures his business; he knows through his training which episodes from myth and story the artists have over the centuries selected for treatment, and returned to time and time again. Moreover his source books anthologise for him the relevant passages from literature. He is able to revise the texts he needs to know. It is worth remarking that the art historian's advantage over his fellows was much less marked in the days when emblem-books and iconologies were a highly esteemed form of reading and study, and when triumphs, masques and charades were a customary form of polite entertainment. Recognition was practised over a 'fair' range of subjects. One recalls perhaps both the space given up to the charade in the first Act of Goethe's *Faust*, part II, and the tedium which that part of Goethe's work now engenders; (one senses also a general reluctance to admit that a number of Goethe's well-known poems are 'emblematic' and presuppose an audience familiar with representational treatments of traditional themes). In short, even if we disregard (as we shall) large allegorical compositions, which may leave even the experts baffled, the literary historian today stands helpless in front of far too many 'subjects'.

So much, then, for the advantage which in theory the connoisseur of literature *should* have when it is a matter of identifying themes from literature in the work of the artists. If that were all I had to say, I should be wasting the reader's time. My purpose here is slightly more complicated. It is to show that the student of literature cannot quickly restore the position either by disparaging reference to the art historian and his source books, or by trying to bring to bear on pictures that extra knowledge he has of literary history and of the intricacies of literary tradition. At least, he cannot do so immediately. He may in fact have to forget his special knowledge and some of his prejudices before he may join usefully in the discussion of works of art at all. To illustrate this I draw on my own experience with Tristan tapestries. I still remember vividly what, as a very orthodox student of medieval German literature, I used to think of them. Those views have long since been rectified, but in the interest of a clear exposition I start again from the beginning.

Let us recall for a moment not only what we know about the *tale* of Tristan and Isolde, but also what we as medievalists know of the history of the *Tristan* theme, and of its treatment by various poets. For medieval literary historians all lines of development lead to one masterpiece of European literature. All other versions and adaptations are 'pre-Gottfried' or 'post-Gottfried'. In Gottfried's *Tristan* we recognise the culmination of tradition in a work of unsurpassed sophistication, containing perhaps even a germ of decay and degeneracy, though that is not generally part of the story as we tell it. The descent from the heights begins in the early Munich manuscript of Gottfried's work itself. Here his diction is tempered to conform with a norm he was deemed by some connoisseur to have overstepped. The end is represented by the *Tragedia von der strengen Lieb Herr Tristrant mit der schönen Königin Isalden* by Hans Sachs of Nuremberg, who not only went back to a tradition earlier and simpler than that of Gottfried, but reduced the story to the final moral that one should 'save up one's love for marriage'. If we now hear that certain tapestries of the fourteenth century follow not Gottfried, but a hitherto not finally identified version, we can scarcely avoid thinking of that chapter in which the descent from the heights was duly registered. In doing this we forget certain factors of, I think, fundamental importance if the arts are to be compared at all. Particularly we forget that even Gottfried's *Tristan* uses the swiftest and (technically) the easiest method of presentation, that of narration in words. The art of tapestry on the other hand follows one of the slowest and most laborious of methods ever invented: stitched pictures. We all too easily overlook the fact that the twenty-two pictures of the tapestry known as *Wienhausen I*,[1] 'narrating' Tristan's two journeys to Ireland, his fight with Morold, his fight with the dragon and his return to Mark's court with Isolde, probably occupied more hours of work than the copying of all the more than twenty extant Gottfried manuscripts. Such a disproportion between invested labour and story almost passes comprehension.

[1] Wienhausen near Celle, Hanover; a tapestry of the beginning of the fourteenth century, further details below.

Let us spend a moment on this question of disproportionate expenditure of labour. Recalling the decoration in illuminated Irish and Northumbrian manuscripts, masterpieces of the goldsmith's craft, and – coming back towards our subject – liturgical objects of all kinds, copes, pluvials, altar-cloths, is one to ascribe an *aesthetic* value to technical skills and perhaps the 'secrets' of crafts? I am myself inclined to do so. I am at any rate in some difficulty when asked to distinguish between the work of a Master of the Woodcut and his engraver (for instance Hans Holbein and Hans Lützelberger). Drawings and drafts (for woodcuts, gold and silverwork, furniture and buildings) are working-hypotheses, at one stage possibly even advertisement or sample, then master-pattern and finally an approximate record. The master knows what he can entrust to the more practised hand of his 'technician'. He sets him some tasks which he knows to be feasible and others which are to be tried, and while the work is being carried out, he continues to plan other things. If the division of labour remains, and the master never lays a hand on the work in progress, it is to me an open question who is the artist. The 'conception' of which the theorists speak leads a very marginal existence at times. In the end one must, however, be persuaded, and indeed it is difficult to see how we shall get back to *Tristan* tapestries until we are.

But returning to *Tristan*, we observe that the twenty-two pictures of *Wienhausen I* reduce the story we are familiar with (through a courtly romance of some twenty thousand lines, unfinished) to the duration of little more than a longish anecdote – to what the motif-researcher calls a 'simple form', or nearly that. This reduction we have to associate in our minds, as was already stated, with an increase of technical effort. We can never do real justice to the situation. Within a few minutes or in half an hour (after several hours perhaps if we understand the techniques involved) the tapestry can only claim our attention as a series of pictures. The colours may be splendid, but what do the pictures represent? There is occasionally something sadistic about the short shrift we give to those who have taken the trouble.[1]

---

[1] With better technical knowledge one can probably quote more extreme cases of the insensitivity or cruelty of aesthetic verdicts. We may be dissatisfied with the 'ductus' of an artist whose work has been in a furnace, and find a representation of the Crucifixion done in *cloisonné* somewhat crude in its outlines. On the other hand the lavish use of the most expensive materials, and fantastically intricate workmanship expended on an object associable with superstitions rather than faith, may inhibit the aesthetic judgment entirely: there is simply nothing to be said.

We finally 'read' the pictures of *Wienhausen I*, all twenty-two of them, as though their purpose were to narrate and little more. We read the inscriptions with a certain tolerance and difficulty. Stitched captions are not easy to read. The more than thirty coats-of-arms in four bands dividing the rows of pictures scarcely claim our attention. After about an hour the modern observer has had enough, and buys a reproduction so that he can examine the pictures further and finish his reading of the three or four sentences. 'But in the fourteenth century everything was different, people had time . . .' At this point I will risk the remark that we are generally too ready to accept this *cliché* without due questioning. Was everything so different in the Middle Ages? People were not so harassed and had patience . . . they could listen to a four-hour sermon . . . frescoes and tapestries, statues and paintings were the layman's Bible. Very well then, let us continue. With the help of the pictures of *Wienhausen I* the story of Tristan and Isolde was narrated, episode by episode – by whom? Have we reliable evidence of this? Have we the scene in which a narrator stands before this or a similar tapestry, telling the story to an audience which at every 'Hear now how Tristan . . .' concentrates afresh? I am naturally asking for trouble in suggesting that this whole conception is a myth, for the evidence is clearly there for something of the kind: the very existence of all the hundreds of frescoes in churches, the serial pictures and sculptures representing *Genesis*, the story of Joseph, of David, the New Testament Miracles and of course the Passion story. And then there is the theologian's *topos* too, of pictures as the people's book.[1]

[1] There is always a risk that this *topos* will attract evidence which does not directly support it. A case in point is the so-called *Pictor in Carmine*, to which I shall want to refer again. What concerns us here is the letter of recommendation which precedes the work itself.

The author, possibly one Adam of Dore (Herefordshire), writing about 1200, complains of the 'presumption and licence of those artists before whose inane images layfolk stand about gaping in our cathedrals and churches' (*inanes . . . picturas . . . presertim in cathedralibus et baptismalibus ecclesiis, ubi publice fiunt stationes*). There is a suspicion that by *inanes picturas* the author means grotesques (M. R. James, p. 145, see below), and a further one that he is in any case quoting St Bernard. This is not good evidence of pictures as the layfolk's Bible. It is, however, evidence of the layman's attention to some kinds of images of ecclesiastical art.

As for the work itself, it consists purely of text. It is a fully written out 'programme' of subjects of the kind the author would recommend for treatment. The number of projected pictures is no less than 646 (no doubt a 'significant' number): 138 New Testament texts, each with two or more typologically significant Old Testament texts in support: all these were to become pictures. M. R. James doubted whether the programme was ever executed, and I myself find a quarter

We now come back to *Wienhausen I* and try again to determine
what association the tapestry had with literary tradition. I think we
have the *choice* of seeing it as a series of pictures before which the
reciter of a ballad-like version of the story stands, referring to each of
the pictures as he reaches it with a stylised gesture: roughly (very
roughly) in the manner of the ballad-monger (*Bänkelsänger*) down to
the nineteenth and even twentieth centuries.[1] *Or* one imagines the
owner of the tapestry or a custodian displaying the *tapestry* as a proud
possession. In his elucidation the technique and the craftsmanship of
the tapestry receive attention, and so do the coats-of-arms. But sooner
or later the custodian turns to what is really interesting, the representation of 'the well-known story of Tristan and Isolde'. (That was
presumably what the visitors wanted to hear and talk about. Crafts are
always something of a mystery, coats-of-arms are interesting up to a
point, tapestries as such are familiar enough.) 'Here one sees how
Tristan . . .' Certainly the custodian will allude to the incidents of the
story as they occur in the pictures, in the terms he has become accustomed to use; it is not the first time he has explained the tapestry. Yet,
if we may draw on whatever situations seem analogous to us, this never
becomes a recital of any tangible Tristan poem or work. It is throughout an explanation of pictures, with reference to a central narrative
tradition, about which any dogmatic assertions will in these circumstances not be socially acceptable. A visitor may venture the remark
that one does not generally read that Tristan fought with Morolt
'against Marke's wishes', as the *titulus* on the left in the third row states.
Others may agree, but this will have been felt to be an interruption,
producing roughly the same effect as when we are reminded that there
is another when someone has sung a traditional song. A few
questions may be asked and observations offered, about the wonderful
dragon, and the ships (how many are there? – all different). The con-
versation finishes as it began, as a discussion of the artist's cunning, and
the patience . . . etc.

---

of a mile of panels somewhat unlikely. Adam of Dore was clearly a literary man.
The *Pictor in Carmine* is a typological essay, working in Adam's own 'researches'.
It was successful as a work in its own right. An artist would have shown greater
restraint in matters of typology. The work is transmitted in thirteen English MSS
of the thirteenth century. M. R. James's edition appeared in *Archæologia*, XCIV (new
ser. XLIV, 1951).

   [1] Readers may annotate this remark in the light of sub-literary and folk traditions
they know: the stipulation here is a ballad *text* and a set of *pictures* representing the
'tragic story', i.e. ignoring the music of the ballad.

The reader will make his choice between these two alternatives (recital of a poem, explanation of the tapestry) when he has seen the tapestries or reproductions of them (details of reproductions below). But despite all that has been said in these reflections and digressions, the purpose of which was to mitigate the literary historian's strictures on the artist who designed *Wienhausen I*, it is still permissible for us, as literary historians, to observe that he did not follow Gottfried's version, nor did he use Eilhart von Oberg's adaptation of the French *estoire* only. It is a matter of rather more serious concern that the Low German text incorporated in the design shows 'more than one misunderstanding of the course of the story as it is represented *in the pictures*', and that 'the *tituli* cannot be the work of the artist who designed the series'.[1] We have in *Wienhausen I*, therefore, evidence of a *Tristan* version which we cannot identify, and of uncertainty about the plot of the story in any case. Even so, we may not *directly* infer a decline in literary taste and standards, for the designer had to consider what could be treated in this medium and within this reduced compass. Gottfried himself would have understood the choice of a simpler model than his own work, for no less than his contemporary Priest Eberhard he showed an interest in tapestries. (The passage is familiar. Gottfried has particular words of praise in his literary review for Bligger von Steinach, the author of a work, since lost, with the title 'the Tapestry' (!); and for his exquisite choice of words – *wunsch von worten*: 'one would like to see them framed in a border of Greek tapestry-work'.) As for the translation of the story into more balladesque terms, Gottfried himself had not hesitated to recognise an element of farce in some of the capers of hero, heroine and their enemies. Tristan is traditionally a master of every kind of cunning.

The choice of the Tristan story for the tapestries of a *convent* still requires a word of comment. Wienhausen is still a convent ('Damenstift', Cistercian originally). The tapestry was made there and was never in any other ownership. A study to be mentioned below refers to a 'modified range of themes in the tapestries of the period (the fourteenth century), which is extended from biblical subjects to include chivalrous and bourgeois and even popular matter'. I would say that just as some of the biblical, mainly Old Testament stories – Esther, Judith, Susanna and the Elders – came to be understood as being

[1] Friedrich Ranke, *Tristan und Isold* (Bücher des Mittelalters, ed. Fr. von der Leyen, Munich, 1925) p. 276. Plates 2–4 are of *Wienhausen I*.

more simply 'historical', those traditional secular stories of love which pointed a useful moral became more acceptable and virtually innocent, particularly if aristocratic. Such tales are sad, tragic and serious. (Tales of common life are at best cautionary, generally vulgar.) Then there is the simpler challenge of subject, and the excitement of working out a pictorial solution. *Wienhausen I* is finally a 'glorious work in radiant colours', as Friedrich Ranke, the editor of Gottfried, wrote in the appendix to his book on '*Tristan* in the Middle Ages'.

*Wienhausen I* may or may not be a masterpiece of its kind. It is difficult for us in literary studies to forget its date, which to us is 'late', its place of origin and the *presumably* provincial standards of draughtsmanship of the artist who drew the designs. It must like other tapestries take its place among tapestries. I wished simply to stress that we must remember the limits of our brief as literary historians. The ladies of Wienhausen were under no kind of obligation to assure themselves that their homage was to the greatest of the poets who had treated the story of Tristan and Isolde.


*Supplementary Notes on Section 2.* The Wienhausen tapestries were long thought to be based on Eilhart's version, a view found in the *Tristan*-book of W. Golther of 1907. Friedrich Ranke noted deviations from the story as told by Eilhart, op. cit. p. 276.

The standard work in which to examine pictorial details of *Wienhausen I* is Marie Schütte, *Gestickte Bildteppiche und Decken des Mittelalters*, vol. 1 (Leipzig, 1927) 3 ff and plates 1–8. A solid table will be required for the use of this volume.

The best starting point, however, is the recent article of Jürgen Ricklefs, 'Der Tristanroman der niedersächsischen und mitteldeutschen Tristanteppiche', in *Niederdeutsches Jahrbuch*, LXXXVI (1963) 33–48, available in most university libraries. It has a handsome coloured folding plate showing *Wienhausen I* in its entirety. *Wienhausen III* of about 1360 is more modestly reproduced.

Ricklefs' article gives an account of further 'Tristan' treatments: (a) a white linen embroidery (*Weisstickerei*) of the early fourteenth century from the village church of Emern (Kreis Ülzen), now in the museum at Lüneburg; (b) an Erfurt (or Würzburg) tapestry of about 1375; (c) a further Erfurt example (about 1375), now in the Victoria and Albert Museum.

With the pictures of the Wienhausen tapestries Ricklefs has compared: (a) *texts*: Eilhart, Gottfried, the Icelandic *Tristramsaga* and the

Middle English *Sir Tristram*, also the French prose romance; (*b*) *other pictures*: the miniatures in Eilhart and Gottfried manuscripts,[1] and woodcuts found in early printed versions of the German prose Tristan. So far it has not been possible to establish the missing source – either for the version of the story given by the tapestries, or for the sequence and number of pictures. Ricklefs is to pursue his researches, but he seems to me to regard the problem as mainly one of literary history (see his title), as though a further romance must be found. So far he has not considered the problem of 'reduction'. Was it possible to reduce so complicated a story to manageable size without editing it? Was such a story sacrosanct in matters of motivation (e.g. 'against Marke's will') by the fourteenth century?

Two final remarks. The *Tristan* tapestries are in fact most honourably mentioned in even a relatively short encyclopaedia article on 'embroidery'. On the subject of Tristan and Isolde tapestries in a ladies' convent: this has been made the subject of an amusing short story *Sie kennen Aphrodite nicht* by Horst Wolfram Geissler (Ullstein, Frankfurt/Main – Berlin, 1965).[2]

## 3. MUSPILLI

One will not even look for a medieval work of art corresponding in every detail of content to the Old High German poem on the Day of Judgment which we call *Muspilli*. Indeed 'it would seem unlikely that we should ever find a source of any kind', Herbert Kolb writes, at the end of his re-examination of the poem.[3] In Kolb's view the *Muspilli* is a work showing a marked individuality and independence; he can only account for it at this time (namely in the late eighth or early ninth century) by assuming a Bavarian origin.[4] Kolb's arguments convince me, although it is in fact immaterial for the purposes of the discussion here whether the poem was written in Bavaria or elsewhere in Germany. I wish to stress its independence of pictorial sources (except

---

[1] I am grateful to Hellmut Rosenfeld of Munich for drawing my attention to an article of evidently fundamental importance, on the 118 scenes from Gottfried's *Tristan* in the Munich MS cgm 51: Paul Gichtel, *Festschrift für Gustav Hofmann* (Wiesbaden, Harrassowitz, 1965) pp. 391–457.

[2] My thanks to Mrs Marga Black for this reference.

[3] Under the adjusted title 'Vora demo muspille', in *Zeitschrift für deutsche Philologie*, LXXXV (1964) 2–33.

[4] Ibid. p. 33.

conceivably in its concluding lines) and indeed assert that medieval art could not have illustrated its content, even in a series of pictures.[1]

Ecclesiastical art of the Carolingian and following periods offers examples enough of the Day of Judgment. Their formula corresponds to the indications given in lines of the *Carmina Sangallensia* of the ninth century. Leitschuh prints these in his monograph on the repertory of Carolingian art, to which we shall make many references in this book.[2] They purport to describe an actual picture:

> Ecce tubæ crepitant quæ mortis jura resignant,
> Crux micat in cælis, nubes præcedit et ignis.
> Hic resident summi Christo cum judice sancti,
> Justificare pios, baratro damnare malignos.[3]

There are many medieval pictures in which Christ is seen as accuser, displaying the wounds inflicted on him as man;[4] *Muspilli* has exactly this image in its more or less final passage – *denne augit er dio masun, dio er in deru menniski intfenc.*[5] One will no doubt today visualise this scene with the help of familiar medieval pictures, and similarly the awakening of the dead 'from the bonds of the grave', *ar der leuuo uazzon.* Or the sculptured reliefs in the tympanon of a cathedral west door will come more easily to mind.[6] On the other hand there are typical Day of Judgment motifs which the poem lacks; and then of course there are

---

[1] In the German edition I said with unavoidable brevity that I did not support Schwietering's interpretation of *Muspilli*, and implied that I thought his reproduction of the Day of Judgment from Henry II's Evangeliary of 1014 inappropriate (his illus. 9). Here, where I can spare a few more lines, I may state the nature of my disagreement. Schwietering (following the art historian Dehio) records the achievement of the Reichenau school of artists and credits it with the *creation* of what became the typical image of the Day of Judgment. It is, I think, altogether too subtle and dangerous to say that the *Muspilli*-poet did *not* contribute to the evolution of the artist's image but, with Otfrid, is evidence of the state of mind which generated it. ('Der Muspillidichter verhalf dieser Bildidee nicht zum Durchbruch aber gemeinsam mit Otfrid kennzeichnet er die Stimmung, aus der vielleicht auf der Reichenau die bildkünstlerische Weltgerichtsvision geboren wurde' p. 12.) I am a great admirer of Schwietering's work, not only the *Deutsche Dichtung des Mittelalters*; it is unfortunate that in this book I can only deal with points of disagreement. On 'Reichenau', see pp. 337 f.

[2] A fuller account of Leitschuh's monograph, pp. 309 ff.

[3] Leitschuh, p. 68.

[4] In judgment scenes and as 'Man of Sorrows', see pp. 111, 126 ff.

[5] Then he will display the wounds which he received as man.

[6] Schwietering, plate VII, illus. 63; Beckwith, illus. 202.

the elements in the poem which Kolb has stressed and characterised, and which make it seem to him an individual work largely independent of models of any kind.

The poem is incomplete. The poet may, as he approached the final lot of the blessed and the damned, have referred to the angel with the sword and balance. By that point he is recalling and endorsing familiar traditions. We are concerned here rather with the seventy-odd lines in which he battles his way through to that point, and then finally stops preaching the special sermon he has for his contemporaries, possibly particularly for Bavarians. It is this earlier content which we shall not find in art, and indeed which would have been in more than one sense 'impossible' in art.

Kolb reminds us that the poet, in describing the duel of Elias (Elijah) and Antichrist first presents it in a way which corresponds to the opinion of some, and is wrong! That is as a judgment of God (a *judicium dei*), in which Elias as the champion of God and the just should be the victor and bring Antichrist, the champion of the 'old enemy' and Adversary (*Satanas*) to a fall. As supporters of such an erroneous view, which could only encourage vain hopes, the poet names the *uueroltrehtuuison* which is now taken to mean 'experts in our earthly laws', and Kolb believes the poet will mean particularly Bavarian law. That the experts had addressed themselves specifically to the case of Elias *v.* Antichrist may be something of a fiction, but there is no denying that the poet describes the preparations, and the course of that imaginary contest in vivid terms.[1] 'Men of God' have the right version, says the poet; it is Elias' blood which will be shed, and this he now relates, and the consequences.

Such a content, an ironic statement ('there are some who think . . .') would be impossible in a work of Christian art and probably technically impossible in any case. It would also be difficult to represent unambiguously a contrast between a *secular court*, where an accused's powerful supporters and kinsmen could save him from the consequences of a crime, and the court of the Last Judgment. Similarly it is one thing to remind fellow Christians of a known parable, here that of

---

[1] An English translation of the passage will be found in the *Penguin Book of German Verse*, introd. and ed. by L. W. Forster (1957) pp. 6 ff, where 'pious men in the world' instead of, say, 'lawyers', reduces the gap between the holders of two completely opposed views.

Dives in Hell and Lazarus in Abraham's bosom,[1] quite another to represent in a picture how an affluent sinner might hope to *escape* a similar lot to that of Dives, perhaps through bribery. All these motifs occur in the poem. The task of ecclesiastical art is to state in a clear indicative or imperative what Christian teaching is, and that task alone kept it always fully occupied. Art cannot with propriety 'illustrate' error. For all these reasons I would say that the *Muspilli* poem owes little to the art of the Church for its vivid pictures and rich imagery.[2]

Finally there is the fight itself, between Elias and Antichrist which heralds the sequence of disasters leading to the destruction of the world by fire, and the Day of Judgment. It does not belong to the canon of Christian art in the West. It may be that some scene in medieval art has been claimed as a representation of just this combat, but the art historian's handbooks seem to offer no evidence of this; and we have to remember that we have still not found convincing textual parallels, even in apocryphal Apocalypses, to the events narrated in *Muspilli*. It is a combat in the truth of which the poet clearly believes, and he describes it with a fervour of conviction which makes this one of the few memorable passages of Old High German literature. He revels in the description of the destruction of the world which follows the wounding of Elias. It destroys all the law courts of this world, and their corrupt judges and those who sought to corrupt them. Medieval art is clearly not the source of this idea, which seems to be something of an obsession with this author. He then has some fine touches in his references to the Devil, his record-keeping and duties as spy (*uuartil*) and informer. Vividly as this role is seen, it is mainly derived from verbal, rather than any pictorial tradition. Finally there are the lines about the 'head which shall say' and the 'hand, down to its little finger, which shall speak', revealing the crimes it has committed here on earth. All this, again, is

---

[1] The pictorial formula eventually evolved can be seen in the so-called Golden Evangeliary of Henry III (*Das goldene Evangelienbuch Heinrichs III*), ed. Albert Boeckler (1933) illus. 123; compare also Schwietering, illus. 36.

[2] It may seem unnecessary to say that art does not illustrate ideas which should not be entertained, but, as I put it, above, art does and must prefer the (positive) *indicative*. By its admonitory images it has access to an 'imperative'. By juxtaposition it can offer an 'either-or' disjunction, perhaps also 'if clause' and 'result clause'. Wilhelm Messerer (see Index of Names) has compared a deliberate 'scaling' of images in a complex composition to 'main' and 'subordinate' clauses. One can also cite rhetorical 'figures' which the artist can match. On the whole it is better to let these thoughts occur to one, than to see how far the analogies with grammar and rhetoric can be pressed.

vividly 'seen', but what is recalled is probably the stylised ritual (supported by traditional formulæ) of the medieval trial by ordeal.

Any poet treating the Last Judgment must, however, finally summon all his resources to describe of all 'last things' the very last. He must tell of the fate of sinful man at the Judgment, and before the Judge – *vora demo muspille*. He knows the words he must use. But their sound will die away, and with them the poet's earnest warning. The devotional image of the artist on the other hand shows the Judgment itself, and to the portrayal of the *tremendum judicium* it subordinates any presages and portents. The warning contained in the artist's image remains there for every beholder. It does not fade or die away. The man who 'knows himself a sinner' (*der sih suntigen uueiz*) can only turn away from it, or enter the door beneath the tympanon in the frame of mind required of him.

This is not the place to compare the older literary accounts of the Day of Judgment systematically. The Old Saxon *Heliand* must, as a verse paraphrase of a Gospel Harmony, keep to the indications given in the New Testament;[1] similarly Otfrid, who seems to have made his own individual choice of roughly pericopal readings. Towards the end of the Middle Ages, however, a much expanded basic text was available, incorporating Old Testament prophecies, words of commentary from the theologians and the narrative and enumerative motif of the Fifteen Portents of the Day of Judgment. Here were the makings of Last Judgment plays. In these there may be speaking parts not only for the biblical characters drawn in by this procedure of composition but also for any further figures occurring in *pictorial* representations of the Day of Judgment – angelic trumpeters, angels bearing the *arma Christi*, angels singing God's praise; naturally also Christ as accuser, poor sinners, Mary as intercessor; also the blessed, perhaps proposing to start their Dance to Heaven. And of course there are suitable parts for the Devil and his minions and for the damned. At the end of this section I recommend the Berne *Day of Judgment Play*[2] which in Wolfgang Stammler's edition is fully annotated with constant reference to the parallels in art. In this latter text a more popular kind of Christianity seems to determine what characters shall appear, a thing one could also

---

[1] Its sections lii–liii are based on Matth. xxiv–xxv, Mark xiii, Luke xvii and Revelations.

[2] *Berner Weltgerichtsspiel*, from a manuscript of 1465 in *Texte des späteren Mittelalters*, xv (1962).

say of the *Muspilli*, though with reference to the popular Christianity of an earlier, still missionary age.

*Supplementary Notes on Section 3.* (1) Lines 1–36 of the *Muspilli* deal with the fate of the individual soul immediately after death. The forces of Hell and angels from Heaven contend for possession and lead the soul to eternal fires or to an abode of bliss and everlasting life. This motif and references (in what may be later interpolations) to alms-giving no more than indicate an emergent doctrine of Purgatory. These abodes will generally have been envisaged in the same way as the final Hell and Heaven. There were, however, some pictorial treatments from an early date of 'the departure of the soul from the body', with representations in a surrounding framework of Hell and Heaven, e.g. in the Wiesbaden codex of Hildegard of Bingen's *Scivias*, about 1170, Schwietering, illus. 35. The artists had inherited the mannikin image for the escaping soul and matched it with a diminutive angel. (2) I mentioned in passing a 'Dance of the Blessed'. Schwietering reproduces as his plate IV (in colour) what is taken to be a first sign of such a tradition. See our plate 11a (Cod. Bibl. 22 of Bamberg Cathedral Library, tenth century, 'Reichenau School'). Schwietering gives this particular image the very precise title 'Ascent to the Cross through the sacraments of the Church', that is: an ascent of the faithful on a spiralling rope of cloud from Baptism towards Ecclesia with her proffered chalice. The spiral continues to the Cross and Crucified, and beyond. Some such ascent the later poets have in mind when they refer to a *dance* of the blessed, led or welcomed by (not Ecclesia, but) Mary, with accompanying music of the angels to whom are assigned the instruments and joyful voices of which the last of the Psalms sings. This dance, of which there is scattered but plentiful evidence in later literature, never assumes the firm outlines of the curiously comple-mentary *Dance of Death*: in which Death (a Leveller) leads a long line of dancers (representing Church, from Pope down to mendicant friars alternating with members of the laity, from Emperor down to beggar and infant child), each with a skeleton partner to the charnel house. There was a 'Dance of Death' fresco on the interior wall of the Cimetière des Innocents in Paris from about 1420. We may wish to see it as a some-what remote and distorting mirror-image of the Dance of the Blessed. That possibility can, at any rate, not be excluded from a discussion of origins. For the Dance of Death (*and* for the Dance of the Blessed) see Wolfgang Stammler's *Der Totentanz, Entstehung und Deutung*, 2nd ed. (Munich, 1948). The much larger monograph of Hellmut Rosenfeld, *Der mittelalterliche Totentanz*, Beihefte zum Archiv für Kulturgeschichte,

III (Münster–Cologne, 1954, virtually unchanged in 2nd ed. 1969), should be used with caution; his thesis of a German origin of the Dance of Death is not tenable on present evidence. On the Dance of Death writings of Stephan Cosacchi (Kozaky), see H. Rosenfeld, *Archiv für Kulturgeschichte*, XLVIII (1966) 54 ff (58 ff).

## 4. RELIGIOUS DRAMA AND REPRESENTATIONAL ART

The discussion of the Old High German *Muspilli* led us to pictorial representations of the Day of Judgment, and finally to the use of pictorial motifs by the compilers of later plays; the *dramatis personæ* for instance of the fifteenth-century Bern Day of Judgment play included angels bearing the *arma Christi*. Later we shall be suggesting that the producers of medieval religious plays may have taken certain further hints in matters of *régie* from religious paintings. These various allusions to an influence of *art on drama* in the Middle Ages more or less oblige us to say something about an old theory which at times had the status of an axiom, concerning an important influence in the opposite direction, of *drama on art*. It is generally referred to by the name of its most eloquent exponent, Émile Mâle.

Ever since, almost a hundred years ago, it was first postulated that late medieval artists took some of their scenes directly from dramatic representations, the theory has continued to make its appearance – even in most recent research, and despite many justified objections.

I take this formulation from Dr Elisabeth Roth's study of 'crowded Calvaries'.[1] Dr Roth summarises the arguments which have been advanced in support of the theory since 1860, and rejects them. In my Chapter IV on the Crucifixion, following an entirely different method of enquiry, I have not so much reinforced objections to the 'Mâle theory' as advanced another which makes no use of the argument from realism: indeed it removes some of the *realia* on which that argument

[1] *Der volkreiche Kalvarienberg in Literatur und Kunst des Spätmittelalters* (Berlin, 1958, 2nd ed. 1967) p. 124.

had depended. If an influence of late medieval drama on art is again postulated, it will, I trust, seek to dispense with realism as a criterion and not equate the action in the pictures with what it will have been feasible to enact in plays, particularly in the Crucifixion sequence. The argument from realism was in any case 'out' in its chronology by a couple of hundred years. The same realism is to be found in religious narrative from about 1200, long before the plays.

But first, the most important thing is to recommend the works of Émile Mâle. Because of one thesis, and one in the event unfortunate subtitle, one will not want to dispense with his four-volume history of medieval art in France.[1] Moreover Mâle's thesis has not been demolished, as we shall soon see, but substantially restricted.

My next starting point is a slim volume of 60 pages with, however, 41 illustrations, by Otto Pächt, long familiar in Britain as a writer and lecturer when he was at Oxford, but now Professor of Art-History in Vienna. In *The Rise of Pictorial Narrative in Twelfth-Century England*,[2] Pächt writes:

That the liturgical drama or rather forms of dramatised liturgy have made an impact on medieval art cannot be contested . . . What is still a matter of controversy is the extent and the true significance of this influence, in part the question of how early it made itself felt. E. Mâle, who in his treatment of late medieval iconography had at first [1908] overrated the importance of the mystery plays ('renouvellement de l'art . . . par les mystères') and had later revised his opinion, struck a much more cautious note when he published his *l'Art religieux du XIIe siècle* (1922).

Pächt's own study of English illustration after 1120, by which time the resistance of the new Norman overlords to 'narrative' art had been overcome, leads him to see in the liturgical plays of the time a 'major factor in the twelfth-century revival of pictorial narrative'; that is, in what are called by some scholars 'paraliturgies', liturgies with slightly expanded texts enlivened in the Middle Ages by a certain amount of miming, with the use of costumes. To see what Pächt means by

---

[1] *L'Art religieux du xiie* . . . *du xiiie siècle* . . . *de la fin du moyen âge en France*, and . . . *après le Concile de Trente* (Paris 1922–32). Mâle's publications were a *continuum*, making reference to his ideas by their dates hazardous.

[2] Oxford, 1962, p. 33.

'pictorial narrative' one has to examine his reproductions: III Banishment from Paradise, IV Creation of Adam, V Entombment, VI Descent from the Cross, VII Christ as Pilgrim on the Road to Emmaus, VIII Ascension, IX Doubting Thomas. In each of these plates Pächt juxtaposes pictorial narrative represented by the *St Albans Psalter* (from St Albans, but now in Hildesheim; date – before 1123), and representations of the same scenes by continental artists. Once one has recognised narrative representation as something that clearly 'looks different', one is ready to follow the by no means simple 'syntactical' analyses which Pächt offers, and to understand his account of the origins of the new style. These he explains partly by reference to native (Anglo-Saxon) traditions; partly by invoking the continued influence in England of classical models, of which there will have been more than elsewhere in Northern Europe as a result of the Roman missions of the seventh century. (These will have brought many new books into the country, including illustrated books, certainly more than are now extant or attested.) Finally, however, there is the influence of liturgical drama which simultaneously recited and mimed episodes of New Testament story. For Pächt (as for others before him) this influence is nowhere more clearly to be seen than when one compares the so-called 'Peregrinus' *plays* and the *pictures* of narrative art devoted to the same subject. The costumes of figures in the pictures of the Emmaus scenes are those prescribed by rubrics for the characters in the plays. Most important is the costume of the 'pilgrim'.[1]

According to Pächt, moreover, the gestures of the figures and their groupings in the *St Albans Psalter* and other English illustrations correspond to the paraliturgical texts rather than to the wordings in the Gospels. Here one cannot summarise. We must leave it that Pächt is convinced. There remains the question whether there is thereafter a direct line of parallel development, from liturgical plays and 'pictorial narrative' in the twelfth century down to the Passion Plays (the Mysteries) and the pictures of late Gothic art. It was for this *later* period that the influence of drama on art used to be asserted with particular vigour, and hence the thesis and sub-title 'renouvellement de l'art par

[1] With Pächt I refer to Karl Young, *Drama of the Medieval Church*, 2 vols (Oxford, 1933) I 471 ff. In the rubrics of the Peregrinus play of St Benoît-sur-Loire, Fleury, 'for performance at Vespers on Tuesday of Easter Week', there is an exact description of the costume to be worn by the Disciples and by Christ on his, various appearances (*Ad faciendam similitudinem Dominice Apparitionis in specie Peregrini*, etc., full text in Young).

les mystères'. But meantime we have generally become more aware that there was a flood of *new texts* from about 1200 which in their narrative content at first left the artists helpless. Here was a new textual tradition for which they had not yet elaborated the appropriate images. The texts with which they had to 'catch up', but which medieval drama incorporated almost automatically, had immediately the status of *authorities*. About them – Anselm, Bernard, Bonaventura – we are to hear a good deal in Chapter IV where we shall adhere to current practice and prefix each name with 'Pseudo', Pseudo-Anselm, etc.; we are here talking about the Middle Ages which did not doubt the attributions. In the works in question the events of the Passion are *described* in the detail in which the artists were later to represent them. It therefore no longer makes historical or any other kind of sense to argue from what *actors* (of two centuries later) will have been able to, or have wanted to enact, simply in order to explain the rituals of the Flagellation and the Crucifixion as Gothic art presents them. But – to leave Mâle's theory for a moment – it is equally erroneous to think that either the primitive generalisations of 'Geistesgeschichte' or the subtleties of the history of dogma can explain the 'realism' of the Gothic. 'Changed attitudes towards religion' and the emergence of a 'theology and Christology of suffering' (*Leidenstheologie*) may be inferred from the pictures painted by Gothic artists, but *not* at the same time invoked to explain their narrative content. In Chapter IV we shall look at some of the origins of narrative realism from the point of view of textual history, philologically.

For this last-mentioned reason Pächt's observations on one 'symbol' of the Passion of Christ are of particular interest to us. He sees in the treatment of the 'bitter cup' by the artist of the *St Albans Psalter* a 'foreshadowing' of a generally much later tendency to 'historicize' Christian symbols (see plate 32c). In a woodcut of the *fifteenth* century showing the Agony in Gethsemane one indeed almost expects to see a very real-looking chalice, set on a ledge of rock; just as one expects to see a sword (or seven swords, one for each of the sorrows) in Mary's bosom. These, we would say, have by the fifteenth century become inevitable elements in any treatment of these subjects, and are barely symbols at all. (If one adds that 'one chalice' may be listed among the properties required for a Passion Play of the same period, the tale is more or less complete.) But in the *twelfth* century? Pächt writes:

The English master . . . takes the 'cup of bitterness' literally, externalises the simile [metaphor or symbol] and shows us the chalice standing on a rock in front of Jesus. In this way the contents of Christ's agonised dialogue with the Father in heaven has been made explicit and articulate. . . . Here as in many other ways, English Early Romanesque foreshadows characteristic features of Gothic art. (p. 58)

I would concede that, to us, such a development may seem to be foreshadowed. But what the twelfth century artist intended was, I think, to translate a metaphor into an image which should still refer back to the *word*, rather in the manner of the artist(s) of the Utrecht Psalter than 'with a new realism'.[1] In this picture the comforting angel and Christ both *point* to the chalice (*calix iste*), so that even *iste* is translated into image. Similarly, in another picture, Pilate throws water from his bowl clean over the heads of the Jews,[2] a curious way of referring to two of *their* words (*sanguis ejus*) *super nos*. But is this 'realism', 'dramatic realism' or simple 'literalism', insistence on the sanctity of sacred words?[3]

We still have to enquire whether the Mystery plays, which clearly cannot have produced any 'renouvellement' of art in Mâle's sense, are now to be left out of account. For various reasons I think their influence on art will have been slight, and one has after all to remember dates and chronology. Anyone who thinks that medieval artists represented the Flagellation and the Crucifixion as they did because they recalled how these scenes had been enacted by players, overlooks not only dates but other and more important sources of an apparent realism.

[1] See p. 326 on the Utrecht Psalter.
[2] Pächt, plate XII, 39.
[3] Otto Pächt once expressed to me his amazement, almost horror (I thought) at my discovery of certain presages of the Gothic in the very diction of the ninth-century Old Saxon *Heliand*. The diction is rhetorical, turgid, and the poet is driven by the exigencies of alliteration to sustained overstatement. The *Heliand* in consequence offers early examples of an *intemperate* treatment of the cruelty of the enemies of Christ, his physical suffering, and of the grief of the three Marys. This I pointed out in my article 'Christlicher Erzählstoff' (see p. 70 n.1) where, however, I also stressed that important, characteristic features of the Gothic are *not* present. By way of contrast at this point, and for interest: in the Gethsemane Chapel of Coventry Cathedral one sees through a grille in the form of the Crown of Thorns the comforting angel and the cup of bitterness in brilliant mosaic. The sleeping disciples are relegated to a dark relief, obliquely set. On a free-standing stone altar are the carved letters *Alpha* and *Omega* as the only reference to Christ's presence.

The artists did *not* draw what they had seen enacted. They followed the instructions of the Bible itself on the manner in which the events of the Passion were to be visualised. These are given in the Bible in a number of *sicut . . . ita* formulæ. *As a thief* is taken prisoner, *thus* was Christ seized, and thus, the ecclesiastical artist must have understood, was he to be represented as being treated. Like a lamb to the slaughter, *thus* was Christ led when he had been seized. The Man of Sorrows was *like* a leper. *Sicut latro, sicut ovis, quasi leprosus.* Countless Passion sermons and tracts had translated these comparisons into narrative prose, describing the events, no less violent, in sequence, which linked these images, generally retaining the words of the original biblical simile in a concluding or passing reflection, but often suppressing it. What was to be imagined, every literate Christian knew; and so the artists had to find the graphic counterparts and present ideal images corresponding to the authoritative words. These are 'negative ideal' images. (Ideal images were, of course, always sought for Christ, the Marys and the disciples.) They will certainly not have accepted the postures, gestures or simple antics of more or less talented actors as the ideal.

We have also to bear in mind that artists in the later Middle Ages were making increasing use of models, drawing from life. As the number of those attested as present in the various scenes increased, they had increasingly to *compose* their crowd scenes. 'Crowds' of onlookers, a 'cohort' of soldiery, the behaviour of which was 'wild and insensate' demanded care in composition, a good deal of stylisation and the inclusion of many types. The artist who paints a scene on the Way of the Cross, or at the Crucifixion itself, is therefore *not* concerned to convey the unforgettable impression made on him by a Passion Play. He has to compose a scene in which 'mob' or 'rabble' and 'soldiery' behave as they should. From the examples he finds in his own vicinity and from among the mimically more gifted guildsmen of his acquaintance he selects, I suggest, the models for the various 'negative ideals', the 'enemies of Christ'. *Thus* they looked and *thus* they behaved. In late medieval pictures of the Seizure, the Mocking, the Flagellation, there is also an unmistakable choreographic principle, which far from reflecting stage practice will surely have been a mirror for producers, to which they will have looked for guidance.[1] If despite all these

---

[1] I have changed my mind considerably on these matters in the thirty years or so since I first became interested in 'free elaboration of sacred story'. At this point I mention merely that a stage direction which sticks in my mind from my earliest

considerations some late medieval pictures do in fact suggest 'stage', we probably have to allow that they may commemorate *performances* and be pictorial records. The illustrations in histories of the theatre naturally tend to select pictures of just this type. Heinz Kindermann even envisages the possibility of producers as the painters in some cases.[1]

In this section I have cited no specific examples of Passion pictures. In Dr Elisabeth Roth's monograph (see above) there are dozens of careful descriptions of late medieval Calvaries. Any museum of art or illustrated history of medieval art offers examples in plenty. I earnestly suggest that readers of this book should for a time ask whether these pictures reflect narrative prose in their content and in their mood – or drama.

Finally a brief word about the relationship of drama and art in later centuries, necessarily brief if we are to remember our title. One can scarcely describe a Baroque ceiling or fresco without referring to something characteristically theatrical or even operatic in the stylisation of posture and gesture. To the 'staginess' of the general presence of the actors must be added the scenic qualities of the backgrounds and settings, temples, arcades, expansive flights of stairs, grottos and boscages. Is the 'theatre' in such compositions contemporary theatre only, or is the division into 'zones', so often observed, a late reflection of the medieval Mystery with its upper, middle and lower realms? The artists could scarcely avoid such divisions when they elected to present some historic moment in Christian perspective. The higher instances are necessarily shown above, the Adversary and his minions below. The rest – sorties by the forces of evil and rescue operations – cannot but take place on the fringe of, or in the middle realm of human activity. For all that there seems to be a general tendency to explain such major compositions, and minor monuments such as Plague Columns (*Pestsäulen*) and Trinity Columns, as they are found in such numbers in Austria, by reference to the dramatic productions of Jesuit schools and their medieval antecedents. In all these compositions there is a division into zones. Further, stage architects, who alone disposed of the necessary equipment and labour forces, were entrusted with the design and execution of ceiling paintings and frescoes. This is perhaps a late and unexpected vindication of the influence of theatre on art.

reading (*Chorus Judæorum canat, si vult*) now seems to me not to be evidence of any licence, but of the strict control kept on 'tumult' in the plays.

[1] *Theatergeschichte Europas* (Salzburg, 1957) I 471 (final section of Kindermann's Notes under heading 3).

# III

## FORTUNE[1]

WE tend today to look upon 'fortune' as a trivial idea, or we associate it with a good deal of fine rhetoric and the posturings of men of action who hold the stage for a while. In this chapter we shall consider Fortune wherever and in whatever guise she may appear, as a personification of the poets, a concept of the thinkers and historians, and as an image of the artists – without prejudice. We shall learn that in the Middle Ages 'fortune' was both what we might now call the irrational principle in history *and* a perfectly valid Christian concept. That is not generally known, and rarely said except perhaps as one of those countless things which 'may be said' without in any way seriously influencing our thinking. Fate and fortune mediate between Divine Providence and man's Free Will. That at least was the view of Boethius. St Augustine thought otherwise. That constituted a dilemma for medieval man. The Christian West has not fully resolved it. The problem is one of modes of thinking. A good deal of this chapter will be given up to a more adequate statement and illustration of the problem. For the rest we shall be concerned with the iconography of Dame Fortune, and her Wheel which is an important key to her role. (The picture of Fortune's Wheel incorporates a view of history – one kind of history.) Her role is in fact more or less decisive in all human affairs. Fortune is on the one hand the force determining the course and the outcome of all political and military action. This means the fate of dynasties and kingdoms, and the success or failure of all wars and campaigns including crusades, insofar as kings and their armies, or the

[1] Under this heading I have written and said a good deal during the last ten years. It has, however, not been in my power to prevent my essays on Fortune and the related problem of medieval historiography from appearing in print in reverse order and first in German. The present situation is that my recent study on medieval historiography, already in print, is for English readers still forthcoming, even though its thesis provides the framework for this chapter. The German title of the study in question is *Augustinus oder Boethius? Geschichtsschreibung und epische Dichtung im Mittelalter – und in der Neuzeit*, part I (Erich Schmidt Verlag, Berlin, 1967). In the short title used in this chapter (*Augustinus oder Boethius*) the interrogation mark is omitted.

advisers of Popes planned them and carried them out. On the other hand Fortune's more petty interventions in men's daily lives suggest and sustain the idea that her principal purpose is to frustrate and be generally vexatious. We shall, however, have to approach our subject more gradually and methodically, reviewing a good deal of familiar matter on the way and disposing here and there of prejudices.

Before we begin our enquiry, we must note that the Germanic peoples already 'had words for' some of the concepts which we shall discuss, *inter alia* for both 'fate' and 'fortune'. The native words changed their meanings as the converted peoples came to terms with their heathen and heroic past (the Migrations), and faced the future as Christians and the rulers of Europe.[1] As we shall repeatedly refer to German works of about 1200, we may note that the Middle High German word for 'fortune' is an old word of this kind, *sælde*. This is Old High German *sâlida* (Anglo-Saxon *sæld*). Less frequently we shall have to refer to 'fate', which is *wurt* in Old High German (*wurd* Old Saxon, *wyrd* Anglo-Saxon); there is also *wêwurt* for 'ill-fate', and *unsælde* for 'misfortune'.

## 1. FORTUNE'S WHEEL: THE MEDIEVAL IMAGE OF DYNASTIC HISTORY

Many medievalists would no doubt be prepared to accept the correlation implied by this heading without any particular demonstration. Namely, that the image of the Wheel of Fortune reflects the medieval conception of *secular* history as the rise and fall of dynasties: history is cyclical. That is precisely my difficulty here, that this conclusion is obvious, whereas the medieval conception of dynastic history, and indeed of 'fortune', is the subject of some misunderstandings. There is therefore an element (but not more) of tactics in starting this exposition at a point unfamiliar to most medievalists, namely with Otfrid of Weissenburg (to whom we have already referred, and shall refer again). We shall find his historical observations worthy of our attention.

---

[1] Gerd Wolfgang Weber's study of Anglo-Saxon 'wyrd' takes King Alfred's translation of Boethius as its starting point and powerfully supports the arguments of the present chapter, which it quotes in first edition: '*Wyrd*'. *Studien zum Schicksalsbegriff der altenglischen und altnordischen Literatur*, Frankfurter Beiträge zur Germanistik viii (Bad Homburg, Berlin, Zürich, 1969).

### A *Otfrid of Weissenburg*

Otfrid – a monk of the monastery of Weissenburg in Alsace, is the author of an 'Evangelienbuch', as we call it, a verse paraphrase of the Gospels in five Books, written in the period 863–871. It offers a mixture of New Testament narrative, and interpretations of the kind one would expect from the pupil of Rabanus Maurus, generally assigned to separate sections headed *mystice* or *spiritaliter*. In one of these passages Otfrid refers to life in this world as a banishment or exile which we owe to our pride (*ubarmuati*).[1] 'Man longs for his lost home', says the poet, to which he can return only by 'a different way', like the Three Wise Men whose story he has just told; they avoided Herod's court (etc.). This is, of course, all commonplace, but we continue. Otfrid will have meant by 'banishment' something akin to the exile of heroes in Germanic lays (for instance of Hildebrand), but for all that have visualised it under a very different image. He saw himself and his fellow Christians no doubt standing disconsolate before the barred gates of Paradise, which are guarded by an angel holding a flaming sword, or by the Cherubim of Genesis (standing on a wheel). We have such images in illustrations to (respectively) the Old German *Genesis* in the Millstatt manuscript and in the St Albans Psalter and elsewhere.[2] There is nothing surprising in all this. But Otfrid's Gospel Book is preceded by a number of dedicatory prologues and concluded by an epilogue. These we need to consider in turn.

First of all there are acrostic verses of considerable technical ingenuity on the subject of Louis, King of the Franks. 'Louis the brave, most wise, rules the whole of the Eastern Kingdom, as it is right that a King of the Franks should: God grant him health (*heili*), happiness (*sâlida*) and joy (*freuuida*)'. Here *sâlida* may be 'fortune', but in context it is more probably 'happiness', scarcely, however, the *salus æterna* invoked in the Latin prayer in the title of this particular dedication. All that I want to stress at this point is the very different sentiment. There is no lament here that life is an exile. Words then follow which claim, in roughly the same strain as the later *Ludwigslied*, that it is the Christian God who has assigned to the Franks so brave and noble a ruler, but also sorely tried him![3] Let us notice this emphasis on trials and the related statement that King Louis is 'in repute' (*in ahtu*) 'of David's lineage'.

[1] *Evangelienbuch*, I 18.
[2] Cf Otto Pächt, *Pictorial Narrative*, plate III.
[3] Cf 'Caesar and David', pp. 102 ff, 129 f.

This may sound to us to be an inordinately bold statement for a poet to make, but it was for all that evidently permissible in the eulogy of Frankish kings. Next follows an assertion that the well-being of the Franks is assured 'as long as we hold and keep him sound' (*unz uuir haben inan gisuntan*). This latter thought is probably an echo of a pre-Christian and Germanic belief in the special sanctity or divinity of kings.[1]

If the second of these two passages offers a more 'optimistic' view of history than the first (life under the King of the Franks is no banishment, but a *felicitas*), there is something approaching downright pride at being a Frank in the next prologue, bearing the significant title: *Cur scriptor hunc librum theotisce dictaverit*.[2] This is a key document in our German studies. Here the monk Otfrid states with complete assurance that the Franks need not fear comparison with the nations of Antiquity, the Greeks and the Romans (the Medes and Persians), unless it be in the difficult and obscure art of composition in hexameters – 'the Frankish language is as yet unschooled and has not been subjected to rules'. He claims superiority for the Franks and their country in wealth and power, and in skills and knowledge from agriculture *via* warfare to theology. What is lacking at this moment, says Otfrid, is Christian poetry in Frankish, to match the religious poetry of the Romans, by which we know (from a Latin letter of recommendation) that he means Prudentius, Juvencus and the Christian Latin poets generally. It is this lack which his Gospel Book is intended to make good. He reserves his humility formula for later, and calls upon his readers to rejoice that the word of God will now 'sound forth in Frankish tongue'. It is therefore by no means a fantastic context in which Otfrid, a man of considerable monastic learning in any case, claims to have 'read indeed in reliable historical accounts' that the Franks are of the line – not of David this time but – of Alexander, 'who subdued the whole world and scattered his enemies'. This is not a mere matter or repute (again *ahta*, see above) but of kinship (*sibba*). And: 'No nation has frontiers with the land of the Franks which does not stand in fear of their displeasure, and pay

---

[1] On this theme a good deal has been written. In an essay by Kurt Dietrich Schmidt (originally 1941) it is treated under the title 'Germanische und germanisch-christliche Geschichtstheologie', reprinted in *Geschichtsdenken*, pp. 76 ff.

[2] 'Why the author wrote this work in the vernacular.' (The adverb *theotisce* is based on *theot*, 'people'. The name of Otfrid's language is 'Frankish', see below.) What I call 'the next prologue' here is in fact 'the prologue' (*Evangelienbuch*, I 1), the passage on Louis being a dedication preceeding the work itself.

them tribute to preserve the peace.'[1] One might have expected quite different thoughts on the subject of Alexander from the monk, something on the vanity of all earthly glory – and a little Christian humility.

Finally there is the epilogue to the Gospel Book, addressed to two monks of the monastery of St Gall. For them Otfrid has indeed a truly monastic *abrégé* of history, from Abel through the patriarchs to Christ's disciples and the apostles of the primitive Church, down to St Gall himself and the monks now in the monastery he founded. It looks as though Otfrid has a different kind or 'line' of history, according to his addressee, the King, the people of the Franks, the *confrères* of St Gall. That is roughly the case, but for better reasons than that Otfrid was no great thinker or historian.

As is known without these examples from Otfrid, there was more than one view of history in the Middle Ages (let us consider only the Christian West). Normally two only are considered. First there is the official Christian view, based on the teaching of St Augustine in the *City of God*; secondly what we find in secular history-writing: a more or less optimistic or pessimistic 'view', and a technique based on 'the Roman historians'. We say that Einhard followed Suetonius in his *Vita Caroli Magni*. This is all very well as far as it goes, but I hope to show that this simple twofold division is inadequate and misleading. Otfrid's words about life here on earth (a banishment in a vale of tears) are Augustinian, to be sure, and similarly his monastic lesson in history for Werinbert and Hartmut of St Gall. His praise of Louis is Christian in spirit, but it is not history. What then about the descent of the Franks from Alexander? There are many problems here. We take the argument forward a step.

Otfrid praises Louis as a *defensor fidei*. That is not Christian history, 'Heilsgeschichte' or any other kind of history. It is characterisation. Otfrid was not entitled, nor was any other medieval author, to determine the place of his 'most Christian ruler', or any other ruling power, in God's plan of salvation for mankind, no matter how pious that ruler might be, and however eager he might be to hear his Christian virtues extolled. That would have been *magnanimitas*, or 'ubarmuati' as Otfrid would have called it.[2] As for the reign of Louis,

---

[1] I suggested above (p. 56) that this statement may reflect familiarity with pictorial representations of the lands offering tribute, see plate 14a (Ottonian, fully a century later than Otfrid's lines).

[2] On *magnanimitas*, a word perilously poised between 'high-mindedness' and 'arrogance', see Heinz Löwe, 'Regino von Prüm und das historische Weltbild der

Otfrid is content to say that it was a blessing that God had destined Louis to be King of the Franks. That again is not history, not an account of the reign; it tells us nothing of the *res gestæ* of Louis. And what Christian writer could presume to say that Louis' reign (a blessing for his subjects) was the beginning, the middle or the end of a chapter of history that God was himself writing 'through his faithful servant'? To elaborate the point, Otfrid does not say that after the lapse of six Ages of the World and the foundation of the Church, and after the election of the people of the Franks to be the *defensores fidei*, Louis – despite all machinations of the Devil – was continuing God's work. Otfrid does not 'place' Louis in history according to any such scheme. Just how rare the works are which make such claims on behalf of any ruler or people, we can perhaps gauge from the reluctance of scholars until recently to discuss at all the *Annolied* of about 1085, which represents Archbishop Anno of Cologne as having had a pre-ordained role to play in the fulfilment of God's purpose – in and around Cologne! It is an instructive document for the student of medieval historiography.

B *Medieval Genres of Historiography: 'after Augustine', 'after Boethius'*

It seems to me that we need a new term, to balance 'Augustinian historiography' and to characterise positively those works which call themselves *Gesta*, and do in fact deal with 'things done' (*Gesta Francorum, Ottonis,* even *Regum Britanniæ,* etc.); a term which tells us what they are, rather than what they are not. This would be the kind of history, presumably, in which Otfrid had read of the descent of the Franks from Alexander. I think we have to reproach ourselves for not having recognised long ago that beside 'Christian history according to Augustine', the Middle Ages wrote a good deal of 'dynastic history according to Boethius'.[1] The latter is also Christian in spirit, but it can

Karolingerzeit' (1951) in *Geschichtsdenken,* pp. 91 ff. On 'determining the place' etc. I allow my statement to stand, despite the instruction I derive from a thesis on 'medieval determination of the present' by Amos Funkenstein, *Heilsplan und natürliche Entwicklung, Formen der Gegenwartsbestimmung im Geschichtsdenken des Mittelalters* (Munich, 1965).

[1] My apologies to readers who have seen my monograph.

deal with day-to-day events. These are the two principal medieval genres of history-writing.

Dynastic history according to Boethius is not a genre acknowledged by the professional historians, or, if they have recognised it, they have not so named it as to attribute it to its originator. I think they would find such a designation useful. Such at any rate is the impression I get from reading their essays, particularly those in which they have to characterise any *medieval* historian who makes extensive and evidently serious use of the term 'fortune'. They are clearly not satisfied with the parallels they find in the Roman historians. We shall see later that it was not from the Roman historians that medieval writers took the *idea*. They took the *word*, and some of the phraseology that went with it; they already had the idea of fortune from Boethius, and this is one, but only one of the reasons for which I suggest that we should recognise the genre 'dynastic history according to Boethius'. It seems to me that practically the whole of medieval history-writing concerned with 'real history', and what is more important for students of literature, practically the whole of medieval narrative poetry (*story* telling) belongs to the Boethian genre. In saying this I obviously include many works which had hitherto been assigned to (if any) the 'Augustinian' genre: because they were Augustinian 'in spirit', or because it would be wrong to classify them as purely secular in their ideas and ideals. Scholars have in fact often allowed themselves to be seriously misled, by pious dedications, prologues and epilogues, by intercalated prayers, monologues of characters and speculations of authors about the ultimate fate (Heaven or Hell) of friends and enemies, heroes and villains, as though these were things done, *acta, gesta* – history, story. They have then gone to the *Patrologia Latina* in search of parallels to these various pious digressions, and, having found them, inferred that their source wrote his *history* or his *story* in the perspective of 'Heilsgeschichte'. They forgot that the Augustinian economy of history is more than an attitude of piety, and more than an attitude towards history. It is a self-contained system, a paradigm of history, which is unaffected by any single 'life' or career until the Church has recognised it (by declaring the 'hero' *sanctus* or *beatus* or a martyr), and thereby included it in the history of the City of God.

The choice of the Augustinian genre obliges an author to take the following view of history: That history began with the Creation, and that from the Fall of the Angels until beyond the Day of Judgment it is fore-ordained by the triune Godhead. God's providence is responsible for the course of all that happens in time. But the only events which ever become history within this system are those which the Church elects to remember, and on which it has passed its verdict. The memorable history of the world since Christ's Ascension is Church history, *sub specie æternitatis* it is 'Heilsgeschichte'. In respect of datable events, there are for instance the Church's Councils and the victories of the faith itself over the heathen. There are the *res gestæ* of those heroes which the Church canonised or declared martyrs (among these there are some who were kings). Church history is also the infinitely detailed chronicle of the never-to-be-forgotten battles waged against the faith by the Devil through the heretics, the main attack being still to come in the Antichrist. On the evidence of the *Etymologies* of Bishop Isidore of Seville (seventh century) there can scarcely be a chapter of history (in this sense) so frequently revised and drilled as 'the heretics and their heresies' – for page after page, the names and a specification of each of these perils which the Church had survived.[1]

As for dynasties and the kingdoms they founded, it is not admitted by Augustinian historiography that they had any other role or destiny than in their time to be the furtherers or the opponents of the City of God. They have no other *fama* or *infamia* now than this. It is known that dynasties rise, and that dynasties fall; one can name them and say that they were held to be great. But on the dynasties of old God had pronounced his sentence clearly, or, as in the vision vouchsafed to Daniel, through enigmatic symbols. For the rest, the only clear lesson of *dynastic* history contained in the Bible is that of Hannah's prayer in the Old Testament, in the 'First Book of Kings' – confirmed in the *Magnificat* in the New Testament:

> Dominus mortificat et vivificat, deducit ad inferos et reducit. Dominus pauperem facit et ditat; humiliat et sublevat. Suscitat de pulvere egenum, et de stercore elevat pauperem, ut sedeat cum principibus et solium gloriæ teneat.[2]

With these words before them, spoken by Hannah, the handmaid of the Lord, and echoed by Mary the Mother of the Lord in the *Magnificat*,

[1] On Isidore of Seville's view of history as this is reflected in the *Etymologies*, cf Arno Borst, 'Das Bild der Geschichte in der Enzyklopädie Isidors von Sevilla', in *Deutsches Archiv für Erforschung des Mittelalters*, XXII (1966) 1–62. On heresies, *Etymologies*, book VIII v 1–70.

[2] I Sam. ii 6 ff; Luke i 46 ff.

the historians of the Middle Ages were faced with a dilemma and a warning against any rash inferences. Are the vicissitudes of dynastic history interpretable in a Christian sense? Are they even worth recording? Is the *only* history what the Church in its wisdom and with the guidance of the Holy Spirit will deem memorable? Dynastic history is, unless man is to stand finally condemned for his *superbia*, not immediately interpretable in terms of the divine economy of history. It was in this sense that Eusebius, having made due allowance for Constantine and Helena, wrote his *Ecclesiastical History*. It was in this sense that Augustine after the fall of Rome wrote his *City of God* which states the only view of history which the Church of the West will henceforth entertain (suitable adjustments having been made at an early date to discount Constantine's preference for a new Rome across the water). Augustine stresses at the same time the danger and the hopelessness of attempting any detailed interpretation of terrestrial history as the fulfilment of scriptural prophecies, whether those of Daniel or St Paul.[1]

And now Boethius. In his *theological* works (*De Fide Catholica, De Trinitate*) Boethius *accepted* Augustine's interpretation of history, or, as I should prefer to say, he 'confessed' it, and so too did all writers in the area of the Western Church throughout the Middle Ages. In this Augustinian scheme – to come now finally to our subject – Fortune plays no part at all, and the equation of dynastic history with the rule of Fortune, toward which we seem to be steering, is in all essentials correct. It is only with the help of the concept 'fortune' that the dynastic historian can break the silence imposed by the words of Hannah's prayer. But for this purpose the Roman and pagan idea of fortune is naturally useless.

---

[1] This did not prevent the Middle Ages from producing a vast amount of 'symbolical' or prognostic history. Modern historians are interested in it as evidence of various ideal schemes of world government, etc. The 'correct' view nevertheless prevailed. There is a preface to the Old High German translation of Boethius by Notker III of St Gall (*d.* 1022) which endeavours to place the 'author of the work about to be presented'. It begins: 'St Paul said to those who in his time were expecting the Day of Judgment, that it should not come until the Roman Empire perished and Antichrist began to rule.' Having referred to Boethius as one of Theoderic's victims, Notker (following Remigius) then quickly runs through the dynasties down to 'our own times'. 'The Roman Empire has now perished, as St Paul prophesied.' At that point he *stops*, and turns to his Boethius text. In other words 'Heilsgeschichte' is known *up to* the present. Notker does not speculate further, or attempt to define the present. See p. 173 (below).

For Augustine in the days before his conversion (for Augustine the academic, that is), 'fortune' was an indispensable idea. After his conversion he had to manage without it. In the *City of God* Fortune is represented as being a tawdry deity, little more than a talisman, of pagan Rome, now fallen and superseded by the Rome of Peter and Paul. As such Augustine dismisses her at an early stage in the *City of God*.[1] Thereafter he has no use for Fortune, either as a goddess or as a personification of chance, the unforeseen. In his scheme of history Fortune is not an 'instance'; she has no responsibilities, no rights, no role. For Augustine dynastic history is consequently an irrelevance. Similarly for Boethius – in his *theological* works. In these he never uses the term, nor does he operate with the idea. He 'confesses' St Augustine's scheme of history, even though *intellectually* he could have accounted for it as a work produced in a given historical situation.

In the *De Consolatione Philosophiæ* of the same Boethius, the Boethius whom Theoderic had seized in 524 as one suspected of complicity in an underground movement of the Roman aristocracy, there is, on the other hand, not a single overt word about the Trinity (though perhaps one clear allusion), nothing about the Mother of God, Christ, the Bible, Sin, Confession, the Sacraments. There is not a word about the Christian religion or the Church in the service of which he wrote the theological tractates. Scholars used to think that he could therefore not have written the tractates, and our school history books continue to express admiration at the Christian morality of the heathen, 'last of the Romans'. *Instead* there is a complete Christian philosophy, using only the Christian philosopher's terms. We shall see that these include the Christian God (but not the Trinity, which is as yet a matter of faith), Providence, Fate, Fortune and Man. Man has Free Will; he has 'virtues' and powers of reasoning which he exercises in the recognition of various 'goods', of which the highest, the 'summum bonum' is 'beatitude'. This is a closed scheme, distinct as a scheme from that of the theologian. No great harm is done, therefore, if in our school teaching we continue to stress the Christian ethic of Boethius. More misleading is the idea, still entertained by some scholars, that medieval writers who provided their Boethius with a handful of Christian glosses had somehow superseded him – the philosopher whom we at the same time credit with the intention and the ability to reconcile Plato and Aristotle! The glossators were bunglers who with their

[1] Book IV, ch. 18.

'compare howevers' failed to recognise that moral philosophy and theology remain discrete systems of thought, which means – to return to our subject of history writing – that whereas St Augustine could (had to) banish Fortune from his scheme of history (as the fulfilment of God's purpose in the 'City of God'), Boethius, dealing with mortal man and his lot, had to find a proper place for Fortune. We have already seen (above) that he did. His *De Consolatione* thereby provided the framework within which dynastic history could be intelligently and rationally discussed and assessed. But let us recall what is common to *both* Christian systems as we find them in the *City of God* and in *De Consolatione*: God, his Providence, and Man, a Christian with a Free Will. We may ourselves add as a comment on these systems that man can think rationally and systematically. He can also recognise the limitations of all systems of human knowledge. He can in the end, when neither the philosopher nor the theologian satisfy him, either write some poetry or go out and make some history!

According to the scheme of history expounded in *De Consolatione* all temporal events are foreseen by God, the *spectator cunctorum*, as Boethius calls him in Book V, the final book. To this God Boethius, the prisoner of Theoderic, is finally enjoined by Philosophia to address his *prayers*. We do not hear his prayers *in this work*. When the philosopher prays he puts on another person and, ideally, writes a different work. So it remains with the majority of medieval writers. By the year 1400 things have changed slightly but not completely. The poet of the *Ackermann aus Böhmen*[1] could not reserve his prayers for a different work. I quote a few lines from the thirty-fourth and last chapter of this dialogue between a bereaved husband and Death. It is a long prayer in which, as the commentators have not tired of reminding us, there is nothing about the Church, the Mother of God, the comfort of the sacraments, and only once, breaking the scheme, of 'Jesus'. That is to say, the prayer is addressed almost exclusively to God as Providence, and so the author remains within the Boethian genre.

... seal of highest majesty, keystone of heaven's harmony ... planet holding sway over all planets, sovereign influence of the stars, law obeying which the orbits of heaven can never forsake their cardinal

---

[1] The work was referred to above, p. 32.

governance, perfect mould of all thoughts, true and restraining centre of all circles, sole knower of all human minds . . . hear my prayer.[1]

## c *History and Story*

It matters very little where we turn in medieval literature, we shall find, I think, that any epic or narrative work, unless it is still pagan in story and ethos (which is the final verdict always on the *Nibelungenlied*, and those Eddic lays which reflect it in its earlier stages) falls into one of the two categories, according to Augustine *or* according to Boethius. Biblical stories are necessarily Augustinian when they are retold by medieval writers; similarly the legends of saints. Universal histories, beginning with the Creation and generally exhausting themselves long before 'the modern period' is reached, are also clearly Augustinian. The rest seems to be Boethian. Though not superficially Christian, but heroic, tragic, fatalistic, even the *Hildebrandslied*, one of the most venerable of our heroic lays, is Boethian if the following interpretation is accepted, in which I take the opportunity of putting some of the old words (see above) into their context.

What God in his providence and his own timelessness has foreordained, all created things experience in the world of time as Fate (Boethius). In our older German poetry, for instance in the *Hildebrandslied*, God is *waltant got* (God omnipotent) or *irmingot* (Lord God of all). Man's fate or destiny is called *wurt*. If it is disaster, as in the case of Hildebrand and Hadubrand, the word is *wêwurt* (an evil fate). Fate becomes event in the moment when man *acts*; in the words of Hildebrand, *wêwurt skihit* (an evil fate befalls, happens). Whatever seems arbitrary or irrational about this particular fate, for instance that

---

[1] Complete translation by K. W. Maurer, *Death and the Ploughman*, (Euston Press, n.d. [1948]), adapted here. The German text: 'sigel der aller höchsten majestat . . . besliessung des himels armonie . . . planete gewaltiger aller planeten; ganz wurkender einfluss alles gestirnes, twang vor dem alle himelische ordenung aus irem geewigten angel nimmer treten mag . . . aller sinne ein feiner einguss, rechter und zusammenhaltender mittel aller zirkelmasse, einiger erkenner aller menschen gedanke . . .'

About two generations earlier than the *Ackermann aus Böhmen* is the full-page picture of the God of Providence in the *Holkham Bible Picture Book*, ed. W. O. Hassall (London, 1954) fo. 2, see plate 1a. God enthroned in the midst of the Universe he has created. In his right hand he holds the compasses (see 'centre of all circles' in the quoted text, above) with which he traces the path of Sun and Moon. *Above*, enthroned, Lucifer, with angels offering homage (*right*) or turning away from him (*left*). *Below*: the jaws of Hell. The subject is 'God's Providence from the Beginning of Time (Fall of the Angels)'.

circumstances have brought a father and his son face to face between two opposing armies, and are such that the son must 'know' that his father is dead (*tot ist Hiltibrant*), that is, according to the paradigm we find in Boethius, rather the work of Fortune: it is *infortunium*. But an Old High German equivalent of the later *unsælde*, uttered in a curse upon a malign fortune (*unsælde sî verwâzen*) would sound indeed strange. That would be a degree of sophistication of thought and sentiment inappropriate in the heroic context. For Hildebrand, faced, after thirty years of life in exile, by his own son, who taunts him with cowardice and subterfuge, it can only be Almighty God himself (*waltant got*) who had decreed this encounter. It is the fate of *both* of them – father and son – which is to be enacted. Hildebrand's words *wêwurt skihit* are a heroic, or rather a soldierly *fiat voluntas tua*. The hero was in historical fact a Goth, the poet a Lombard; and both were Christians. The poetic convention required an older, but not a pre-Christian and pagan ethos to be suggested. I know that it is not a suggestion generally acceptable to my colleagues in German studies that we should discard completely our somewhat Eddic or possibly Wagnerian ideas of the Germanic hero under stress; but sooner or later we shall have to come to terms with the words of the lay as we have them, and forget the pathos. At any rate it should in future be legitimate to recall that the Hildebrand who in the lay spoke the words *wêwurt skihit* is the faithful champion who stood forth before the army of Dietrich, in real history that same Theoderic who was to have Boethius, the author of *De Consolatione Philosophiæ*, murdered in Pavia. That is to say: the Boethius who, at the beginning of the sixth century, taught the Christian West that Fate is God's will. Men (Kings, their counsellors, their generals, individuals) learn what their fate *is* when, in the exercise of free will, they *act*.[1]

[1] In an article entitled 'Notes on Fate and Fortune (for Germanisten)', contributed to *Medieval German Studies, presented to Frederick Norman* (London, 1965) pp. 1–15, I wrote slightly more fully about the christianised conception of fate in the *Hildebrandslied* (Norman himself already having insisted that *waltant got* is the Christian God, and that the poet was a Christian). I went on to discuss the solecism of which the *Heliand* poet was guilty in trying to use this same christianised idea in his re-narration of the story of Christ's Passion, particularly the Agony in Gethsemane, and the defection ('fore-ordained') of the 'faithful followers' in the hour of need. I took Johannes Rathofer mildly to task for ignoring the teaching of Christian moral philosophy in his discussion of 'the idea of fate in the *Heliand*', which he unquestioningly took to be heroic and Germanic (*Der Heliand, theologischer Sinn als tektonische Form*, Niederdeutsche Studien, IX (Cologne and Graz, 1962)).

To repeat: in the very moment when man acts, he fulfils the decree of Fate. He acts generally in circumstances which demand a quick or daring decision (a *temeritas*). His deed is a consequence of his exercise of free will. The 'event' is, however, often a mockery of his *reason*, bearing no discernable relation to his *merits*, or those of his enemies, *or* to his ideas of *justice*. As for his hopes of salvation and his immortal soul, he knows, and the Church in its teaching tells him – 'that is another matter'. It belongs, to revert for a moment to the terms we were using, to the Augustinian economy of thought and of history. Fate, which is so swiftly and regularly invoked by political man, cannot be evaded. It cannot be escaped either, even by those who elect to forsake this world, thus or thus. No man can know in advance the outcome of *any* action. The dramatists have repeated this in endless rhetorical variations, bodying it forth with 'figures' from any age, often those of Antiquity. Here is Schiller, *Wallensteins Tod* (Act I scene iv):

> Nicht ohne Schauder greift des Menschen Hand
> In des Geschicks geheimnisvolle Urne.
> In meiner Brust war meine Tat noch mein;
> Einmal entlassen aus dem sichern Winkel
> Des Herzens . . .
> Gehört sie jenen tück'schen Mächten an,
> Die keines Menschen Kunst vertraulich macht.

The mysterious 'urn of fate' and the hand of man dipped into it are here simply classicising flourishes with which a Protestant poet embellishes a Catholic general's soliloquy, as he weighs the *pros* and *cons* of defection from the Empire. (When he acts, disaster follows; it was already on the way.) We are so familiar with 'fate and fortune', 'chance', 'opportunity', time and its 'forelock' from the rhetoric of the dramatists of the post-Renaissance world, that it is difficult to adjust ourselves to the stricter 'systematic' use of the corresponding terms in the centuries from Augustine and Boethius (say 420–520) down to and including Boccaccio, Petrarch, Dante (and perhaps beyond).

We now repeat the Boethian scheme of history as a hierarchy of instances, namely: *God*, his *Providence*; the *Fate* of all temporal things and beings – including man; *Fortune*; the *Free Will of Man*. This paradigm was known to every medieval author as being the only one available for works of non-theological content, for the rational interpretation of 'real' history (history proper), or for the composition and interpretation of all kinds of *fictions*. There is therefore only a very restricted area within which the author of a chronicle or a narrator of fictions can move and manœuvre. Here, within the limits he sets himself by his very choice of subject, he must show his mastery. He must show what he can 'make of' the subject, and the records assigned to him – his sources. He shows it in what we conventionally call characterisation and motivation. Glancing back at the paradigm, he deals with the exercise of free will and the 'fortune' which attended it – in campaign, enterprise, adventure.

By history I mean in this context some continuous record of *gesta*, and not, for instance, those arbitrarily selected events which might be recalled in support of a thesis, say a theory of the Christian state; and when I refer to narrative literature I have in mind works dealing mainly with 'adventure', for instance the courtly romances of Chrétien de Troyes, or in second generation Hartmann von Aue; and not Wolfram von Eschenbach's *Parzival* or the so-called *Jüngerer Titurel*. In these two latter works the attempt is made to bridge the gap between a traditional dynastic history (of the Grail kings) and a kind of 'Heilsgeschichte', with something resembling a Lodge in place of the Church. (A further word below on such attempts.[1])

### D *Boethius*, De Consolatione Philosophiæ

Unfortunately our medieval disciplines seem to have ignored Boethius' doctrine of history. The *De Consolatione* appears generally to be regarded as being a 'moral' work, offering solace in adversity, or an *Ars Moriendi*, or as a schoolbook (in the modern sense). There has probably never been a schoolbook so influential. It was read for a thousand years, and, we must assume, examined. Most of us can recall some of those who translated it: King Alfred, Notker of St Gall, Jean de Meung, Chaucer, Queen Elizabeth. What is more to the point is that *De Consolatione* must have gone through the schools in thousands of digests, lists of themes, tabulations and perhaps diagrams. We cannot demonstrate this in the customary way, of course, with references to still extant manuscripts. But if anyone had asked, for example, Walther von der Vogelweide (who had not had a clerical schooling at all, so far as we know) what are the 'three principal goods', we know what he

[1] A much fuller statement in *Augustinus oder Boethius*, I, pp. 71–84.

would have answered. His answer is in fact the subject of his most famous poem; it is one of our 'lines' to expound it. What has not been recalled by the commentators is that 'the three goods' is also the theme of book III of *De Consolatione*, or more exactly the theme there is *opes* and *honores*, with some obvious insertions between these two end terms for the many transitory goods of this life on earth, and *beatitudo* as the *summum bonum*. Walther's words in his reflexions are *êre* (*honores*) and *varnde guot* (*opes*), with, as the good excelling them all, 'God's Grace', *gotes hulde*. In answer to a Boethius question this would not have been strictly correct. Walther was guilty of no more than a venial sin, a *mélange des genres*. In answer to the question he had himself asked (how one should live in this world) his answer was correct, and any court chaplain would have given the same answer. That is what poets and court chaplains are there for – to provide sound advice based on the best authority, but cutting across the dividing lines between theology and academic philosophy, advice which a good Christian may follow on weekdays. (God in his providence has so divided the week that those who are not called to forsake the world can address themselves, according to the day of the week and the time of day, to the one or to the other scheme of history.) The argument of Boethius, book III, was therefore known to Walther von der Vogelweide. How he learnt it we cannot say. It was simply what was taught. More important than that Walther *did* know book III (however imperfectly and indirectly) is the fact that his editors hitherto didn't.

In assessing the influence of authors like St Augustine and Boethius one looks for evidence of the *use* of their ideas, not for copies of their works or quotations from them. The influence of Augustine is to be seen in the general acceptance of his interpretation of history throughout the writings of the Western Church. His doctrine was used, *De Civitate Dei* was not quoted.[1] The same is the case with Boethius. His work taught the only Christian doctrine of history which was applicable to the story of dynasties, individual kings and princes; and to Arthurian adventurers and the heroes of Antiquity when they re-emerged in the later Middle Ages. But to stress again the point we were making, St Augustine on Church history and Boethius on secular

---

[1] The historians of political theory in the Middle Ages seem to be embarrassed to find so few quotations from the *City of God*. That is exactly as matters should be, if a teaching has been really influential, cf. Johannes Spörl, 'Mittelalterliches Geschichtsdenken als Forschungsaufgabe', in *Geschichtsdenken*, pp. 1–29, especially p. 19.

history were so fundamental as to be scarcely quotable at all. They were quite simply what was taught.

Boethius provided the Christian Middle Ages, and to a very considerable extent the modern world too, with a system of ideas and terms with which alone it is possible to write *all* history from a Christian standpoint: with which it is possible to treat the fate of individual leaders and the lot of great dynasties; the decline of the Frankish line and the rise of the Saxons, the victories of Saladin, usurpations, catastrophies, the accidental drowning of a most Christian Emperor returning from a Crusade, assassinations. All these events God in his wisdom and providence had evidently fore-ordained, men electing in the exercise of their free will so to act that these things came to pass. It is Fortune which *as* the last instance *in* the last instance determines the choice of action which man will make and the outcome. Fortune determines, in short, the course of 'real history', that very history which to Augustine was irrelevant, just as Fortune had no part to play in bringing about the City of God. But for Boethius Fortune is not a totally free agent, and there are limits to her powers. Fortune is the instrument of Divine Providence, which at any time may place her under restraint, halt her course, bridle her. (Medieval artists often draw the bridle.) This is the respect in which Boethius' interpretation of 'fortune' made a complete break with the tradition of Classical Antiquity.

The medieval Fortune has in common with her predecessor a name, a number of standing epithets ('blind', 'fragile', etc., *cæca, vitrea, fragilis, volubilis errans*), and several *topoi*, 'favourer of the unworthy' (*indignorum fautrix*) etc. That means (*pace* Ernst Robert Curtius) that the Fortunes of Antiquity and of the Middle Ages have little in common, for the subordination of Fortune to the intentions of Providence is a new conception, and moreover Fortune is in the Middle Ages seen under an entirely different image, derived from Boethius.[1] Modern readers may think that the subordination to Providence is not an idea easy to sustain, but eight hundred to a thousand years is not a bad life-span for an idea difficult to sustain. Neither the Stoics nor the Epicureans had been able to find a role for Fortune at all in a divinely ordered universe; she belonged to the world of 'matter', beyond any divinity's concern – not a satisfactory solution. The role assigned to her by Boethius is one she retains down to Boccaccio, Petrarch and Dante, and the poet of the *Ackermann aus Böhmen*. What the early Renaissance

---

[1] See below and Appendix B.

authors have to offer is rhetorical variations on Boethius's themes, or elegant vulgarisation of his ideas.[1]

'What development is there in the idea of Fortune?' is a question I am often asked. This I always assume to be an invitation to say that there was some notable advance from *simple* medieval ideas towards a final sophistication in the Renaissance. But to continue, there *is* a development. As we approach the Renaissance there is less readiness to accept Fortune's rule, and more vociferous indignation at her injustices – among those she has not favoured. Others who believe they have struck a lucky vein seek to exploit their chances, and plan by careful attention to the propitious moment (opportunity, *occasio*) to 'outwit' Fortune and make her subservient, possibly permanently, to their purposes. The old tag that a man may 'fashion' his own fortune (as *faber fortunæ suæ*) becomes an influential philosophy. This is, in a way, a return to the classical conception of Fortune, with some complications. It presupposes in some respects a sceptical attitude toward the tenets of the Christian faith. Stoically to defy Fate is tantamount to refusing God his way, and attempts to outwit Fortune are attempts to evade God's Providence. This all implies a trust in a *dæmon* which may prevail, and so make the consolations of philosophy seem an academic irrelevance. (This all considerably enlarges the scope of *metanoia* and *melancholia*, but that is another story.) But to return to the Middle Ages! Among the ideas (and ideals) of Classical Antiquity which were re-interpreted by the Christian West we have to count, therefore, not merely *imperium*, *Cæsar*, *Roma*,[2] but also *fatum* and *fortuna*. These christianised terms (together with *salus*) absorb some of the nuances of the Germanic terms used to translate them – *wurt*, *sælde* and *heil*.

At the same time, those of us who come to medieval studies through German literature will be unanimous in feeling that the *native* words are always richer in their associations, more 'poetic' than the Latin terms for which they now stand substitute. The poets use *sælde* and *heil* with a depth of feeling and a resonance with which they did not even seek to invest the loan form, *fortûne*, or the words with a similar meaning reaching German *via* French, as did 'chance', 'adventure'. It was particularly with the help of the older native words that the poets gave expression to their heart-felt longing for 'happiness here on earth',

---

[1] One of many conclusions to be drawn from Klaus Heitmann, *Fortuna und Virtus. Eine Studie zu Petrarcas Lebensweisheit* (Cologne, 1958).

[2] And *renovatio*, with P. E. Schramm, see p. 103 n. 1.

and 'salvation' hereafter. In both these contexts German poets used the words *sælde* and *heil*. Happiness here on earth and salvation hereafter cannot be gained by mere prowess, or by 'virtues' of any kind; one cannot 'earn' or 'deserve' them as the due rewards of worth. The outcome is always unpredictable. One can *wish* for happiness; one can *pray* for God's grace. Whether they are vouchsafed depends, in the one case as in the other, the educated layman must always feel, on something that one calls – what? German writers say 'sælde' which means, shall we say, 'fortune – perhaps more'. One must be *fortunatus*, destined to be lucky. Of a hero of romance the poet can say that in the end he *had* 'sælde'. In saying this, he has not been blasphemous. 'Happiness', even 'happiness ever after', a 'lasting' *sælde*, which is the philosopher's *beatitudo*, is the final lot of the hero of romance. Any statement *before* the hero has completed his course that he is 'sælic' includes the hope that his good fortune will hold. The element of 'wishfulness' is so strong in such contexts that 'Wish' itself may materialise as a personification. With complete confidence, indeed as a statement of fact, the poet can assert that the hero has this, namely every conceivable perfection, and the complete approval of all right-thinking men. This may provide an effective prelude to a final chapter of accidents and of cruel misfortune, in surviving which the hero will display still further virtue and seem to *deserve* his final good fortune and happy retirement from further action.[1] There is a close correlation, therefore, between 'wish' and prayer, between fortune and *grace*. Medieval man could not but feel that an element of luck entered into his *final* destiny, and that it was by the grace of God that he was occasionally favoured by Fortune.

[1] On the role of 'chance' in Hartmann von Aue's tale of Gregorius, and the 'instances' (God as Providence, Fate, Fortune) which control his destiny, I wrote in the article for Frederick Norman to which reference was made above, p. 180 n 1. The story of Gregorius was not an easy one to accommodate within either of the available schemes of history, for the hero, born of an incestuous union and having committed incest himself, becomes, after a period of stupendous penance, (a fictitious) Pope. The story is not a chapter in the history, or an approved legend of the Church. In any case Hartmann was a layman. For these reasons the Boethian scheme had to be used. But how? *Sin* and *penance* are not part of the Boethian scheme. Hartmann prises open a crack, as he must, if his story is to be told at all. He introduces the Devil as *agent provocateur* and the Holy Spirit to set in train the quest of the emissaries of Rome who will fetch Gregorius from his rock. For the rest, what Hartmann is pleased to call the 'heil' (salvation) of his hero depends at every turn on chance, coincidence and seized opportunities: the outcome of any of these is *sælic* or *unsælic* (fortunate or disastrous), see p. 206. The story remains within the limits of the Boethian scheme, liberally interpreted.

E *Fortune in* De Consolatione Philosophiæ

For every student of the Middle Ages, whether he is primarily a historian, a literary or art historian, or is simply a medievalist, *De Consolatione Philosophiæ* should be prescribed reading. That is easily said. The Latin is beyond most of us now, the translations available (until quite recently) in English are archaic, the full text has its *longueurs* and passages of considerable difficulty.[1] Summaries of the argument of *De Consolatione* are generally uncompromisingly philosophical, while introductions to Boethius devote most of their space to defining the place of the work in the history of medieval philosophy (Neo-Platonism). For us in literary and historical studies such a scholarly approach is not very helpful; in a way it is unsuitable. The argument of books IV and V, the most 'important' no doubt, is beyond the technical range of any but the metaphysical poets, quite beyond the scope of historians and artists of any age. In book III, dealing with the various 'goods' and the 'highest good', Boethius parts company with all except the more tenacious didactic poets and the moralists. It is in book II that he writes at the level of poets and dramatists; historians can understand him and the artists can illustrate his ideas in a telling image. Book I, finally, is more or less straightforward autobiography, presented in the framework of a dialogue. There is a good deal of fine rhetoric in prose and in verse. That may seem an excessive simplification, but it indicates what parts of *De Consolatione* are more or less immediately accessible to men of letters. The later books will always have seemed to be the philosophical justification of book II. We are not being unscholarly if we profit from hindsight in this way. Great works are influential, not on their own terms, but as edited by those who use the works.

We must afford the space here to look again at the famous passage in book II of *De Consolatione*, the great dialogue 'of Fortune' which Philosophia holds with the imprisoned Boethius. In order to instil her remedial doctrines, Philosophia for a time harangues her patient, using the arguments of Fortune, whom she indeed impersonates (and in the

---

[1] There is a full analysis (in German and Latin) of *De Consolatione* in *Augustinus oder Boethius* I 99–153, in which those parts are more fully reproduced which seem to me to have been particularly influential. The translation of V. E. Watts (Boethius, *The Consolation of Philosophy*, Penguin Classics L 208, 1969) is most welcome, but of course far too late to be referred to otherwise than by its title in this volume.

process satirises). The prisoner is to learn to distrust Fortune's 'blandish-ments', even when she presents them with all the engaging persuasive-ness of rhetoric. At the same time the dialogue is intended as a respite and interlude; 'stronger potions are to follow' for which the patient is clearly not yet ready.[1] After a few preliminary flourishes 'Fortune' delivers herself of the following *defensio*:

With what cause do you, O man, charge me with injustice in daily complaints? What wrong have I done you? Dispute with me before any judge concerning the possession of riches and dignities, and if you can show that these ever belong to mortal man as his own, I will im-mediately concede that those to which you lay claim were indeed yours. When Nature brought you from your mother's womb, you were possessionless in every respect, and you immediately passed into my care (etc.). [The argument continues on the theme: 'Man has only the *use* of the things which Fortune grants him'. Next, Fortune's 'right' of mutability.]
The heavens may release the full light of day, or conceal it beneath clouds of darkness at night. The year may in its seasons cover the face of the earth with flowers and fruits, or envelop it in mists and cold. As is its right, the sea will at one moment be quiet and calm, in the next disturbed with storms and waves. Why then should I be bound to a constant state, so contrary to my ways, merely by the insatiable desires of men?
This it is in my power to do, and this is the game I play at all times: I turn the wheel at speed, and delight in sending what is at the bottom to the top, and what is on top to the bottom (*hæc nostra vis est, hunc continuum ludum ludimus, rotam volubili orbe versamus, infima summis et summa infimis mutare gaudemus*). Go, if that is your wish, to the top (*ascende si placet*), on the condition that you will not hold it to be an injustice, if, following the rules of my game, you have to descend again. Am I to believe you do not know my ways? How Croesus, King of the Lydians, who had recently lorded it over Cyrus, was soon to find himself in desperate straits, and would have burnt at the stake, had a downpour of rain from the heavens not saved him? Had you forgotten how [Amelius] Paulus was moved to tears by the plight of King Perses, his prisoner? What else does the outcry of the tragedians

---

[1] The medical figure is sustained throughout the five books, and was remem-bered. *De Remediis* was the title later preferred to *De Consolatione Philosophiæ*. (Students of German will again be reminded of *Der Ackermann aus Böhmen* by the following extracts.)

lament but the indiscriminate blows of Fortune which overthrow flourishing kingdoms (*Quid tragœdiarum clamor deflet nisi indiscretu ictu fortunam felicia regna vertentem*)?[1]

The historians among my readers will be shocked, no doubt, by the submission of this passage as evidence of the Boethian view of history. This is surely very thin 'documentation' – a bare half dozen cases, even if we take in Fabricius, Brutus and Cato from *Metrum VII* which follows. There are, however, several points to be considered. Let us first note that when Boccaccio, some eight hundred years later, offered fifty to a hundred times more historical 'cases' in *De casibus virorum illustrium*, he could find no other lesson of history. So much for the value of documentation. Next, the picture of Fortune, that is of history and, by implication, history writing, is satirical. Fortune claims to know everything about the course which events have taken. She is responsible always for the outcome. She is 'what happens'. In claiming that her doings are the subject of tragedy too, she implies that history writing is man's attempt to come to terms with events by a purging of the emotions; it is the service of a Muse. Through the device of satirical impersonation Philosophy assigns history to its subordinate place among the works of which rational man is capable. Dismissing dynastic history with a handful of obvious examples Philosophy moves on. Political and all other kinds of history as they are enacted and chronicled will provide further examples – of the turning of the Wheel of Fortune.

The medieval historian who undertook to write the story of a dynasty took the Boethian scheme of history as his framework.[2] The scheme itself incorporates a view of history; it is *given* in the genre 'after Boethius'. The historian's remaining task, technically more demanding than the choice of genre, was the actual commemoration and

---

[1] Notker of St Gall's commentary on *tragœdia* runs as follows: *tragœdie sint luctuosa carmina, álso díu sint, díu sophocles scréib apud grecos, de euersionibus regnorum et urbium, únde sínt uuíderuuártig tien comoediis, án dîen uuír iô gehórên letum únde iocumdum exitum.* Úns íst áber únchúnt úbe dehéine *latini tragici* fúndene uuérdên, sô uuír gnûoge fíndên *latinos comicos* (Altdeutsche Textbibliothek, XXXIV 70). [Tragedies are sad poems such as Sophocles wrote concerning the overthrow of kingdoms and cities; they are the opposite of comedies ... which always end happily. It is not known whether any Latin tragedies are to be found; there are plenty of comedies.]

[2] This is true even of Otto von Freising, despite his title in one work: *Chronica sive historia de duabus civitatibus.*

'illustration' of the dynasty. For this he drew on his training and a tradition of history-writing. Here his models were indeed the Roman historians, and these modern scholarship has generally been able to identify. They gave him plenty of guidance on how to write history professionally, but not how to see history, or how to understand it.

The story of the dynasty can begin in a remote past, anywhere on the time-scale of terrestrial history as this is known. That may mean 'beginning with Alexander' as in the historians whom Otfrid had consulted, or Frankus (as in Fredegar's *Chronicle of the Franks*, and the *Annolied*), or Brutus (Geoffrey of Monmouth). Francus and Brutus, the founders of France and Britain, were both reputed to have been among the heroes who left Troy in the following of Aeneas. This bold assertion of origins has, however, the 'unfortunate' effect of committing the chronicler to what must be the burthen of his epilogue, whether he actually writes it or leaves it for a continuator, namely 'vanity, all is vanity'. But meantime there could be the long and generously pro-tracted narrative of the *res gestæ* of the dynasty, its conquests and achievements, its just claims to fame. There were the deeds of the almost patriarchal founders, the reigns of the ruling prince's immediate forebears, the recent golden years of peace. Then alas, some reference had to be made to the trials of the present, the machinations of enemies – their envy. It is basically a long-drawn-out *laudatio temporis acti*, a pessimistic reading of history, the lesson of which, a moral lesson, was so clearly to be seen in the image of the Wheel of Fortune.[1]

This is not to say that the medieval historian could get no guidance from Augustine on the treatment of *secular* history, as well as of ecclesi-astical history. Rather that Boethius offered in *De Consolatione* the complete range of terms which the historian needs for the presentation and interpretation of the vicissitudes of political life; he offered also the memorable image of Fortune and her Wheel, the inescapable lesson of history.[2] It is of course true that Boethius utters in the same work an

[1] Pictures of the Wheel of Fortune are frequent in illustrated manuscripts, not only of *De Consolatione Philosophiæ*, but also of the *City of God*. Since Augustine will have nothing to do with Fortune, the pictures must in the latter case be satirical, though it is hard to see in what way they are: perhaps by a greater insistence on a 'two-faced' Fortune, Janus-headed or half black, half white. The truth is that even disparaging reference to Fortune attracted the familiar picture in the artist's repertory. See A. de Laborde, *Les manuscrits à peintures de la Cité de Dieu*, etc. (Paris, 1909), plates III (right), XIXa, XXIIa and d, XXXb, LIX, LXIV.

[2] The more common 'formula of four', *regno, regnavi*, etc., is replaced in the Fortune-picture of the *Hortus Deliciarum* (see plate 6a) by a rhetorical variant

earnest warning against history itself, that is against accepting Fortune's invitation to mount her Wheel and take the consequences. Boethius no less than Augustine considers the fame and glory of peoples and their regents to be illusory. All Christian teachers, the Preacher in the Bible, Augustine, Boethius, are depressingly unanimous in this. But Boethius had argued his case rationally; one could part company with him and be no more than foolish, not heretical or blasphemous. He had special advice to offer, 'remedies', for those whom Fortune had brought to a fall. For princes, however, and their advisers and their poets, the time for the remedies seems always to have been 'not yet'. There is a time for everything. Boethius had need of his remedies, they seem to have argued. He had failed in his attempt to make history, and his misfortune was complete. Any fame he was to have would take account of his end, which was failure. The prince is meantime still on his throne. He may succeed. His reign may be glorious.[1] It will, however, not be remembered as glorious unless historians make it memorable. Not all careers are remembered as illustrations of the 'vanity' of man's endeavours. There are also those who are to be remembered when we are enjoined to 'praise famous men and our fathers in their generations'.[2]

F *Fortune in Medieval Romance*

That was, I admit, a very lengthy introduction to 'fortune in the Middle Ages'. I have associated Fortune's story, already largely

---

reflecting (I think) the words of Hannah's prayer (above, p. 175). They are *glorior elatus* (=regno), *descendo minorificatus* (regnavi), *infimus axe premor* (sum sine regno) and *rursus ad alta vehor* (regnabo). Compare in Hannah's prayer *solium gloriæ teneat; dominus mortificat; (in) pulvere, stercore; dominus deducit . . . et reducit.*

[1] Opposite the picture of Divine Providence in the *Holkham Bible Picture Book* is a full-page picture of Fortune, see plate 1b. Fortune, crowned, a Queen, stands behind a large wheel indicated in schematic outline; she holds it by two spokes, to turn it apparently without effort. On the wheel, above, a king with crown and sceptre: *Regno*. Right: a king falling from the wheel, his crown and sceptre preceding him: *Regnaui*. Below, crushed by the wheel, a king without crown: *Sum sine regno*. Left: a male figure reaching up to take a crown: *Regnabo*. Clearly as the text in Boethius may have prescribed such an image, it was a stroke of considerable ingenuity whereby some artist of the (early?) twelfth century determined that the kings should be four in number, to represent dynastic history in its full cycle, and found the 'suppletive' *sum sine regno* to link past and future tenses of the verb 'to rule'. This image and the 'formula of four' swept the field; there are endless variants on the image but only one regular variant on the formula, see last note.

[2] Ecclesiasticus xliv.

familiar, with a historiographical thesis (Augustine–Boethius) which was unfamiliar in the form in which I have presented it. It may be that with less dogmatism I could more quickly and easily have demonstrated that we have to take medieval preoccupation with fortune more seriously, as evidence of an endeavour to interpret history in a Christian sense. Let us now turn to narrative literature in the Middle Ages. I think that in future we shall have to show greater care in our choice of terms. Particularly we should more or less absolutely refuse to characterise any work of secular literature, and any work written by laymen for laymen as 'Augustinian'. To put it the other way, narrative literature *uses* the Boethian scheme of history. It recounts the exploits and successes, the perils and misfortunes, renewed successes and final 'happiness ever after' of heroes and heroines in purely Boethian terms. With the attainment of *beatitudo* their story (history) ceases. In other words Fortune is the highest of the powers which the narrative poets can effectively involve in the *story* they have to tell. Prologues, monologues, asides and epilogues are another matter. They are not story. They are not true commentary. They are good *wishes*.

It is of course impossible here to embark on a survey of the principal medieval romances in turn. I simply cite Arthurian romance as a clear case of 'fortune' narrative. After the vicissitudes of 'adventure' which the hero positively *seeks*, there is as his final reward a 'happy ending', lasting happiness, to all intents the *fortuna manens* of Antiquity. This is, as was already indicated above, the only thing which even the most enthusiastic writer dare imagine or wish for his hero. There is no serious reference to the hero's soul. The hero drops in at chapels on the way, before the day's adventures begin, because he is *such* a knight. This has nothing to do with his story. Easter and Whitsuntide are dates in his social calendar, not in his liturgical year. This assertion brings us immediately to the question of the Grail romances, particularly Wolfram von Eschenbach's *Parzival*.[1] In the course of his early adventures Parzival reaches the court of King Arthur, so achieving the degree of success which is the normal goal of the chivalrous knight. Arthur's court is the source of *sælde* (fortune). If the court of King Arthur is the normal goal, what does Parzival seek (or does Wolfram seek for him) when he leaves the court again? In what kind of relationship do Grail and Grail-Kingship stand to the 'hierarchy of instances'

[1] A fuller account of *Parzival* in Boethian terms in *Augustinus oder Boethius*, with particular reference to the hero's 'change of heart' on a Good Friday.

according to Boethius on the one hand, Augustine on the other? Trite as it may seem to say so, the Grail community is a kind of Church, the institutions and *ordo* of which Wolfram has accommodated to such an extent to those of the Church proper that he comes at times dangerously close to blasphemy. At the same time it is a community which Boethius might have postulated for those who elect to follow the *vita activa*, combining high ideals of conduct and government with religious observance, indeed deepest piety. For its own members, including the Grail King, it has a stringent code, but *contempt* of the world and celibacy are not demanded. Temperance, self-discipline, honourable conduct – and noble blood are.

Let us recall that common to both the economies of Christian history are God's Providence and man, man having a free will. This means on a strict reading that Parzival's career is not, as some colleagues seem to think, guided by Divine Providence, but by the men of free will who worked on the tradition concerning Parzival; and of these Wolfram is the greatest, and the most headstrong. Wolfram is not St Augustine; he is not writing 'Heilsgeschichte'. He is also not writing a tract, either a religious or a philosophical tract, but a final series of *adventures* for Parzival. In Wolfram's *Parzival* the hero fulfils the 'fate' which the poets had been at work evolving for him. It was the highest which could be devised for him short of a blasphemous and presumptuous assertion of his sanctity. (Church history does not know Parzival, cannot know him.) The sustained fiction of the Grail community as a kind of Church (and of a knight destined to become its 'King') is a *temeritas* which can succeed only if the poet himself has *sælde*, which means *inter alia* the avoidance of disaster. In a work on this scale and with these idealistic pretensions, disaster would have been the displeasure of the official Church. (The final verdict is always with the Church, if it elects to speak.) After all that his hero has achieved, he will, Wolfram trusts for his hero's sake and for his own, '*not* have jeopardised' his soul. That would be a 'fortunate' issue for both of them.

Wolfram the *poet* cannot invoke a higher instance than Fortune. When he pauses to deliberate before his audience ('what will the hero do now?'), he pretends to consult Dame Adventure. Of his final achievement in completing his work he says he has 'brought his hero to the goal which *sælde* (fortune) had destined for him', and 'done a useful piece of work'. As for Parzival's great religious crisis, which to us modern readers, and no doubt to Wolfram's contemporaries, seems the very centre of the story, it determines the mood and frame of mind in which Parzival enters on his Kingship. From the point of view of *story* it is in fact purely *episodic*, and without any consequences of its own. Or the consequences are absorbed by the story of the hero's 'fortune'. Tradition already had it that Parzival won the Grail despite a neglected opportunity, which, if seized, would have caused it to fall into his lap – for fortune is not 'earned'. The failure on the first 'occasion' was a vicissitude of fortune, having nothing to do with any kind of guilt, as a vast secondary literature on 'Parzival's guilt' has so adequately proved.

Wolfram's struggles with this tradition led to a work (a 'life') in which fortune is made to seem to serve the hero. Divine Providence may have ordained that there should be a Parzival tradition in Western Europe, to be taken up by a short succession of generations which held the chivalric code to present the highest ideals of which man was capable. It was Parzival's fortune to have Wolfram as his last historian. Parzival becomes Grail King after final vicissitudes which Wolfram, lacking satisfactory sources at this stage, planned for him. Despite the first neglected *opportunity* (*owê daz er nicht vrâgte dô* – 'alas, that he did not ask the Grail King then and there what he ailed'), and the ensuing *metanoia*, Fortune, *alias* Wolfram, must lead the hero a second time to the Grail, 'the overflowing font of all goodness *in this world*'. The Grail, says Wolfram, is a *thing*, and about this thing, which in the end he seems to have visualised as a portable altar,[1] he has the most remarkable information to offer, which he claims to have from his mysterious source 'Kyot'. About its custodians he has some pretty strange lore too. The whole tradition is, however, by comparison with anything which the Church acknowledged, a fiction. None the less Wolfram made this fiction the vehicle of his most serious and responsible thoughts on knighthood, an institution to which the Church never gave more than grudging acknowledgment. The poet hopes, as I said, that he may share the fortune of his hero:

'I have now brought Parzival', he says, 'to that goal which Fortune had after all destined for him. Any man who reaches the goal of his life in such a way that his soul is not lost to God through the fault of the body, and yet contrives to win the admiration of his

[1] See p. 69.

fellow-men through worth and honour, has laboured to good purpose.'[1]

Actually the words are 'has done a good job', by which Wolfram meant that if Parzival had made the effort, so had he too. Of the 'salvation' of his hero, Wolfram was not so convinced that he did not start on the career of his next hero Willehalm (Guillaume d'Orange) with relief and a sense of liberation, for on this hero the Church, he believed, had already spoken. His hero was *beatus*. There is an entirely different atmosphere in the *Willehalm*. For all that, Wolfram did not complete the story. I do not think he could have completed it. This is not the point to argue the case in detail. It was, I think, a case of mistaken identity. The new 'humanity' which demanded that Willehalm should treat the heathen as medieval chivalry had learnt to know him, vitiates the poet's attempt to tell the story of the hero whom the Church had beatified: namely the champion of the faith who had not hesitated to slaughter the heathens like cattle, just as the paladins of Charlemagne had done according to the *Rolandslied*.[2] From the point of view of Western civilisation Wolfram's *Willehalm* is great story-writing. It is not Augustinian.

And now a final word on dynastic history. What other meaning can one read into Book XVI of the *Parzival*, than that in a more perfectly ordered world it would be Providence herself, and not fickle and inconstant Fortune, which determines dynastic successions, and sends out, as thrones fall vacant, suitable candidates from some special institution of her own? So that whereas ordinary mortals might rejoice at the appearance of a Swan Knight, a higher dynasty, that of the Grail Kings (rather like the Community of the Tower in *Wilhelm Meister*, or an invisible 'Lodge' elsewhere) would know that provision was being made for the welfare of a nation temporarily bereft of a ruler. This leads to the thought that the Western world may have cast many a sidelong glance at the Byzantine Empire, not only to envy the more impressive ceremony of the Eastern rite.[3] The schism might be the work

[1]
     ... *Parzivâl[s], den [hân ich] brâht*
dar sîn doch sælde het erdâht.
swes lebn sich sô verendet,
daz got niht wirt gepfendet
der sêle durch des lîbes schulde,
und der doch der werlde hulde
behalten kan mit werdekeit,
daz ist ein nütziu arbeit. (827, 17 ff.)

[2] sam daz vihe, sam di hunte, *Rolandslied*, lines 5421, 5423.

[3] Believed to be reflected in the Grail ceremonies (Konrad Burdach).

of the Devil himself, as the Eastern heresies certainly were, but Fortune, always the favourer of the unworthy (*indignorum fautrix*) might have taught the Eastern world a better history lesson, and a better solution of the problem of Church and State.

## 2. OTHER PICTURES OF FORTUNE

We are now familiar enough with the Boethian conception of history and with the medieval image of Fortune derived from book II of *De Consolatione*. History consists of 'cases' (falls), preceded by ascents. This is the cycle of history, which repeats itself. Later, history will be seen to follow the line of a spiral and not to repeat itself exactly. 'Decline and Fall', 'Untergang des Abendlandes' and other titles nevertheless show that history continued to be seen under roughly the same image as in the Middle Ages. There are other similarities. Until quite recently the character of individual leaders was regarded as a clue to their success or failure; particularly an ability to see and seize opportunities was essential for success in 'policy'. It may sound impossibly archaic nowadays to say that a statesman 'had' or had not 'fortune', but when Lord Attlee, summing up Churchill's career, said 'he was lucky',[1] he reiterated what since Antiquity has been history's only serious lesson: leaders must have fortune or go. Other terms have been brought up to date. *Occasio* is still seized (openings are exploited) at the propitious moment (by those who have an uncanny sense of timing), and so on. The old battle of the Vices and Virtues (Prudentius), or the realisation of the City of God (Augustine), have as the background been replaced by the more recent 'conflict of ideologies'. History is still interpreted preponderantly morally, so that we generally deplore opportunism, while recognising opportunity as the main factor in decision making. Even computerised 'critical path analysis' has no other intention than to outwit Fortune; it produces a strategy. There is, therefore, it would appear, nothing simple and primitive in historical thinking in the Middle Ages. The apparently so naïve image of the Wheel with its *regno, regnavi* contains, moreover, an element of self-mockery, present too, perhaps, in some of the final admissions of modern historians: for instance that history is only communicable in the form of literary fictions (Toynbee), or that it is self-revelatory (Collingwood).

[1] *Observer*, 31 Jan. 1965.

For more than a thousand years after Boethius secular history was held to consist entirely of 'falls'. Consider the late work of Boccaccio (1313–75), *De casibus virorum illustrium*, which, I am told, nobody reads today. In a German translation by Hieronymus Ziegler, printed in Augsburg in 1545, the title-page runs as follows:

Fornemste Historien vnd Exempel von widerwertigem Glück, merklichem vnd erschröcklichem Vnfahl, erbärmklichen Verderben vnnd Sterben grossmechtiger Kayser, Künig, Fürsten vnd anderer namhafftiger Herrn. In neun Büchern durch den fürtreflichen hochberümbten Historischreiber vnnd Poeten Iohannem Boccatium von Certaldo in Latein beschribn . . . jetzt zum aller ersten von Hieronymo Ziegler fleyssig verteütscht, Augsburg 1545.[1]

The principal Histories and Examples of adverse Fortune, notable and alarming Disgrace, miserable Ruin and Death of all-powerful Emperors, Kings, Princes and other famous men, in nine books . . . by the most excellent and illustrious writer of history and poet Iohannes Boccaccio, in Latin, now for the first time diligently rendered in German, etc.

To recommend Hieronymus Ziegler's book, the publisher, Steiner of Augsburg, employed not only the horrific diction of this title-page. He utilised also some of the Fortune engravings he had had from Hans Burgkmair and the so-called 'Petrarca-Meister', an artist whose work is of true Renaissance sophistication.[2] Even so, this artist uses the medieval Wheel of Fortune as image. By comparison, Georg Pencz's woodcut for Hans Sachs' poem 'Das waltzend Glück' of 1534 is undistinguished (see plate 8a).[3] We may note, however, that it shows, beside a well-drawn and mechanically sound Wheel of Fortune, a hand of Providence in the clouds above, which has Dame Fortune's 'game' under firm control. This is in keeping with Boccaccio's understanding

[1] B.M. Catalogue: 10604g[8].

[2] On the Petrarca-Meister, see Walter Scheidig, *Die Holzschnitte des Petrarca-Meisters zu Petrarcas Werk Von der Artzney beyder Glück des guten und widerwärtigen, Augsburg 1532* (Berlin, 1955).

[3] In the German ed. I treated Georg Pencz's woodcut as an illustration of Ziegler's Boccaccio of 1545. This was a lapse. According to Heinrich Röttinger, *Die Holzschnitte des Georg Pencz* (Leipzig, 1914), p. 43, illus. 16 (cat. 33) it is, like several other Pencz woodcuts, a Hans Sachs illustration. (It exists in one copy in Erlangen Univ. Library.) Though one will hardly dispute a very close association with the Hans Sachs poem one cannot be certain which is the source, the woodcut or the poem.

of Fortune and, despite the date (1534), still 'according to Boethius'.[1] In the book itself countless cases of famous men who 'fell' are duly chronicled. From the alphabetical index one may quote Adam, Alaric, Alboinus, Boethius himself, Brutus, Caesar, Coriolanus and 'Pope Johannes, a woman'. The spreading of the net is remarkable. The lesson of history is pressed home by the sheer weight of the examples. It may be objected, of course, that this is not a serious approach to history-writing, but we shall not get very far if we stop to consider what the true task of the historian is. It is of considerable incidental interest that late medieval artists seized upon a couple of Boccaccio's statements about Fortune, to produce at long last alternatives to the old picture. Dame Fortune once appeared in his study, he says, to wave 'a hundred arms and just as many hands' at him, and warn him of the consequences of attributing all the world's misfortunes to her. The manuscript copies of *De casibus* often show a Fortune intended to be of terrifying aspect, with six to twelve hands and arms (cf plate 4a). As an iconographical innovation this image has had a great success with the art historians. I do not think it occurs outside this one context, in which case it remains, like the other new image, a 'Fight of Fortune and Poverty', a Boccacio illustration rather than a Fortune iconography.[2]

As far as I know, modern historians do not have nightmares of this kind, in which Fortune (History) herself demands an account of their doings. They probably do not dream either of a 'Realm of Fortune'.[3]

The title-page of Niklas von Wyle's translation (1468) of the Dream of Fortune (*Somnium Fortunæ*) of the later Pope Pius II (Enea Silvio Piccolomini, 1405–64) runs:

Vorred Nicolai von Weyl / der zwölfften Translation. Wie Enee Siluio / der Babst Pius genañt / ward: traumet / das er inn das reich der Künigin Frawglück kommen were: vnd wie er sehe alle stånd der welt: was sie mit jm redte / vnd wie Frawglück zůerwerben were.

---

[1] Cf *Augustinus oder Boethius*, I 39–45.

[2] See Appendix B, p. 216.

[3] In Appendix B I come back to this subject, pp. 217 f. The most influential text appears to have been a passage in the *Anticlaudianus* of Alanus ab Insulis (*d.* 1203) which draws the threads of an old tradition together: Fortune's realm is henceforward a remote island surrounded by treacherous seas and accessible only over drawbridges. It has two castles, one splendid, the other in ruins, or one castle, part of which is perilously unsafe. Whether this same motif occurs later than in J. A. Comenius' *Labyrinth of the World* (1631) ch. 23, I do not know.

Niklas von Wyle's Preface to the Twelfth Translation: How Enea Silvio, who was elected Pope Pius, dreamed that he had entered into the Kingdom of Queen Dame-Fortune, and how he saw all the estates of this world, what she said to him, and how Dame-Fortune is to be won.

The edition by H. Steiner (Augsburg, 1536) has as its frontispiece the corresponding Fortune picture of Hans Burgkmair the Elder (see plate 8b).[1] A Janus-faced Fortuna rides through the air on her throne which is fitted on one side with a Wheel of Fortune. The throne hangs by cords from the skies: again a reference to Providence's control, one thousand years after the *De Consolatione*.

Having illustrated *inter alia* the longevity of the *typical* Wheel of Fortune image we come now to a consideration of some of the variants, the main thing about which is that we should recognise them as such – as variants. They are not 'pictures of Fortune', but they show 'the fortune of X'. They do not present the course of history as a generalised concept, but refer to 'individual' moments or specific phases of history. Of the variants we need only a few examples here.

In order to refer to a specific historical situation, for instance to present an opponent with the image of his coming fall in a pamphlet or broadsheet, the artist has to adapt or replace the four kings of the traditional Wheel of Fortune. In order to wish luck to a faction, on the other hand, or to congratulate an individual on some success (or succession), the allusions to the mutability of Fortune have to be reduced in some way, or cancelled completely. At the risk of being tedious I repeat that these variants are in the nature of things not typical Fortune pictures.[2] To register all the variants would require a sizeable monograph. For the purposes of this chapter the formulation may suffice that when a text refers simply to Fortune (for instance in the *Carmina Burana* or the *Roman de la Rose*) – and not any particular individual's fortune, the typical image of Fortune with her Wheel will generally be used.

[1] See also Arthur Burkhard, *Hans Burgkmair der Ältere* (Berlin, 1932) plate LVI and van Marle, *Iconographie profane*, illus. 224.

[2] Any statement in art-history books that Fortune is occasionally represented by the figure of a youth (for instance, in a fresco of Schloss Lichtenberg, late fourteenth century, van Marle, *Iconographie*, etc., illus. 227) should without ceremony be deleted. The young man in the fresco is certainly turning the Wheel of Fortune, but *against* Fortune. The message is clearly a *wish* that the young man may succeed in so doing – in fashioning his own 'fortune', despite Fortune. It expresses the confident hope that he will be *faber fortunæ suæ*. This seems to me to be one artist's attempt to offer, if not an equivalent image, a suitable substitute for the smith at his anvil!

For the *Ship of Fools* or *Reynard the Fox*, or in the pamphlets produced during the Peasant Revolt or the Thirty Years War, the artists will draw the Fortune of the Fool, of Reynard, of the Peasants, the Protestants, with *parti pris* for or against the title hero. The position of the passengers on the Wheel will represent the present or proximate state of some important confrontation. There are in fact infinite possibilities. I therefore offer two examples only to illustrate this point, adding a third, not directly connected, to round off the main story of this chapter. Of my two examples one is very early, the other late. In both the Wheel of Fortune is modified to serve in the representation of specific moments in history. My third returns to the more general 'lesson of history' as the rise and fall of the great. It does not use the Wheel image, but recalls the lot of Job.

## 3. HISTORICAL CASES

A  *The Fortune of Tancred (and the Hohenstaufens)*

The *Sicilian Chronicle* of Peter of Eboli was written about 1197 for Henry VI.[1] The poet's dates are about 1160–1219. There is only one manuscript, copiously illustrated. The theme of the Chronicle is the fall of the anti-king Tancred. It is a remarkable work, treating in Latin verse and in pictures the events of the years following the death of William II (the Good) of Sicily in 1189. There are pictures to match an event in each of the sections into which the Chronicle is divided, but unfortunately none to illustrate the coronation of Tancred – typified in the text as being the 'crowning of an ape':

> ecce vetus monstrum, nature crimen aborsum;
> ecce coronatur simia, turpis homo.[2]

[1] The Chronicle was edited by Ettore Rota as *Petri Ansolini de Ebulo de rebus Siculis carmen*, Rer. Ital. Scriptores XXXI 1 (Città di Castello, 1904) and almost simultaneously by G. B. Siragusa as *Liber ad honorem Augusti*, Fonti per la storia d'Italia, Scrittori XXXIX–XL (1905). The sole manuscript is Cod. 120/ii of the civic library of Bern, cf Otto Homburger, *Die Schätze der Burgerbibliothek Bern* (Bern, 1953), pp. 120 ff, where there is a colour reproduction of Tancred under the Wheel of Fortune (plate VII). Other pictures from the same manuscript in several places, e.g. *Shorter Cambridge Medieval History*, illus. 124–6 and *Neue Propyläen Weltgeschichte*, II (1940) 316, 317, 321.

[2] The later emblematists knew a corresponding image, see plate 5b, from Otho van Veen's *Qu. Horat. Flacci Emblemata* (Brussels, 1607) p. 155. Cf Philipp von

The chronicle of events is borne along by the author's fanatical hatred of Tancred, his intemperate adulation of Henry VI and his almost messianic expectations of Henry's son Roger (Frederick II). For the rest, it is an impressionistic account of events in Sicily, and events elsewhere as seen from Sicily, among them the capture of Richard Cœur de Lion. This is dealt with in word and in image, the latter having the caption: *illustris Rex Anglie a Ierosolemis rediens captus presentatur Augusto.*[1]

Now Tancred's fall or 'case'. Let us note first that there is an early picture, about quarter of the way through the Chronicle, showing Tancred as having fallen from his horse which has stumbled, clearly an evil omen. A title says this is Tancred's 'fortune', see plate 4b. Of more direct interest to us are the final and the penultimate pictures.[2] Let us take the final one first, which – so the author thought – showed the lesson of history which was to be learnt from the glorious career of Henry VI. The subject is Sapientia sitting in judgment on Fortune, who looks somewhat bedraggled and has lost her crown, see plate 3b. How the two characters come to be in these roles of final arbiter and *persona non grata* we learn from the previous scene. Here, in a picture at the foot of a page, Tancred writhes in the dust. His plight is that of the king 'without kingdom' or 'crushed beneath the wheel' of the typical Wheel of Fortune (see plate 3a). It is a chariot wheel without any mounting. Fortune is shown (head and shoulders only) on top of the wheel. She does not vouchsafe her victim a glance, but supplicates admission to the entourage of the victor, Henry. The household he has assembled consists, however, of the Virtues, and Sapientia rejects on Henry's and their behalf Dame (or Queen) Fortune's plea. What is perhaps even more interesting to us is that Henry died two years later, and that was to all intents the end of the Hohenstaufen dynasty. For the

---

Zesen's *Moralia Horatiana*, an adaptation of van Veen, published with the engravings of the 1607 edition by Guido Pressler (Wiesbaden, 1963) in 2 vols, our picture I 99 (cf II 45). The Horatian motto 'Fortuna non mutat genus' is interpreted to mean roughly 'even when crowned, an ape is still an ape'. Fortune is shown in the garb of a Roman matron; she is blindfold. Her draperies billow from her girdle like a full sail. In her left hand she holds an antique rudder. Beside her is the ape in royal robes, holding a sceptre. The realistic background (street, houses, a canal) emphasises the strangeness of the foreground group.

[1] *Shorter Cambridge Med. Hist.* illus. 126, upper and lower halves.

[2] The plates in Rota's edition are IX (Tancred's horse), LII (Tancred under the Wheel), LIII (Sapientia arraigns Fortune).

dynasty there was no further fortune, but only 'nemesis'. Fortune had after all turned her wheel and betaken herself elsewhere. That is *not* in the chronicle. A further reflection is that Henry had sent Tancred's widow to Hohenburg in Alsace, where under the abbess Herrade of Landsberg one of the most famous of all medieval illustrated books was compiled, the so-called *Hortus Deliciarum*. Let us not spoil a good story by too close an attention to dates. The picture of the Wheel of Fortune in that volume will have given the new member of that distinguished group of ladies food for thought, Christian we may trust, see plate 6a.

If these concluding remarks are thought to be a little flippant, I would reply that the professional historian may relate the career of Henry VI in Sicily and this 'turning point in Western European history' with a generous admixture of *fortuna* and *occasio* commonplaces. 'The new pope was the man to make the most of his opportunities; but it was Henry VI's failure to make the right concessions at the right time which ushered in the nemesis of 1198–1215. The responsibility for the catastrophe which followed Henry VI's premature death cannot be thrown on to a blind, malignant fate [fortune?]: it rests on Henry's own shoulders.'[1]

### B *Gustavus Adolphus of Sweden*

Now an example from the time of the Thirty Years War. It is interesting both because of the persistence of the Wheel image with the four kings and the familiar *regno*-titles, and of certain baroque complications. This time I will give details of the drawing in the form of instructions, which any reader with time to spare may care to follow, comparing the result with plate 6b. The task is to represent pictorially the events of 1618 to 1630 – particularly the Swedish intervention – from the standpoint of the Holy Roman Empire. The title of the picture is 'The Great World-Clock of the Roman Empire': *Deß Romischen Reichs Grosse Welt Vhr*. The Empire is to be represented by a tower. But first, putting the point of a pair of compasses in the centre of the page, one draws two large concentric circles, leaving a band wide enough to take the Roman numerals I to XII twice over, XII at the top, XII again at the bottom. The tower itself (with the inscription *turris tremulus* on a band below the battlements) represents the Holy Roman Empire. What one draws is

[1] I was careful to explain to Geoffrey Barraclough exactly what use I wanted to make of this quotation from *Origins of Modern Germany* (Oxford, 1947) p. 204. I am grateful.

*1a Divine Providence*
Holkham Bible Picture Book
(English, *c.* 1330)

*1b Fortune's Wheel*
Holkham Bible Picture Book
(English, *c.* 1330)

*2a Fortune's Wheel*
Gregory's 'Moralia in Hiob' (Spanish, late ninth century; added drawing, French or English, twelfth century)

*2b Fortune's Wheel*
*Carmina Burana*
(Bavarian, mid-thirteenth century)

*3a Emperor Henry VI attended by the Virtues. Fortune's plea rejected. Tancred crushed by Fortune's Wheel*
Peter of Eboli's 'Sicilian Chronicle' (Sicily, *c.* 1197)

*3b Henry VI on Sapientia's throne. Sapientia arraigns Fortune. Tancred under Fortune's Wheel*
Peter of Eboli's 'Sicilian Chronicle' (Sicily, *c.* 1197)

*4a Six-armed Fortune (Fortune remonstrates with Boccaccio)*
Boccaccio, *De casibus virorum illustrium* (French trans.), Book VI, Ch. I (France,
*c.* 1475)

*4b Tancred's Fall
(Fortune)*
Detail from Peter of
Eboli's 'Sicilian Chronicle'
(Sicily, *c.* 1197)

5a *Fortuna redux*
Engraving by Nicoletto
da Modena (North
Italian, *c.* 1500, Bartsch
xiii, 38)

5b *Fortune with crowned ape*
('*Fortuna non mutat
genus*')
From Otho van Veen's
*Qu. Horat. Flacci
Emblemata*, Brussels, 1607

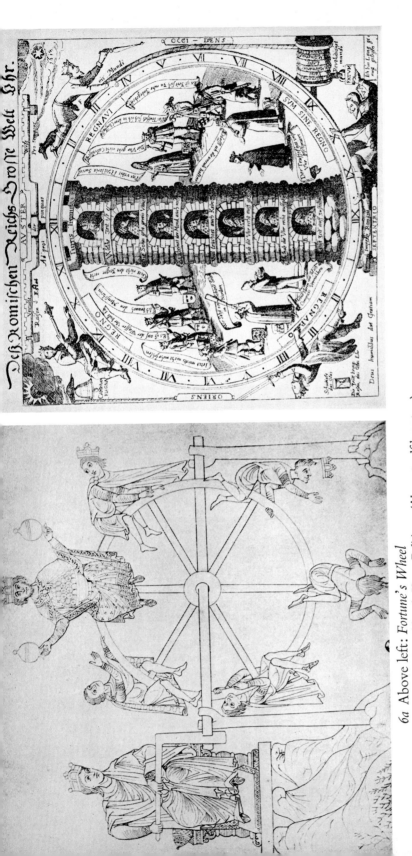

6a  Above left: *Fortune's Wheel*
Herrade of Landsberg's *Hortus Deliciarum* (Alsace, twelfth century)

6b  Above right: *World Clock of the Holy Roman Empire (with seven-storied electoral tower, the Fortune of Gustavus Adolphus, etc.)*
German broadsheet, c. 1632

7a  Below left: *Nemesis (the so-called Great Fortune)*
Engraving by Albrecht Dürer, 1503 (Bartsch 77)

7b  Below right: *Fortune with spinning-wheel and sphere (Fortune as Lachesis)*

*8a Fortune's Wheel*
Woodcut by Georg Pencz (1534)

*8b Janus-headed Fortune
enthroned, with Wheel*
Engraving by Hans
Burgkmair the Elder, *c.*
1515 (Bartsch 124)

*Walther von der Vogelweide*
'Manesse' anthology of Minnesang (Swiss, *c.* 1320)

9b *David as Lawgiver and/or The Judgement of Solomon*
Beatus page (initial E) of the 'Windmill Psalter' (East Anglia, late thirteenth century)

9c *Psalmist with cithara, Anima*
Illustration of Psalm xlii (A.V. xliii), verses 4–5.
The Stuttgart Psalter (Northern France, early ninth century)

9d *The Vision of Ezekiel*
Amiens Cathedral, relief medallion, 1225–35

*10b King David as Psalmist*
Beatus page of Carilef Bible (Norman? 1088–96)

*10a King David as Psalmist*
Beatus page of the Portiforium Oswaldi (Norman?

11a Left: Dance of the Blessed (Ascent to Heaven through Church and the Redeemer) Commentary on Canticle, Proverbs, Book of Daniel (Reichenau, end of tenth century)

11b Above: David lamenting the death of Saul and Jonathan Pudsey Bible (Durham?, c. 1153–95)

*12  Story of Job. (Bottom right) Job as Patron of Musicians*
Centre panel of the Altar of St Job, by the Master of the Barbara Legend (Rhenish, *c.* 1485)

13a *Albrecht Dürer, drawing. Self-portrait as Man of Sorrows (Type II), 1522*
Bremen, Kunsthalle (now 'missing'—Lippmann 131)

13b *Albrecht Dürer, drawing. Adaptation of Man of Sorrows (Type I), c. 1510*
Bremen, Kunsthalle (Lippmann 130)

14a *Imperial portrait. Otto II (or Otto III) receives the homage of Germania, Francia, Italia and Alemannia*
Registrum Gregorii (Reichenau or Trier, *c.* 983), by the Master of the Registrum Gregorii

14b *Man of Sorrows, seated. ('Sessio' or, popularly, 'Christ awaiting cruxifixion')*
Statuary group. St Nizier, Troyes (Aube), *c.* 1500

15a Christ, Peter and the Woman of Sam
(adapted from 'Annunciation at the
Well'?)
Ivory panel from Maximian's Cathedra
(Eastern Mediterranean, early sixth century)

15b Annunciation (Mary with
distaff)
Ivory panel from Maximian's
Cathedra (Eastern Mediterranean,
early sixth century)

15c Annunciation, Mary reading Psalter
Ivory (School of Metz, second half of ninth century)

16a *Animation of Adam. Christ as the Wisdom of the Father, Adam, the Holy Spirit with Trinity sceptre*
Old German 'Millstatt' Genesis (Millstatt, Carinthia, *c.* 1220)

16b *Trinitas Creator*
Herrade of Landsberg's *Hortus Deliciarum* (Alsace, twelfth century)

*17a  The Holy Trinity:
'Throne of Grace' (with
symbols of the
Evangelists and suppliant
donors)*
Würzburg-Ebrach Psalter
(German, *c.* 1200)

*17b  Dedication of book to
St Peter (Peter with
'PETRUS' staffs)*
Illustration of the Gero-
Codex (Reichenau, *c.*
965–970)

18a 'Thou art Peter': Peter receives his 'keys' (PETRUS-monogr
Evangeliary of Otto III (Reichenau, c. 997–1000)

18b Peter's Denial
Side panel of sarcophagus (Rome, fourth century)

19a *God receives the soul of David*
Design based on an illustration of Psalm lvi (A.V. lvii) of the *Utrecht Psalter*. Ivory cover of the Psalter of Charles the Bald (Goldschmidt I, 406, Reims, c. 870)

19b *Presentation of the Codex Egberti to Egbertus, Archbishop of Trier, by Keraldus and Heribertus (artist and scribe) 'of Reichenau'*
The Codex Egberti (Reichenau School, c. 985)

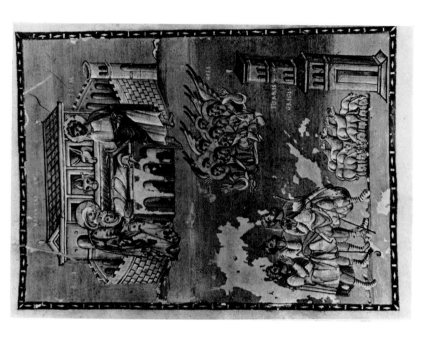

20a Scenes from the trial of Christ: Peter's Denial
(John xviii 13–xix 1). (above) Peter, Christ
'whom Annas condemned'; (centre) Peter and
the 'hostiaria'; (below) The Flagellation

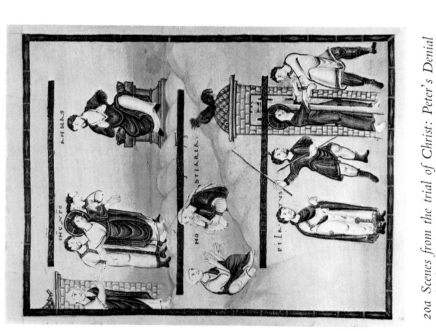

20b (above) Nativity in Bethlehem
(below) The Glad Tidings to the Shepherds;
the Tower of the Flock (Turris gregis)

21b *The Deposition and Entombment, with 'Joselp'
and Nicodemus*
The Codex Egberti (Reichenau School, c. 985)

21a *The Crucifixion.* (above) *'Symon' bears the
Cross;* (below) *Stephaton's lance-thrust, 'Dis-
mas' and 'Gesmas' crucified beside Christ*
The Codex Egberti (Reichenau School, c. 985)

22a Above: *Healing of the Blind Man at the 'Aqueduct' of Siloe*
The Codex Egberti (Reichenau School, c. 985)

22b Right: *Old Testament types of Christ: (Abraham and) Isaac, Moses as Standard-Bearer, Samuel*
Chartres Cathedral, North Transept, Central Portal, c. 1215

22c *Standard-Bearer with 'Dragon'*
Illustration of Psalm lix (A.V. lx), title verse
Psalterium Aureum (St Gall, 841–872)

22d *Moses raising the Brazen Serpent (or Dragon)*
Psalter illustration, 'Psautier de Saint Louis' (Paris, 1255–7

*23a Majestas Domini with symbols of the Evangelists and the Twenty-Four
Elders*
Benedictine monastery, Moissac (Tarn-et-Garonne), *c.* 1110

*23b and c Dame World ('Frau Welt') side and rear views*
Worms Cathedral, South Portal, fourteenth century

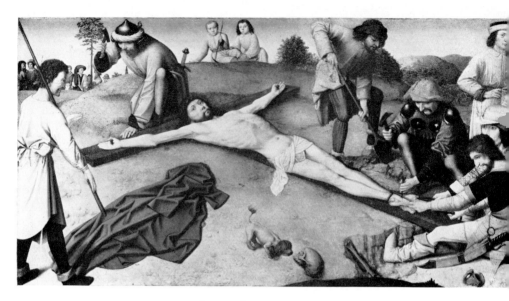

*24a Nailing to the Cross (jacente cruce)*
Gerard David (c. 1450–1523). Panel, 19″ × 37″

*24b Nailing to the Cross (erecto cruce)*
Fra Angelico (1387–1455) and assistants. Fresco, Florence, S. Marco, 'cell 36'

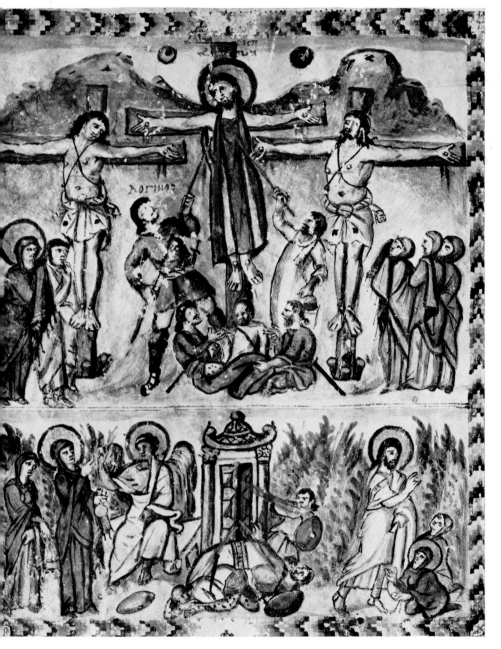

*25 The Crucifixion ('historical')*
Rabbula Gospels (Syrian, A.D. 586)

*26a Crucifixion on Palm-Tree Cross: (Ecclesia), The Virgin, John, (Synagogue), etc.*
The Salisbury Psalter (Salisbury?, mid-thirteenth century)

*26b The Crucifixion ('allegorical')*
Weingarten Gospels (Winchester?, 1025–50)

27a *Nailing to the Cross: Tubalcain in his Smithy (a late essay in typology)*
From German block-book version of the fourteenth-century 'Speculum Humanae Salvationis'

27b *The Forging of the Nails*
Holkham Bible Picture Book (English, *c.* 1330)

27c *Nailing to the Cross*
Holkham Bible Picture Book (English, *c.* 1330)

28 *The Crucifixion* (typological):

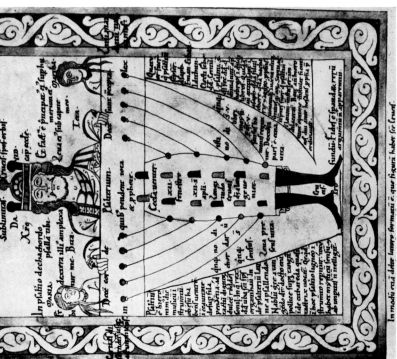

29a *The Crucifixion ('typological')*
Page of a Biblia Pauperum (Upper Austrian, c. 1330)

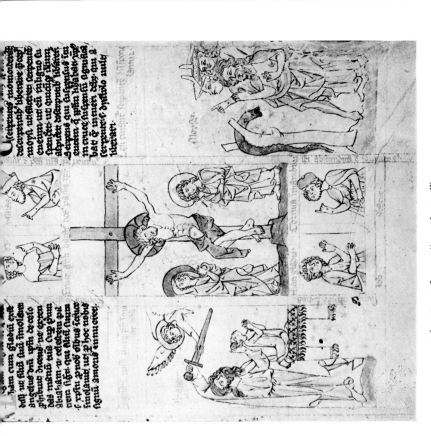

29b *David's Psaltery as Type of the Crucifixion*
Psalter illustration (South-east Germany, twelfth century)

*30a  The Crucifixion (in 'crossbow' likeness)*
By 'Grünewald' (Mathis Nithart, d. 1528)

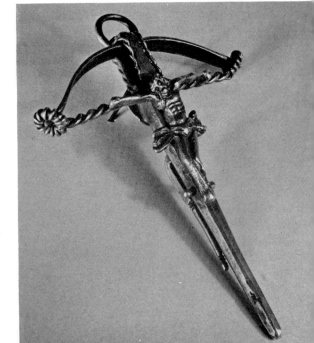

*30b  Crossbow Crucifix*
Archer's badge, silver
7 × 5 cm.) (South
German, early six-
teenth century)

31 *Descent from the Cross*
*God the Father with the soul of Christ and banner of the Resurrection, Mary,*
*Nicodemus (?), Joseph of Arimathea (?) on bent palm-tree, John*
Sandstone relief. The 'Extern Stones' (Externsteine), near Paderborn, *c.* 1130

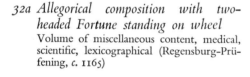

32a *Allegorical composition with two-headed Fortune standing on wheel*
Volume of miscellaneous content, medical, scientific, lexicographical (Regensburg-Prüfening, *c.* 1165)

32b *Madonna and Child Midwives, Joseph)*
D-Initial (Office of the octave of the Nativity) Sac tary of Drogo, Bishop of (826–855; Metz, *c.* 842)

32c *The Agony in Gethsemane*
St Albans Psalter (St Albans, England, *c.* 1120–30)

the seven-storied Tower of *Grammatica*[1] or, if this cannot be recalled, the chessboard castle. It is itself well constructed, but the foundations are seven layers of large undressed stones, without mortar. At the window in each of the seven stories is an Elector, asking a 'time' question; the one in the upper story asks 'what time is it now?'

In drawing the clock dial we at the same time drew the rim of a wheel, which is turned, not by a Goddess Fortune but by a special mechanism. There is a heavy rope running part of the way round the rim to the drum of a windlass, bottom right, and on the end of the rope (after several turns round the drum) there is a weight, labelled 'Fatum', which Gustavus Adolphus (not yet crowned) holds on the palm of his hand. He is climbing on to the wheel at the point ('twenty past') where the wheel-rim has the additional inscription *Svm sine regno*. Experimentally we must let this weight go, to see what happens in time. The rope turns the dial-wheel, and the king moves to the *regnabo* position where he is also depicted (he is now crowned and holds a sword). He travels thence to his next two positions. In the corner of the square opposite his *regno* the sun of the Empire is eclipsed (Gustavus Adolphus holds a sceptre); it shines again (top right-hand corner) where Gustavus Adolphus still has his crown but holds a bauble, at *regnavi*. To the right and the left of the tower, in semi-circles, are twice six figures, the Catholic powers (Pope, King of France, etc.) to the right, Protestants to the left. The picture needs no further commentary here. We can ignore the many other details and the scrolls giving the words of the various characters involved in this piece of history. The mechanical problems of the wheel are only dubiously solved.[2]

### c *Retrospect: Belisarius*

In conclusion I draw attention to a development which was in time inevitable. The too openly didactic picture of the Wheel of Fortune with its four kings gave way to the image which must always have been

[1] See *RDK* I 350.

[2] The picture will also be found in Eugen Diederichs' *Deutsches Leben der Vergangenheit in Bildern*, II 275, fig. 927. I am grateful for reference to this picture, and help in interpreting it, to my colleague Dr W. A. Coupe. I support his identification of the King as Gustav Adolphus, not Frederick V (as in Diederichs). Another broadsheet of 1621 (*Deß gewesten Pfaltzgrafen Gluck vnd Vngluck*) uses the typical Wheel of Fortune image to depict the fate of Frederick V. I draw attention to Dr Coupe's monographic study, *The German Illustrated Broadsheet in the Seventeenth Century*, Bibliotheca Bibliographica Aureliania, XVII, 2 vols (Baden-Baden, 1966), particularly I 15 ff, 168 ff.

in the background of men's minds, to be used tragi-comically as soon
as that should be seemly: the wretch sitting at the wayside in his
misery, the mockery of passers-by.[1] We have already considered this
image in considerable detail with reference to Job, Jeremiah and the
Man of Sorrows.[2] Its associations kept it sacrosanct. It was not said of
these figures that they had suffered 'misfortune'. They had fallen on
evil days, the victims of sufferings of various kinds unrelated to those of
ordinary human experience. They were prototypical sufferers. By the
seventeenth century the situation had changed. It was some hundred
years since Luther had referred to Job's sufferings as his 'Unglück' in the
preface to the Book of Job. Towards the end of the century the popular
Viennese preacher, Abraham a Santa Clara was able to speak of the lot
of Justinian's famous general Belisarius[3] as follows:

What Envy is, what Envy does, was learnt by Belisarius – that
world-famous leader in war: after he had vanquished three quarters of
the world, after he had defeated in Asia Cosroes the Persian king, in
Africa Gilimer, in Europe the Gothic monarch Theodatus; after he had,
near Rome, slain in one day nine-and-sixty thousand of his enemy;
after he had by his indomitable valour brought the Roman Empire to
the greatest prosperity and honour, and subdued everything about him
except the envious ones –
   Who were so displeased at Belisarius's glory and fortune that they
burrowed so long like moles, scratched so long like hens in the sand,
rummaged so long like bees in the garden, that they finally turned the
heart of the Emperor and brought Belisarius into disgrace, so that
finally the mightiest hero of the world had his eyes put out, so that he
could weep bloody tears at men's envy –
   Poor Wretch! who had to lose his eyes before he could see how
sharp are the teeth of the Envy of Courtiers. His wretchedness grew
until he had to beg his crust from those who passed by, and he counted
over and over again the few pence in his wooden bowl –
   For whom, before that, whole kingdoms had been too cramped a

---

[1] Dante's use of the image in the *Vita Nuova* was merely blasphemous, see
p. 126. J. A. Scott says 'dangerously close to blasphemy' in 'Notes on Religion and
the *Vita Nuova*', in *Italian Studies*, xx (1965) 17–25 (p. 24).
[2] pp. 111, 126 f.
[3] Jakob Biedermann wrote a *Comico-Tragœdia* on Belisarius in 1607. (*The Times*
gave him a third leader on 13 March 1956, 1400 years after his birthday. He had all
the qualities required of generals, 'courage, health, youth, knowledge of humanity,
luck'.) Abraham a Santa Clara, *Judas der Erz-Schelm* (1686 ff), from which see the
excerpts in *Deutsche National-Litteratur*, XL 98 ff.

space. I can well believe he often sat on a stone at the corner of the street, and set up his cap on his stick, and twirled it round and round, and considered the Fickleness of Fortune.

I do declare, Fool Belisaire was made aware that Virtue's share when Envy's there, is traps and pitfalls everywhere. So it is, the more's the pity, and here's the moral in his ditty:

> Give to poor Belisarius,
> In God's name, don't be hateful,
> A bit of bread to make him glad,
> A proper beggar's plateful.
> The man is blind, so treat him kind,
> He can't do aught about it,
> Before his Fall, a Generall,
> Poor Devil, now he's routed.[1]

[1] Was der Neyd, wie der Neyd hat erfahren Bellisarius, dieser weltkündige Kriegs-Fürst, nachdeme diser über drey Theil der Welt triumphirte, nachdem er in Asia den Persischen König Cosroen, in Affrica den Gilimer, in Europa den Gothischen Monarchen Theodatum obgesiget; nachdem er bey Rom in einem Tag neun vnd sechtzig tausend der Feind erleget, nachdem er das Römische Reich, vermittelst seines vnüberwindlichen Heldenmuths in höchsten Glück vnd Ehrenstand gesetzt, vnd alles überwunden, aussgenommen die Neyder, welchen das grosse Lob vnd Glück Bellisarij also missfallen, dass sie so lang vntergraben, wie die Maulwurff, dass sie so lang gegrüblet, wie die Hennen in dem Sand, dass sie so lang alles durchsuchet, wie die Bein in dem Garten, biss sie endlich das Hertz dess Kaysers vmbgekehrt, den Bellisarium in Ungnad gebracht, dass zur Letzt dem mächtigsten Welt-Helden die Augen seynd aussgestochen worden, damit er den Neyd mit blutigen Zähren möchte beweinen, der arme Tropff, nachdem er keine Augen mehr hatte, konte erst recht sehen, was der Hof-Neyd für scharpffe Zähn habe, sein Elend wachste so weit, dass er auch das Bettlbrod von den Vorbeygehenden samblen müst, vnd zehlte gar offt seine wenige Pfennig in seinem hültzeren Schüsserl, deme vorhero gantze Königreich zu eng waren; ich glaub gar wol, er seye offt auff einem Eckstein der Gassen gesessen, seinen Huet auff seinen Stecken gesetzt, selben offt vmb vnd vmb gedrähet, vnd darbey das wankelmüthige Glück betracht, fürwahr, fürwahr hat Bellisar, der arme Narr, so gantz vnd gar, ja Sonnenklar, genommen wahr, dass Neyds-Gefahr, die Tugend plage immerdar, diss folgende Liedl gesungen:

> Gebt doch dem Bellisario,
> Ich bitt vmb Gottes Willen,
> Ein Stückl Brodt, so ist er froh,
> Und kan den Hunger stillen,
> Der blinde Mann, nimbt alles an,
> Daran ist gar kein Zweiffel,
> War vor dem Fall, ein General,
> Jetzund ein armer Teuffel.

# APPENDIX A: SUPPLEMENTARY NOTES ON FORTUNE IN MEDIEVAL LITERATURE[1]

(1) Fortune with her great Wheel and four figures of kings is a very specific image. It becomes fairly frequent in the work of *artists* from about 1190. It seems to have taken some fifty to sixty years for the poets to assimilate this picture and harmonise it with more general Fortune lore, and in Germany it is only the post-classical writers who seem to have this particular Fortune image in mind when they comment on a 'case'. In Heinrich von dem Türlin's *Krône* there are repeated references to *Gelückes* or *der Sælden rat* (or *schîbe*), lines 299, 2766–79, 6017–82, 15041 ff, and to Fortune's Castle 15654 (see p. 218).[2] Further references: *Jüngerer Titurel*, stanzas 1430 (1432), 1478 etc.; Wirnt von Gravenberg's *Wigalois* 31, *12* ff, 51, *38* ff. It is pointless to quote the texts without retelling the career which called for a fortune gloss. The instances cited are covered by the general statement (p. 192) that Fortune governs Arthurian story.

The Middle Ages were naturally not restricted to Boethius for their Fortune lore. He had little cause in *De Consolatione* to recall the more optimistic doctrines of 'opportunity' and the fruitful moment (*occasio* and *Kairos*). These were to be found in simpler school texts and collections of sayings (for instance 'Cato'). Boethius was not concerned either with 'neglected opportunity' and 'rue' (*metanoia*). From Hartmann von Aue's *Gregorius* one can see that these ideas could all be used in the context of Christian didacticism. When the fisherman's wife insists that the destitute Gregorius should be given shelter, it is because he is the first, and 'might be the last' stranger to whom they may show charity. She later fears that Gregorius may miss his *chance* of martyrdom, and he shows a similar concern (lines 2848 ff and 3072).

(2) Fortune with her Wheel is an allegorical figure. Cumbersomely equipped she can do very little, beyond the turning of her wheel. In a

---

[1] These notes correspond to pp. 122–3 and 129–32 in the German edition.
[2] I am grateful to Rosemary Wallbank (of the German Department, University of Manchester) for these references to *Diu Krône*.

narrative context someone must chance upon her in a remote place, or see her picture. She cannot very well have a part in story, since she makes story. Her role is to be held responsible – in soliloquies and the like.

(3) Synonyms for 'fortune'. Particularly in the later Middle Ages the poets know more words for the fortuitous than there are discrete ideas in that area. This is partly the consequence of word migration. There are no sharp divisions to be made between Middle High German *geschicht* (happening, fateful happening, *sors*) and *sælde, gelücke, fortûne, schanze, âventiure* (and the corresponding negatives, however expressed). One could only define these various terms closely by analysing the situations or events to which they are applied. There are rapidly diminishing returns from such exercises. Essays on *sælde* (generally, and in such specific contexts as the beginning of Hartmann's *Iwein*) and most recently on 'Glück'[1] have had a very mixed reception.

(4) How do medieval writers deal with the 'fortune' in which the *heathen* places his trust? The evidence varies, naturally, with the identity of the heathen and his Christian relevance. The question immediately becomes one concerning his god or gods, and the kind of providence he believes in. First, Aeneas. Heinrich von Veldeke's *Eneit* is a completely Christian work in the same way as Boethius' *De Consolatione Philosophiæ*, that is: without one word of reference to the Christian religion or the Christian Church. The 'gods' of the national epic of the Romans are retained (as in Heinrich's immediate source, the *Roman d'Énéas*). It is quite clear that they are kept as the appropriate 'antique' equivalent of the Divine Providence in which Christians believe. It would have been a gross *mélange des genres*, however, for the poet to have referred at any point from the Rome founded by Aeneas to the Rome of Peter and Paul. Since the foundation of Rome is his destiny, any 'cruel chance' in the story of Aeneas must remain an episode. But Dido? What of her? She is treated by the German poet as 'an outstandingly piteous martyr of an irresistible dæmonic love'. This interpretation was first put forward by Hugh Sacker in 'Heinrich von Veldeke's

---

[1] W. Sanders, *Glück. Zur Herkunft und Bedeutungsentwicklung eines mittelalterlichen Schicksalsbegriffs*, Niederdeutsche Studien, XIII (Cologne and Graz, 1965). This study appeared too late for more than an added note in *Literatur und darstellende Kunst* (p. 145). Dr Sanders took what is, as he says, chronologically the latest of the German words in this semantic area. (It never succeeded in asserting itself, and it remains associated with Fortune's more trivial and chance favours.) He considers the word in excessive isolation.

conception of the Aeneid', in *GLL* x (1957) 210 ff. In the following
volume of *GLL* ('On coming to terms with Curtius', see p. 61 n. 2) I
reinforced Sacker's interpretation, arguing, as in this chapter generally,
from 'two kinds of history'. Marie-Luise Dittrich has since made this
position unassailable in her contributions to *Zeitschrift für deutsches
Altertum*, xc (1960–1) and in later writings.

Coming now to the real pagans, the enemies of Christianity. The
Middle High German term for *their* 'fortune', in a small number of
important texts, is not *sælde* but *wîlsælde*. The first element in this
compound (*wîl-*) has attracted a good deal of attention. This has
hitherto been taken to refer to the transitory nature of the *sælde* to
which other religions aspire, as opposed to the lasting bliss in which
Christians are most interested. It is true that Old High German *wîla*
can mean the 'passing moment'. In the Notker-Glossary of Sehrt,
*uuil-uuendigi* is expounded as 'changeability within a short period of
time', roughly 'fickleness'. Schwietering[1] thinks, with reference to one
particular context, of 'fortune governed by the (momentary) con-
stellation at the *hour of birth*'. I am not myself entirely happy with
either of these interpretations, for the Fortuna invoked in the temples
dedicated to her in heathen Rome was a Fortuna *manens* or *stabilis*, see
p. 212. We may assert that 'uuîla' is a *short* period of time; it is in fact
sufficiently neutral to translate and render *fortuna stabilis, manens*, even
if only fortuitously. To refute this, better evidence will be required than
that very long passage in the *Kaiserchronik* from which the lexico-
graphers have taken their lead. But whatever proves to be the correct
interpretation of *wîlsælde* the following is of relevance, namely
Boethius on the subject of *fortuna manens*: it too is transitory! *Lasting
fortune is transitory.*[2]

'In the hour of death even that fortune which was to have lasted
vanishes and proves to have been a fortuitous happiness' (*nam etsi rara
est fortuitis manendi fides, ultimus tamen vitæ dies mors quædam fortunæ est
etiam manentis*). This important statement is carefully and correctly
rendered by the medieval translators I have looked at (Notker and
Chaucer), and by an otherwise anonymous 'I.T.' of 1609. Notker: *Sîn
énde íst îo dóh téro sélbôn sâldôn énde, níunt folle-gîengín sie ímo únz tára*
(man's end is, for all that, the end of those same fortunes, even though
they had served him to that very hour); Chaucer: Yet natheless the

---

[1] *Deutsche Dichtung des Mittelalters*, p. 89.
[2] *De Consolatione* ii, *Prosa* iii, last sentence.

laste day of a mannes lif is a maner deth to Fortune, and also to thilke
that hath dwelt; Anon. 1609: yet the end of life is a certain death, even
of that fortune which remaineth.[1]

It was clearly not the Fortuna *fragilis, vitrea* (etc.) of the Roman
satirists whom the medieval writers wished to disparage in the context
'religion of the heathen'. Heathen religions are inferior because they
see the highest good in a 'stable fortune', that very 'happiness ever after'
which medieval writers, no less than their modern successors as writers
of fictions, made the final lot of heroes and heroines.

(5) Fortune's Wheel, as the Middle Ages had learnt to see it with the
help of Boethius, had to compete with another wheel image. The
faster this disc or wheel turns or runs, the better. This is called *gelückes
schîbe*, for which see the Middle High German dictionaries under
*schîbe*. (*Schîbe* can, however, also be used of the ideally stable wheel of
Fortune, *der sælden schîbe*.) Having suggested that the allusion might be
to some medieval game (German edition) I now draw attention to the
*velocissimus cursus* of 'prosperity', to which Boethius refers when he
reflects on his happiness hitherto.[2]

(6) There are various interpretations of the *ambigui vultus* of Fortune,
thus designated, but not described by Boethius at the beginning of
book II. She may be shown facing two ways with Janus head, or with
a second, old and ugly face visible only from behind. Sometimes her
face is half black, half white (*velut luna*, according to the *Carmina Burana*).

It is obvious that Fortune would come to be associated with Frau
Welt (Dame World), but this was not brought about by the invention of a mediating paraphrase describing *neither* of the ladies. It is too
simple to say that the 'two sides' of Fortune correspond to a 'near side'
and a 'far side' (= the beyond) of the World. The essential feature about
Dame World is not an abstract mundanity, but a back covered with toads
and reptiles, plates 23b, c. The connection was established by the
discovery (*inventio*) of common traits, which the artists then represent
by attributes of Voluptas and Luxuria.[3]

---

[1] The sources: Notker, Altdeutsche Textbibliothek, XXXIV 86; Chaucer,
*Complete Works*, ed. F. N. Robinson, 2nd ed. (Oxford, 1957) 332b; Loeb Classical
Library, *Boethius*, p. 187.

[2] *De Consolatione* II, Prosa iv.

[3] Walter Veit in a report 'Toposforschung' in *DVJSchr* XXXVII (1963) 120 ff,
offered the mediating formula, which must be rejected as quite inappropriate in
the discussion of medieval images. This contribution added nothing to W.
Stammler's account in *Frau Welt* (1959).

(7) The poets say that 'Fortune is round' (*sinwel*), and history is represented by the Wheel as being cyclical. This roundness may go into the nobler sphere, which in its turn may be *said* to be, but not convincingly represented as being of glass – until the artists use colours naturalistically. In drawings the sphere appears to be of stone. See also p. 222 and Shakespeare quotation, below.

(8) Medieval romance deals at length with the court of King Arthur. His knights are, however, far from being courtiers. They seek their fortune in adventure 'abroad'; they do not compete for place at the court, unless it be Kay (Keie) the Seneschal, or an intruder. The Tristan story, particularly Béroul's, comes nearer to a portrayal of court life. The Fortune of the courtier becomes a central theme in the drama of the Elizabethans and the German Baroque. Lear's words: '... and hear poor rogues / Talk of court news; and we'll talk with them too, / Who loses, and who wins, who's in, who's out', may stand for all quotations.[1] Among many passages in Goethe's *Tasso* which are meant to suggest Renaissance Italy (rather than Weimar), one may count the great debate between Statesman and Poet (Antonio and Tasso) on the relationship of merit and fortune in a world subject not to Providence, but to the will and favour of absolute princes. In discussions of this kind, the image of Fortune may be that of the Renaissance artists after about 1460 – the goddess is blown along on her ball by changing winds, over the waves or through the air. It may, however, still be the medieval Fortune with her Wheel. That is by then a somewhat hoary image, but more serviceable. A further alternative is to let some loquacious character tell all that he knows about Fortune as a 'moral' (Fluellen):

By your patience, ancient Pistol, Fortune is painted plind, with a muffler before her eyes, to signify to you that fortune is plind; and she is painted also with a wheel, to signify to you, which is the moral of it, that she is turning and inconstant, and mutability and variation; and her foot, look you, is fixed upon a spherical stone, which rolls, and rolls and rolls; in good truth the poet makes an excellent description of it: Fortune is an excellent moral.[2]

[1] *Lear* v iii.          [2] *Henry V* iii vi.

## APPENDIX B: ICONOGRAPHICAL SURVEY AND BIBLIOGRAPHICAL GUIDE

In this survey and guide I make use of the article on Fortune which I prepared for the *Reallexikon zur deutschen Kunstgeschichte* fourteen years ago. The main outline of Fortune's story is presented here under more conventional headings, and without reference to the historiographical thesis of the foregoing chapter. Pictures already discussed are occasionally referred to again. Since this appendix is largely bibliographical, I have, where it seemed appropriate, included full titles of monographs and articles in the main statement 'above the line'. Where the treatment is more discursive I have tried to keep the text readable and made use of footnotes.

### (i) General

A. Doren's Warburg lecture of the early twenties is still the best introduction to Fortune in the Middle Ages and the Renaissance.[1] The four studies of H. R. Patch of roughly the same date contain a vast amount of material but are occasionally insecure in matters of interpretation.[2] R. van Marle's account stands out by the adequacy of its illustrations.[3] Doren and van Marle together offer some thirty Fortune pictures, Patch several more, of which those in the medieval volume (1927) are the most valuable. For Germanic and native German tradition, Jacob Grimm's *Deutsche Mythologie* should be consulted under 'Sælde' and related headings.[4]

### (ii) Antiquity

There is a massive article on Fortuna and related figures in Pauly-Wissowa, *Realenzyklopädie*, 13th half-vol. (1910) cols 12–42. W. H. Roscher, *Ausführliches Lexikon der griechischen und römischen Mythologie* (1884–1937) I 1500 ff, is more readily consulted. Harry Erkell, *Augustus, Felicitas, Fortuna, lateinische Wortstudien* (Göteborg, 1952) 131 ff, is

---

[1] A. Doren, 'Fortuna im Mittelalter und in der Renaissance', in *Vorträge der Bibliothek Warburg*, II (1922–3) 71–144.

[2] H. R. Patch, *The Tradition of the Goddess Fortuna in Roman Literature, . . . in Medieval Philosophy and Literature, . . . in Old French Literature* (Smith College Studies, III–IV: 1922–3); *The Goddess Fortuna in Medieval Literature* (Cambridge, Mass., 1927).

[3] R. van Marle, *Iconographie de l'art profane du moyen âge et à la Renaissance*, 2 vols (The Hague, 1931–2) II 181 ff.

[4] 4th ed. in 3 vols (1876; reprints 1930 and Darmstadt 1953).

probably too specialised for medievalists, who will find the following essay more illuminating: Georg Pfligersdorffer, 'Fatum und Fortuna. Ein Versuch zu einem Thema frühkaiserzeitlicher Weltanschauung', in *Jahrbuch der Görres-Gesellschaft*, NS (1961) pp. 1–30.

*Fortuna* was originally an epithet ('happy') which could be assigned to *fors* (fate), itself neutral. A personified Fortuna became a Roman goddess with sanctuaries in Præneste and Antium. In St Augustine's day there were eighteen Fortune temples in Rome (see below).

Roman art did not represent the inconstant and fickle *fortuna meretrix* of the satirists and moralists, but *fortuna stabilis, manens*. The Middle Ages inherited the satirical tradition, partly through Boethius, who, as we have seen, ridicules Fortune's pretensions in the dialogue of book II in *De Consolatione*: partly, however, through the simpler school texts and collections of sayings. Medieval didactic poets inevitably include 'fortune' in their repertory, for instance Spervogel,[1] Walther von der Vogelweide,[2] Freidank,[3] Heinrich Wittenweiler.[4]

The *Fortuna stabilis* or *manens* of Antiquity was rediscovered (dug up) during the Renaissance. She is represented in Roman art as a stately matron, seated or enthroned. The attributes which in a satirical context would refer to her mutability (sphere, wheel, rudder, ship's prow) are here all shown at rest. Other attributes: cornucopia, serpent of Hygæia, dolphin of Neptune, caduceus of Mercury, wheatsheaf of Ceres – all allude to the sphere of activity or interest of the devotee (trade, commerce, agriculture etc.), or to other favours (health, understanding, genius) considered to be in Fortune's gift. During the Empire Fortunes were mass-produced for house altars or for the quarters of the legions in the provinces and overseas. Many are associated with thermal baths (*fortuna balnearia*). Augustine's account in *De Civ. Dei* IV and V is of a completely vulgarised deity, often little better than a talisman.

### (iii) *The Christian Middle Ages*

General. Beside Doren's essay (above) and Patch (1927) there are important older works by Wilhelm Wackernagel[5] and Karl Weinhold.[6] About the word *sælde* in Middle High German there is a dissertation of Th. Scharmann.[7] German literary historians incline to attribute too

---

[1] *Minnesangs Frühling*, 21, 29.    [2] L. 55, 35.
[3] Bezzenberger, 110, 15 ff.    [4] *Ring*, 9317.
[5] 'Das Glücksrad etc', in *Kleine Schriften* I (1872) 241–57.
[6] *Glücksrad und Lebensrad* (1892).
[7] *Studien über die Sælde*, diss. (Würzburg, 1935).

lofty a meaning to *sælde*. Wolfgang Stammler's succinct statement on Fortuna in the Middle Ages[1] is more to the point.

(1) There are several passages in the Bible which remind *us* of fortune *topoi*,[2] but in the Christian view of history, fortune is irrelevant (and what we call the Old Testament view of history is *ex hypothesi* inaccessible to medieval Christendom). It is consequently a serious (i.e. interesting) lapse of which we have evidence in one of the earliest drawings of Fortune and her Wheel (complete with *regno*-formula), see plate 2a. It was drawn on the empty lower half of a page in a Spanish copy of the *Moralia in Hiob* of Gregory the Great. The artist was clearly copying from a source – fairly crudely, what he took to be an apt commentary on the lot of Job.[3] According to Alfred Boeckler, whose opinion was sought on my behalf by the editors of *RDK*, the artist responsible for this drawing (and this solecism) was 'French or English, certainly not Spanish'. Luther's preface to the Book of Job contains (I think, for the first time) a clear and intentional reference to Job's calamities as his 'Unglück'.

The Psalmist's words: *pone illos ut rotam* (see 11, below) led to some wheel pictures in illustrated Psalters, and reflections on wheels in commentaries (including Notker's), about which I hope to write more fully in due course. This is, let us say, 'a different wheel'.

(2) Apart from a later lucky pouch (*Glückssäckel*) and a lucky hat (*Glückshaube*) there seems to be nothing in the fortune lore of Germany which might be of popular origin. (The chap-book hero Fortunatus has a learned name, the hat and the pouch.) German folk-lore knows of no personification of 'luck', despite all the prints and woodcuts and widespread use of a Wheel of Fortune design on the backs of playing-cards from the fifteenth century to the nineteenth.[4] Fortune with her Wheel is to country-folk no doubt a silly picture; that of the naked goddess on her ball is 'rude'. Fortune can mean little to people who live by calendars and almanachs; 'fortune-telling' is also a science.

(3) Fortune's appearance (see p. 209). Compared with the *ambigui vultus* of Boethius, the 'black and white' specification given by Albertus

---

[1] *Aufriss*, III 671 ff.

[2] Eccles. iii 1 ff, viii 14, ix 2; Isaiah xxxviii 12 ff.

[3] M. R. James, *Descriptive Catalogue of the Latin MSS of the John Rylands Library* (Manchester, 1921) MS lat. 83, fo. 214b.

[4] Richard Beitl, *Wörterbuch der deutschen Volkskunde*, 2nd ed. (Stuttgart, 1955) p. 267; *Handwörterbuch des deutschen Aberglaubens*, III 879; H. R. d'Allemagne, *Les Cartes à jouer*, 2 vols (Paris, 1906) passim.

Magnus is unmistakable: *dimidium nigrum et dimidium album propter eufortunium et infortunium.*[1] This established an in any case more or less 'given' relationship with the moon (*fortuna velut luna* according to *Carmina Burana*).[2]

In the Middle Ages Fortune is represented as a Queen, of serious aspect. She has, though rarely, been mistaken by scholars for the Queen of Heaven. Whether she is given crown and sceptre, shown blindfold, with wings etc., depends on whether the artist intends to identify or to describe her. She is often 'gigantic' by comparison with man; *or* man is her 'toy' (the victim of her 'game'). A late Fortune (with wheel) wearing a modern clock as crown is something of a curiosity.[3]

(4) Older representations of the Wheel of Fortune. About a dozen important miniatures of the late twelfth century offer the typical iconography (*large wheel*, kings on the wheel, *regno*-formula). A two-headed Fortune standing on a *small wheel* in a MS from St Emmeran is untypical, and seems to have had little success outside works of art history, see plate 32a.[4] It reminds us of the Fortune of Antiquity, but the iconography is at least in part determined by its context. The typical Fortune would not have provided the required 'end rhyme'; Fortune has to be in size and outline comparable with Potentia and Voluptas, below her in the same picture. The only further example known to me of a medieval Fortune standing on a small wheel decorates the Chansonnier of Jean de Montchenu (*c.* 1460–76).[5]

Two figures only (presumably 'fortune' and 'misfortune') on Fortune's wheel are to be seen in a Schulpforta MS (Lat. 10) of about 1180 (a *De Civ. Dei*).[6] One King on Fortune's wheel is (typically) Alexander, but the context may determine otherwise.[7] When there are

[1] Cf Patch (1927) p. 43 n 4 = *Physicorum*, II ii 11.
[2] ed. Hilka-Schumann (Heidelberg, 1930) i i 35.
[3] *Zimmernscher Totentanz* (*c.* 1560), fo. 58 of MS 123 of the Fürstlich Fürstenbergische Bibliothek, Donaueschingen.
[4] This is clm 13002 of the Staatsbibl., Munich; van Marle, *Iconographic profane*, II, illus. 207, p. 182; Alfred Boeckler, *Regensburg-Prüfeninger Buchmalerei* (1924), illus. 15, text pp. 18 and 90 ff; G. Dehio, *Geschichte der deutschen Kunst* (1919–24) Textband 360, Tafelband 1338.
[5] Jean Porcher, *French Miniatures*, etc., trans. Julian Brown (London, 1960) plate LXXXIII = MS Rothschild 2973, fo. 1 (Bibliothèque Nationale).
[6] Cf p. 190 n 1.
[7] G. Cary, *The Medieval Alexander* (Cambridge, 1956) plate V; see also D. J. A. Ross, *Alexander historiatus*, Warburg Institute Surveys, I (London, 1963) for Alexander in art generally.

six figures on the wheel, as in Villard de Honnecourt's sketch-book[1] or the *Hortus Deliciarum,*[2] the figures above and below are ideally static (in glory, in misery); motion through the other positions is represented by two figures each.

Probably the most famous and most frequently reproduced Wheel of Fortune is in the Benediktbeuren song-book (*Carmina Burana*), where it was added to embellish the section devoted to Fortune poems, see plate 2b. The passage on Fortune in the *Roman de la Rose* is conventional.[3] It often attracts a picture of Fortune with her Wheel, which then reappears in an illustration of the *Roman de la Poire* (*c.* 1270).

The Wheel may appear without a mount, or be mounted in many different ways, more realistically towards the Renaissance and with attention to mechanical proprieties. But schematic (outline) wheels are often encountered. A drive through gears (to obscure the direction of travel) is rare. Fortune turns the wheel with a crank, or she holds two spokes, or the rim, or she spreadeagles herself to be the spokes herself. She normally stands to one side of the wheel, but occasionally swings it from within.[4] Only rarely are the victims in a tread-mill wheel.[5] A Wheel of Fortune without Fortune may indicate a changed viewpoint, but no inferences are possible.

After Dante's account of Fortune in the *Inferno*,[6] Renaissance artists often assigned to her the nobler sphere, which may still be turned with a crank, or rolled, or it may simply be present as part of a composition uniting several attributes of Fortune. In the *Genealogia Deorum* Boccaccio associated Fortune and Lachesis (among the Parcae).[7] Even a homely spinning-wheel may therefore contain an element of learned allusion. This will be the case in Hans Sebald Beham's *Fortuna 1541,* see plate 7b, in which Fortune is identified by (*a*) the stone sphere, (*b*) the spinning-wheel, (*c*) the mannikin, successor to the *regno*-King, (*d*) the ship (mercantile adventure).

The 'formula of four' (*regno, regnavi* etc.): the variant *glorior elatus* (which conceivably alludes to the words of Hannah's prayer, see p. 175)

---

[1] ed. H. R. Hahnloser (Vienna, 1935).
[2] Cf above, p. 190 n. 2 and plate 6a.
[3] ed. E. Langlois, 5 vols. Société des Anciens Textes Français (Paris 1914–24) 3980–90.
[4] Cf Patch (1927) plates VI, VIII (=Honorius Augustodunensis, *PL* CLXXII 1057).
[5] *JWCI* VI (1943) 44 and plate.
[6] VII 67–9.
[7] ed. Vincenzo Romano (Bari, 1951) pp. 13, 27.

is not restricted to the *Hortus Deliciarum*. In the rather more complex Fortune image of a Cambridge manuscript[1] one reads the formula with *glorior elatus, descendo minorificatus,* but the variants *rursus ad astras* (for *rursus ad alta*) and *teror* and *feror* for *premor* and *vehor*.

(5) In a short didactic poem attributed to Gottfried von Strassburg ('das gläserne Glück') fortune is said to be made of glass.[2] This idea is of less frequent occurrence than one would think. Fortune is *sicut glacies* in the *Carmina Burana*,[3] unambiguously *vitrea* however in the *Sentences* of Publius (or Publilius) Syrus,[4] i.e. in the gnomic one-line treatment of a minor school text.

(6) There are several late medieval books (beside Boccaccio's *De casibus* and Petrarch's *De remediis utriusque fortunæ*) which are generously illustrated with Fortune pictures. Apart from, for example, Henry Martin's edition of *Le Boccace de Jean sans Peur,* with several Fortunes among his 150 reproductions of miniatures[5] one will accordingly want to see those illustrating the *Épitre d'Othéa* of Christine de Pisan[6] and the *Estrif de Fortune et de Vertu* (1477) of Martin le Franc.[7]

Fortune with many arms; the Fight of Poverty and Fortune. These motifs were referred to in passing, above, p. 198. They occur in the text of *De Casibus* in book VI i, and book III i respectively. Whereas the former image (Fortune with six to twelve arms) is comprehensible and makes sense even when freely glossed, the second (Fortuna lying defeated on the ground, Poverty triumphing) is comprehensible only as a text illustration. If anything falls flat here, it is not Fortune but Boccaccio's invention.

Late medieval illustrations of Boethius (*De Cons.*) show a series of

---

[1] Cf E. G. Millar, *La miniature anglaise* (Paris, 1926), plate 54b for the picture, more complicated than most by the introduction of Sapientia who contests Fortune's claim that chance governs all events on earth (*mundana casu aguntur omnia*); 'nichil in mundo fit casu'. Millar calls the work in which the miniature occurs an *Imago Mundi*. See M. R. James, *A Descriptive Catalogue of the MSS in the Library of Corpus Christi College, Cambridge* (Cambridge, 1912) I 137 ff, item 66: it is a two vol. miscellany in which the Fortune image occurs on fo 66 as frontispiece to a *Historia de origine Anglorum . . . ab Adam.* Date of the miniature: early thirteenth century.

[2] The text and an essay by Karl Stackmann, 'Gîte und Gelücke', in *Festgabe für Ulrich Pretzel* (Berlin, 1963) pp. 191 ff.

[3] Hilka-Schumann (Heidelberg, 1930) I i 35.

[4] *Publilii Syri Sententiæ,* ed. R. A. H. Bickford-Smith (London, 1895) p. 13, 214 *Fortuna vitrea est: tum cum splendet frangitur.*

[5] Paris, 1911.

[6] ed. J. van den Gheyn (Brussels, 1913).

[7] ed. Alphonse Bayot (Paris, 1928).

apparently realistic scenes (court, court of law, market place), according
to the course taken by the dialogue, the most important scene, however, still being that where Philosophy appears to the author in his
prison.[1]

(7) Misfortune, always more striking in its real occurrence than
fortune, has its own images. For all that they remain less familiar and
are unable, as images, to compete with the in some way cancelled
image of Fortune. We had, above, the example of Tancred's stumbled
horse which had thrown its rider, but more memorable was the later
image in the same work of Fortune's wheel which had run over him
(isolating, as it were, *infimus axe premor*). In the *Jüngerer Titurel* Albrecht
von Scharfenberg risks the figure of Synagogue's stumbled horse:[2] *Ir
pferde sint geswichen | die bein und ist bestruchet, | die sælde von ir geslichen*
('the legs of Synagogue's horse have collapsed under her in a stumbling
fall, and fortune has forsaken her'). Here there is perhaps a reminiscence
of Pharaoh's pursuit – an unhappy image, in that Synagogue is not
customarily visualised as mounted in the first place.[3] In an early
eighteenth century picture-book claiming that the Christian world *also*
has its hieroglyphs, and translating various Bible quotations into a
rebus-cum-emblem picture language, 'misfortune' is rendered: (a) by
the prefix *Un*- before a conventional Fortune (on winged ball, holding
a sail), (b) by a female figure in tunic, holding two snakes in raised right
hand, a spinning-wheel with figures (see above, H. S. Beham) in her
left.[4]

(8) Island Kingdom and Court of (Queen) Fortune. To the outline
statement above (p. 198 n. 3) the following may be added. The fully
developed tradition of an island kingdom is present in the *Anticlaudianus*
of Alanus ab Insulis.[5] It exploits memories of the Fortunate Isles,[6] and
the sail, wind and tide metaphors and similes of fortune lore. Together
these suggest a remote island realm. As for the 'court' Fortune holds,

[1] Cf Emile van Moé, *Un ms. à peintures de Boèce* (Paris, 1937), with parallels from
other MSS.

[2] Stanza 558 in Werner Wolf's edition, DTM 45 (1955).

[3] Exod. xv 1ff, Isaiah lxiii 13. Synagogue riding on an ass (*asinus stultus et laxus*)
as in the *Hortus Deliciarum* (Straub-Keller, plate xxxviii) is scarcely to be associated.

[4] Heinrich von Wiering, *Courieuse oder sogenannte kleine Bilder-Bibel* (Hamburg,
1705) p. 51. The text translated into hieroglyphs is Sirach xi 14: 'Es kommt alles
von Gott, Glück und Unglück', etc. Luther; *bona et mala* in the Vulgate.

[5] Book VII 405 ff, ed. R. Bossuat, Textes Philosophiques du Moyen Age, I
(Paris, 1955).

[6] Cf Isidore, *Etymologies*, XIV vi 8.

Boethius refers in passing to Fortune's household; music, wealth and honour are her 'servants' (*musica vernacula laris nostri; opes, honores . . . famulæ nostræ*).[1]

A full characterisation of Fortune makes some kind of reference to her reversals, and includes an antithetical figure appropriate to the general context: two urns or phials, one upturned: a castle, partly in ruins, two castles, one in ruins;[2] two attendants, one in rags. These are appropriate when the subject is 'realm' or 'court' of Fortune, while for good measure Fortune herself may still be represented as literally 'two-faced', see 10, below.

(9) That Fortune should be 'without heirs'[3] is probably to be interpreted to mean that among her blessings there are gifts and talents which cannot be left like worldly goods to any successor. That is a theme in Walther von der Vogelweide's elegy for Reinmar: 'Alas that wisdom, youth, beauty and virtue cannot be bequeathed' (*Owê daz wîsheit unde jugent, / des mannes schœne noch sîn tugent / niht erben sol*); the poet's skill also perishes with him.

(10) At the end of the fifteenth century Dame Adventure (Frau Aventiure) appears in art: with black-and-white face, like Fortune: enthroned, turning what was Fortune's wheel. *Heure* and *Malheure* (*Gheluck* and *Ongheluck*) appear as heralds at either side of her throne; *Malheure* is in rags and tatters; for instance in French and Dutch illustrations of the *Danse aux Aveugles* of Pierre Machault. The 'aveugles' are Death, Love and Fortune.[4]

(11) Other Wheels with Figures. Not every wheel with figures is a Wheel of Fortune. The figures in the sectors or around the rim may represent the Ages of Man, the order of Nature, the Prophets, the Disciples, the Evangelists; add the Zodiac and astrolabes. The monumental Wheel Windows of medieval churches and cathedrals (Amiens, Beauvais, Basel etc.)[5] probably soon came to be recognised as Wheels of Fortune, but the earliest, Beauvais (about 1160), clearly had originally another subject. The figures are now badly weathered. The one at the top is clearly *not* Fortune, but probably a personification of the 'justice of the Lord' or an avenging angel. The biblical text underlying

---

[1] *De Consolatione*, book II, *Prosa* i and ii, *Metrum* ii.

[2] Fuller treatment of the 'realm', with reproductions from medieval miniatures in Patch (1927) ch. 4.

[3] Heinrich von dem Türlin, *Die Krône*, l. 299.

[4] Paul de Keyser, *Gentsche Bijdrage*, I (1934) 34 ff.

[5] Cf van Marle, illus. 217 ff.

this and some other wheel images may be *pone illos ut rotam*.[1] This should not be taken to mean that the Church rejected the profane image of the Wheel of Fortune. Later ecclesiastical art treats the subject even in the interior of churches.[2] There are also various Fortune frescoes in churches in England and Scandinavia.

### (iv) *From the Middle Ages to the Renaissance*

The transition to the Renaissance is characterised in German art by a freer treatment of the traditional *medieval* Fortune motifs, and by a characteristic modernity of draughtsmanship.[3] A light-hearted variant on the Wheel of Fortune is Dürer's 'Glückwunsch' for Melchior Pfinzing (L 51), in which Fortune sits on the top of the Wheel while atelier assistants with their various instruments travel round. There is no suggestion of misfortune for any, but rather of a merry-go-round for all.

### (v) *Renaissance*

(1) From about 1460 there are two possible iconographies in Italian art. There is an antique Fortune – a Roman matron with rudder and cornucopia, usually preferred for medaillions, which may have a Christian motto, for instance *deo duce, virtute comite, fortuna favente*; and indeed God's head in a blazing sun duly subordinates 'favouring Fortune' to God's guidance. Then there is a neo-mythical Fortune, a young, naked woman, initially distinguishable as Fortune solely by her attributes, but for all that, expressive of men's ideas on fortune. She is clearly intended to be an enigmatic figure. This Fortune stands on a sphere (ball). She holds, according to her physique, anything from a merest wisp of voile to a substantial sail with beam and rigging. She has often been confused with Occasio on the one hand, or Venus Marina on the other.[4] With or without wings she sails on her globe across the sea,

---

[1] Psalm lxxxii 14. The Beauvais window in Joan Evans, *Art in Medieval France* (O.U.P. 1948), plate 115.

[2] See the Siena mosaic reproduced in van Marle, illus. 213.

[3] On Georg Pencz, see p. 197, above, and van Marle, illus. 225; compare also Hans Weiditz' *Fortuna* for Ulrich von Hutten's *Ad Caesarem Maximilianum* (1519), Doren, illus. 12. The outstanding examples, however, in the work of the so-called 'Petrarca-Meister', see p. 197.

[4] Cf p. 120.

or over the land, or through the air, driven by the winds. She some-times blows energetically into her own sail (Peter Vischer the Younger). Or her craft is a *dolphin* or a *horizontal wheel* (=whirlpool). The texts (if any) accompanying the Renaissance Fortune are of epigrammatic brevity. This new image is, however, difficult to bring to bear on any scene representing human affairs. This is probably one reason for the long persistence of the medieval image with the pamphleteers, and in the rhetorical apostrophes of Fortune in Renaissance and later authors.

Hans Sachs would seem to have been familiar with practically every Fortune iconography we have mentioned so far,[1] similarly Shakespeare, on the evidence of Fluellen's speech, p. 210 above.

The 'congratulation' ('Glückwunsch'). A picture of about 1466 which has attracted more attention than it deserves, represents the 'happy voyage' of two newly-weds, and refers through the ship to the family business.[2]

(2) The great masters of the Italian Renaissance seem not to have chosen Fortune as a subject. The best early Italian work is an engraving of Nicoletto da Modena of about 1500, a *Fortuna redux*: Fortune on her ball has drifted to the shore where a herma indicates that she may be made fast. This is presumably the fortune of the merchant venturer, see plate 5a.[3] An allegorical picture of Andrea Mantegna (d. 1506)[4] represents Fortune as a grossly fat naked woman, while Giovanni Bellini (d. 1516) shows her as a blindfold harpy, standing on two balls, holding two urns, *La cieca Fortuna*.[5] It may be that the latter image contributes to the grotesque monster appearing in the title-page of Grimmelshausen's *Simplicissimus* (1669), a work in which Fortune provides not only the theme but the structural principle.

Apart from the greeting for Melchior Pfinzing (above), Albrecht Dürer drew a Fortune known as *Das kleine Glück*, and of course the *Nemesis* of 1503. The two latter are a German 'translation' of the image created by the Italian Renaissance. Dürer's immediate successors for a time follow his example in making Fortune a Northern slattern, but then prefer the Italian alternative (if Fortune is to tempt, she should be

---

[1] Cf Helene Henze, *Die Allegorie bei Hans Sachs*, Hermea XI (Halle, 1912).
[2] See Doren, illus. 14.
[3] It must be left to the art historians to work out the complex relationship between Dürer and Nicoletto in the treatment of Fortune and the use of Fortune models in other compositions.
[4] Paul Kristeller, Andrea Mantegna (Berlin-Leipzig, 1902), illus. 131-2.
[5] *Allegoria*, Gallerie dell' Accademia, Venice.

seductive). Urs Graf, however, shows Fortune as a soldier's whore;[1] his debt to Dürer's Fortunes includes the use of a goblet as the symbol of sensuality or intemperance.

### (vi)  Miscellaneous Addenda

A long list could be made of non-typical Fortune iconographies, and of verbal traditions concerning Fortune for which an exact pictorial counterpart will not readily be found (and *vice versa*). There are also contaminations of various kinds. Here there will be room only for a few indications. The chariot assigned to Fortune may in origin be the chariot of the festive procession: in Goethe's *Harzreise im Winter* (stanza 4), it perhaps belongs to her as of right, though forming part of the Prince's procession 'along a well prepared route'. In a ranting speech of Egmont, and in the Sturm und Drang poem *An Schwager Kronos* the chariot in full career seems to me to belong, in context, as much to Fortune as to Phaeton. Various commonplaces concerning fortune (and misfortune) generate an image of Fortune on horseback, whereby a loose association with 'vaulting ambition' is established. On the other hand the idea of a special fortune of horsemen (*fortuna equestris*) had been familiar since Antiquity. Holbein drew an equestrian Fortune who lays low her victims with arrows fired from the bow.[2] On the other hand again, the 'slings and arrows' of an outrageous fortune are relatively rare in pictorial art. It is an idea that will have occurred to many, that Fortune's gifts may be shaken from a tree, but I know of no pictorial representation of this before Cartari's *Imagini* (Venice, 1571) p. 571. This, and a number of other images I have encountered in early iconographical handbooks, have made me possibly excessively suspicious of all compilers – Cesare Ripa (*Iconologia* 1593), Gregor Reisch (*Margarita Philosophica*, Basel, 1508), M. de Prez (*Dictionnaire Iconographique*, Paris, 1756). They seem to me to offer a good many pictures which may be last-minute innovations, pictures the artists should have drawn, witty ideas they should have had.

*Final notes*: (a) I have not endeavoured to deal with Fortune associated, whether through words or through images, with various *games* (chess and games of chance), nor with Fortune as a figure in complex allegories or compositions (for instance in a *Tabula Cebetis*). (b) Readers interested in my final quotation from Abraham a Santa Clara on

[1] Gesamt-Katalog 334 = Inselbücherei 664, illus. 2.
[2] Woltmann, II 93.

Belisarius,[1] will want to see a Fortune picture of 1606 which Gertrude Bing discussed. Fortune herself is shown seated on her stone sphere by the wayside, where passers-by mock her.[2] In Ludvig Holberg's *Jeppe på Bjerget* (iv, 1) Jeppe sits in his misery on a muck-heap. The stage directions say that he turns his broad-brimmed hat in his hands as he laments his lot (cf. Belisarius). (c) Though I have often been pressed to extend my survey to include the Fortune theme in music, I do not feel competent: I mention merely that the *motette* is the form apparently favoured.

[1] Cf pp. 204 f.
[2] *JWI* i (1937–8) 304 ff and plate 46.

# IV

## THE CRUCIFIXION

MANY medievalists before me have had to ask the question with which this chapter begins, namely: how could the one word which we find in the Vulgate, *crucifixerunt* ('they crucified him') give rise to the pages of description of the Crucifixion which we find in medieval devotional writings, and to the gruesomely 'realistic' representations of late medieval art: 'how they nailed our Lord to the Cross'? Moreover, how we are to explain the remarkable *agreement* between the various texts, and again between texts and pictures, when the ritual which they describe or depict contains so many details which we find it hard to account for at all? Not the least of the difficulties is that our various medieval disciplines introduce us to the problem at a point where whatever development there has been is virtually complete, or they allow us to see only the concluding stages where the representations become 'still more realistic'. Without all too great difficulty we contrive to find our way back to the point where there is evidence of a more stable textual tradition, which we associate with a somewhat shadowy corpus of thirteenth-century works, or chapters in works, attributed to St Anselm, St Bernard, St Bonaventura. Most investigators are content to leave it at that.

What is now urgently needed is a clear statement of the sources of this 'common lore' of about 1200–50 concerning the Crucifixion. Fully half of this chapter is devoted to this one problem. It is, however, useless simply to name the sources. We have to learn or re-learn how to read and understand them when they are put before us. We shall on the other hand be successful in our enquiry, I think, if we keep to strictly 'philological' methods. This is, if we keep to *texts*, and read and understand them as they were understood in the Middle Ages. The modern reader must be set aside for the time being. We must let words again mean what they *meant*.

With the modern reader we must set aside also anything which he claims to know about the great changes which took place in the temper and tone of religious life in the twelfth and thirteenth centuries in

Western Europe. This knowledge is not wrong. We must none the less think without it for a time, lest we find ourselves involved in circular argument, seeking first an explanation of the art of the Gothic in a *sentiment religieux*, and then finding the same sentiment reflected in art. For the duration of this chapter, therefore, we know nothing at all about the 'spirit of the Gothic'. As for a 'theology of suffering' (*Leidenstheologie*), we have not heard of the idea. Nor do we know anything about 'late medieval realism'. We shall first of all isolate the words used down to about 1500 to describe the Crucifixion – the verbal tradition, and endeavour to solve the problems which it raises. Once we have worked out the origins of that tradition, we may, if we still wish to, draw again on our knowledge of religious and devotional life in the Middle Ages, and write appropriate commentaries on individual texts and pictures from the standpoint of whatever kind of history it is we favour: history of dogma, of piety, of the human spirit.

In the same categorical strain it must also be said that it is premature to speak of 'apocryphal' or 'legendary' elements in the Crucifixion as medieval authors described it or painters depicted it. We shall find that the common lore of which we have been speaking enjoyed an *authority* during the latter part of the Middle Ages which was never accorded either to the principal books of the Apocryphal New Testament or to legends. Medieval writers and artists 'knew' simply that everything of which they wrote, or which they portrayed, happened exactly thus, yet I should surmise that by the period 1200–1300 there was not an author or an artist, and scarcely a theologian anywhere in Europe who could have given a full and adequate account of the sources of this knowledge. There was no history of the branch of scholarship of which this assured knowledge represented the findings. It was all the more carefully transmitted for that reason.

Most readers will be startled to hear that the gulf between the single word of the Evangelists and late medieval descriptions of the Crucifixion can be bridged; particularly any reader who for the moment had forgotten that the Gospels offer indeed only one word in the context of sacred *story*. The Apostles themselves, however, and the Fathers of the early Church had from the outset provided *crucifixerunt* with explanatory paraphrases and figurative synonyms in considerable number. We shall soon have to look at some of them in detail. And by the date 'around 1200' which has already established itself in our minds as a turning point, when a few important *narratives* of the Passion begin to emerge, the theologians had written whole libraries of biblical commentary. (One needs only to recall the two-hundred-and-nineteen volumes of Migne's *Patrologia Latina* which cover roughly the period up to around 1200.) Once we are aware of the general structure of patristic scholarship, and when certain established conventions of interpretation of the biblical word have become familiar, we shall begin to see *which* among the paraphrases of *crucifixerunt*, and which glosses on it, impose order on the accumulated Crucifixion lore. We shall indeed be able to bridge the gulf of which we spoke a moment ago. Or, more accurately, we shall rediscover the bridge; it was always there. It is not, perhaps, a structure to inspire immediate confidence in the modern reader. It is at least two (some say four, or three) stories high. By 1200 it was considerably weakened by excessive use and certainly rotten in parts. Luther declared the whole thing a menace, but occasionally (not only in his early days) nipped across, armed with a hook to catch Leviathan. Medievalists have to be prepared to observe the proper use of this bridge, with the same assiduity as they must discount the findings of nineteenth-century biblical scholarship. With the Middle Ages they must regard the Old Testament as a Christian work, believe that one Isaiah only wrote the whole of *Isaiah*, that David wrote the Psalms. There is no such thing as *Ur-Mark*, there is no Synoptic problem, and so on.[1] The medievalist must be able to make his knowledge contemporary with the works he studies.

In this chapter our concern will be with medieval textual (and pictorial) tradition concerning the Crucifixion, which we shall seek to explain and justify in purely medieval and Christian terms. This means, *inter alia*, as the references to the bridge foreshadowed, that we shall take medieval belief in the multiple sense of the scriptural word

---

[1] Recently a valuable monograph appeared with the title, *Die Illustration der Luther-Bibel 1522–1700*, by Ph. Schmidt (Basel, 1962) with 400 illustrations. Everything the author writes about the artists and publishers involved in editions of Luther's Bible up to 1700 is most scholarly and highly interesting: on Lucas Cranach the Elder's illustrations of the *Neues Testament deutsch* (1522), on the use of copies of old woodcuts from Koberger for the *Neues Testament Adam Petri zum dritten Male* (1525), and a good deal else. What he writes about the 'typology' of some of the older pictorial sources utilised, particularly about the *Biblia Pauperum*, is, on the other hand, first of all Lutheran. 'Catholicism could think of nothing better to do with the Old Testament', he says, in expressing his distaste for typology (p. 34). For my part I find it natural that works of the fourteenth and fifteenth centuries should see the Old Testament as it was generally seen before the Reformation, and that they should accord no particular priority to the Gospel of St Mark.

seriously. Our handbooks of medieval studies never tire of telling us about the 'literal or historical', 'allegorical' and other senses in which the biblical word was understood in the Christian Middle Ages, and they generally offer an illustration or two, almost inevitably the four senses of the word 'Jerusalem'. Most writers on medieval matters leave it at that: at a statement and a brief illustration of the doctrine, which they seem for the rest to find quaint. Failure to take the doctrine of multiple interpretation properly into account, coupled with modern prejudice in favour of the literal and historical sense of the biblical word is precisely the reason why we have hitherto not been able to recognise the true origins and the development of Crucifixion iconography.[1]

My main task in this chapter is to expound a thesis and communicate findings. This will in itself prove difficult enough. Most of the difficulties are inherent in the subject. I trust I have not added to them by serious inadequacies of exposition. It is, however, possible that some readers will be troubled by my insistence that we must follow strictly

---

[1] There have been many attempts in the past to explain the iconography of the Crucifixion: in the handbooks of the theologians, of ancient historians and art historians, and in the prefaces to editions of medieval texts. Because the material to be considered in any comprehensive enquiry is so vast, the explanations offered have generally been brief – a few sentences, a paragraph, a few columns in an encyclopaedia of Christian archaeology. Most writers are content to make simple assertions of what they think to be the likely explanation.

In the following pages I offer a thesis which I hope will be found acceptable. It was first the subject of my private discussions and an exchange of essays with the late T. W. Manson in Manchester in 1946–7. For his timely rectification of some of my notions concerning the composition of the New Testament (particularly my bolder inferences from the Evangelists' use of the 'argument from prophecy') I shall always be grateful. The thesis was then submitted in a paper and in a lecture delivered in Britain and in Germany in 1952 (Sheffield, Manchester, Kiel, Hamburg, Göttingen, Münster), finally in an article 'Das gotische Christusbild', in *Euphorion*, XLVII (1953) 16–37. The article is frequently quoted, and I have noted with gratification that a number of scholars have accepted its main thesis and some incidental findings of relevance to their own studies. For the rest, I am asked when the book is likely to be ready which I stated to be 'in preparation'. All I can say is that if ever the book is finished it will, in the main, be a compendious documentation of the thesis argued in the article of 1953 and now in this chapter. The thesis has stood the test of twenty years of my own fairly sustained reading. What has encouraged me as much as generous expressions of agreement is to know that Professor Kurt Ruh of Würzburg, starting originally like me from a single late medieval Passion tract, had arrived at methods of *text* interpretation similar to mine. I shall, however, not endeavour to draw either his tract or any of 'mine' into the main exposition, for they all pale into insignificance beside the works which we shall finally find to be responsible for the Christian tradition of the Crucifixion.

philological method. Here I can make no concessions. What texts said in their time they must be accepted for the purposes of this investigation as saying. Finally, no findings resulting from a methodical enquiry may be rejected merely because they are unwelcome.

## 1. HISTORICAL PICTURE AND HIERATIC IMAGE

The subject of this chapter is the iconography of the Crucifixion, not (or not primarily) of the Crucified, that is *Christi crucifixio*, not *Christus crucifixus*. The Evangelists say that Christ was crucified, or, more accurately, that 'they crucified him'. That is the report of something which happened on Golgotha, an event. The artists of the later Middle Ages depicted the event on countless occasions. Meanwhile we call such a picture, conventionally, a *historical* picture. The much more familiar image of the Crucified on the Cross is a hieratic or devotional image in which the crucifixion (a 'fastening to a cross') has already been completed and is not represented as an event. We must naturally allow that any pious Christian may, according to the nature of his piety, make the historical picture the subject of his devotions. The Stations of the Cross (which we shall discuss in a moment) provide perhaps the principal example of historical images (pictures, reliefs, statuary) associated with devotions. Or, conversely, he may contemplate the devotional image of the Crucified and in his meditations recall the events which had gone before. Some sacred pictures contain only an element of event or action: Christ commending Mary to John, or speaking any of the 'Seven Words'; these are generally felt to be devotional images. Both the Crucifixion and the Crucified have, as images, their textual correspondences in the words of the New Testament understood in their primary 'literal or historical' sense, namely *crucifixerunt* and *consummatum est*. It was perhaps necessary to say that even *consummatum est* has a first, literal and historical meaning which is not in any way cancelled or reduced in its historical content by 'higher' interpretations.

Readers will have sensed, from their reading of this chapter so far, that it will be quite impossible for us to proceed chronologically with this account of Christian tradition concerning the Crucifixion. There is, for instance, no correlation between early and late periods on the one hand, and any preference for the lower (historical) or higher (e.g. allegorical) interpretation of the biblical word on the other. Any such preference which we may think we have noted in a given period leaves out of account all the preaching and teaching of which we have no records. There will have been a constant interplay of different kinds and levels of exegesis throughout the whole period from about 400 to 1500. This long chapter will therefore have its own logic and organisation, which I shall not waste time in explaining. It will simply emerge as we proceed. As for the many digressions, we shall make them whenever a matter we have chanced upon, or have been dealing with for some time, can be more or less finally disposed of. Towards the end of the chapter we shall then be relatively unencumbered and able to concentrate attention on a somewhat unexpected series of conclusions. And now, to return to the exposition: for a time we shall be considering the biblical word understood in its first 'historical' sense, and dealing with questions which can be answered without any elaborate commentary. We had already mentioned as perhaps the most familiar 'historical' treatment of the Crucifixion in Christian art the so-called Stations of the Cross. Let us deal now with the Stations.

### The Stations of the Cross

Many a reader will have asked what the origin and the *authority* of the Stations of the Cross may be. The answer which the Church holds in readiness for questions relating to this or analogous expressions of popular piety is: the Stations are 'not canonical'. Of the three falls on the Way of the Cross, of the Sudary of St Veronica and of Mary's swooning the New Testament says, as one knows, nothing; but in the Catholic world still, 'the pious may believe' (that these things happened, etc.). In the Middle Ages these and other accretions to the Gospel story were glossed with the words *pie creditur* or *fertur*. The Church distinguished between *vera* (canonical) and *credenda*; and *non verum sed credendum* is a medieval equivalent of 'apocryphal'. When the Pope a few years ago visited the Holy Places, one of his most exacting tasks in the trying circumstances as they were reported was to say nothing concerning the Stations which went beyond *pie creditur*. No Catholic, Protestant or agnostic heard him say, or read him to have said, more than this.

On the Stations of the Cross, of which there is evidence in Western

Europe from the later Middle Ages, one will find a certain amount of information (on the number and the identity of the various Stations) in any reference work. We need rather more than this for our purposes. There is a series of eight articles in Didron's *Annales Archéologiques*[1] on the Stations, in which a useful piece of initial guidance is given for an understanding of this tradition: 'L'église, qui procède toujours avec sagesse et maturité, s'occupa fort tard du chemin de la croix'.[2] Finally ('fort tard') the Church resolved to bring this popular commemorative devotion, so much more readily followed than the Liturgy, under its supervision, to regularise it, and to ensure that pictorial representation remained within a generously determined norm in respect of workmanship and style. As for the authority of the main Stations, there was little it could do, and just how tenuous the authority may be, has in any systematic account discreetly to be revealed. The swooning of Mary, for instance, 'remonterait au moins à l'époque constantinienne et laisserait encore de nos jours, dans une pierre que l'on vénère un témoignage de sa véracité'.[3]

The Crucifixion itself, one should note, is often represented as being carried out with the cross on the ground (*jacente cruce*). For this the authority is of an entirely different order, and is patristic. We shall discuss it in considerable detail, below.

The historical origins of the Stations are fairly clear. The present-day devotion of the Stations is the authorised form of a tradition which was already being worked out in earliest Christian centuries in the Holy Land itself. It began as a mainly *verbal* tradition associated with the Holy Places; it finished as a mainly *pictorial* tradition. The former was evolved by the custodians of the Holy Places and the guides to them. Of this we have evidence in the first reports of pilgrims.

The most notable of these reports is the *Itinerarium Egeriæ* (or *Peregrinatio Ætheriæ*) of about 400.[4] It is at the same time a most important source for the early history of the Liturgy, for it tells us of forms of the office which were already in use at the various sacred sites. What distinguishes the emergent tradition of the Stations from the commemorative ritual of the Liturgy is preoccupation with places, distances, incidents, things, and a concern to complete the authentic Way of the Cross as a devotion. What was told at the various points on the Way incorporated the relevant details of the New Testament

[1] xx–xxiv (1860–64).    [2] xx 320.    [3] xxiii 109.
[4] ed. Otto Prinz, 5th ed., *Sammlung vulgärlateinischer Texte* (Heidelberg, 1950).

account, but it also drew on the apocryphal Infancy Gospels (while these themselves derive at least some details of setting from traditions associated with the sacred sites). Some features, for instance that there were three Falls, have no scriptural foundation, but were no doubt always part of the tradition of the Stations. When this came to be transplanted to Europe, the scenes and the episodes had to be visualised. Hence the strength of the pictorial tradition. The verbal tradition (mainly meditations for the Stations) shows a preoccupation with the number of paces separating the episodes on the Way (the *Meditations* of St Bonaventura are meticulous in this), and sculptured reliefs devoted to the Stations may be sited on buildings in such a way that the 'original' distances are maintained.

Meanwhile there were various 'vestiges' of the Way of the Cross (and the Passion) which were unique to the original sites. Some of these will always have seemed trivial, and may have been an embarrassment when early enthusiasm had led to the building of special sanctuaries. Great importance attaches, however, to one relic: the *marble column* of the Flagellation which from the days of St Jerome was virtually 'gospel'. In Christian art it can no more be omitted than the animals in a Nativity. It has no scriptural justification. It had no other authority than that Jerome vouched for its identity as the 'column to which our Lord was bound', and that it could be shown as a relic.


## 2. *HISTORIA* AND HISTORY

We come now to what appears to be the most urgent question for many modern readers. They believe they have a simple, straightforward question to ask about the Crucifixion, and they want a straightforward answer. I hope that in this chapter they will find their answer. It will not be straightforward. The heading of this section indicates, moreover, that the question and answer *cannot* be entirely 'in line'. And now, a fresh start.

Anyone who has read even one account of Christian art knows that the devotional image of the Crucified on the Cross is much older (it is some eight hundred years older) than any unambiguously 'historical' picture showing 'what happened', whether in the latter the cross is represented as lying flat on the ground, or already erected and fixed in position. He probably knows too that before the fifth century the

Christians hesitated to represent Christ on the Cross pictorially at all. The Cross itself, on the other hand, or rather a cross was a symbol sacred to Christians from apostolic times. And so in the mind of every observer there arises at some time the question: was Christ 'in fact' crucified as Christian art testifies? This apparently so modern question has been asked by Christians for about a thousand years or longer! The answers which have been given since the beginning of the modern era have almost without exception been wrong. Either completely wrong (and often perversely wrong-headed), or right and wrong at the same time; for if an *answer* is to be completely right, it must be the answer to a correctly formulated question. Early Christians and the Christian Middle Ages asked the right question (no doubt together with wrong questions), and heard it answered in accordance with Christian knowledge. They accepted the answer. Namely, Christ was 'in truth' crucified in the manner which the authoritative texts of the Church describe, and which ecclesiastical art then represents. These – the texts and the pictures – are our subject, and we must concentrate our questions on them. These are our 'facts'. Our questions, even today, must be properly formulated questions.

The Crucifixion of Christian art is not a Roman or a Jewish crucifixion but 'Christian and biblical'. It is *sui generis*. It is 'biblically true', and consequently not susceptible of direct annotation in the light of what in ordinary parlance we call 'historical sources'. At this point some readers may want to stop reading. Others may think, as I do, that the last statement is the most important one in this book. Any comparison of the testimony of Christian art with sources *other than* the Bible, the works of the Fathers of the Church, the Liturgy and perhaps hymns, will always be 'interesting'. It can never lead to any other conclusion than that if malefactors were crucified thus or thus in Antiquity, Christ was believed to have been crucified differently. The correct question to ask is therefore not '*how* did the Romans' or '*how* did the Jews' execute (perhaps crucify) those whom they had condemned to die by a shameful death? but '*why* did Christianity believe the Crucifixion of Christ to have been carried out in the manner stated by the theologians (and the poets after them), and represented by the artists in their sculptures, carvings, paintings, drawings?' The answer to this latter question cannot be more clearly formulated than in the apparently paradoxical assertion that the 'historical picture' (see above) of Christian tradition is *not* in the customary sense of the term historical.

Hence the title of this section 'historia and history'. (From each of these nouns we need a derived adjective. I shall use 'historical' in inverted commas when I intend it as the adjective of historia.) That is to say that the academic historians cannot give us any help in explaining the Crucifixion because their sources relate to crucifixion. One of the first modern historians, Justus Lipsius, proved – involuntarily – that the academic historian is the last person we should consult. He himself showed only an imperfect understanding of the nature of textual evidence. Any reader who possesses a copy of the New Testament with historical notes will perhaps at this point care to look up John xix 17, bajulans sibi crucem. If the note includes any remarks on Roman or Jewish crucifixions – particularly if the information is attributed to 'Lipsius' – it should be provided with a cautionary interrogation mark and read critically. It is factually correct, but it is irrelevant. It belongs to a different system of history.

If we are to explain the Christian 'historical' picture, we must keep to the facts of Christian tradition, which are to be found first of all in texts. We shall be considering quotations from Christian works up to about 1500. We shall be asking two questions. What was written in the various centuries about the Crucifixion? – and where do we find the statements? It is not a matter of indifference to know in what kind of Christian works the statements are made. There is a hierarchy or order of statements. We need to know whether the words we read are the 'word of God' uttered by a prophet of the Old Testament, or the words of Christ himself, or the words of the Evangelists who wrote their eyewitness accounts under divine inspiration. They may, however, be words of interpretation (of the Old Testament, of the New Testament) offered by the early theologians known as the Fathers of the Church. They may be words of the divine service (Liturgy). They may be the words of a hymn of the early Church, or words spoken in a sermon by a preacher whom the Church subsequently canonised. They may be the words of a visionary (for instance St Bridget), or finally (in the fifteenth century) the assertions of some enthusiast speaking on his own behalf or for some sect, and impatient of the reticence of the Church and the preaching orders. We are, in short, concerned to know the authority of the statements we may find in the vast volume of writings which constitute Christian tradition down to about 1500. As for 'authority' in any strict sense, a sharp line has to be drawn, I think, between Liturgy and hymn, with rapidly diminishing credence for the words of saints, visionaries and enthusiasts. By comparison with the authority of the Bible, of patristic exegesis and the Liturgy (on the *Crucifixion*), the statements to be found in the Jewish, Greek and Roman historians (on *crucifixions*) have no evidential value – *except* for the crucifixion of the *two thieves* on Golgotha. The Jewish, Greek and Roman sources (even though 'contemporary' with the New Testament) are otherwise of concern only to the historian, whose business is with the facts of the ancient world. The facts with which we are concerned are Christian tradition as it is. This is accessible to us through texts and pictures which are there, confronting us. These are facts which the historian cannot explain; he lacks the relevant training. The modern theologian is in difficulties also, since, whether Catholic or Protestant, he has forgotten beyond recall, or is reluctant to recall, the theology (Christology) which is contemporary with the pictures and the texts.

The same two questions, suitably modified, have also to be asked with reference to *pictures* of the Crucifixion. We must ask *where* Crucifixions are to be found. If we disregard for a moment the image of the Crucified behind the altar (the 'absolute' devotional image) it seems to me that the art historians have hitherto not given much attention to the context of the Crucifixions they reproduce in their handbooks: whether they come from illustrated Psalters or from illustrated Evangeliaries (Gospel Books). A vast number are from Psalters. I do not for a moment suggest that medieval artists drew and painted a different Crucifixion for each of these, or that the devotional image was appropriate in the one case, the 'historical' one in the other. But if, in the whole of the pre-Reformation period, the Church said with one voice that the Passion Psalms *described* the Crucified (and his Passion), while the Evangelists *confirmed* the fulfilment of Old Testament prophecy (in one word – *crucifixerunt*), then the Crucifixion picture is logically (historically too, I think) in the first place a Psalm illustration. By the time the reader has reached the end of this chapter he will find this assertion in no way startling. Christian art in fact evolved many of its images in the context of Old Testament *prophecy* of New Testament events.

Be that as it may, the really momentous developments came around 1200. First of all in devotional literature, then about 150 to 200 years later in art we have the beginnings of Gothic, which is characterised by the translation or transposition into 'epic' terms of what had long been known in detail concerning the Crucifixion. It became the subject-matter of *narrative*, later of narrative art, finally of *dramatic* art, and the whole 'story' could be re-enacted by the players of Passion plays. In other words a body of traditional 'historical' knowledge received, as it were, a long-delayed *imprimatur*. For this we have no doubt to invoke those changes in religious feeling which hitherto we were inclined to make responsible for the *content* of the texts and the pictures themselves. The time was ripe for the release, both of the knowledge and of the crowding formulæ which were its vehicle. The faithful recited them endlessly, first the clergy and the orders, in Latin to one another, then in the vernaculars to wider congregations. Sacrosanct formulations which had once given expression to the hope that the hands and arms of the Saviour stretched on the Cross would 'draw all things' unto him were precipitously transposed into the 'historical' mode, and understood to mean that at the Crucifixion the enemies of Christ dragged at his hands, arms and legs until 'they might count all his bones' as had been prophesied. This development in the sense in which the biblical word could be, and henceforward was understood, I have just called for convenience a transposition. We shall soon have to look at this development much more closely and define it more precisely. It is a translation of ancient prophecies, metaphors, similes, symbols of the Crucifixion into 'history'. But before we go on to any more detailed examination of these developments, we need to hear more about the Crucifixion in the art of the Middle Ages. Some of the things I have been saying, particularly about 'history' and history, will be relevant.

## 3. THE 'REALITY' OF CHRISTIAN ART

My next starting-point is a passage in the *History of our Lord as exemplified in Works of Art*, by Anna Brownwell Jameson[1] – the best treatment of the subject there has been. It is a source of special gratification to be able to quote from this work, now over a hundred years old, with the same assurance as it was recommended to me about fifteen years ago by a member of the Warburg Institute. (I already knew it, but had not wanted to admit that I had been using anything so out-dated.) There is not the space here for quotations long enough to convey a proper impression – of the fine restraint and sensitivity with which Mrs

---

[1] 2 vols (London, 1864). By the same author, *Legends of the Madonna* (1852, reprinted 1903), *Legends of the Monastic Orders* (1850), etc.

Jameson introduces her readers to this 'most painful of all chapters' in the story she has to tell. We must go straight to the passage we need. Here are a few lines in which Mrs Jameson refers first to crucifixion as a form of capital punishment in the ancient world, and then characterises the Crucifixion of Christ as it is represented in Christian art, asking what may be the 'reality' of this latter scene.

Two causes prevent our viewing [this event], even if we would, through the medium of common and absolute reality: the reverence of ages . . . and the disuse of ages. Art furnishes a third cause; for she herself refuses to bring this scene within the conditions of reality.[1]

This statement as I have abridged it is perhaps too subtle for us today. In more vulgar modern idiom this means that we 'cannot visualise exactly what in fact happened' – for two reasons. First, reverence: we are reluctant to relate so sacred an event to what knowledge we have of practices in the ancient world. Secondly, crucifixion as a capital punishment belongs to the remote past. It was abandoned, says Mrs Jameson, long ago, and we do not care to think of it. In other words, Mrs Jameson would have given only limited assent to the views of those modern scholars who recognise in the scene a 'realism' which they think characteristic of the Gothic. To her it is all 'more or less a convention'. With a sure instinct she suspects behind the apparently so realistic depiction of a gruesome ritual a reality strange, not only to us, but to the medieval (and later) artists themselves. For all that, Mrs Jameson was keenly observant of details.

Doubts about the reality of the artists' Crucifixion scenes tend nowadays to be more crudely expressed, as doubts concerning physiological and mechanical proprieties: whether it 'could have happened' or 'could have been done' thus. One can (with distaste) read modern investigations of connoisseurs of Christian art who happen to have physicians or an anatomist among their friends and advisers. They are always eager to point to the 'footrest', which, though not attested in historical sources, 'will have been necessary'.[2] Such scholars are however still looking for that reality which, as Mrs Jameson recognised, art refuses to depict. Even so, they are less at fault in their method than those who seek to elucidate the details of the Crucifixion of Christian

---

[1] II 137 in the 4th edition (1888).
[2] There was, they may have read, often a kind of mercy-seat (a saddle: *cornu*), 'which will have served the same purpose' as the footrest.

*art* with the help of a shroud for which the claim is made that it is genuine. If the evidence provided by the shroud coincides with the evidence of the pictures, the shroud is, I should say, thereby proven a forgery. It can *ex hypothesi* not be both 'historical' *and* historical.

'Art herself refuses.' Mrs Jameson knew as well as anybody with what an array of ladders, ropes, hammers, nails, wedges, and borers (bradawls) the artists of the Middle Ages (and Dürer) tried to bring the Crucifixion within the conditions of *some kind of* reality. But what reality was thereby portrayed has long been problematic to us, and, as I have already hinted, it is possible that late medieval artists could not themselves have explained on what authority (other than 'St Anselm' – or 'St Bonaventura says' etc.) they drew as they drew. Their pictures, they knew, were 'true', whether they represented the crucifixion thus (*jacente cruce*) or thus (*erecto cruce*).

The reality of the Crucifixion is, as we said above, not the reality of the ancient world, though this was known to the earliest Christian artists (and was first rediscovered for the modern world by the patient researches of Justus Lipsius). It is also not a reality familiar to the European Middle Ages. The 'gallows of the cross' has in origin nothing to do with the gallows, but is a simple word for word translation of *patibulum crucis* (see below). The reality of the Crucifixion is a painfully reconstructed 'historical' reality which the Christian world owes to the *biblical* researches of the Fathers of the Church. Its only source is the Bible, but the Bible interpreted in a way which has passed more or less entirely out of use since the Reformation and Counter-Reformation. To grasp this, Protestants and agnostics have to learn to read and understand the Bible from a more *Catholic* point of view, and then join the Catholics in reading and understanding the Bible as the *medieval* Catholic world understood it.

We will first examine (or rather display) the *results* of patristic scholarship – the 'recovered reality'. As soon as we are reasonably familiar with the results we will examine the *method* of recovery. Read carefully, the texts we shall be considering themselves tell us where we should seek their sources. We need no new heading. The 'reality' of the artists is also – and was first – the reality of the authors.

As a result of centuries of endeavour to establish the full 'historical' sense of the biblical word (the literal or historical sense is by no means to be equated with what is obvious to anyone), two *different*, and not readily reconcilable accounts of the events on Golgotha were known by about 1200. Let us for safety's sake say that they were known to the clergy and the orders. These were the events held to be confirmed by the Evangelists in their word *crucifixerunt*. In both these accounts the transposition of Old Testament prophetic words, metaphors, similes and symbols into 'history', of which we spoke a moment ago, was already complete. All descriptions of the Crucifixion, down to the end of the Middle Ages, and all pictorial representations are based on one or the other of these: *or* writers *use* one and refer to the other as an alternative. The one account sees the Crucifixion, which is by now always a *nailing* to the cross, carried out *jacente cruce*, with the cross on the ground. We have it in its simplest form in the so-called *Dialogue with the Holy Virgin* of Pseudo-Anselm. The other ritual, a Crucifixion *erecto cruce*, is found in the *Meditations* already referred to of Pseudo-Bonaventura. The Crucified on an erect cross is – if one uses every scrap of evidence available – an image which had been known to Christendom for well-nigh a thousand years, let us say for several centuries. It is the *Meditations* which *relate* exactly *how* Christ was nailed to an already erect cross.

PSEUDO-ANSELM. By 'Pseudo-Anselm' we generally understand a *Dialogus S. Anselmi cum B. V. Maria* of which, by the middle of the thirteenth century, there were copies in practically every monastic library in Europe. Where it was *not* found we have to allow that it may have been known but rejected in favour of the alternative, see below. The Latin text is generally quoted in modern works from Migne's *Patrologia Latina*,[1] but Migne's text has no particular authority by comparison with other Latin and the countless vernacular versions. The work is of unknown authorship. There is some justice in the popular ascription to Anselm, the monk of the Norman monastery of Bec who became Archbishop of Canterbury, for the Marialogical writings of Anselm's pupil and biographer Eadmer (*c.* 1055–1124), and of Anselm's nephew, also an Anselm, enjoyed widespread success.[2]

PSEUDO-BONAVENTURA. The text of the *Meditationes Vitæ Christi* is to be found among the inordinately influential 'spurious' works of the

[1] *PL* CLIX 271 ff.
[2] Cf R. W. Southern, *St Anselm and his Biographer* (Cambridge, 1963). On German adaptations of the Anselm Dialogue, see Kurt Ruh, *Bonaventura deutsch* (Bern, 1956) p. 30.

Seraphic Doctor.[1] The question of the authorship of the *Meditations* cannot be taken up in any detail here. I refer to the short but incisive statement of Kurt Ruh in his study of Bonaventura translations[2] where, drawing on investigations of P. Columban Fischer, he stresses again that the author cannot be the Johannes de Caulibus whose name still lingers on in reference works.[3] The Chapters *De Passione* (73–85)[4] certainly go back to Bonaventura's own day, and could well be his own work. And in any case it is *not* the 'Meditations on' the Passion with which we are concerned in this study of origins, but the *events* on Golgotha and the ritual of crucifixion. These are not the invention of any *one* writer, but represent, as we shall see, a solution evolved by the Church Fathers long before Bonaventura's day.

Among *important* texts transmitting the 'solutions' more conveniently attributed to the Anselm-Dialogue and 'Bonaventura', is the 'Rhythmical Life of the Saviour', South-east German (?), *c.* 1200.[5]

Let us now look at the text of 'St Anselm' where the Crucifixion is described in careful detail. This may be visualised with the help of the Flemish artist Gerard David, 1450–1523, whose treatment of the crucifixion *jacente cruce* is in the National Gallery, see plate 24a.

(a)  *The Crucifixion* jacente cruce

(. . . et nullus evangelistarum scribit.) Cum venissent ad locum Calvariæ ignominiosissimum, ubi canes et alia morticina projiciebantur, nudaverunt Jesum unicum filium meum totaliter vestibus suis, et ego

---

[1] *Bonaventuræ Opera Omnia*, XII (*spuria*) (Paris, 1868) cols. 509 ff. Nicholas Love's translation, *The Mirrour of the Blessed Lyf of Iesu Christ* is edited by L. F. Powell (1908). A translation, with reproductions of the copious illustrations of an early Italian version in Isa Ragusa and Rosalie B. Green, *Meditations on the Life of Christ*, etc., Princeton Monographs in Art and Archeology, XXXV (Princeton, N.J. 1961).

[2] *Bonaventura deutsch* (Bern, 1956) pp. 269 ff.

[3] See Margaret Deansley, 'The Gospel Harmony of John de Caulibus or S. Bonaventura', in *British Society of Franciscan Studies* X (1922): the *Meditationes* were translated into English 'long before the death of John de Caulibus, nearer in fact to the death of S. Bonaventura in 1274'.

[4] Separately edited by Sister M. Jordan Stallings, *Meditaciones de Passione Christi*, etc. (Washington D.C., 1965).

[5] *Vita Rhythmica Salvatoris*, ed. by A. Vögtlin, Bibliothek des litterarischen Vereins in Stuttgart, CLXXXI (Tübingen, 1888). It offers the Crucifixion *jacente cruce*. Vernacular (verse) adaptations of this work are known to students of German literature – by Walther von Rheinau, Bruder Philipp, Wernher ('the Swiss'), see the literary histories.

exanimis facta fui; tamen velamen capitis mei accipiens circumligavi lumbis suis. Post hoc deposuerunt *crucem super terram*, et eum desuper extenderunt, et incutiebant primo unum clavum adeo spissum quod tunc sanguis non potuit emanare; ita vulnus replebatur. *Acceperunt postea funes et traxerunt* aliud brachium filii mei Jesu, et clavum secundum ei incusserunt. Postea pedes *funibus traxerunt*, et clavum acutissimum incutiebant, et adeo tensus fuit ut omnia ossa sua et membra apparerent, *ita ut impleretur illud Psalmi*, Dinumeraverunt omnia ossa mea.[1]

In about ten lines of print we have here what purports to be an account of the Crucifixion. It *begins* by stating that the enemies of Christ first laid the cross on the ground, and *ends* with the assertion that they pulled so violently at his limbs that the words of the Psalmist (were *or* should be) fulfilled: 'they counted all my bones'. In longer Passion plays the Crucifixion sequences can *begin* with the ordering and the making of the cross and the nails, as it were with the pre-history. (This may be expanded to include the whole 'Wood of the Cross' tradition, going back to *Genesis*! – but that is usually considered to be a story in itself.) Sooner or later the point is reached where the completed Cross, borne by Jesus to Calvary, is laid or thrown upon the ground.[2] Next (generally) the *holes to receive the nails* are bored. This is a somewhat enigmatic procedure – until we have established its source. This motif happens to be lacking in the text we have quoted from Migne. I consider it possible that it was omitted in this particular text. 'Logically', one might be inclined to think, these holes were 'invented' to provide a plausible justification for the dragging of the limbs with ropes. Chronologically, however – but we said we would keep first to the

[1] '(. . . though none of the Evangelists records this). When they had arrived at that most ignominious of places, Calvary, where dead dogs and carrion were thrown, they stripped my only son of all his clothes, (at which) I swooned; but taking my head-cloth I bound it about his loins. Thereupon they laid the cross on the ground and extended him upon it and drove in first one nail so thick that it filled the wound it caused, and no blood could flow. Then they took ropes and dragged the other arm of my son Jesus and drove in a second nail. After this they dragged his feet with ropes and drove in one very sharp nail, and he was so stretched that all his bones appeared, so that the words of the Psalm were fulfilled: "they counted all my bones".' (= Caput x).

[2] 'Thrown': I introduce this variant so that we may annotate it at once. I do not myself look upon 'thrown' as primarily an intemperate addition to the humiliations inflicted on Christ. One should *first* consider whether in the Old Testament anyone or anything which prefigured Christ or his Cross was thrown to the ground. Some readers will know at once what incident I have in mind.

'historical' sense of biblical words, and that means we shall have to come back to the 'holes bored in advance' at a later stage in the exposition. In Passion Plays the men entrusted with this gruesome office are only too ready to correct their mistakes of measurement and drive in their crude nails with cruel hammer blows; or it is said that they bored the holes too far apart intentionally. We shall see that this latter 'cruel invention' was required for the purposes of illustrating an important teaching going back to St Jerome at least. But in time the ritual is completed, and in the end someone – not an executioner – will say that this was all done in order that the words of the Psalmist should be fulfilled: 'they counted all my bones' (*dinumeraverunt omnia ossa mea*).

This is *one* version of the Crucifixion. It was preferred by the compilers of Passion Plays. It had the advantage of not inviting the objections of reverent craftsmen, whose ideas on what is mechanically feasible were always better respected than ignored. Medieval and later artists (including Dürer) did not eschew it, and I have already mentioned Gerard David. His treatment makes no concessions. His subject is the passivity of the Crucified and the blank incomprehension of the executioners who 'know not what they do'.[1] But for good reasons the Church has generally preferred the alternative solution, if 'preferred' is the correct word; 'alternative' *is* correct.

And now we turn to 'Bonaventura' and the text of his *Meditations*, a work which has been called the 'Gospel Harmony of the later Middle Ages'. It was, however, apparently better known in Italy, France and England than in Germany; or rather it was displaced in Germany by the much more compendious *Vita Christi* of Ludolf of Saxony which exploited the *Meditations*.[2] The passage we are to consider is from chapter 78, which according to the art historians is the basic text for the iconography of the Crucifixion in the art of the later Middle Ages.

This *opinio communis* of the art historians, to be found in every handbook, extends to Bonaventura's influence on the iconography of virtually any incident in the Passion story. In respect of the Crucifixion

[1] I have often wondered what may be the feelings of visitors who are scarcely inside the National Gallery when they come upon this picture, for which their upbringing (in the majority of cases Protestant or Nonconformist) provides no preparation. I have noted also that the same picture on the sleeve of an LP record of the *St Matthew Passion* strikes some modern observers in its *unfamiliarity* as being more 'factual' than the usual devotional image.

[2] Cf Kurt Ruh, *Bonaventura deutsch*, 270 ff. [Ludolf of Saxony died 1378].

it causes me some embarrassment.[1] Fra Angelico (1387–1455) offers a literal translation of the text of the *Meditations* into pictorial terms, see plate 24b. But his Crucifixion, following the text, shows a short ladder in front of the Cross on which Christ still stands, arms outspread, facing his enemies to pronounce his 'Father forgive them'. This image remains quite *untypical*. It is a picture one has 'not seen before'; one scarcely ever sees anything resembling it. I can consequently not understand how we are to maintain the thesis that Crucifixion *iconography* was profoundly influenced by the *Meditations*. If the meaning is merely that Bonaventura established the *priority* of the Crucifixion *erecto cruce*, that may well be true. Certainly the Western artists seem to have accepted his solution, or rather his re-statement of an approved solution of the ritual of the nailing. At the same time they have generally chosen to represent a moment which Bonaventura does not recognise, when the (æsthetically offensive) short ladder before the Cross has been removed, but not the two longer ladders used to reach the cross-beam. The short ladder is not only an ugly feature to contemplate; it has to reach to a point above the footrest, and so obscure it, as indeed it does in Fra Angelico's picture.

(b) *The Crucifixion* erecto cruce

Observe carefully the manner of the Crucifixion. Two ladders are set in place (*Hoc modum crucis diligenter attende. Ponuntur duo scalæ*), one behind the right arm, the other behind the left arm of the beam, which the evil-doers ascend with nails and hammers (*super quas malefici ascendunt cum clavis et martellis*). And then another ladder is set up in front, reaching to the point where the feet are to be fixed (*Ponitur etiam alia scala ex parte anteriore, attingens usque ad locum ubi debebant pedes affigi*). Note these details. The Lord Jesus is compelled to ascend the cross by this short ladder (*Compellitur Dominus Jesus crucem ascendere per hanc scalam parvam*); he does whatever they demand, offering no resistance or protest (*ipse autem sine rebellione et contradictione facit humiliter quidquid volunt*). When Christ reaches the top rung of the short ladder he turns, opens those royal arms and extending his most beautiful hands, he stretches them up before his crucifiers (*aperit . . . illa regalia brachia, et extendens manus pulcherrimas, in excelsum eas porrigit suis*

---

[1] Nowhere more than in Émile Mâle, who, having overstated the case for Bonaventura, relegates 'Anselm' and the Crucifixion *jacente cruce* to a quite inadequate footnote in *L'Art religieux du xiii<sup>e</sup> siècle*, 8th ed. (1948) p. 40 n. 3.

*crucifixoribus* . . . ) 'Behold me, my Father' (*Ecce, hic sum, Pater mi*') [An evil-doer on the ladder behind the right arm of the Cross seizes Christ's arm and] fixes it firmly to the Cross (*eam cruci fortiter affigit*). Then the one who is on the left side takes his left hand and pulls and extends it as far as he can, applies another nail, drives it in and strikes it home (*ille qui est in latere sinistro accipit manum sinistram, et trahit quantum potest, et extendit, et alium clavum inmittit, percutit et configit*). [All the ladders are removed. The body of the Lord hangs] suspended from the nails alone which transfix his hands (*solis clavis infixis manibus*). [One of the executioners runs forward, drags down the feet and drives an enormous single nail through both feet.][1]

In a Middle English adaptation of the *Meditations* by Robert Manning of Brunne (*c.* 1315–30)[2] the pulling of the legs is 'justified' by the statement that 'they had bored the holes too far apart'. They pulled *til þe cros kraked, alle þe ioyntes brasten atwynne.*

This pulling of the limbs is clearly not primarily the expression of a readily definable religiosity. What the various writers intend is to show *how* the words of the Psalmist came to be fulfilled: whether the cross was on the ground or erect. And that is why 'Bonaventura', having described the Crucifixion *erecto cruce* down to the last detail could go on to say, 'but there are others who hold that the *modus* of the crucifixion was otherwise'. He then describes more briefly a crucifixion *jacente cruce*: 'this you may, if you wish (*quod si magis placet*) prefer'. But in the one as in the other case: '*Ecce crucifixus est Dominus Christus . . . ita in cruce extensus . . . ut omnia ossa dinumeraverunt*', as Christ had prophesied through David. Still more clearly, in the Passion Play of Brixen,[3] centuries later, David himself goes onto the scene at the completion of the Crucifixion and 'rhymes' as follows:

Als ich am 21. psalm zwar
Gesprochen hab frey offenwar:
Seine hend und fues sy haben
Gar jemerlich durch graben,

[1] ed. col. 606. The passage is translated with no abridgment in Ragusa and Green (see p. 238, n. 1) p. 333–4. I have abridged particularly the loquacious prayer – more nearly seventy than seven words.

[2] ed. J. Meadows Cowper, EETS (1875) 610 ff.

[3] The youngest text, in the appendix to J. E. Wackernell, *Altdeutsche Passionsspiele aus dem Tyrol* (Graz, 1897) p. 409.

Das im alle seine gepain
Gezelt sein worden allain:
Secht Nu all zu diser frist,
Ob ietz sölichs nit geschechen ist!

As I said indeed clearly and openly in my 21st Psalm, 'They have pierced his hands and feet', so that 'every single bone has been counted'. Look now, all of you, has it not all now happened at this very moment?

### (c) Provisional Conclusions

What is new, I think, in my treatment of the two modes of the Crucifixion as we find them in the *Dialogue* and the *Meditations*, is the emphasis I have laid on the common elements, and their concentration on the formula '*ita . . . ut*', 'as it was prophesied, thus was it fulfilled'. We moderns are more conscious of a contradiction, the irreconcilability of *jacente cruce* and *erecto cruce*. But may we see a contradiction when the Middle Ages treated the two solutions as alternatives, and if medieval writers and artists made their choice as they were finally invited to do in the *Meditations*? No doubt there were occasions when the alternatives were held to compete with one another, but the record we have is *not* one of debate and dispute. Truth resided evidently in the fulfilment of prophecy, the moment of 'consummation'. The two rituals were tolerated side by side because *either* of them allowed the faithful (finally) to see the *one* fulfilment.

The two accounts are consequently variants of basically one *ætiological* story, but, by comparison with the folk-lorist's ætiological stories, there is one important difference. The 'events leading to the known result' – or the 'pragmatic series', as such pre-histories have been called – are not the *invention* of imaginative story-tellers, but the discovery (Latin *inventio*) of biblical scholarship. The premature boring of the holes to receive the nails is *also* fulfilment of prophecy, as we shall see in due course. Such an ætiological story is therefore naturally not the work of *late* medieval writers, nor of any *individual* writer, but the result of the combined endeavours of the Fathers of the Church from earliest times to harmonise the various prophecies of the Crucifixion in one 'historical' sequence. They finished with two for all that.

Equally naturally, even this result will not have been achieved at a first attempt.

About 350 Bishop Hilary of Poitiers showed uncertainty. He was ahead of, or not abreast of developments. He believed and said, as the Middle Ages would not say again, I think, before the fifteenth century, that Christ was fastened to the Cross with nails *and ropes*.[1] In Jerome and Augustine, and in the works of the theologians down to the end of the Middle Ages, we find the Crucifixion of Christ carried out with nails only. The thieves are a different matter. Whether it is a Crucifixion *erecto* or *jacente cruce*, Christian art *always* conforms to this tradition of a *nailing*. The ropes used for the pulling of the limbs were, without doubt, in late medieval times, of necessity used in the actual performance of Passion Plays (the nailing was simulated); but they are then no more than a producer's device. This is a vital, but difficult point, appreciation of which is not facilitated by the frequent *metaphorical* use of the words 'fetters', 'bonds', for the nails throughout the Middle Ages. More on these matters below.

The poets and the artists take, therefore, as their subject-matter what was in fact the outcome of the scholarly endeavours of the Fathers to harmonise prophecy. From about 1200 these findings, converted into 'history', were prefaced in devotional writings with the note: 'lacking in the accounts of the Evangelists',[2] and made accessible to an ever widening public. Not primarily to encourage a more fervid piety or a deeper compassion. What characterises the Crucifixion story is, in either version, its capacity to *convince* rather than to move: and its complete coherence and compatibility with the Church's Christological teaching. Small wonder, since this was its origin. If, therefore, at a rudimentary pragmatic level the purpose of the 'release' of these two narrative versions may have been to put an end to speculations about the 'things over which the Evangelists had passed in silence', the stories were also intended to propagate *true doctrine*, in the same way as, a thousand years or so before, the narratives of the Infancy had been evolved both to put an end to unauthorised pseudo-Gospels and to propagate the only correct doctrine concerning the divinity and humanity of Christ. The New Testament apocryphal books, *Pseudo-Matthew*, the *Gospel of Nicodemus* and the rest, *also* end each episode with the declaration that prophecy was hereby fulfilled. They are *also*

---

[1] *PL* x 352.     [2] See the 'Anselm' quotation, 238 (below).

ætiological stories. At the level of 'history', therefore, the Church from about 1200 allowed it to be taught that on Golgotha these things happened thus, or thus – but not in any third way.

We have naturally not yet explained the origin of all the apparently realistic motifs in medieval Crucifixions. There is still a good deal to be said about 'the holes bored too far apart'. It will also be clear that the ætiological explanation will not in itself suffice. We have postponed some explanations in order to be able to examine the product, for a rapid orientation. We took the quickest route from the one 'historical' word *crucifixerunt* to the still (or again) fully 'historical' account of an Anselm or Bonaventura. We kept to the biblical word understood in its first 'historical' sense. We learnt that certain words (like *dinumeraverunt* etc.) are not *less* true for being in the Old Testament and prophetic. Rather the contrary.

At this point it may be objected that the Crucifixion story as told in Pseudo-Anselm and Pseudo-Bonaventura preserves no trace of the scholarly origins to which I have repeatedly alluded, and that its style is simple and popular. The style shows rather a studied simplicity. The more one reads in medieval exegesis, the more disciplined, the less free and popular will devotional works, even the enormously inflated texts of the later Passion Plays, appear. The two variant versions of the Crucifixion story seem to me, in short, to reflect faithfully the conclusions of the Fathers of the Church, duly translated into appropriately simple narrative terms.

By now we have clearly suggested that the Fathers of the Church themselves must have visualised the nailing to the Cross in the same way as, seven or eight centuries later, Pseudo-Anselm and Pseudo-Bonaventura and the artists of the Gothic. No other conclusion is possible. (Only the final 'realisation' of certain details is *late* medieval.) As philologists, however, we may not suggest solutions when the facts of textual history are there for us to examine. We must consider the words and wordings of biblical texts, the Liturgy, the writings of the Fathers themselves and the later theologians. For the sake of completeness we must then go on to the authors, poets, and the artists who illustrated any of these, used them as sources, or were, as we say, inspired by them.

Nothing can be clearer, however, than that up to about 1200 it was the Church itself which, to recall Mrs Jameson, 'refused' to have the

Crucifixion *represented* under the conditions of any 'reality' whatsoever. But for centuries before that date, for almost a thousand years, it had *had to know* how the Crucifixion was to be *imagined*. The enemies of Christianity, the doubters, but also the faithful had ensured that, by their questions and challenges. How the Church saw the Crucifixion is in fact already reflected in the very choice and arrangement of the lessons and Psalms of its Liturgy. Furthermore the Fathers of the Church had to have a clear conception of the Crucifixion *as a procedure and ritual* if they were to write coherent commentaries on the books of the old Testament, most particularly on those words of the prophets and the Psalms which formed part of the Liturgy of Holy Week and Easter, the commemoration of Crucifixion and Resurrection.

Why was there this emphasis always on the *Old* Testament and prophecy – in the Liturgy, and in early exegesis? Merely to 'save' the Old Testament for Christianity? The reason why attention was directed primarily to the Old Testament, and for the comparative neglect of the New, is to be found in Christ's own final teaching of the Apostles. Christ stated: '*all things must be fulfilled* which are written in the law of Moses, and in the prophets and in the psalms concerning me':[1] *necesse est impleri omnia quæ scripta sunt in lege Moysi, et prophetis, et psalmis de me*. This was taken universally to be Christ's own *instruction* to study the Old Testament. This instruction, and the paradigmatic *examples* Christ had given in his own teaching of 'things' to be fulfilled, and the manner of their fulfilment (e.g. Jonah's three days in the belly of the whale were 'fulfilled' in the three days in the tomb before the Resurrection), are the foundation of patristic Old Testament scholarship. This consists in large measure in an exhaustive search for those prophecies to which explicit reference had been made *neither* by Christ *nor* by the Evangelists. The task of scholarship was to find and recognise the *omnia* and prove their relevance (that they were *de me*). It is in the course of just such study that the Church evolved, *inter alia*, its mental picture of the Crucifixion.

For this task a special faculty was required. St Paul called it a *discretio spirituum*,[2] a 'discerning of spirits' according to the Authorised Version. To St Augustine[3] St Paul's words meant a special ability to discern the deeper spiritual meaning of the scriptural word. But the *facultas* (authorisation) to pursue such investigations lapsed, it would seem, with the last of the Fathers, i.e. at the end of the period we call patristic;

---

[1] Luke xxiv 44.    [2] I Cor. xii 10.    [3] *De Civ. Dei*, xviii 32.

and in theory at least there were no further speculations on these lines.[1] The Church then deemed that this particular task of interpreting prophecy had been well and truly completed. To judge by the reluctance of modern translators and commentators of Augustine (on *Psalms*) and Gregory (on *Job*) to persevere in rendering and annotating all the speculations to which the *discretio spirituum*, coupled with the search for *omnia de me*, gave rise, the decision to close this chapter of historiography may well seem to have been taken somewhat late. What is more important is that all the main findings of this first era of biblical scholarship were transmitted as a coherent corpus of authoritative clerical lore. This includes the 'historical' Crucifixion as a *verbal* tradition. As for Christian *art* up to the end of the patristic age, there are as yet few devotional images of the Crucified, and there are *no* representations of the Crucifixion as a 'historical' event. This position is then held until about 1200 when certain texts of which we have already spoken were released. The matching pictures followed.

And now, for general orientation, a glance at subsequent developments in the modern era. The whole of patristic learning and its product was submitted to fresh scrutiny at the time of the Reformation and the Counter-Reformation, which was also the time of the humanists – with far-reaching consequences. These we must try to state in summary form. Luther rejected the methods and most of the findings of patristic scholarship. As for Christ's own instructions concerning the relevance of the Law, the Prophets and the Psalms (*omnia da me*), the reformed Churches accepted as fulfilled only those prophecies which the Evangelists had themselves confirmed as fulfilled. The Evangelists had clearly exploited prophecy in their accounts of the Nativity, the Ministry and the Passion. Some episodes of the New Testament were therefore 'not historical in the customary sense'. There is consequently a drastic reduction in the amount of story which the reformed Churches will tell in their teaching or see represented in their pictures, if any. This determines their attitude towards medieval religious art. They find much of it apocryphal or legendary in content.

The Catholics had begun, even before the Counter-Reformation, to discard whatever seemed excessively medieval in the teachings of the principal Fathers. The science of typology then becomes something

[1] In this general account I have to ignore Rupert of Deutz (d. 1129). I deal with his historiographical method in *Augustinus oder Boethius* II.

characteristic of the Church's past, to be cherished as hallowed tradition in the main but not necessarily to be rehearsed in current teaching. The inherited narrative tradition is kept under discreet supervision and not added to, either in word or in image.

For the humanists there were special problems arising from methods of textual study learnt elsewhere. The Bible as a corpus of writings was the legitimate object of critical and historical scrutiny. In such a context the 'argument from prophecy' was revealed as a method the use of which could be observed in the New Testament. The humanists could not use it themselves. It has no evidential value. (Later *acta* and *gesta* cannot be attested in earlier *scripta*.) That is the end of the matter.

Today the Christian Churches continue to make fullest use of the Old Testament, particularly the Psalms,[1] and to sing ancient hymns and follow a liturgy almost as old as Christianity itself. They also provide a teaching which enables their members to understand fully what is involved in this adherence to *textual* tradition. They are less able to explain the works of Christian *art* which they have inherited from the past. Insofar as Christian art narrates, it tells a story for which the authority can now only incompletely be recalled. That has, in fact, by now been the situation for several centuries. This uncertainty cannot be better illustrated than by considering the efforts of Justus Lipsius.

## 4. HISTORY AND *HISTORIA* – THE MODERN DILEMMA (Justus Lipsius)

It is understandable if most modern readers still want to know, or want to know in addition, what *really* happened on the Way of the Cross and on Golgotha. Instead, therefore, of merely repeating the assertion that any such enquiry will *not* help us in our studies of Christian literature and art, let us look at the efforts of Justus Lipsius (1547–1606), one of the first modern historians. He tried to find the answer. Let us see how he fared. His aim was ostensibly a 'reciprocal illumination' and reconciliation of two historical disciplines: an older Christian discipline of biblical study (for which his distaste is ill-concealed), and the modern critical examination of authenticated sources, with

---

[1] Psalm xxi/xxii remains the Good Friday psalm of the reformed Churches because it is in mood and general tenor appropriate and was quoted by Christ. The words remain, however, the Psalmist's words and ard not held to describe the Crucifixion as for instance St Augustine had said, *PL* xxxvi 169.

particular reference to one subject: 'The Cross'. From the viewpoint of the philologist, who is at any time prepared to look at written evidence with the historian, the researches of Justus Lipsius were, to put it mildly, at times ambivalent. He failed to recognise that not all sources provide evidence of one kind; they do not all contribute to one and the same 'truth'.[1]

Justus Lipsius was born in 1547 at Issche near Brussels and went to school with the Jesuits; he then studied, at first in Louvain. During the short period of his early, brilliant professorship in Jena (1572) he turned Protestant, later Calvinist and after further vacillations finally Catholic again. His most influential work bears the title *De Constantia* (1584).[2]

Lipsius was without doubt a brilliant scholar. When he returned on urgent advice to Louvain in 1591, according to the biography based on his correspondence, he had declined professorships in France, Spain and Germany, and a tempting research post at the Vatican on 'any terms he cared to name' (*stipendio et viatico, quod ipse defineret*). It was none the less vexing that at a time when he needed to show himself a good Catholic again, he could in all his works not point to anything on a Christian subject. He was (and remained) a classical philologist and ancient historian. He had written monographs on gladiators (1582) and

[1] Christian archæologists today do not try to write two kinds of history at once, but sometimes experience difficulty in making clear to the less scholarly devout that there *are* two kinds of history. Though there is much that remains obscure to them, they do not confuse, as Lipsius did, sources and records on the one hand, and on the other hand the documents and monuments of more than a thousand years of Christian tradition. See, for instance, Ferd. Cabrol and Henri Leclercq, *Dictionnaire d'archéologie chrétienne*, III 2, col. 3045 ff, on the 'cross' (*in Antiquity*), and VIII 1, 1149 on the 'instruments of the Passion' (*in Christian tradition*). It is, however, surely discretion carried to extremes when a contributor to Pauly-Wissowa's Encyclopaedia writes, under 'Cross': 'it is highly improbable that the cross (in Antiquity) necessarily, at all times and everywhere was of the shape which is so familiar to us today and which the Fathers of the Church describe'. This remarkable statement is evidence of the panic which seizes some scholars when, like Lipsius, they find there is no foundation for the 'cross as we know it' in records of the kind we call historical.

For Lipsius I refer readers to my article 'Justus Lipsius' *De Cruce Libri tres* (1593), or The Historian's Dilemma', in *Festgabe für L. L. Hammerich* (Copenhagen, 1962) pp. 199–214: it offers an analysis of *De Cruce*, with a running critical commentary on its treatment of Christian tradition, and quotations to which in this résumé I can only allude.

[2] The translation of Sir John Stradling (1594), *Tvvo Bookes of Constancie, written in Latine by Justus Lipsius*, was edited by Rudolf Kirk and Clayton Morris Hall for 'Records of Civilisation', Rutgers Univ. Press (New Brunswick, N.J., 1939). The first German translation in facsimile, ed. by L. W. Forster, Sammlung Metzler (Stuttgart, 1966).

amphitheatres (1584), on Roman fortifications, ballistic missiles, and coins; and he had edited Tacitus and Seneca. He had also long been working on Roman law, and had dealt *inter alia* with criminal procedure in the ancient world. Before the year of the publication of *De Cruce* in 1593, however, he had written nothing, or rather 'mere drafts, not worthy to be preserved in the temple of Memoria', on crucifixion (and the Crucifixion). It seems, however, either that the 'drafts' which Lipsius half acknowledged in this way have not disappeared without trace; or that grateful students took steps to see that some of his more notable observations in lectures on crucifixion, and the Crucifixion as it is represented in art, reached a wider public. The University Library of Cambridge possesses copies of a work purporting to be of origin 'Cambridge, 1592'[1] with the title *Justi Lipsi Tractatus de supplicio crucis ad historiam Romanam cognoscendam apprime utiles*. There can be no doubt that the 'tractates' on capital punishment, though only a few pages of print all told, will have been extremely useful (*apprime utiles*) to anyone wishing to know more about Roman history. They can only have been an embarrassment to the humanist in need of rehabilitation, for he had on this evidence apparently committed himself in public to the view (which he never relinquished) that 'Christian artists know nothing at all about Roman crucifixions' (*ergo pictores ignari prorsus antiquitatis*).

What Lipsius objected to in particular was the cross-bearing as it is represented in Christian art, in which the cross is always shown complete with its cross-beam. He was at that time not to be shaken in his conviction that the word 'cross' (*crux*) does not mean a cross as we understand it at all. It is *any* instrument of capital punishment and has no particular shape or structure. Anything (or any form of torture) which brings about the death of the victim is a *crux*, Prometheus's rock and chains, for instance. ('Cruciform' derives its meaning from the Christian 'Cross'.) And if a malefactor under sentence of death was made to carry anything to his place of execution, then it was indeed *called* a 'cross': what he in fact carried was at most the cross-beam, sometimes a kind of 'stocks'. This is still the view of Christian archaeologists today, and appears to be the correct reading of the very varied historical evidence. Roughly the same is true of the Flagellation and the Cruci-*fixion* itself: the historical evidence of all the many variations

[1] I have not been able to pursue this matter. The present wording reflects an earlier conviction that the attribution must be spurious.

in practice, at different times and in different parts of the world of Antiquity (Jewish, Greek, Roman) does not provide any exact parallel. Nothing can be done about this, except to *recognise* that Christian tradition *is as it is*, and seek to explain why this is so. Lipsius failed in the attempt. What is tragi-comical about this situation is that while Lipsius was preparing his major work *De Cruce* in three Books, his Jesuit friends seem to have showered him with quotations from the Fathers of the Church, so that he could 'work them in'. I surmise that in so doing they drew his attention to problems which they themselves wished to see solved, for instance *jacente cruce* or *erecto cruce* (which was correct?), with three or with four nails (what was his view?), with or without footrest? That was his dilemma. He understood document evaluation for the purposes of historical research. He was quite incapable of taking superseded, *patristic* methods of scholarship seriously. He could of course not *use* such methods for his own researches. It was none the less reprehensible that he did not recognise, or even ask, what might have been the nature and purpose of patristic scholarship. For Lipsius sources were sources, words meant what they meant to him – literally. The consequence is that repeatedly during the course of his long investigation, he has to say that the *modus* of flagellation and crucifixion 'must have been different in the case of our Lord'; or '... the Fathers of the Church are of different opinion in these matters, and who am I that I should doubt their views?' That sounds, quoted in this way, like a cautious and well-considered admission of 'difficulties inherent in the subject', and so one would judge, had Lipsius been able to leave it at that. But quoting the Fathers when they make use of allegorical interpretations, and when they see typological correspondences, he cannot restrain his mirth. These things are to him rather quaint conceits (*inventiunculæ*), and on one occasion he offers 'more in the same strain, since these things are so amusing'. The further irony here is that Lipsius' advisers may have *encouraged* him to discredit some of the final trivialities and *curiosa* of typology in its decline, and furnished him with the useful examples: it had become an irrelevance. Lipsius shows just as little interest in Old Testament *prophecies* of the Crucifixion. In short, he threw away the very evidence he needed if ever he was to explain the Crucifixion of Christian tradition. It was evidently too early, even for a scholar of Lipsius's stature, to see that Christian knowledge is a self-sufficient economy. Imagining, as he seems to have done, that he would discover an explanation of Christian tradition *en passant*, and having, as we said just now, discounted the only sources which could have helped him to a solution of one of his main problems, he could not but get himself into a situation which is no longer tragi-comic but tragic, for in his dilemma he finally belied the principles of his *own* scholarship. For instance in his treatment of the *stauros* which he finds in Greek sources. He establishes from a study of his Greek historians that execution by means of a *stauros* is an impaling: a *stauros* is a *stake*. He offers examples from secular writings. What he does not even mention is that *stauros* is the word for the Cross of the Crucifixion in New Testament Greek. Even the most courageous investigator might, in his day, have kept silence with him. But there cannot be much sympathy with him when he quotes Christian hymns and a poetic paraphrase of the Gospel of St John as though these were sources of the same kind as his Roman historians, and when he confirms the findings of the Fathers by referring to Christian art and *vice versa*. This is pure clowning. This kind of thing happens, however, when – and *only* when – he is attempting to deal with problems of Christian tradition. *This only* drives him to these devices.

After making a careful analysis of the evidence and the arguments submitted by Lipsius, and having considered the many copperplate engravings in which Lipsius had shown all the modes of crucifixion of which he had found evidence, or which he postulated or considered possible, I come to the reluctant conclusion that *De Cruce* is only marginally a work of strict scholarship. It comes dangerously near to other categories of writing. (The same author wrote, soon afterwards, two pious booklets on local sanctuaries which are mawkish to a degree.) For all that we had to consider *De Cruce* here. It illustrates the historian's dilemma when he is confronted with facts and evidence of different orders, only one of which is accessible to him and his methods. For his own subject – history – Lipsius assembled a remarkable corpus of evidence, Jewish, Greek, Roman, *inter alia* on crucifixion in the ancient world, for the critical examination of which he showed tenacity and acumen. His material was still drawn on and his findings were quoted down to the nineteenth century. For the history of tradition (what the modern historian might call myth-making) and for theology, poetry and art and *their* history he showed no understanding.

The final impression is of an uneasily contemptuous humanist, bowing himself out with an ingratiating smile or smirk. Within ten years of his death even the encomia of his supporters prudently class

*De Cruce* among his works 'on Antiquity'. In the long debate on his Christian orthodoxy they did not mention it. The work was flayed by George Thomson of St Andrews in a broadside of 1606. The best evidence of his orthodoxy which his supporters could adduce was his deathbed confession.

## 5. *HISTORIA* AND THEOLOGICAL EXEGESIS

*Crucifixerunt eum.* Warned by the example of Justus Lipsius, we will now give more attention to what the Church Fathers had to say. We can, however, dispense with actual quotations almost entirely, for only in the rarest of cases shall we be concerned with any individual Father. What we are mainly interested in is the finally approved interpretation of *crucifixerunt*. This emerged after early debates on Christ's human nature, as an opinion shared by the leading Fathers, and of course only *such* an interpretation could ever be taught and become the subject-matter of Christian hymns and ecclesiastical art. By that time all the prophecies, and all the types and prefigurations which were ever to be authoritatively associated with the Crucifixion had been established and 'proved'. Our task is therefore to rehearse what were theological commonplaces of the period up to and about 600 and then beyond that date. In the interest of a clear exposition we will continue to start wherever we can from the biblical word in its historical sense. Gradually expanding the scope we shall then include those 'shadows and figures' which, from the beginning of exegesis, were held to refer, though sometimes more darkly, to the events of the Passion, particularly the Crucifixion. For those readers who already know a good deal about these matters I mention in advance as a 'dark' prophecy the words of Habakkuk, *cornua in manibus ejus.*[1]

In the New Testament one reads *crucifixerunt*, 'they fastened him on a (*or* to a) cross'. Of the shape of the cross and the manner of the fastening (*fixio*) – with nails, for instance – there is no direct evidence. But the Fathers and every theologian after them could 'prove' the nails;[2] they could also prove the shape of the cross.[3] The grammatical subject

[1] Habak. iii 4.

[2] Psalm xxi 17, 'they pierced my hands and feet' is the key text, supported by the evidence offered to the doubting apostle Thomas, who was shown the imprint 'of the nails'. This proof is so often encountered in the pages of Migne that it must have been a set subject of instruction and examination.

[3] See below.

of the verb *crucifixerunt* is, on the evidence of New Testament story,
'the Jews who had conspired against Jesus'. Of their 'wild and
insensate' behaviour at the Seizure, on the Way of the Cross and at the
Crucifixion, the Passion Psalm (xxi, verse 13 and following) speaks
metaphorically and prophetically: 'many bulls have compassed me . . .
dogs have encompassed me' (*circumdederunt me vituli, . . . canes, tauri
pingues obsederunt me*). Such were the men who crucified him.

Equally important are Christ's own prophetic words in his teaching
of Nicodemus:[1] 'And as Moses lifted up the serpent in the wilderness,
even so must the Son of man be lifted up' (*sicut Moyses exaltavit
serpentem in deserto, ita exaltari oportet Filium hominis*). This comparison
involves a serpent, figuratively a likeness: *sicut serpens – ita Filius
hominis*. We will deal with this later. This is not a 'historical' statement.
That still leaves, however, *oportet exaltari* which, prophesying what is
to happen, *is* 'historical'. The impersonal *oportet* declares the Son's
acceptance of the will of the Father, his obedience. In the presence of
his enemies Christ again used *exaltari* of his Crucifixion: 'When ye
have lifted up the Son of man . . .' (*cum exaltaveritis Filium hominis*).[2]
The Crucifixion is, therefore, on New Testament evidence a 'fastening'
(*-fixio*) to a 'Cross' and an 'exaltation'; Christ was to be 'lifted up'. To
the impersonality of *oportet* corresponds the incomprehension of the
enemies of Christ, who will 'know not what they do'. They fulfil the
will of the Father in their treatment of the Son, who is obedient unto
death; at the Crucifixion they raise him aloft.

None of these statements requires any gloss. That the Cross was of
wood and heavy, is, one would think, clear enough from the New
Testament narrative; but it is, for all that, of wood and heavy for
many reasons which are *not* primarily 'historical', but theological and
Christological. This is a subject I propose to treat only briefly here,
stressing merely that from the Carolingians down to the end of the
Middle Ages there were artists who saw no reason at all why the cross
borne by Christ (and by Simon) on the Way should be shown either as
heavy, or indeed as the cross on which he was to be crucified. He may
carry a light processional cross, see plate 21a. This should suffice to
show that there was no universal, overwhelming interest in 'historical'
realism. As for the shape of the cross, that again was not a purely
'historical' question. In a 'historical' context the Cross of the Crucifixion is of a shape to conform with the posture of Christ in the attitude

[1] John iii 14.          [2] John viii 28.

of prayer, that is of the *orans* with arms fully outstretched.[1] There are other reasons, which we shall discuss, why the Cross of the Crucifixion should be 'cruciform'.

To these primarily 'historical' statements concerning the Crucifixion all others had to, and did conform. By this I do not suggest that there was a hierarchy of statements. Merely, that the search for *omnia de me* could in the nature of things not lead to results contradicting the clear statements of the New Testament (*crucifixerunt, oportet exaltari*), or the principal Passion Psalm ('they pierced my hands and feet', 'they counted all my bones'). What other indications does the New Testament offer of the *manner* of the Crucifixion? There are some *few* others, but in each case one has to consider whether the words characterise the intention of the Jews, or the voluntary compliance of the Son with the will of God. Here we can do little more than mention the terms, for they provide only a number of glosses on the Crucifixion, not primary 'historical' statements. First let us consider the verb 'hang' (*pendere*), and the derivatives of *pendere*.[2] These all refer to the 'ignominious death' of the Old Law[3] as a hanging on a 'tree' or 'gallows', in Vulgate Latin on a *lignum* (*ignobile*) or on a *patibulum*. That is, these words refer to the crucifixion intended by Christ's persecutors, and the Crucifixion as it appeared to them in their 'blindness'. Their purpose was, of course, frustrated.

Then, more important again, Christ's Crucifixion is an 'ascent' of the Cross. This one might infer from the words of mockery 'let him descend from the cross' (*descendat*), but there is better evidence than these unwitting remarks. There are the authoritative words of the Bridegroom in the Song of Songs, *ascendam in palmam*.[4] From the earliest days of the Church these words of the *Canticle* were seized upon. The hanging from a gallows (or a tree) intended by Christ's enemies was in fact a voluntary and 'victorious' ascent; indeed of a tree, but of a palm-tree, not the *lignum ignobile* of the Old Law. Associations such as this provide, however, as yet no 'history'. They

---

[1] As has often been pointed out, like Moses before the victory over the Amalekites, Exod. xvii 12 ('Aaron and Hur stayed up his hands . . . and his hands were steady until the going down of the sun').

[2] Cf *suspendentes eum*, Acts v 30, and the prophetic text *Elegit suspendium anima mea et mortem ossa mea*, Job vii 15.

[3] *mors turpissima* is the expression in *Wisdom of Solomon* ii 20, the only significant evidence, I believe, to be taken from the Apocryphal Old Testament.

[4] Cant. vii 8.

furnish words of thanksgiving and rejoicing, but they 'tell' nothing which has not otherwise been told.

A short digression – on *palma*. This addition of what must have been a welcome metaphor to the names and designations of the Cross, raises the question of the origins of the Church's diction generally. It is important to remember that however rich, imaginative, colourful and poetical – or highly rhetorical – it may seem to us when we encounter it in prayers and hymns, it is in the main learned in origin. A science of typology is reflected in its antithetical figures. The figures of Christian poetry declare a theology and Christology. They are the outcome of theological argument and learned debate. That is the reason for this digression. What the Church sang when it 'gloried in the Cross' with St Paul, was always compatible with its 'historical' knowledge of what happened at the Crucifixion. For some conception of the rhetoric of the early Church which did not survive, one has to look at the hymns and Odes assembled in scholarly studies of 'apocryphal' material. Their figurative language proved to be unacceptable to the Church. Not because it was too poetic, but (no doubt) because its figures were at variance with the evolving doctrines of the Church.


## 6. PREFIGURED *HISTORIA* (TYPOLOGY)

We must now slacken the pace considerably. In limiting our main attention so far to the biblical word in its 'historical' sense, we have possibly suggested that an explanation of the texts of Bonaventura and Anselm is already within our reach, and that the Church was primarily concerned to recover 'history' as quickly as possible, to fill out the meagre accounts of the Evangelists. Almost the opposite is the case. Urgent as it had been for the Church in its patristic age to establish and know in detail the manner of Christ's Crucifixion, its main endeavour was thereafter to stabilise that knowledge in its correlation with an evolved theology and Christology of considerable complexity; and for the rest to resist and *delay* all tendencies to rehearse mere 'history', or to amplify it with any new discoveries.

Perhaps we may see the Church's belated (and unsuccessful) endeavour during the Carolingian period to forbid all further use of the Apocryphal New Testament in the same light. The stories had served their purpose. They were now an embarrassment, because of their tone and style, not to speak of their homely realism (the incredulous midwife of the Nativity, the bread-winning of the Holy Family in Egypt, the Childhood miracles). They were a potential nuisance too in that they seemed so openly to advertise 'fulfilment of prophecy' as a legitimation of narrative invention. Among the steps taken to educate the devout to a better understanding of Christian tradition generally, and at a level higher than that of *historia* which had once been thought to be the limit of layfolk's understanding, we may surely count the outburst of typological teaching and representation towards and in the twelfth century. There is, for instance, the preparation of typological 'programmes' for *pictorial* treatment, to which devotional literature *in the vernacular* may offer the textual counterpart: for instance the Early Middle High German poem which we call the *Ezzolied*.[1] Whereas in an earlier Strassburg version of about 1063 there is little typological lore, typology provides the main content and much of the 'poetry' of a revision (Vorau) of about 1120. If this popularisation of typology was intended, among other things, to stabilise Christian narrative by providing it with a wealth of fairly easily assimilated, learned associations, it succeeded in its purpose only temporarily; for after the 'controlled release' discussed above, the 'historians' were soon again at work, making fullest use of all the material (the 'parallels') which the Church had now made so readily accessible. But before considering those later developments, let us look at some examples of approved typological method.

## (a) *Typology in the Art of the High Middle Ages*

The art historians prefer to begin their treatment of medieval typology with an analysis of major pictorial programmes as we may encounter them for instance in church windows. Here we shall take a single work executed on a small scale, and deal with it in some detail. There is an enamel processional cross in the King Edward VII Gallery of the British Museum (near the Sutton Hoo exhibits), see book cover. It comes from the Rhine-Meuse area. It has a square pictorial plaque at each of the four ends of the cross, and a fifth at the intersection, all of them clearly 'prefigurations' – but of what?

[1] Cf p. 27.

*Above:* Moses and the High Priest Aaron (their names are given), standing right and left of a column on which a serpent (?) is decoratively balanced; or is it a dragon? At any rate the picture illustrates Numbers xxi 8–9, where a 'fiery' (or 'brazen') serpent is set up on a pole by Moses.

*Right:* The painting of the door-post and lintels with the blood of the 'lamb without blemish', the *agnus* [*sine*] *macula* of Exodus xii 7. The mark made is a 'Tau' cross. The words *signvm Tav* are also given in the picture (they are not to be found in Exodus).[1]

*Below:* The 'two spies' who, having been sent by Moses into the land of Canaan, return bearing a 'cluster of grapes upon a staff' (*uva in vecte*), Numbers xiii 24. The names of the spies are given above the picture as Caleb and Joshua.

*Left:* The Widow of Zarephath (*Vulgate* Sarephta), who, according to the text of Jerome said to Elijah: *En colligo duo ligna ut ingrediar*. The English Authorised Version also says 'I am gathering *two* sticks (that I may go in and dress it for me and my son, that we may eat it and die).' Luther rather maliciously says 'one or two sticks'. This is III Reg. (= I Kings) xvii 12. The two sticks form an X which the Widow (standing erect) carries.

*Centre:* Jacob, crossing his hands (Vulgate: *commutans manus*), blesses Ephraim and Manasseh, Gen. xlviii 14. The A.V. says 'stretching forth', but the 'crossing' of the hands is implied in the 'cancellation' of Joseph's intentions.[2]

This work is ascribed to the Master of enamels, Gottfried of Huy (Godefroid de Claire) of the monastic school of enamellers from which Nicholas of Verdun also came; *his* principal work is the Klosterneuburg altar of about 1185.[3]

Before we consider this 'learned' composition for the immediate purposes of our investigation, I should like to intercalate at this point

---

[1] Cf p. 118.

[2] 'cancellation': to 'cancel' is literally to 'cross' out with a cross or crosses, see dictionaries.

[3] On the Meuse Valley Cross, see the old B.M. *Guide to the Medieval Antiquities* (1924) illus. 44, text pp. 81 ff; or Ernst Kitzinger, *Early Med. Art in the British Museum* (1955) illus. 38 and p. 86. The guide to the Klosterneuburg altar by Floridus Röhrig, *Der Verduner Altar*, published by the monastery, Stift Klosterneuburg, 2nd ed. (1955) with *fifty illustrations*, is an exciting and scholarly introduction to medieval typology.

a question of more particular interest to students of German literature, and consider what might be the answer to it. How many of our Middle High German poets would have understood the symbolism of this cross? Walther von der Vogelweide, Wolfram von Eschenbach? – I doubt it. Hartmann von Aue? – I think, certainly. Hartmann's description of the emaciated hero Gregorius on his rock, 'one could at once have counted all his bones, large and small, showing through his skin',[1] shows him so familiar with the biblical-liturgical words *dinumeraverunt omni ossa mea* that he could accommodate them in the text of his own reasonably pious tale. It was a bold thing for him to do, but in line with his general attitude to sacred lore, which is often more nearly frivolous than the *opinio communis* of our studies allows. Of the same emaciated Gregorius Hartmann had just said, 'One could compare him as follows: imagine someone to have spread a sheet of linen over a thornbush . . .'[2] That is again a 'reserved' simile, normally used in elucidating the symbolism of altar and altarcloth, the two being associated with the ram caught in the thicket, and the body of the sacrificial lamb stretched to the 'four horns' of the altar. Coming immediately before the 'counted bones', this is an allusion to Christ. No other interpretation is possible. Hartmann would, I think, have been able to interpret the Meuse Valley Cross. But let us get back to our subject!

Let us now consider the intentions of the artist who designed the cross, and call to mind the glosses which a contemporary cleric would have been able to offer. Without any further researches a theologically trained cleric would have been able to speak for an hour, or compose a tract, on the five prefigurations – *without* using the word *crucifixerunt* at all. His subject would be 'Man's Redemption and Salvation' or 'The Glorious Cross', for all five images refer to promise, blessing, healing, and there is no representation of Abraham's sacrifice. After the briefest

---

[1] *Man möhte im sam gereite | allez sîn gebeine | grôz unde kleine | haben gezalt durch sîne hût. Gregorius*, 3462 ff.

[2] *ich glîche in disen sachen | als der ein lîlachen | über dorne spreite* . . . More immediate explanations invoking the outward appearance of extreme asceticism, or recalling household linen spread to dry or bleach, are, I think, wayward simplifications. They falsify our picture of Hartmann, moreover, making him seem all too simple and sincere. Hartmann's 'lamb and lion' asides in his *Iwein*, his three ladies with their unguents who restore Iwein to life, and Lunete's declaration ('I know that my lord is alive') all verge on the blasphemous and were intended to tease the more devout members of his audience. See my article 'On coming to terms with Curtius', in *GLL* XI (1958) 375 ff.

reference to the Old Testament stories (these could be assumed both known and recognised in their images) the interpretation would remain at the level of 'allegory', roughly as follows:

The pictures in the horizontal line (widow, Jacob's blessing, the painting of the doorposts with the blood of the lamb) give the interpreter his lead for a long disquisition on the *shape* of the Cross – of *this* cross also, and then on the meaning of the four arms (four dimensions, four directions), with the inevitable citation of 'I draw all things unto me', *omnia traho ad me*, etc. Next, the brazen serpent (?), the cluster of grapes, the two spies. For some of the wide-ranging reflections to which these images give rise, we are not yet (within this chapter) equipped to deal. I will therefore assume most of these to be known from general familiarity with Christian lore (the true vine, the mystic wine-press 'trodden alone', the two spies as the two Testaments, etc.), and concentrate on the serpent-dragon problem – as the expositor would have to do also. Why do we see a dragon at all?[1] This is the point where we need to have this matter explained and disposed of.

With prophetic reference to his death on the Cross, Christ had said in his teaching of Nicodemus:[2] *sicut Moyses exaltavit serpentem . . . ita oportet exaltari Filium hominis*. This is a difficult statement, but clearly one carrying authority. The medieval theologians did not ignore it, or dismiss it as colourful rhetoric, or as 'poetry'. But the Mosan cross does *not* represent the Crucifixion in any of its pictures.[3] We have, therefore, I believe, to think again, or harder. The one thing given in this image *and* in the Chartres statuary group is most certainly *not* a serpent raised on a staff and prefiguring the Crucifixion, but a dragon set on a column. How are we to interpret this? We must go back to the source.

What does the Old Testament in fact say about Moses and his 'serpent'? The text says indeed that he took a serpent, but that it was 'of brass' and that he 'set it up as a sign', *posuit eum pro signo*. What sort of a serpent, however, and what sort of a sign, and sign of what? If one looks up 'sign' in the seventh-century encyclopædia, the *Etymologies* of Bishop Isidore of Seville, one finds a whole section 'on signs' (*De Signis*). It is in fact an article on *standards*, military standards. Reading

[1] See the previous remarks on Moses with a dragon on a column, p. 89, Chartres Cathedral, cf plate 22b.

[2] Cf p. 254, above.

[3] Only the enamels are preserved (mounted now on a perspex cross!). My interpretation would be only slightly modified if there had been a Crucifix on the reverse side.

into the article one sees that both a column (*pila*) and a dragon (*draco*) are also standards. Indeed the dragon is the original standard.

DE SIGNIS: . . . Draconum signa ab Apolline morte Pythonis serpentis inchoata sunt . . . Pilam in signo constituisse fertur Augustus, propter nationes sibi in cuncto orbe subjectas . . .[1]

If the *draco* as a standard goes back to the slaying of Python by Apollo, and the *pila* to Cæsar Augustus because of his dominion over all the nations of the world, it must be evident that what Moses raised 'as a standard' was only apparently a serpent on a staff: in reality and in a deeper historical sense it was a *draco* set on a *pila*. We were therefore not wrong when we persisted in seeing in the Chartres group a fluted column with a dragon on it. The Meuse Valley Cross shows a column with at least a *rampant* brazen serpent, perhaps even a dragon. Certainly not a limp or a writhing snake.

In another part of his encyclopædia, where his subject is not standards but reptiles, Isidore says that the *draco* is the largest of the *serpentes*.[2] Perhaps readers may recall the problems of 'meaning' raised in our minds when we first encountered the dragon, and were considering the kind of lexical entry which would be required to deal with this situation. But to come back to the Mosan cross. In this context the otherwise synonymous *serpens* has to give way to the *draco*, or something very like one (a rampant serpent). The dominant idea of the composition is the Cross as a standard, as banner. There is no suggestion of the reptile *serpens*. This is after all a processional cross, a banner itself, borne aloft before the choir as it marches in, singing the words of the old processional hymn, *Vexilla regis prodeunt* ('the royal banners forward go'). Marching behind this *vexillum* or *signum* the choir may feel it is repeating the victorious way of the children of Israel into the Promised Land. If it is also reminded of the fiery column of which the Old Testament speaks more explicitly, that will be legitimate. *Vexilla regis* is still sung.[3]

Perhaps it is felt that this interpretation is too bookish and recondite. I must admit that I was relieved to find clear evidence that the *draco* as a standard could also be visualised in a less stylised form by at any rate one medieval artist, see plate 22c. Of this very military-looking

---

[1] *Etym.* XVIII iii.    [2] *Etym.* XII iv 4.
[3] *Hymns Ancient and Modern* 96, *English Hymnal* 94.

group in the *Golden Psalter* (841–72) Franz Friedrich Leitschuh said in his history of Carolingian painting, 'a mounted troop led by a standard-bearer with a standard, a dragon'.[1] One may still wonder whether this is merely historian's lore.[2] In a final example from a much earlier Christian century we have evidence of a clearer memory of the real *dracones* of the late Roman world. There is a hymn by Prudentius (d. *c.* 410) devoted to two Roman legionaries who forsook their military service to follow the banner of Christ, and paid the penalty. He sings of them in the *Peristaphanon*, as of early Christian martyrs:

> Cæsaris vexilla linquunt, eligunt signum crucis,
> Proque ventosis draconum quos gerebant pallis
> Præferunt insigne lignum, quod draconem subdidit.[3]

They forsake Cæsar's banners and seek out the standard (*signum*) of the Cross, and instead of the wind-filled cloth dragons which they had been bearing, they raise that ensign-tree (*insigne lignum*) which subdued that [other] dragon.

This is a good example of the 'conceit' in early Christian poetry. It calls for alert attention to the play on *signum*. This brings *lignum*, which in the context of the Crucifixion is *ignobile*, into the same semantic field as *vexillum*: it is now a *lignum insigne* which I hope to have rendered acceptably as 'ensign-tree'. There is the final play on the word *draco*, the Devil, whom we may see here as the artists so often represented him, transfixed or pinned down by the point of the standard, generally the banner of the Resurrection. And so one may continue to speculate, noting as we look back at our material that the column in the plaque of the Meuse Valley Cross is not fluted (as in the Chartres group) but bears a spiral decoration. Its capital is, for a standard, generous, and recalls rather the Tree of Life in Eden, and the spiral would then be the serpent – and so on.[4]

An analysis of the further pictures on this processional cross would lead us too far away from our main subject, to which we gradually

[1] Full title of Leitschuh's work, p. 309 n. 2. The *Psalterium Aureum* is in the Library of the Chapter of St Gall.

[2] The later 'dragoons' have not hitherto been thought to derive their name from this form of standard, but from the nickname of a 'fire-breathing carbine'. [On dragon standards, A. T. Hatto in *GLL* xxii (1968) 25–9.]

[3] *Peristaphanon*, ed. Dressel, I 34 ff.

[4] With the spiral decoration compare the tail of the dragon in plate 22d.

return by asking whether it is this same 'sign' or another cross which is
raised during the ceremony of the Mass. 'In fact' a different cross is
raised. What have medieval writers to say about the cross raised when
the officiating priest takes up the posture of the *orans*?

Thereupon the priest stretches out his arms to their full extent. That
means that our Lord was stretched upon the Holy Cross so direly that
one might have counted all his bones through his skin.[1]

These are the words of the Franciscan preacher Berthold of Regensburg in a sermon on the Mass, about 1270. The priest re-enacts the
raising of the Cross which he himself re-presents as *orans*. The con-
gregation are to see in him Christ stretched on the Cross. This is not a
sign or promise of triumph and victory but 'history': this 'happened'.
The associations are entirely those of sacrifice, immolation. History is
not to be forgotten in the process of 'glorying in the Cross'. That had
also been the message of the Old English *Dream of the Rood*. In that
poem the glorious Cross, which has been extolled in words derived
from the hymn *Pange lingua*, enjoins the visionary to remember too the
inglorious tree which it had first to be. At this point, after the quotation
from Berthold of Regensburg, I think it appropriate to repeat what
was said a few pages ago, namely that the posture of the *orans* – older
than Christianity itself[2] – is the real explanation of the 'cruciform'
Cross of Christian tradition. Christ's prayer, 'Father, forgive them'
(*pater, dimitte illis*) determines the image of *Christus orans*, and to this
the Cross itself must necessarily conform.

If it is now objected that my interpretation of the symbolism of the
Mosan Cross, though medieval enough and instructive, was too long –
longer than we need, I can only reply that I wanted to *show* this kind
of lore in the same way as, above, I displayed the 'straightforward
narrative' of Pseudo-Anselm and Pseudo-Bonaventura. Having done
that I recall that only a relatively short period separates these works:
they all fall into the fifty or so years around our critical date 'about

---

[1] Dar nach strecket der prister die arme sere von ime: daz bezeichent daz unser
herre gedent wart an das heilege cruce als ser, daz man allez sine gebeine gezelt
mohte haben durch sin huet. For this quotation see the text printed in F. J. Mone,
*Schauspiele des Mittelalters*, 2 vols (1846) II 357. Compare St Augustine on Psalm
lxxii 5: '*in nomine tuo levabo manus meas*': . . . *levavit pro nobis Dominus noster manus
in cruce et extensæ sunt manus ejus in cruce*, PL XXXVI 755.
[2] Cf above, Moses before the Amalekites.

1200'. Next, though our first instinct is to say that there is a world of difference between the two modes of contemplating the Cross and the Crucifixion, and that a 'gulf' separates 'simple narrative' on the one hand and clerical lore on the other, that is about as far from the truth as one can get. What we have been dealing with so far, whether 'history' or symbolism, was *all* clerical lore. The difference was one of levels and orientation, not between popular and learned. If difficulty is to be the criterion, it is the Church's historical teaching which calls for discipline and restraint in those commissioned to retell it. The symbolical and typological lore is by comparison easy to learn and handle; it is plentiful, it is well organised. It is at any time a satisfying exercise to recall the 'types'.

The real difficulty will prove in the end not to be that of seeing the connections between 'history' and its prefiguration in 'types' and prophecies, but of discrimination. Here pictures are helpful. They 'hold' their images. The dangers begin when images, perhaps particularly typological representations, are allowed to recall those Old Testament words which Crucifixion narratives had declared, or were soon to declare, 'hereby fulfilled'. On the whole it will appear that ecclesiastical art exercised a restraining influence; but it could not *halt* the speculations of those who thought in words about the Crucifixion at whatever level, for word traditions cannot be 'fixed' with the same finality. How and for how long, as he meditated, was the pious Christian expected to distinguish between a victorious and redeeming brazen serpent (or dragon) and the 'worm and no man' of the Good Friday Psalm, which, according to the Church's own teaching, was equally prophetic of the same Saviour, albeit under another aspect, as 'the rejected of men'? The difficulties of discrimination must have been aggravated when the Church's teaching had to be repeated in the vernaculars, where 'worm' can mean *worm*, *serpent*, and, for that matter, *dragon*. By what means can language (any language) single out the 'duel' fought between Life and Death on the Cross when the verbs available to describe the duel mean either to 'wrestle' or to 'writhe'? The 'overcoming of Death' and the 'throes of death' can be treated in appropriately distinguished and stable images; ambivalence in words can only be avoided in the larger context of a poem or a hymn, which, with or without music, can establish a mood; but even that can only be done successfully on certain days of the liturgical year. On the remaining days the texts are still there for further thought on what may be their meaning. How long could the door-posts be smeared with the blood of the Lamb, brought into association with the Cross (marked indeed with a *Tau*) and not suggest a Cross itself drenched with blood? The chalice of Ecclesia and the basin of the *fons pietatis* were one consummation, at the level of *allegoria*. The blood-drenched Cross is not an invention of the Gothic, but one may certainly speak of a Gothic innovation when narratives relate and pictures show what 'must be' the 'history' behind these allegories.

Long after it had become possible to tell and show all that 'the Evangelists passed over in silence', typological teaching continued. It became more superficial, as we shall see in the next section. The compilers of Mystery Plays meantime found roles for the prophets, who declared their prophecies and re-enacted those of their deeds which had pre-figurative significance. It is wrong to imagine that such didactic scenes will have had little popular appeal. There is on the contrary plenty of evidence in devotional literature that typology could generate new poetry of a humble kind. I have drawn attention elsewhere to Laments of Mary in which the Mother of Christ, approaching the Cross with John, asks: 'Dear Cousin, what is that I see hanging on the tree? Is it man or worm? It twists and writhes in great agony.'[1] I mention as a curiosity, and as evidence perhaps of a finally debased tradition of the serpent as 'type' of the Crucifixion, that according to a recent dictionary of German thieves' cant, a wayside crucifix is, or was until recently, called an 'aufgeschlangelter Bink'.[2] Bink means 'man'. 'Aufgeschlangelt' contains a last reminiscence of the serpent, remembered perhaps in the wording of a Passion Play.


## (b)  *Typology in the* Biblia Pauperum (*fourteenth century*)

There have been objections to the continuing use of the term *Biblia Pauperum* ('Armenbibel'), and Picture Bible (*Biblia picta*) is recommended by some writers. We should not think of a 'poor man's Bible'. That does not alter the fact that the Picture Bibles are unmistakenly a late phenomenon. In respect of the Christian learning they transmit they are the last representatives of a tradition which was already over a

---

[1] 'Christusbild', pp. 34–5. The German rhyme is in fact between 'Wurm' and 'Sturm' (=*certamen*).
[2] Siegmund A. Wolf, *Wörterbuch des Rotwelschen* (Mannheim, 1956) p. 36.

thousand years old. They rehearse this tradition in the final form of an illustrated primer for the use of clergy in the instruction of layfolk. Even if one follows the art historians in their datings and treats typology proper as something which began as late as the grandiose programmes of Abbot Suger of St Denis (d. 1151), the Picture Bibles must be held to mark a final decline, in which the meaningful antithetical pairing of Old Testament 'type' and New Testament 'antitype' has given way to something simpler: a bare juxtaposition of *parallel incidents* or scenes from Old and New Testament with an added lesson. Moreover the Picture Bibles aim to provide 'all the examples', always a sure sign that a tradition is being finally worked out. All the Old Testament parallels which were needed to match the memorable New Testament episodes, canonical and apocryphal, were duly found and incorporated. For all that, 'poor' as the Picture Bibles may be in so many respects, they are not 'the end'. On the contrary, the end of the line had already been reached a century earlier in the Anselm *Dialogue* and the *Meditations* of Pseudo-Bonaventura (and similar works), with their systematic 'historisation' of all tradition, including tradition derived from prophecy, concerning the Crucifixion.

The Picture Bibles elect therefore to keep alive the Church's teaching concerning history,[1] albeit at a more modest and homely level than in such works as the Meuse Valley Cross. The Picture Bibles do not isolate 'story'. They temper history with the lesson of types and prefigurations, and type and antitype are made to look as alike in general outline as tradition will permit. For all that, even this quite rudimentary teaching was by the fourteenth century merely a learned gloss on 'the facts' as these were known from other sources at least equally learned and authoritative. Everyone knew 'what really happened' on Golgotha.

When all these reservations have been made it must still be conceded that *Biblia Pauperum* is not an appropriate designation for the Picture Bibles. It does not do justice to the artists and the commissioners of these works. One is in any case reluctant to disparage works which have provided, and still provide so many students of the Middle Ages with their first introduction to typology. Under two headings, below, I offer analyses of pages from Picture Bibles, one devoted to the Bearing

---

[1] Inverted commas for 'history' and 'historical' will now be used only where ambiguity might still be possible.

of the Cross, one to the Crucifixion, so that we may observe how these subjects are treated. The treatment is anything but purely historical.[1]

### The Bearing of the Cross

The source here is a *biblia picta* of the monastery of St Florian in Austria of about 1310.[2] The Bearing of the Cross is represented in a central medallion, see plate 28. The following prophecies are associated with this episode in the Crucifixion story, each of them attributed to a prophet represented by his head only:[3]

> Jeremiah: (a) Sicut ovis ad occisionem ductus est.
>     (b) Ego quasi agnus mansuetus.
>     (c) Mittamus lignum in panem ejus.
> Solomon: Opprimamus virum justum.

From the days of the Fathers these prophecies had been referred to the Passion of Christ. 'Like a lamb to the slaughter' will seem apt enough as a simile, even to us today, but 'let us put wood in his bread' (in the Authorised Version, 'Let us destroy the tree with the fruit

---

[1] There are three slim, handsome volumes devoted to a facsimile addition of Codex Vindobonensis 1198: *Die Wiener Biblia Pauperum*, ed. by F. Unterkircher, G. Schmidt and J. Stummvoll (Verlag Styria, Graz-Vienna-Cologne, 1962). The pictures of this MS served as models for the enamels added to the Klosterneuburg Altar (see above) when it was rebuilt about 1330. Compare also Gerh. Schmidt, *Die Armenbibeln des XIV. Jahrhunderts* (Graz-Cologne, 1959). This latter is a copiously illustrated study of Picture Bibles. The text is probably fully accessible only to specialists. Section B on 'situation rhymes' and 'picture assimilation' may, however, be more generally useful. See in addition the article 'Armenbibel' in *RDK* where older titles (not repeated here) will also be found.

In appendix 1 to Hans v.d. Gabelentz, *Die kirchliche Kunst im italienischen Mittelalter* (Strassburg, 1907) there is an 'ideal' *Concordia veteris et novi testamenti*; Mrs Jameson (op. cit. II 417 ff) also offers a comprehensive review of Old Testament-New Testament juxtapositions in the *Biblia Pauperum*. As for the *Concordantia Caritatis* (see *RDK*) and the *Pictor in Carmine* (M. R. James, in *Archæologia*, NS XLIV (1951) 141 ff), see above, p. 151 n. 1. I prefer to treat these two exhaustive and systematic programmes of typological learning with extreme caution. They provide, interesting though they may be, primarily evidence of themselves.

[2] This Cross-Bearing is reproduced and discussed in Gerhard Schmidt, *Die Armenbibeln*, etc., plate 2 (lower half)=St Florian, Stiftsbibliothek, Codex III, fo. 6v.

[3] (b) and (c) are Jerem. xi 19; (a) is in fact Isai. liii 7. The Vulgate text of Sap. ii 10 is *opprimamus pauperem justum*.

K                 P.L.A.M.A.

thereof') has always seemed remote from the event to which it is supposed to allude, and there is no 'historical' paraphrase which can mediate satisfactorily. It was generally taken to mean, 'let us make him (the Host) bear the wood of the Cross'.

Apart from *prophecies* of the Bearing of the Cross there are pre-figurative *types* to make up the composition and fill the half page. These are given full pictorial treatment. There is on the left Isaac carrying the wood of *his* sacrifice, and on the right the Widow of Zarephath carrying her two sticks crossed in the form of an X. The emphasis is, however, not on the shape of her burden (as it was in the Mosan cross) but on the carrying of it. Of the two Old Testament episodes which are written out in brief, I leave the story of the Widow to the reader and his magnifying glass. The story of Abraham and Isaac is told more or less according to the Vulgate:[1]

> Legimus in Genesi: Quad cum Abraham et Ysaac pergerent simul et Abraham portauit gladium et ignem, Ysaac uero qui ligna portauit Christum significabat qui lignum crucis in quo immolari pro nobis voluit suo corpore proprio portauit.

But even in this reduction more words are used to associate the incident with Christ's Cross-Bearing than to tell the story itself. This is followed by the 'lesson':

> Ligna ferens Christe te
> presignat puer iste
> fert crucis hic lignum
> Christo reputans sibi dignum.

This, with the story of the Widow, is the content of the page (half a page). The Bearing of the Cross as an image is firmly associated with the *image* and the story in words of Isaac's and the Widow's bearing of their burdens of wood, and with certain Old Testament prophecies which are not pictorially rendered. These various associations provide a modestly learned framework of reference for the Bearing of the Cross. It is clear from this example that the Picture Bible is not primarily or even incidentally concerned to add to the story of the cross-bearing, or to add any realistic detail to its pictorial representation.

---

[1] The text is offered without editorial refinements.

*The Crucifixion*

This time our source is a Budapest manuscript from Upper Austria, about 1330.[1] The central picture in this composition (see plate 29a and compare plate 28, right) represents a Crucifix – a three-nail crucifixion. Here I shall have rather more to say about the prophecies adduced, and refer more briefly to the types.

(*Above, left*) David: foderunt manus meas et pedes meos, dinumer. etc.
(*Above, right*) Isaiah: oblatus est quia ipse voluit et peccata nostra ipse portauit.
(*Below, left*) Job: numquid capis Leviathan gladio.
(*Below, right*) Habakkuk: cornua in manibus ejus, ibi abscondita est fortitudo ejus.

These prophecies call for the following comments. David is quoted for his twenty-first Psalm to which we have referred throughout. Note that '*dinumer. etc.*' is sufficient to represent *dinumeraverunt omnia ossa mea.* Isaiah is given the words *peccata nostra* instead of *dolores nostra.*[2] The other two prophecies require fuller annotation. The words of Job on the 'drawing out of Leviathan with an hook' (here 'with a sword'),[3] and those of Habakkuk concerning 'horns coming out of his hands'[4] and the 'hiding of his power' – taken together – gave the authority for endlessly repeated variations on the theme of the 'Divine Angler' with his *line* (the genealogy of Christ), the *bait* (Christ) and the concealed *hook* (the Cross) on which the Leviathan (the Devil) was to be caught. This patristic 'conceit' is to be found down to and including Luther who had the good sense not to make fun of it. It seems later to be superseded by what has been called the 'mouse-trap theory of the Redemption'.[5] It is equally important to know that these somewhat whimsical ideas of the Fathers laid up stores of difficulties for the later serious theologians, in that it is not acceptable to think of the Redemption as a plot contrived to deceive the Devil ('Überlistung des Teufels'). The deception of the Devil was already strongly suggested in the Apocryphal *Gospel of Nicodemus* (or 'Acts of Pilate') part II, where

[1] G. Schmidt, op. cit., plate 12b.    [2] Isai. liii 7.
[3] Job xl 20 = A.V. xli 1.    [4] Hab. iii 4.
[5] Is the mousetrap the late medieval painter's substitute image for something impossibly 'unrealistic' which could not be accommodated to a 'homely' setting?

there is panic in Hades during the Trial and Crucifixion of Christ. The patriarchs and prophets have begun to assemble near the gates, Lazarus has been lost. It was inferred in the Middle Ages that the Devil was prompted in his panic to seek through Pilate's wife to stop the Trial of Christ. Engaging as the idea may be that the Devil had misread the signs, it has unwelcome corollaries for the theologians. The most frequently reproduced picture of the Divine Angler occurs in the *Hortus Deliciarum*.[1] We refer to this picture in German studies because a stanza in the *Ezzolied* shows the poet to be perfectly familiar with this piece of clerical lore. That leaves the 'horns in his hand(s)' in the prophecy of Habakkuk unexplained. We come back to the 'horns' later.

The 'types' represented are, to the left of the Crucifixion, Abraham's sacrifice: an angel seizes Abraham's sword to stay his hand (the story is also told). To the right we see Moses' raising of the serpent on a Y-shaped branching staff or pole. This is a very different image from that of the Mosan Cross, properly so, for the context here is 'sacrifice', not victory or triumph. The text assures us, it is true, that 'the contemplation of this image is a remedy against snake-bite, it can save us from Hell'(!), but for all that, the serpent is no *draco*. It is equally not a 'worm' (*vermis*), and the body of the Crucified, though accommodated to the line of the prefiguring serpent does not 'writhe'. In short, there is little or nothing here showing preoccupation with 'what really happened'; there is no undue emphasis on physical suffering.

If one now extends 'Picture Bible' to include such other fourteenth-century works as the *Speculum Humanæ Salvationis* and the *Holkham Bible Picture Book* of about 1330,[2] we shall find rather more to put us in mind of realistic details in the art of late Gothic. In the *Speculum*, of which there are different redactions, there is more which lends itself to 'realistic' exploitation than in the *biblia picta*. The Holkham Bible Picture Book – a unique manuscript – remembers the lesson of typology, but has already absorbed it into story and is silent about types and prefigurations. We shall, however, deal with these two works only to the extent that we need them for our main enquiry. Indeed I consider

---

[1] Straub-Keller plate XXIV, Schwietering illus. 32.
[2] I class these only loosely together. There is no overt typology in *Holkham* (see below), the text of which I am editing for the Anglo-Norman Text Society. On the *Speculum*, see below.

only one picture from each, with the help of which I carry our story of a general trend towards 'realism' one step forward. I am concerned with the creation of certain *roles*, and the invention of *things* which were needed to complete the 'ætiological' version of the Crucifixion story. It is in this sense only that I use the term 'realism' in the remainder of this chapter.

In the *Speculum* we encounter an Old Testament figure who had long been waiting in the wings to be called upon to play a New Testament role, namely Tubalcain. His image had long been known. He is in the gallery of Old Testament figures to be found in a fully illustrated Genesis, for instance the Old English *Cædmon Genesis*, or on a Cathedral West front. He was obviously predestined to become the smith who made the nails of the Crucifixion. In the *Speculum Humanæ Salvationis* he is represented in his smithy with his two apprentices, see plate 27a. He supervises their work. They are hammering at a piece of iron on an anvil. These are according to the title of the picture, the 'inventors of the art of the smith and of melody',[1] which at once tells us that Jubal and Tubalcain have become one person – as in the *Cædmon Genesis*[2] – but immediately split up again into a master and his servants. This scene in the smithy is to the right of a scene representing a Crucifixion *jacente cruce*, where one old man and two young assistants each drive in a nail. The title of this composition is 'Christ crucified foretold his death in figures'.[3] That is surely remarkable, but the Middle Ages knew many things which we have forgotten. The only Passion prophecy which can be associated with the work of the smiths and music-makers is to be found in Psalm cxxviii, verse 3. The Vulgate Latin is *supra dorsum meum fabricaverunt peccatores*. The Authorised Version reads 'the plowers plowed upon my back'. A far cry still, modern readers will think, from anything that we would recognise as music-making or forging or nailing. That is precisely the point. We said that Tubalcain had been waiting a long time to be called upon. In the end he seems to have come in on half a cue, claiming as a *faber* the right to play this role. (The Fathers had *always* determined the meaning

---

[1] *Inventores artis fabricariæ et melodiarum.* Our plate 27a corresponds to fo 50 in the blockbook *Speculum humanæ salvationis*, facs. ed. by Ernst Kloss (Munich, 1925). In the critical edition of J. Lutz and P. Perdrizet (two vols, Leipzig, 1909) the same juxtaposition of Tubalcain with apprentices and a Nailing to the Cross will be found in plates 45 and 132 (clm 146; Paris, MS Bibl. Nat. fr. 6275).

[2] Cf p. 291 n. 1.

[3] *Christus crucifixus mortem suam figuris predixit.*

of *fabricaverunt* in the light of *supra dorsum meum*, as the work of 'plowers' who drew deep furrows on Christ's back at the Flagellation, and when they stretched him on the Cross.) In the *Speculum* 'fabricatores' is the appropriate name for Tubalcain[1] and his apprentices who make music on the anvil with their hammer blows, which they continue to deliver at the Crucifixion. We shall soon see that music-making is perhaps a dominant idea among all the principal similes, metaphors and symbols of the Crucifixion. Violence is done to sacred texts here only in the association of music-making with the work of *peccatores*, but even this makes sense in the end. The music-making of the sinners is that of cruel hammer blows on crude nails, again the intention of the enemies of Christ. For the moment we are concerned, however, with roles and things. The exegetes have now found their smith, the hammers and a source for the nails.

If the modern reader thinks that this is all an unnecessary digression, and that it is enough to say that there *had* to be nails and hammers at the Crucifixion if Doubting Thomas was later shown the 'imprint of the nails', then I am afraid I have to say that the modern reader has still to make his first acquaintance with the exegetical methods of Christian theologians in the Middle Ages. Any self-respecting theologian would have rejected with contempt the suggestion that he might make rationalistic inferences of this kind. Christ's instruction had been that *all things* concerning him were to be sought in the Old Testament.[2] But the exegete's task is not yet complete. There clearly had to be a smith; he had found him, the *first* smith. That makes him eminently *suitable* as a type, but at the same time *impossible*, because there is no corresponding New Testament antitype for him to prefigure. Providentially however, his final role is to *do nothing*! In the fully evolved ætiological story there had to be some good cause why the smith *could not* make his nails as requested by the wicked Jews, and why therefore – the nails being needed in a hurry – his wife had to make them. If in the end the Christian faithful prove to be the *fabricatores*, it is indeed a venial sin.

---

[1] Tubalcain + Jubal, see above.

[2] The proof of the nails was given above, p. 253 n. 2. The hammers are more or less justified by reference to Tubalcain, but for them and the pincers of the Deposition there is no acceptable proof-text. It is interesting to see what 'objects' can be included in a complete array of the *Arma Christi*: the column of the Flagellation, the lance, Stephaton's rod and sponge, the vinegar bucket, etc.; the ladder, hammers, nails and pincers; the dice, Peter's cock, the cheek-smiting hand (mailed), Christ's beard, Judas's kiss, cf Timmers, *Symboliek*, illus. 58; *RDK* s.v.

They invented *ex nihilo* the smith's wife, calling her Hedroit (I have not discovered why), or Isault, presumably so called after another woman who had shown a certain crude ingenuity in the handling of red-hot iron. And so we learn that the smith, approached by the Jews, finds his striking hand smitten with some foul disease (see plate 27b reproducing the Holkham Bible treatment of this scene). His vicious wife leaps forward and says that she will make the nails. It is not surprising that they are crudely fashioned, blunt at the point but sharp at the edges. Not only does the Holkham Bible show (Isault) at her forge; it relates this whole episode in Anglo-Norman.[1]

## 7. THE ORIGINS OF LATE MEDIEVAL REALISM

The purpose of the last long section was *inter alia* to show that the Christian Middle Ages did not hasten with all possible speed to evolve and propagate a purely historical account of the Crucifixion. The release of the approved historical accounts (Anselm, Bonaventura –

---

[1] The text must as yet be read in the facsimile edition of W. O. Hassall (London, 1954), fo. 31r (lower half). The smith's wife is Isault in the *Mystère de la Passion* (Angers), ed. O. Jodogne (Gembloux, 1959), where the episode is very fully told. Somewhat arbitrarily I extend this footnote to accommodate the only treatment to be found in this book of the *three-nail Crucifixion*. A good starting-point and general introduction to this subject (of considerable dispute) is the article by K. A. Wirth, 'Dreinagelkruzifixus', in *RDK* or Elisabeth Roth, *Der volkreiche Kalvarienberg* 2nd ed. (Berlin, 1967) pp. 26 ff. Early opponents of this iconography called the three nails an invention of the Cathars, see Arno Borst, *Die Katharer* (Schriften der MGH xii) (Stuttgart, 1953) p. 128. While naturally acknowledging the importance of the number three, I still incline (as in 'Christlicher Erzählstoff', p. 287) to associate the transition from four-nail to three-nail Crucifixions in the thirteenth century with the portrayal of Christ dead on the Cross. This required not only a bowed head and closed eyes, but for completeness also crossed feet. What was said in theological debates and at synods is *retrospective* rationalisation, the solution of a dilemma which had become an embarrassment. We have one important text, the *Vita Rhythmica Salvatoris* which explains the three nails in narrative terms, i.e. ætiologically: Christ refused to have his legs parted. In *Christi Leiden in einer Vision geschaut* (see next note for edition) the *fourth* nail is driven in, but through *both* feet which are crossed only after the third nailing. In provincial carvings the head of the fourth nail has occasionally been filed away, leaving one foot apparently unnailed. In Middle High German poetry around 1200 we already find three nails referred to in a poem dubiously ascribed to Walther von der Vogelweide (L 37, 4) and in Wolfram von Eschenbach's *Willehalm* (108, 3). There will never be a finally convincing solution of this problem.

there were others, less influential) was, I have suggested, meant rather to put an end to speculations and to stabilise matters, at least for the clergy and the orders. Because of the continued adherence to the doctrine of the fourfold sense of the Biblical word, we may not assume either that there was a slow and inevitable development towards *historia*, 'historisation'. Mainly for these reasons I declared at the beginning of this account that we should not attempt to treat our subject chronologically. But now, as we reach the half-way mark in this chapter, we find ourselves dealing increasingly with 'late' phenomena, and what was a strategy of exposition now begins to conform to what was the historical sequence of events. None the less we can still not proceed purely chronologically. There is a category of Cross and Crucifixion symbolism which I have reserved for the final section of this chapter. There the story is not one of development but of collapse and disintegration. We therefore continue with the exposition along the lines we had been following, but, to repeat, we shall now be dealing increasingly with traditions concerning the Crucifixion in their late and final decline – towards *historia* and 'realism'.

In the concluding stages, say from 1200 (or 1250) to 1400 (or 1450) we have always to allow for the presence and the influence of the incorrigible historian and 'realist' among those transmitting inherited tradition. This is the man who 'sees' behind every shadow and figure the historical factor which alone explains things finally and fully to his satisfaction. If *he* hears, for example in the words of the prophet Jeremiah, that Christ was 'carried' to the slaughter like a lamb (*quasi agnus mansuetus ad victimam portatur*), he sees what others have not wanted to see, namely the carrying. He interprets that Christ was driven along by so turbulent a crowd of his enemies that he 'never once properly set his foot on the ground'.[1] He could not be contradicted when the commemorative Liturgy varies these words and attributes them to Christ himself: *eram quasi agnus innocens, ductus sum ad immolandum.* When are these words remembered? At Matins on Thursday of Holy Week.[2] 'Led' and 'carried' are evidently both true. Christ was 'led', understand 'carried along'.

[1] Also brachten sy in zo der portzen der stede, dat he nye eynen rechten trit mit synen voissen gedede, Dan sleiffen vnd kechen, bis sy in brechten in Annas huys. *Christi Leiden in einer vision geschaut*, ed. Pickering (Manchester, 1952) 66, 28–31.

[2] It is not possible in the restricted compass of this chapter to demonstrate the *contribution of the Liturgy* itself to the evolution of the Gothic Passion tradition. It must suffice to recall that the prophecies of the Passion were virtually from the

For such an exegete history comes first, and everything is or may be history. What the Church is prepared to *sing*, he is prepared to *say*. What is true can be said and told without embellishing figures, unless these provide a striking likeness, possibly reinforced by an authoritative *sicut – ita*. He finds that there is much that Anselm and Bonaventura had overlooked, or they were concealing something. He can improve on their accounts. We shall have to consider some of the results of his endeavours. But at the same time there were others in his day, less intent on research, who got a better hearing because they 'saw' better and even more clearly, and were more eloquent in the telling of what they saw. These are the spirits who claim attention in our histories of religion and popular piety. They found the words to stir and move.

So that these undoubtedly important developments shall not appear here in the dangerous isolation they so often enjoy in our handbooks, I shall stress as I go along what I believe to have been the intentions of the *artists* of this and the immediately following periods, for there can be no doubt that the apparent 'detailed realism' in the visions of visionaries and mystics (say from 1180 to 1350 or 1400) results in large measure from all too fervid contemplation of the images of Christian art. There is often a clearly wilful 'historisation' of what the artists had intended to be seen as symbols and allegories.

To illustrate these observations, let us start from the words of the hymn of Venantius Fortunatus, Bishop of Poitiers (*c.* 600):

Flecte ramos, arbor alta, tensa laxa viscera

Bend, O lofty tree, thy branches, thy too rigid sinews bend.[1]

---

beginning included in the office of Holy Week. Isaiah liii ('Man of Sorrows') and Isaiah lxiii ('Who is this that cometh from Edom, with dyed garments from Bozrah. . . . Wherefore art thou red in thine apparel and thy garments like him that treadeth in the wine-fat?' 'I have trodden the winepress alone') have the status of New Testament readings. Because of his prophecies of the Passion, Isaiah was unofficially declared *quasi Evangelista* or 'the fifth Evangelist'. Throughout the Middle Ages the Mass was, moreover, interpreted from the viewpoint of the history of the Passion. The officiating priests were held to enact the sequence of the Passion story, see the section 'Die mittelalterlichen Messerklärungen' in Adolph Franz, *Die Messe im deutschen Mittelalter* (Freiburg, 1902; reprint Darmstadt, 1963) pp. 333 ff, or the corresponding passages in Jungmann, or Yrjö Hirn, *The Sacred Shrine, A study of the Poetry and Art of the Catholic Church*, (orig. 1909; rev. English edition London, 1958), ch. 5, 'The Mass'.

[1] *Hymns Ancient and Modern* 97, *English Hymnal* 96, part II in each case.

These are lines from the Eastertide hymn, *Pange lingua*. From its earliest days the Church had seen the Crucified with sinews stretched on the Cross, his bones so visible that they could be counted, and had called for compassion with him. Pious Christians countless times prayed to the Cross, imploring it to bow – in homage to its victim, to bend and show mercy, 'be softened'; and occasionally visionaries saw how the Cross did bow in response to their earnest supplications. This vision came to be particularly associated with St Bernard. Others held that 'that might not be'; for instance the poet of the Old English *Dream of the Rood*. The authoritative image remained: *tensa viscera* and *dinumerata ossa*. But a train of thought more generally associated with this image was of the Redeemer, who in the posture of an *orans* and as Bridegroom 'drew all unto him' in accordance with the words: *omnia traham ad meipsum*. 'This he said,' says St John, 'signifying what death he should die.'[1] Such was to be the response to the cry uttered in the *Canticle*, 'trahe me post te, curremus . . .'[2]

Kneeling before such a Crucifix the faithful might also meditate on the length, breadth and height of the love of the Redeemer,[3] and on the dimensions of his Cross. Such was the devotion of the Cross, whether the medieval artist intended his image to show or allude to the *patibulum* of the Old Law, the Tree of Victory foreshadowed in the *palma* of the *Canticle*, the trellis of the True Vine, the staff or column of the Brazen Serpent, the altar of the Lamb, the throne of the King, the pulpit of the High Priest. I must say a little more about this list of possible allusions in medieval images.

If the artist thought particularly of the 'numbered bones' of Psalm xxi, he drew or carved a body taut on the cross with ribs displayed, but at the same time he might avoid a purely 'historical' representation by making the Cross recognisably a palm-tree Cross (plate 26a). His picture was then only in part historical, mainly allegorical. More allegorical Crucifixions illustrating *ascendam in palmam* had been attempted by early masters of ivory carving, with the Saviour putting a resolute foot on a step on the Cross, or on the rung of a short ladder, about to mount the Cross voluntarily. But as we have already indicated, the palm-tree Cross was found to be a more satisfactory way of associating the Bridegroom of the *Canticle*, the antecedent mounting being then more discreetly alluded to by a 'kind of step'. This same step, modified in shape and size and glossed with the help of a chalice

[1] John xii 32–3.        [2] Cant. i 3.        [3] Ephes. iii 18.

could alternatively indicate rather the altar of sacrifice, whereon Christ is then the perfect Sacrifice. Or it could 'mean' the footstool beneath the feet of the King who ruled from the Cross. Or yet again it might indicate the pulpit of the High Priest. Meanwhile the only satisfactory reference to the Brazen Serpent, 'like which' Christ had said that he would be 'raised up', was by making the hanging body of the Crucified follow the serpentine line of an S or Z, see plate 26b.[1]

These may all have been artists' intentions. There was nothing an artist could do to prevent his picture being interpreted in the light of what it 'in fact showed'. The artist's purpose and intentions, even the very subject of his image, could and can always be more or less arbitrarily misunderstood and reinterpreted by anyone 'so minded'. A contributory factor in the artist's defencelessness was no doubt that he was not always certain what the various traditions and conventions of representation meant, or had once meant. Though it takes us a little out of the way, I should like at this point to refer to the unusual iconography in the Descent from the Cross on the so-called Extern Stones (*Externsteine*) in the Teutoburg Forest near Detmold. This is one of the most remarkable and spectacular Christian monuments in Europe (plate 31). The Extern Stones themselves are a bizarre group of sandstone rocks with cavernous chapels which may in origin be pre-Christian. What interests us here is the monumental relief with life-size figures representing the Descent from the Cross, the date of which has been estimated as about 1130. Some of the figures are both weathered and mutilated, but there can be no doubt about the determination of the principal iconographical features. Mary and John flank the central group consisting of Joseph of Arimathea and Nicodemus at the deposition. God the Father has received into his arms the soul of Christ (represented as a child) and at the same time holds the banner of the Resurrection. Sun and Moon peer over a veil. But what is Nicodemus (?) standing on to assist in the deposition? This cannot be anything but a palm-tree, bent over under the weight of Christ's follower.[2] This is a

---

[1] The S-line was no doubt often preferred on purely 'stylistic' grounds, and were style and not iconography our subject here, we should say 'Byzantine', just as we might invoke *cloisonné*, should we wish to consider the 'counted bones' with reference to the effective use of materials and the exploitation of techniques.

[2] This palm-tree was the subject of scandalous misinterpretation in the Nazi period, when it was claimed as a clear representation of the Germanic 'Irminsäule'. Goethe, however, was not fooled. He recognised the tree as a tree, but he claimed it, I think, as the palm-tree of his favourite emblem-books, not as the *palma* of the *Canticle*. 'One of those engaged in taking down the body appears to

curious misapplication of the text *ascendam in palmam* from the *Canticle* which, according to the Church, refers to Christ's victorious ascent of the Cross. The example took us indeed somewhat out of our way, and was not strictly relevant. The artist was, I think we may safely say, at fault in the matter of the palm-tree and out of touch with standard practice in using the conventional soul symbol in the representation of Christ's death on the Cross. The uncertainty of the artists (generally) may be in part responsible for their tendency to accumulate non-historical elements in their depictions of the Crucifixion. They show not only Sun and Moon covering their faces with a veil, and the rent curtain of the Temple, but also Church with her chalice and Synagogue with broken lance beside Mary and John as flanking figures (plate 26a). There may also be a serpent at the foot of the Cross and Adam's skull for good measure. These all serve to counterbalance, diminish or even cancel the more historical details such as bucket and sponge, dice, pincers, hammers and the rest. The final, composite image is then clearly not intended as a 'historical' record.[1] It is not so much a depiction of the scene on Calvary at a given moment as a sermon on the Crucifixion. But there is scarcely a medieval representation of the Crucifixion which can frustrate the intentions of the historical rationaliser, when the rationaliser has set his mind on 'history'. The point now, of this long preamble is that the artist who had represented the Cross as a palm-tree (or any kind of tree) had no means of refuting those who quoted him in support of their contention; namely, that the wicked Jews had not even taken the trouble to plane their cross. 'They could not wait; they preferred it to be thus.' They 'pulled his body over the stumps so that the wounds bled again', thus fulfilling the remembered prophecy that the 'plowers plowed deep furrows' upon his back,

---

have stepped on a tiny tree which has bent down under the weight of the man, whereby the tedious ladder is avoided' (Hamburg ed., xii 208): Ein den Leichnam herablassender Teilnehmer scheint auf einen niedrigen Baum gestiegen zu sein, der sich durch die Schwere des Mannes umbog, wodurch die immer unangenehme Leiter vermieden ist.

[1] Paul Thoby, *Le Crucifix des Origines au Concil de Trente*, (Nantes, 1959 with a supplement) offers illustrations of 400 Crucifixes and a systematic 'objective' analysis of each. The author tries in addition to establish for each century the typical form of the Cross, the typical posture of the Crucified, etc. Thoby derives his types from 'historical' and 'allegorical' representations without differentiation. I add without any intention of malice that I have found this study a valuable guide to what investigators with entirely different interests may see in works of Christian art.

etc. The same interpreters knew that the Brazen Serpent is the sign of the victory of the Redeemer, see plate 26b. They also knew that the victory was preceeded by an 'agony' ending in the death of one who had called himself 'a worm and no man'. No doubt the artist had represented or alluded to the victory, but for all that his S-line meant the serpent locked in battle *and* the writhing worm. Was one not enjoined to remember *both* images of Christ, not only Christ in victory, or glory at the Transfiguration, but also in his humiliation, the rejected of men who 'hath no form or comeliness'.[1]

Here, surely, the reader must by now think, we should pause to reflect on the changes in religious feeling which gave rise to these tendencies. They clearly betoken a coarsening of sensibility or the debasement of a theology of suffering ('Leidenstheologie'). That would, however, still be premature, and it would make our argument circular. The interpreters who thought along the lines we have just indicated were, after all, still *exegetes* of a kind. There were precedents in past tradition for their methods, even for their 'argument from the image', see below. There are other reasons in addition why we may not stop to enlarge on the signs of a decline in 'taste'. First of all we have not yet completed our account of the sources of medieval Crucifixion tradition. There are, secondly, other writers, to whom we have alluded, following different methods. They visualised the Crucifixion in scarcely less drastic terms. They are still held (by some) in high esteem because of their sheer *visonary power* and the literary qualities of their revelations.

The peculiar gift – in this context – of visionaries, is to see and respond to the sufferings of Christ during the Passion with an intensity and fervour which moves and convinces. They may indeed profoundly influence religious feeling in their own time and thereafter. They may become Saints of the Church. That does not absolve us from the duty of scrutinising the content of their visions, to consider what its sources may be. Let us not become deeply involved in visions as such, or in a discussion of the way of life of those who from time to time were granted them. It is a fact of textual and iconographical history that what the many visionaries of the later Middle Ages saw, coincides for the greater part with what Anselm in his *Dialogue* and Bonaventura in

---

[1] Psalm xxi 7: *Ego autem sum vermis, et non homo; opprobrium hominum, et abjectio plebis.* Generally quoted *vermis sum,* etc. Isaiah liii 2: *Non est species ei, neque decor.*

the *Meditations* had already related, and the artists had meantime drawn or carved. The rest (what else they saw) was, in the main, soon forgotten. There is only a very small number of innovations to be attributed to the visionaries of which we may say that they entered into or modified central tradition, for instance the 'vision of St Bernard', in which the Crucified leans forward to embrace the Saint.

Just as in a previous chapter we found the apparently boundlessly ecstatic vision of Hildegard of Bingen to consist almost entirely of quotations from or allusions to the *Canticle* and *Ecclesiasticus*, so the Revelations of St Bridget (1303–73) prove on a close examination of the texts attributed to her[1] to be a mosaic of reminiscences: of her readings of all kinds (Bible, Liturgy, Hymns to the Virgin and the older Passion narratives) – and of the works of ecclesiastical art as she had meditated upon them. Imagining herself then in the role of the Mother of Jesus – she had visited the Holy Places – she related what she saw and felt in the Cave of the Nativity (with the help of *Pseudo-Matthew* and its derivatives), on the Way of the Cross and on Calvary (with the help of current narrative traditions). Her visions differ in their iconographical content from the tracts of Anselm and Bonaventura in that she takes as given and describes what they had been concerned to demonstrate and teach. By her time the common tradition of the Passion was anybody's for the effective retelling.[2] St Bridget's *Revelations* were more successful, if only on the evidence of her canonisation, than other more or less contemporary works in the same or in related genres. In St Bridget there is a balance of sentiment and vivid narrative, emotional fervour and callousness, which other writers did not strike. But literary history is not our task here. For all that, there is, as far as I can see, only one iconographical trait in her image of the Crucifixion which may be claimed as peculiarly hers. That is her insistence that the abdomen of the Crucified was so

---

[1] St Bridget wrote in Swedish. For safety's sake I refer to the Latin text of her Revelations, prepared for her canonisation in October 1391 (edited as *Revelationes cælestis seraphicæ matris S. Birgittæ Suecæ*, Munich 1680). About the versions in the various vernaculars (e.g. German and English) I can offer no more than an impression that they are all much nearer to the Anselm-Bonaventura tradition, but *en masse* completely beyond editorial aid. The passage in the first German print (Lübeck, 1496) which I quote in the next note is not to be found in the Latin. On the state of the English texts, see EETS 178, pp. xix ff.

[2] When Suso, Ludolf of Saxony and St Bridget had written their various works, Anselm and Bonaventura were no longer really quotable as sources and authorities.

shrunken and desiccated as to be a concavity – *Venter dorso inhærens consumpto humore quasi non haberet viscera.*[1] It must also be conceded that her account moves with a freedom that suggests independence of sources. She had absorbed her sources into her experience. With these she had, however, also absorbed some of the speculations of the realists and 'historians' concerning physiological possibilities. St Bridget *saw*, for instance, that the weight of Christ's body discernably enlarged the wounds in his hands. It is not possible to say with certainty whether it was St Bridget or her German translator of about 1490 who finally 'therefore postulates' that the same ropes with which the limbs had been pulled 'will also have been used for the fastening to the Cross'.[2]

There were others – in plenty – who did not themselves enquire with the students of liturgical texts, or see with the vision of a St Bridget of a Suso. They *saw* merely, willingly, often with a crass realism partly engendered by the ease with which words beget words. Their works are fairly evenly distributed through the countries of Western Europe. They enlarged their compassion to include the victim of indignities and brutalities *however* described, for 'no one can describe . . .'

In the accounts and representation of the Passion in the pre-Reformation period there is a final accession of 'historical' details for which – now that we are familiar with a number of exegetical procedures – explanations can be suggested. There is not the space here to deal with them all, or to deal with any of them properly. By 'properly' I mean specifying the innovation, and then 'justifying' it by reference to Old Testament prophecy and the related symbols. Merely to name

[1] The influence of St Bridget of Sweden on the religious art of the later Middle Ages has been asserted, but generally on the basis of a direct comparison of her text with the pictures of the late Gothic, ignoring her sources. Where there are close correspondences in mood and in iconographical detail (perhaps a *venter dorso inhærens*), one should first ask whether this is Crucifixion iconography or 'St Bridget illustration'. In the case of the Nativity scene, the mysterious light for which St Bridget has been held to be the source is in fact present in the *Infancy Gospels* and in the *Narrationes de Vita et Conversatione Beatæ Virginis Mariæ* (etc.) edited by Oskar Schade (Halle, 1870).

[2] alzus wert hyr ghesat ein cruzifix so alze de here an dat crutze wart ghebunden unde ghenegelt. (*Sunte Birgitten Openbaringe*, Lübeck 1496, fo. cxivr, see my article 'Christlicher Erzählstoff', p. 285 n 2.) This is the fifteenth-century testimony of a belief in nails *and* ropes which I spoke about above, p. 244, with reference to St Hilary of Poitiers (fourth century). I know of no instances between these two dates, and, as I have said, the artists clung to the truth of properly authenticated tradition; they did not represent their surmises. I owe this reference to the Lübeck print to the late Prof. William Foerste (*d.* Sept. 1967).

the cases, for instance the *spike-block* fixed to the hem of Christ's robe during the bearing of the Cross,[1] or the violent crossing of Brook Kedron, or the Crucifixion on an insecure cross which 'over-balanced',[2] gets us little further. What does not cease to amaze me is that Albrecht Dürer included so many of these late discoveries of over-enthusiastic 'historians' in his *Grosse Passion* and the *Grosser Kalvarienberg* of 1505.[3] In the latter work, a 'simultaneous' picture of the whole Way of the Cross represented as a 'serpentine', he includes even the breaking out of Christ's teeth before the Crucifixion. This is a grossly literal and transparently pseudo-historical exploitation of a verse in the Lamentations of Jeremiah, 'he hath also broken my teeth with gravelstones'.[4] This example may suffice.

Before we begin our last section in this chapter we shall be wise to recall that emphasis on the physical suffering of the Saviour is not an innovation of the late Middle Ages. From the days of the early debates on Christ's humanity it was an article of faith, written indeed into the text of some early creeds,[5] that Christ suffered not only 'physically, not figuratively' (*corporaliter et non umbratice*) but 'as never a man before'. There are countless passages in Migne's *Patrologia Latina* dealing rhetorically with the 'sum' of his *physical* sufferings. By 'rhetorically' I mean that it appears to have been a set literary (and no doubt spiritual) exercise to *rehearse* the human weaknesses (hunger, thirst, fatigue), and the more than human sufferings of Christ as man according to some stylistic pattern. One finds the *summa* as a series of nouns with a single adjective, of verbs in the passive with a superlative adverb, as rows of participles, and so on. Or one could, or at any rate St Bernard could, substitute for each torment in turn the old Testament prophecy of it.[6] Virtuosity of this kind must on any reckoning seem hazardous. There is plenty of evidence, even in earlier centuries, of readiness to accept

[1] I mention this, as in *Festgabe Hammerich* (see p. 249 n. 1), p. 210, because James Marrow (at present Research Fellow in the University of Reading) will write at length on this subject.

[2] The 'formula' for this is indicated in 'Christusbild', p. 36 n 41.

[3] Fr. Winkler, *Die Zeichnungen A.Ds.* (1936) II, plates 317 ff. Reluctantly I have suppressed a plate reproducing the drawing (genuine) of the tooth-breaking because it is interpretable only with the help of the finished picture (dubiously Dürer's) and Breughel's adaptation.

[4] Lament. iii 16: *et fregit ad numerum dentes meos*; Luther: Er hat meine Zähne zu kleinen Stücken geschlagen.

[5] Cf A. Hahn, *Bibliothek der Symbole*, 3rd ed. (1897) pp. 209 ff.

[6] See 'Christusbild', p. 28.

this hazard. In the *Opus Paschale* of the fifth century Sedulius enjoined the faithful to 'believe' that at the Scourging Christ's back was 'ploughed with lashes and torn with insults'.[1] His reference to furrows is a passing reference – of gruesome realism – which he seeks to cancel by adding the boldly figurative 'torn with insults', so leading his readers back to the sacred words of the Psalm and the Liturgy (Passion Sunday): *supra dorsum meum fabricaverunt peccatores*. Unless one allows that such calculated risks were successfully taken in Sedulius' day, we shall have to seek the origins of Gothic 'realism' in the fifth century! Later centuries continued to take these risks, relying on the ability of the Church to preserve the distinction between words of prophecy *sung* in commemoration, and the same words used in the context of continuous *narrative*. When Christ said 'sitio', for instance, he said only this word. The words of the Passion Psalm xxi were being fulfilled. They are: *lingua mea adhæsit faucibus meis*. These were not yet drawn into the syntax of a historical statement. The weakness of this distinction is that the Liturgy offers examples of such adaptation, and in the course of time many words of prophecy became 'simple words' and spoke their message in whatever context they were used. All that was required was to imagine Christ himself quoting prophecy. He had then said 'I thirst; my tongue cleaveth to my jaws'. The final stage is reached in the Passion tracts where 'his tongue cleaved' etc., because of the exhaustion he had suffered on the way.

One further thought before we sum up this section. From earliest days the Church had known of a *necessary* connection between the words *flagellatus* (or *flagellis cæsus*) of the Evangelists and the 'stripes' (*livores*) of Isaiah's prophecy, 'by which we are healed'; and between the Man of Sorrows scourged by his persecutors, and the prophecy that his appearance would be that of a leper. It was only in the later Middle Ages that writers wrote out in full how that prophecy came to be fulfilled. They *named* each part of the body on which, from the crown of the head to the sole of his foot, no part was left whole, and they virtually counted the 'forty-less-one strokes'[2] they saw, and counted the wounds and weals which made him appear 'like a leper', *quasi leprosus*. Or they observed the flowing blood of him who 'trod the wine-press alone'. A development in 'religious feeling' no doubt, but the writing

[1] PL xix 720: *Christum pro mundi salute passum fuisse iam credite, qui flagris [terga] sulcatus, obprobriis lacessitus. . . .*
[2] 2 Cor. xi 24.

out was done in fulfilment of a *task*, apparently assigned in Christ's own words, *necesse est impleri*.

Anyone proposing therefore, to write seriously about the *sentiment religieux* of the later Middle Ages should not forget the accumulated formulæ of a thousand years of study, or the ease – facility even – with which the resources of rhetoric could be invoked in the final stages for a full account of all that had become known. As a check one should consult the works of contemporary artists. They were less able to treat their subjects at length and in full detail. They were less likely to fall victims to their own technical virtuosity. But anyone who has examined a fair range of Crucifixes, Entombments and Pietàs of the fourteenth and fifteenth centuries knows that the artists too, in the end, accepted the challenge to portray Christ having suffered 'as never any man'. This is the only satisfactory explanation of those late medieval images which we find 'revolting' They were intended to be revolting.[1]

At this point the reader will feel with me that in our endeavour to reach an understanding of Crucifixion iconography, we have been under an often oppressive restraint. It would have been welcome if from time to time we could have interrupted this exposition and granted ourselves a respite, to look in detail at the treatment of our subject in some hymn, or poem or painting. But there it is, we should have lost the thread. Perhaps we have lost it without any such digressions. We have covered a lot of ground since we made medieval interpretations of *crucifixerunt* the starting point of our search for the reality which medieval artists and writers *did* represent. It is a reality different in every respect, as Mrs Jameson said, from 'common and absolute reality'.

There are certain 'things' among the 'things concerning me' with which we still have to deal. They are the most important of all, but they will, I trust, after this long preparation, no longer be found the most difficult. They are two *symbols* of the Crucifixion: the Harp and the Bow, which at an early date were claimed to be both symbols and *likenesses*. The harp as a likeness of the Crucifixion seems to have been more or less completely forgotten since the Reformation. And if anyone in German studies today refers to a 'simile of the bow' he probably means an involved and not very helpful passage of a dozen lines in Wolfram von Eschenbach. Without better knowledge of the *harp* we shall not solve the problem of the pulling with ropes and the

---

[1] An example in Schwietering, illus. 130. The churches of the Rhineland are not alone in continuing to display these images.

'holes bored too far apart'. There is also something to be learnt about the music-making of God, and about the Cross and the Crucified – his harp – at the Crucifixion. We should, I take it, also be glad to understand better the symbolism of 'Grünewald's' Isenheim Altar. Without knowledge of the *bow* we shall not know what that painting represents, nor how it represents it.

## 8. HARP AND BOW

Among the *omnia de me* to be referred to Christ's Crucifixion are, according to the Fathers of the Church, not only prophetic words, actions and situations, but also certain things; *omnia* is a neuter after all. Some of these things are musical instruments, the origins of which are generally held to be mythical, whatever tradition they occur in. Musical instruments abound in the Old Testament. The Fathers may have thought it particularly important to dissociate the harp from Orpheus and Apollo and invest it with Christian associations. Whether that was an important consideration or not, the harp was in the end probably the most influential of all Christian symbols – of the Crucifixion as a 'historical' event. We seem, as I said, collectively to have forgotten this.

For the purposes of this chapter a harp is a *cithara*. A concordance of the names of musical instruments occurring in the Old Testament, that is in Hebrew, in Septuagint Greek, in Vulgate Latin and in the vernacular translations, is in itself a highly confusing document. If one then adds some of the names in non-biblical sources (in medieval poetry, or in medieval handbooks of musical theory) the situation is well-nigh hopeless. Add then pictures, both from pre-Christian art and from medieval illustrated Psalters, and finally the opinions and theories of modern scholars, there appears to be little hope of ever finally associating names and identifiable instruments. There are few areas in which scholars are so dogmatic: in telling us exactly how to distinguish the various instruments. Fortunately we shall be concerned in this chapter only with harp and psaltery *lore* in the works of the Christian writers, who said with quite remarkable unanimity what this lore *means* in exegetical terms. Conversely there is nothing in this chapter to help the musicologist, and much which may usefully alarm him.[1]

[1] I have noted that what I wrote on the harp and the Crucifixion in 1953 ('Christusbild') has been taken seriously by Hugo Steger (in *David Rex et Propheta,*

We start by looking at *Cassiodorus*. His dates were about 477–570. For many years, until 540, he was chancellor to the Ostrogothic King, Theodoric. He was the historiographer of the Goths (his history of the Goths is lost; we have only the abridgment of Jordanes). He was also an eminent literary scholar and book collector, but for whose efforts there would have been no manuscripts for Carolingians to copy, and no subject Classics as we now know it. He also wrote an influential Commentary on the Book of Psalms.[1] One explanation of this astonishingly varied career and this literary output is to be found in his dates. He lived to be over ninety, spending the years of his retirement in his monastery of Vivarium at Squillace, which appears (with its baths and research library) to have been a highly civilised establishment. What interests us in this section is Cassiodorus on the subject of the harp. There are two passages for our consideration. One of these is famous, not to say notorious, while the second – a matter of a few lines – has been passed over more or less unregarded. With such a preamble I obviously mean that it is the second which is more useful to us in our enquiries. We need the first, however, as a foil and as an introduction to more serious things.

In 507 Cassiodorus wrote on behalf of his master Theoderic to Boethius, who was at that time about twenty-seven years old (Cassiodorus was, say, thirty):[2] 'The King of the Franks, Lutwin (Clovis) is asking us urgently (*magnis precibus*) to find him a harp-player (*citharoedus*).[3] With no more than this as his excuse Cassiodorus launches into an essay on the harp. It is one of the more famous purple passages of the early Middle Ages; Cassiodorus himself calls it a *voluptuosa digressio*. I abridge as follows:

---

1961) and by Egon Werlich (*Der westgermanische Skop*, diss. Münster, 1964). Namely: anything said about the harp in general or about David's harp in particular by a *theologian*, and any drawing of *David*'s harp, is likely to be useless or worse to students of musical instruments. This note is supplemented from time to time in the following pages.

[1] In German studies we come across him because his master was Theoderic, our Dietrich von Bern, and because his Psalm Commentary was used by Notker of St Gall in his annotated translation of all the Psalms. (Notker also consulted Jerome and St Augustine, or all three authorities in a conveniently glossed Psalter.)

[2] The letter is edited in *MGH: Auct. Antiqu.* Tom. XII (1894) = *Cassiodori Senatoris Variæ*, pp. 70 ff.

[3] The next letter says somewhat abruptly that the post is being advertised: *citharoedum destinavimus expetitum.*

'What may one say of the harp-player?' – He 'soothes the savage breast', etc. (*tristitiam noxiam iucundat, tumidos furores attenuat, cruentam sævitiam effecit blandem*). There follows a discussion of the properties of each of the modes, Doric, Phrygian, etc., and of the efficacy of Orpheus' music. 'But this is all said of music made by man in his skilful striking of instruments' (*sed hæc omnia humano studio per manualem musicam videntur effecta*). Cassiodorus next discusses the song of the poets and their metrical forms; he concludes this section with a sly reference to the song of the Sirens.

'But now to the Psalms! – let us now talk of the Psalter[1] descended from the skies, which a man whose fame is heard throughout the whole world composed; the Psalms are so modulated that they may save the soul (*loquamur de illo lapso cælo psalterio, quod vir toto orbe cantabilis[2] ita modulatum pro animæ sospitate composuit . . . ut his hymnis et mentis vulnera sanentur et divinitatis singularis gratia conquiratur, en quod sæculum miretur et credat: pepulit Davitica lyra diabolum*). The Davidic lyra[3] drove off the Devil from Saul (*sonus spiritibus imperavit: et canente cithara rex in libertatem rediit, quem internus inimicus turpiter possidebat*). Nothing else ever invented has had the power so to stir the soul as does the sweet reverberation of the hollow cithara (*Nihil tamen efficacius inventus est ad permovendos animos quam concavæ citharæ blanda resultatio*).

Cassiodorus next speaks of the *chorda* (here a consonance of many voices), which stirs our hearts (*corda*). He informs Boethius, the foremost musicologist of the Middle Ages, that the harp was the invention of Mercury. He also tells him of the music of the spheres which it is beyond the cunning of the human tongue to describe.

Cassiodorus could, in the context of an open letter, scarcely have gone on to tell Boethius that in the natural philosophy of Antiquity the organs of speech are systematically compared with the various parts of a stringed instrument.[4] The teeth are the *chordæ*, the tongue is the *plectrum*, the nostrils are the 'horns' or *cornua*. (We should compare the parts rather differently today.) We shall need some of this information – particularly on *cornua* – in due course.[5]

---

[1] In this case the Book of Psalms.

[2] Here and in Psalm cxviii 54 *cantabilis* = 'worthy to be sung of'.

[3] Here David's instrument is called a *lyra*, immediately afterwards a *cithara*.

[4] For instance in Cicero's *De Natura Deorum* II 144, 149; cf Isidore's *Etymologies*, x i 51.

[5] This lore passes *via* Avitus (*De Mundi Initio* lines 87–9, cf. MGH: *Auct. Antiqu.* VI ii) into the Old German *Genesis* (Altdeutsche Textbibliothek, 31 (1932) ll.247ff). Then there are Gottfried von Strassburg's words in praise of Bligger von Steinach ('his tongue which bears the harp', *sîn zunge, diu die harpfen treit*), in

It is indeed a strange musicological disquisition which the learned Chancellor sent in the name of the King of the Goths to the even more learned Boethius – the Boethius to whom we devoted so much space in chapter III. In a moment we shall have to look at the second passage, from Cassiodorus' Commentary on Psalms, where I should hesitate to say that he wrote more seriously than to Boethius. There is an element of *voluptuosa digressio* in this passage too. None the less it is a piece of evidence of quite outstanding importance for our understanding of Crucifixion iconography. To appreciate the full bearing of his remarks it will be advisable for us to look again – in the light of our investigations so far – at the text of the Psalm he is annotating, for it is none other than the *Easter Psalm* LVI (A.V. LVII).

The subject of Psalm LVI is 'historically' *David's* situation 'when he fled from Saul', as the titles in our modern Bibles still tell us. Surrounded by his enemies he promises when 'these calamities be overpast' to 'praise thee, O Lord, among the people', and to 'sing unto thee among the nations'. He will 'sing and give praise', seizing first his harp and psaltery which he bids 'awake!':

> Exsurge, gloria mea;
> exsurge, psalterium et cithara.

It is roughly thus that we understand the Psalm today, as a Psalm of David, concerning David's promises to praise the Lord. But on Easter Day, in the Liturgy of Easter Day? We may think it 'applicable to the deliverance of Christ'; the subject is deliverance from death and the grave.[1] Such a restrained interpretation would not have satisfied a medieval theologian. To have insisted that this and no more is meant by the Psalm in this context would have been wilful blindness. At Eastertide the words are *de me*; they concern Christ. They are, it is true,

---

which the allusion to the school lesson is muffled by the assertion of a 'harmony of words and sense'. Much earlier, *c.* 860, Otfrid of Weissenburg, in his letter of commendation to Liutbert, Archbishop of Mainz, had used the old conceit in its more conventional form: 'It is appropriate that humankind should sing the praise of the Creator of all things, who gave them the plectrum of the tongue to sing his praise in the various languages.' – (*Est tamen conveniens ut . . . humanum genus auctorem omnium laudent, qui plectrum eis dederat linguæ verbum in eis suæ laudis sonare.* Erdmann's ed. p. 7, lines 115 ff.)

[1] See p. 290, last section of n. 2.

not immediately 'historical'. They do not *tell* the events of Easter Day; they *sing* the Resurrection. The first two-thirds of the Psalm, however, concern Christ as he awaits deliverance (Vulgate numberings):

2. Miserere mei, Deus, miserere mei;
      quoniam in te confidit anima mea,
      et in umbra alarum tuarum sperabo, donec transeat iniquitas.

3. Clamabo ad Deum altissimum,
      Deum qui benefecit mihi.

4. Misit de cœlo et liberavit me,
      dedit in opprobrium conculcantes me.
   Misit Deus misericordiam suam et veritatem suam,

5. et eripuit animam meam de medio catulorum leonum;
      dormivi conturbatus.
   Filii hominum, dentes eorum arma et sagittæ,
      et lingua eorum gladius acutus.

6. Exaltare super cœlos, Deus,
      et in omnem terram gloria tua.

7. Laqueum paraverunt pedibus meis
      et incurvaverunt animam meam;
   foderunt ante faciem meam foveam,
      et inciderunt in eam.

8. Paratum cor meum, Deus, paratum cor meum;
      cantabo, et psalmum dicam.

There is a wealth of images here to portray the 'dangerous case' of the just man surrounded by his enemies, too great a wealth, in fact, for any simple 'historical' parallel to the case of Christ to be read into them. But in the Middle Ages (and to anyone preoccupied as we are), the men whose teeth are 'spears and arrows' are notably Christ's enemies. (The Cross in the Old English *Dream of the Rood* says with reference to itself 'although I was wounded with arrows': *eall ic wæs mid strælum for-wundod.*) The enemies apparently flashing their teeth may recall the 'hounds' (*canes*) of the twenty-first Psalm. Is there an allusion in the 'pit digged before me' to the executioners on Calvary who prepared a hole for the Cross? If so, it is shadowy indeed. There are snares (ropes?) before the feet of one sore beset (bent), who declares his heart to be 'ready' and to await the passing of the iniquities done to him. The words *cor paratum* recall Christ's *spiritus promptus,* and *donec transeat iniquitas* recalls his prayer *transeat calix iste*[1] in the Agony of Geth-semane. The allusions may remain allusions, and the translations into modern vernaculars may have reduced their directness, but this is still, even in the reformed Churches, the Easter Psalm.[2]

Verse 8 (above) concludes with the words, 'I will sing and give praise' – *cantabo et psalmum dicam*. Christologically interpreted, these words clearly express the intention of the Son on his deliverance from his enemies. This is followed by 'Awake up, my glory, awake, psaltery and harp' (*Exsurge gloria mea; exsurge psalterium et cithara*). On the same interpretation these are God's words, for: Who else than God can have issued such a command? Whom else can God have addressed as 'my glory', than the Son who had just now declared his trust? The words *psalterium et cithara* are consequently *also* addressed to Christ. Himself the psaltery *and* the harp, he is commanded by God to 'awake and rise'. Sung on Easter Day these words celebrated the escape from the bonds of death and the tomb, that is the Resurrection. Within the setting suggested by the Psalm itself, where the just man is beset by his oppressors, the words apply more immediately to the escape (*exsurrectio*) from the restraining fetters of the Cross (the *vincula crucis*, the nails). It is in this latter more narrowly historical context that the Psalm is of such profound influence on the iconography of the Crucifixion.

Presented in this way, this interpretation of the Easter Psalm is no doubt somewhat rhapsodic. In the Middle Ages too we may think that it will have sounded excessively hymnic at a first hearing, but the 'first hearing' remains here as elsewhere a fiction. The exegetes had provided

---

[1] Matth. xxvi 39; or *orabat ut transiret ab eo hora*, Mark xiv 35.

[2] It is not easy to find the answer of the reformed Churches to the question why exactly this Psalm is the Easter Psalm. I mention as a curiosity that in the *Bampton Lectures* of 1878 (*The Witness of the Psalms to Christ and Christianity*), W. Alexander found it 'impossible to construct a Life of our Lord without taking Prophecy into account' (p. 76), but he made only two trivial and passing references to this Psalm. He did not say it is the Easter Psalm, nor does Peake's *Commentary on the Bible* (1962) p. 425. The *New Commentary on Holy Scripture*, ed. Charles Gore, H. L. Goudge and A. Guillaume (1928) p. 359, is more helpful.

In *Helps to the Study of the Book of Common Prayer, A Companion to Church Worship* (Clarendon Press, n.d.), one reads under Easter Week: 'Psalm lvii: The deliverance of God's servant from his enemies; applicable to the deliverance of Christ, and the Christian through Him, from death and the grave.' Of Psalm xxii the same handbook says (Easter Even): 'The sufferings of God's servant in language remarkably like an actual description of the crucifixion' (similarly of Psalm lxix and lxxxviii) [all A.V. numberings].

a firm foundation in a quite sober *doctrine* concerning the psaltery and the harp which it will be right for us to assume known to every chorister. We shall find it even prosaic and pedantic in its simplest form, as it was *taught*. We may not want to do more today than renew acquaintance with this teaching, but we may not ignore it. It is to be found in Prefaces to the Psalter – in St Augustine's for instance; Jerome had had it too. It runs roughly as follows:

Why is this book called a Psalter? It is so called after the instrument of the same name, the *psalterium*, which is distinguishable from the *harp* (*cithara*) in the following respect. While both are stringed instruments, shaped like a Delta (*Δ*), the sound-box of the psalterium is *higher*; it is *lower* in the harp.[1]

It is particularly in interpreting Psalm lvi, however, where the two instrument names are used of Christ, that this 'compare and contrast' exercise is written out in full.

*Exsurge psalterium et cithara*. From the days of Jerome and Augustine down to the Reformation the clergy of the Western Church interpreted

---

[1] Delta harps and psalteries are often to be found in illustrated Psalters. They were presumably drawn to comply with the definition, which goes back to Jerome. *His* researches into forms and shapes were undertaken to elucidate Jubal's two instruments, the *kinnor* and *ugab* of Genesis iv 21. The morphological studies of more modern musicologists, e.g. John Stainer, *The Music of the Bible, with an Account of the Development of Modern Musical Instruments from Ancient Types* (London n.d.), show drawings or representations of Babylonian and Egyptian instruments, including *kinnor* and *ugab*. One can see where Jerome got his ideas of higher and lower sound-boxes. But that is now, for our purposes, an irrelevance except in that *what he wrote* was passed down unchanged for a millennium. It is this tradition which concerns us.

There is a picture of Jubal with his *Harp* (sound-box low down), beside the smith Tubal(cain) at his anvil, in the *Caedmon Genesis*. See *The Caedmon-MS. of Anglo-Saxon Biblical Poetry*, ed. by Sir Israel Gollancz (Oxford, 1927) p. xliii. I am grateful to Dr Egon Werlich for this reference, and for drawing my attention to the partial confusion of Tubalcain and Jubal, see p. 271.

The instruments drawn in the Utrecht Psalter, on the other hand (and possibly in Stuttgart) are *not* governed by exegetical definitions, and they can apparently be usefully examined, see E. Winternitz, 'The Survival of the Kithara and the evolution of the English cittern', in *JWCI* xxiv (1961) 222 ff.

See Stainer, illus. 23–25 for the Egyptian or Assyrian harp. It is interesting to see Jerome's and Augustine's harp lore quoted by Stainer as evidence of instrument shapes in Antiquity, but sad to see him imagining that an account of the *sawtry* in Bartholomaeus' *De Proprietatibus Rerum* (1398) is 'contemporary with Chaucer' (p. 51): it is, in fact, Jerome again, his antiquarian lore, reproduced without the Christian exegesis.

these words as God's call to Christ to 'arise'. This is the Exsurrection (*exsurge!*) from the restraining bonds of the Crucifixion which precedes the Harrowing of Hell and the Resurrection. As for the twofold address, as *psalterium* and as *cithara*, that is Christ as Son of God and as Man. Here in this Psalm and 'everywhere in the Psalms where there is reference to the *harp*', says St Augustine, we are to understand *Christ as man* in his suffering: *caro humana patiens*.[1] He himself repeats this, more briefly or more fully throughout his Psalm Commentary. The *psaltery* on the other hand, the nobler instrument with the sound-box higher than in the harp, means the Christ who performed the miracles of healing.

Lest we should see the lesson of the harp in too great an isolation, I mention now, as something we may perhaps more easily remember, that the skin (*pellis*) of Psalm ciii 2 and the *tympanum* of Psalm cxlix 3 are believed by Augustine to be counted also among the things which are '*de me*', and to refer to the Lord evidently stretched on the frame of the Cross like a drying *fleece*, or *drum-skin*, or parchment *charter* (the chirograph of our Redemption).[2] Thus prepared we are now equipped to return to Cassiodorus and his commentary on the words of the Easter Psalm.

*Exsurge* (or *resurge*) *cithara*. 'The harp means the glorious Passion which with stretched sinews and counted bones (*tensis nervis . . . dinumeratisque ossibus*) sounded forth his bitter suffering as in a spiritual song (*carmen intellectuale*).'[3]

This is surely a remarkable formulation. What promises to be a soaring metaphor is made almost grotesque by the intrusion of the 'counted bones' from the Good Friday Psalm. We may none the less, as philologists, be grateful for this confirmatory evidence that the two principal sources of medieval Christian ideas concerning the Crucifixion are the Psalms xxi and lvi. As for God, the musician who made music on the harp at the Crucifixion (and on the psaltery at the Resurrection),

---

[1] *Enarrat. in Psalmos* (PL XXXVI 671–2).
[2] *PL* XXXVII 1194 and 1341–2 are the fullest statements on fleece and drumskin; the context is Psalm ciii 2, with direct or indirect reference to the Saviour throughout. In the above lines I have compressed into one statement notions more discreetly expressed, but of ubiquitous occurrence, throughout the *Enarrationes in Psalmos*.
[3] *PL* LXX 404.

he is perhaps present in Cassiodorus' designation of the music as a *carmen intellectuale*. This epithet can probably only be used of the music of the Divine Musician. That these ideas, at the sophisticated level of the patristic 'conceit', might provide a challenge to the medieval artist seems on the face of things unlikely. We shall, however, soon enough have to consider this harp and psaltery lore in the simpler forms in which it was taught and explained. Perhaps it is at this point, therefore, that attention should be drawn to a remarkable 'abstract' drawing of *David* himself *as a harp* or psaltery, and simultaneously of the Crucifixion in prefiguration, see plate 29b.[1]

It would be tedious if we were now systematically to log the recurrence of the harp and psaltery lesson, down through the centuries. It is a *commonplace* of even the most modest of the exegetes. Why have we forgotten it so completely? How little attention has been paid to this tradition in the past century can perhaps be most simply indicated by stating that in the main index volumes to Migne there is only *one* reference to the *cithara* as a 'figure' of the Crucifixion. (With due gratitude I remember that it is to the Cassiodorus passage which we have just examined, and in the indexes to individual volumes one will find many more references.) The absence of any real guidance in Migne may explain why in a recent study with the promising title 'Classical and Christian Ideas of World Harmony'[2] there is, so far as I can see, no reference to Christ's Crucifixion as the Christian God's music-making, whereby a central medieval idea of world harmony through music is completely missed. As for my own reading, I have to confess that the illustrative passages from medieval writers which I had assembled by 1953 still seem to me to be the most striking. They are convincing evidence that the harp and psaltery tradition which began with

---

[1] I owe acquaintance with this miniature to Hugo Steger's study *David Rex et Propheta* (1961) in which it is fig. 53a, from a South-east German (?) Psalter of the twelfth century with the commentary of Peter Lombard. It is a verbose allegory in image and words on the ten-stringed harp of David as a type of Christ. Steger has transcribed the interspersed text, p. 232. We are concerned here only with the *possibility* of such an image: evidence that the harp could be *seen* as a cross. This has little to do with 'realism', our topic at present. [The quasi-realistic representation of a figure crucified on a harp in Hieronymus Bosch's *Millennium* may, I hope, by now be held to be at least provisionally glossed. It occurs in the general context of executions on this and other musical instruments, *and* on a banqueting table. The latter is, I think, a profanation of the 'sacrifice' drawn to the four 'horns' (corners) of the altar-table.]

[2] Leo Spitzer (title as given above) (Baltimore and London, 1963).

Jerome and Augustine was still vividly alive a thousand years later.
What I have collected since that date provides little beyond mono-
tonously regular confirmation that the *lesson* continued to be taught
throughout the Middle Ages. I have only occasionally found something
to add to the store of poetry which it inspired. We may certainly infer
that throughout the Middle Ages every cleric and every artist knew
what was to be said about the harp.

In the dry form of a lesson, Cassiodorus's interpretation of *resurge
cithara* is to be found in Notker of St Gall's German translation of the
Psalms, about 1000. This means that at the monastery school of St Gall
the lesson was taught. All Notker's writings are textbooks. Readers of
this book will, however, be better convinced by the following examples
from more literary works, reproduced in the main from my article of
1953, with a few lines restored, and supporting translations. When we
have been able to convince ourselves of the close relationship of harp
and Crucifixion we will conclude the more theoretical exposition, and
examine the final completion of the 'ætiological' story. As readers have
by now surmised, we shall now finally find the solution of the 'holes
bored in advance' and some remaining 'realistic' details.

A late Middle High German poem of about 1300 which we call *Die
Erlösung* (Man's Redemption) sings as follows of David the Psalmist
who himself had sung of the Resurrection:

Iâ der werde godes vrûnt
in deme salter aber sprach
jubilîrende unde jach:
'Surge mea cythara.'
Nû hôret, wie man daz verstâ
dief von sinne scharpe.
Iz quît: 'Stant ûf mîn harpe,
stant ûf mîn psalterium'.
Diz dûdet Iêsum Cristum.
Von des persônen sprach er dô:
'Exurgam diluculo.
Des morgens vrû wil ich erstân'.
Nû sult ir hôren sunder wân,
wie sich das selbe spil
unsem herren glîchen wil.
Die harphe und daz psalterium
sint beide ungespannen dum,

sie sint ungeslagen doup
rehte sam ein lindenloup,
daz von dem boume vellet.
Wer sie gespannen stellet
und slehet dar und aber dar,
ir sûzekeit wirt man gewar
des ordenlîchen sanges,
des sûzen seidenklanges.
In aller wîze det alsus
unser herre Cristus.
jâ sâ der hêre heilant
an daz krûze sâzuhant
gezwicket und geslagen wart,
gespannen unde sêre gespart,
geslagen dar und aber dar.
Dô wart man zuhant gewar
der godelîchen sûzekeit,

die godes vrûnden ist bereit.      und in die werelt uber al
Zuhant der sûzen harphen sanc   der harphen sûzekeit erschal.[1]
hinabe zû der hellen klanc

It should be noted that this passage, the real subject of which is not really David but David's harp and his psaltery (prophetic of the Resurrection), occurs late in the narrative sequence. It is only when David is being liberated at the Harrowing of Hell that the poet enlarges on his subject in this way. The 'historical' account of the Crucifixion has necessarily already been given. It is in strict accordance with the other Crucifixion Psalm, the twenty-first:

Sie zugen ime sîn kleider abe.    Daz volc sach allez jâmer dâ.
An des vrônen krûzes habe      Sie slûgen ime unsûze
der heilant wart gerecket,       durch hende und ouch durch fûze
gesperret und gestrecket        drî quecke nagele und scharf.
an des krûzes arme sâ.          Lôz man ûf sîne kleider warf.[2]

Of about the same date is the *Passional*, a work attributed to the Teutonic Order in East Prussia:

[1] *Die Erlösung*, ed. Fr. Maurer, Deutsche Literatur in Entwicklungsreihen, Geistliche Dichtung des Mittelalters, VI (Leipzig, 1934) 5618–56. **Translation:** The worthy friend of God, David, had in his Psalter declared in jubilation: *Surge mea cithara*. Hear now how that is to be understood in its deep and penetrating sense. It says: 'arise my harp, arise my *psalterium*'. This means Jesus Christ. David had said, speaking in Christ's person: '*Exsurgam diluculo*, I shall arise early in the morning'. Now hear how beyond doubt this music (-making) is to be compared to our Lord. The harp and the psaltery are mute when still unspanned and, unless struck, silent like the linden leaf that falls from the tree. If anyone tightens their strings, however, and strikes them again and again, their sweetness will be heard, their regular song: the sweet sound from the strings. Thus exactly did our Lord Christ. Yes, immediately the glorious Saviour was nailed and fastened on the Cross, spanned and direly stretched, struck again and again, the sweet music of God which he makes for his faithful was heard. The sweet song of the harp at once sounded down to Hell, and throughout all the world the sweetness of the harp's music sounded.

[2] Ibid. 5203–12: **Translation:** They stripped him of his clothes. The Saviour was extended on the frame of the holy Cross, (he was) pulled and stretched to the arms of the Cross. The people saw the sum of sorrow there. Brutally they struck through his hands and through his feet three nails stout and sharp. They cast lots for his garments.

| In den nagelen er sich spien | vnde hat dar vf sin seiten spil |
|---|---|
| als ein gedente seite . . . | durch gedone vollen scharfe |
| Eya mensche nu vernim: . . . | an des cruces harfe |
| Der vater des gewaldis, Got | gespannen . . . |
| nach der minne gebot | [und wil] von suchten bosen |
| Din herze an sich locken wil | als Sauln Dauit dich losen.[1] |

This poem goes on to say that at the Crucifixion all Nature was silenced by the song of the harp. The Father played until the strings broke: *sus wurden alle saiten slaff.* When it is said that the broken strings hung limply, one may perhaps be reminded again of the *serpens*, or the *vermis*. We may, however, also recall the hymn:

> Recordare quod ut vermis
> Ligni tener et inermis
> In altum erigitur.[2]

English readers may by now have called to mind the lines of George Herbert (1593–1632) on Easter:

> His stretched sinews taught all strings what key
> Is best to celebrate this most high day.[3]

The lines from George Herbert may carry more weight than the following from the completely medieval *Philomena* of John of Hoveden (Howden, d. 1275) who was presumably committed by his choice of subject to an exhaustive quest of musical imagery. At the death of Christ on the Cross:

> Lyra luget et vita moritur

[1] ed. F. K. Köpke (Quedlinburg and Leipzig, 1852); my quotations from K. A. Hahn, *Das alte Passional* (1857) pp. 74, 38 ff and 78, 82 ff. **Translation:** He stretched himself between the nails like a tautened string: . . . Now hear, mankind: God, the almighty Father would draw your heart to him, and with that intent has spanned his strings on the harp of the Cross, so that its penetrating notes may reach you; he would deliver you from evil afflictions, as David delivered Saul.

[2] F. J. Mone, *Lateinische Hymnen des Mittelalters* (Freiburg, 1853) II 137, cf Vulgate text of 2 Sam. xxiii 8; *tenerrimus ligni vermiculus* (different in A.V.).

[3] I have the quotation from Rosamond Tuve, *A Reading of George Herbetr* (1952) p. 145, where the poem is discussed, with, I think, full awareness of most of the problems with which we have been concerned. I am grateful to John Danby for drawing my attention to this study almost as soon as it appeared.

or

> Ecce migrat cedrus in Libano
> Cruce Christus, cantus in organo,
> Melos lyrâ, sonus in tympano.[1]

I conclude this brief survey of texts in which the Crucifixion is treated as the music of the harp with a handful of quotations of wider scope. The harp (in one case the psaltery) is associated with divine love, concord, harmony. The texts are widely scattered in time and from quite unrelated areas:

1. In the sixth of the apocryphal Odes of Solomon the opening lines are believed by the editors to read:
'As the wind(?), passing through the strings of the harp causes them to sing, so the spirit of the Lord through my limbs, and I sing of his love.'[2]

2. In his *Flumen abundans* of 1551 Alciati treats the *cithara* as the emblem of *Fides*. When 'faith' is broken the strings of the *cithara* are likewise broken, *concors* and *harmonia* are lost.[3]

3. In stanza 7 of 'Harzreise im Winter' Goethe asks:

> Ist auf deinem Psalter, Vater der Liebe, ein Ton
> seinem Ohre vernehmlich. . . .

These quotations are quite inadequate to prove or to suggest anything, except that, in high relief against a vast background of musical and numerological theory associated with ideas of cosmic harmony, there were simpler images of Aeolian and other harps, to be recalled when the poets down to Goethe wrote of concord and harmony. (What can Goethe's source have been?)

[1] *Johannis de Hovedene* 'Philomena', ed. Clemens Blume (Hymnologische Beiträge, etc., suppl. vol. IV of *Analecta Hymnica*: Leipzig, 1930) lines 442 and 460 ff.

[2] I first noted these lines in E. Hennecke, *Neutestamentliche Apokryphen*, 2nd ed. (1924) I 441. In the thoroughly revised 3rd ed. (Tübingen, 1964) II 582, the translation is relegated to a footnote in favour of, 'As the hand moves through the harp and the strings sound', etc. This is what J. Rendall Harris had already preferred in *The Odes and Psalms of Solomon* etc., 2nd ed. (Cambridge, 1911) pp. 96 ff: 'as the hand [*or perhaps* plectrum] moves over the harp, and the strings speak', etc. He did not want 'wind' in place of 'hand', or any suggestion of the Aeolian harp.

[3] *Emblematum flumen abundans*, (Lyons, 1551) facs. ed. of the Holbein Society (1871), Emblem 16 *Fides*.

And now we return to our exposition. Ideally the harp is a *symbol* of the Crucifixion. That is to say, the harp 'is' or simply 'means' the Crucifixion. In the Old Testament it betokened suffering, *patientia*, as we must surely infer from Job's words *versa est in luctum cithara mea*, 'my harp is turned (*or* attuned) to mourning'. The Middle Ages knew Job as *Hiob citharista*.[1] The symbol becomes a *metaphor* from the moment when the poets, or the exegetes in an imaginative paraphrase, speak of the Crucifixion as God's music-making, which in the hour of Christ's death brought all nature to silence and caused sun and moon to be veiled in darkness. The metaphor is, however, reduced to a *simile* whenever circumstances require its use to be justified. That is when it is challenged, either by those who are wilfully blind, or by those who 'do not understand'. That means *inter alia* in the instruction of the faithful. In the hands of those who were seeking to recover *historia* by the study of *omnia de me*, the symbol or the metaphor had to yield to the reasoned comparison in which 'the Crucifixion is like a harp, *because* ...' The comparison was then *taught*, and the lesson was repeated endlessly, and refined and improved. 'The harp consists of a wooden frame with stretched sinews ...' etc.

It is in the reasoned comparison of the Crucifixion with the harp that we have, fairly clearly, to see the *second* major source of the 'realism' which we find so characteristic of the devotional literature and art of the later Middle Ages. The *first* source we had already identified as being the ætiological explanation of the image of the Crucified already present in the twenty-first Psalm: 'they counted all my bones'. But having said 'first' and 'second' we must immediately cancel the suggestion of the second as a supplement to the first, for the ætiological story was evolved to show not only the counted bones, but also the taut strings or sinews of the harp, the *tensa viscera* which are the fulfilment of the prophecy of the harp. It contrived incidentally to show the fulfilment of other prophetic images ('things' in the Old Testament) to which we have been able to make only passing allusion: the stretched skin of the tympanum, the parchment of the charter, the vine on the trellis – and there are others.

To *these* origins of the 'realism' which we observe in medieval descriptions and representations of the Crucifixion we can only be led back, as I hope I have by now demonstrated, by methods which I should myself call philological: by the study of the contextual meaning

[1] Cf pp. 108 f, 345.

of words.[1] Such a study forces one, if the context is to be properly determined, to ride rough-shod over the lines which are customarily held to mark off our various academic disciplines. My main problem has consequently been that of exposition. Any reader who has followed my story up to this point will doubtless see the way ahead and be able to forecast most of what is still to come. We will none the less not be precipitate. It is now, I should think, clear why the holes bored in the Cross to receive the nails were bored 'too far apart' – and indeed why there would have to be holes at all. And why the nails, as all the details of the Crucifixion were brought into 'register' with the prophetic harp, came to be thick nails, triangular or square in section, sharp at the edges no doubt, but blunt at the points. They were or became the *pegs of the harp*. The legend of the Smith's Wife was evolved to account 'historically' for this *bluntness* of the nails.

And now, finally, the ropes! These have in origin nothing to do with the technical problem of fastening a player to a cross in a Passion play, as has been repeatedly suggested. This 'brilliant solution' of the problem of Gothic iconography has been found on so many occasions, in so many different places, that one could not wish for a better example

[1] We have just now passed the point at which my own investigations began. It may be of interest to know what my initial problem was. I encountered it as the editor of a fourteenth-century German tract on the Passion, *Christi Leiden in einer Vision geschaut*, which Robert Priebsch had edited on the basis of what he believed to be the sole manuscript (Heidelberg, 1936). I had four complete manuscripts and a fragment (Professor K. Ruh's research team in Würzburg have since found half a dozen more, and James Marrow continues to find medieval Dutch translations and adaptations). Christ is said in this tract to have been stretched on the Cross 'as never any *seite* over a *bret*'. Further, that when the spear pierced Christ's side, there was a loud crack 'as when . . . (?)'. The medieval scribes had had their difficulties with the latter comparison. The *lectio difficilior* involved a 'schlieme' which I decided in the end could only be a drum-skin or a stretched sheet of parchment (such as was used for window-coverings) – not a 'faggot' as Priebsch thought. It was *torn* (not thrown) *violently* (not into a fire). From what I have written in these last few pages it will be seen where in the end I located the parchment: among the symbols prophetic of the Crucifixion. This train of thought was determined, no doubt, by the initial conviction that *seite* and *bret* were (or should have been) harp-strings and harp. The *bret* was not the 'Streckbrett' (rack) of the torture chamber on which a man's flanks (*seiten* = costæ) might be stretched, or just any dulcimer ('Hackbrett') with its strings. With the kind of blindness for other things which characterises the *aperçu* I was able to declare to Friedrich Ranke (my teacher in Breslau and our first German visitor after the War) that the Crucifixion of the Gothic is a 'de-symbolised harp of David'. He was convinced after two sentences of explanation. The *aperçu* became a working hypothesis. The rest of the story I have already told in an introductory note, p. 226 n. 1.

of 'polygenesis'.[1] This theory is, I hope, now finally disposed of, leaving only a metaphor to be remembered: the nails (the Christian Crucifixion is with nails only) may be called 'bonds' or 'fetters'. In the Old Saxon *Heliand* they are 'nail-fetters'. They are the *vincula crucis*. As for the ropes (*funes*) used at the Seizure in Gethsemane (*comprehenderunt Jesum et ligaverunt eum*),[2] these ropes were not abandoned or forgotten. They were used, it was universally believed (and generally represented in art) to lead the lamb to the slaughter[3] and for the tying of Christ to the pillar at the Flagellation, and on the way to Calvary whither he was led 'like a thief'.[4] They were finally used (with diminished authority) for the pulling of the limbs, for instance in the Anselm dialogue, as we saw, and then in later adaptations of the *Meditations* of Bonaventura – as the height of the erect Cross was increased, and the feet of the Crucified could no longer be reached. The ropes were welcome as a means of keeping the 'foul hands' of the 'hounds who encompassed him' from further contact, but let us leave such details. Here we can take our leave of the plays, in which the ropes were necessarily used to tie the player whose nailing had been mimed, but I repeat that the words of the executioners ignore them in this function, and the artists ignore them too.

Much more important is the almost incidental solution we now find of the riddle presented by the words of the prophet Habakkuk, 'there are horns in his hands'. At the beginning of this chapter I referred to this as one of the darker prophecies concerning the Crucifixion. I was able to do that with little risk of having a reader who would be sure that he knew in what way these words were understood in the Middle Ages. There is, in fact, evidence in plenty that this prophecy, which, once in the Liturgy, could never be discarded or ignored as meaningless, caused trouble. The Fathers had understood it, but not in one way only. The late Picture Bibles remember it.[5] In full context: *splendor ejus ut lux erit; cornua in manibus ejus*. Of the various interpretations which can be placed upon these words one emerged triumphant at the level of 'history'. It was a meaning of the word *cornua* which must always have been known but which only finally became completely relevant. We must consider the others first, however, for it is the others which the

---

[1] It occurred to Mildred K. Pope and me over tea in Manchester in 193(7?). It will be found in several places in print.

[2] John xviii 12.

[3] Matthew xxvii 2.

[4] Mark xiv 48, Luke xxii 52.

[5] Cf p. 269.

Fathers will have had in mind when the Liturgy was being evolved.

'Horns' associated with light and splendour, as in the words of Habakkuk, are *beams* of light. It will be remembered that Moses had beams or 'horns' issuing from his brow according to Exodus xxxiv 29, cf 2 Corinthians iii 7. Moses had *faciem cornutam*, and so the medieval artists represented him. 'Horns' associated with sacrifice, however, are the horns at the corner of the altar to which the sacrificial offering is bound (*cornua* in this sense is believed to be the origin of English 'corner'). The applicability of 'horns in his hands' to the Christ of the Crucifixion is evident if Christ is seen as the perfect sacrifice; and if one is to 'glory in the Cross', then the horns of light and radiance are again relevant. But there were difficulties in this reading which led some to take *cornua in manibus* as an example of the figure of hypallage, the real meaning being not 'horns in his hands' but 'his hands in the horns', that is in or on the nails or hooks of the Cross (cf. 'God's hooks'). There remains the meaning of *cornua* which assorts completely with the *harp* as prophetic foretelling of the Crucifixion, namely: *cornua* are the pegs of a stringed instrument.[1] To anyone knowing this meaning of *cornua*, Habakkuk's words present no difficulties. Indeed this completes the comparison of the Crucifixion with the harp of David – and helps to determine the shape of the nails which in the end the Smith's Wife forged. This solution accorded well with what had to be said about certain other metaphors and similes of the body of Christ stretched on the Cross: the 'pegged' fleece, the sail on the mast (sail rings are also *cornua*).

The harp had to be treated in such great detail because it was the most influential of all the many medieval symbols of the Crucifixion. It determined Crucifixion iconography in its progress towards 'realism'. Its authority was also unassailable, for according to the Easter Psalm God had addressed Christ Crucified as 'my harp'. But there is also a *bow* to be considered among the many other symbols of the Crucifixion. We should want in any case to know how such a symbol fared, for the

---

[1] At this point I refer us back to a previous note, p. 287, on Cicero's comparison of the parts of a stringed instrument with the organs of speech. This passage is *De Natura Deorum*, II 144, 149. It will be seen that Cicero compares the *cornua* (pegs) of the stringed instrument with the human *nostrils* 'because they are the source of the resonance'. As a good pedagogue I must explain that the harp peg is a protruding *solid horn* (horn positive); the nostrils are *trumpet horns* (horns negative).

bow is 'very like the harp'; *or* it is very like the harp if one elects to determine 'sinew(s) stretched over wood' as the characteristic in each case. The story of the bow as a symbol of the Crucifixion is in fact far more interesting than at this point we anticipate. (But so too are the stories of the other symbols, whether they belong to the skin-fleece-parchment-charter, or to the vine-winepress, or any other group.) I have chosen the bow for a number of reasons, one of which is more purely art-historical than until quite recently I realised. Namely, that of all the symbols of the Crucifixion the bow is the only one which the modern observer can, with real conviction, 'see'. He can see the bow (once it has been pointed out) without being either a historian or devout. The bow also illustrates in an unexpected way the 'realism' of late medieval art. This 'realism' was after all not solely the final outcome of the 'historical' researches of the Fathers of the Church. The bow belongs, in the end, to the 'reality' which, according to Mrs Jameson, Christian art refused to represent. But the bow which intrudes from the world of reality to influence Christian iconography at last, is not the primeval archer's bow, but the late-medieval crossbow. The story in brief is that the archer's bow had, as a symbol of the Crucifixion, no success. The crossbow begins its career in, I think, the early fourteenth century. It celebrated its greatest triumph in Grünewald's Isenheim Altar, see plate 30a. The historical evidence is throughout somewhat sparse, but unambiguous, both of the failure of the bow and the success of the crossbow.

As we turn now first to the archer's bow we may profit from our familiarity with the hieratic image which ecclesiastical art evolved, and say that as a prophetic image of the Crucifixion the ancient bow was foredoomed. The archer's bow must be shown and seen in profile. It cannot be brought into register with the Cross as venerated, or with the Crucified, an *orans*. So much for the *image* of the older bow. As for the verbal tradition, that was never promising either. The Old Testament, particularly *Psalms*, where the air is often thick with darts and arrows, assigns the bow almost exclusively to the wicked, the persecutors and the oppressors. (Folk beliefs support this, of course, but we are not concerned with folk-lore.) The bowman is the enemy of the faithful. That is the general context of the bow. There is however, one important bow which the theologians could not ignore. It is evidently on the side of the righteous man. It is in the blessing spoken by Jacob over Joseph in Genesis xlix 24:

But his bow abideth in strength and the arms of his hands were made strong (*Sedit in forti arcus ejus et dissoluta sunt vincula brachiorum et manuum illius*).

The words must (one can only surmise) have tantalised the Fathers in the early days of their quest for *omnia de me*. The difficulty is (or one difficulty is) that the previous verse says that archers have already shot at Joseph whose bow now abides in strength. The exegetes may seem to us occasionally to have taken Old Testament words out of their context in order to declare them prophetic, but here the proximity of hostile archers seems to have stayed their hand. We concentrate attention therefore on the one resolute attempt of a theologian which I have been able to discover, to associate the bow in the Blessing of Jacob with the Cross of the Crucifixion. I adduced the text in question in 1953. I still find it unsupported. Even more important than the lack of parallels is the absence of allusions to the blessing in accounts of the Crucifixion: this 'prophecy' seems not to be quoted. Perhaps the most important consideration (in retrospect): the text of the Blessing of Jacob is not used in the Liturgy of Holy Week. If I now reproduce this piece of exegesis more fully than before, that is because it seems to me to be the only text which clearly envisages the *old* bow. The author is Gotfrid of Admont (Styria, d. 1169):

Arcus qui ex ligno et chorda, vel cornu et chorda constat, eundem Dominum ac Redemptorem nostrum nobiliter demonstrat. Potest enim designari per chordam sanctissima ejus caro, diversis tribulationum angustiis mirabiliter attracta et distenta. Per lignum vero sive cornu omnipotens ejus divinitas, quæ rigida quoadammodo et inflexibilis ad compatiendum humanis miseriis permanebat, quousque nobilis hæc chorda, sacrosancta videlicet caro Christi, torqueri opprobriis et illusionibus trahi atque distendi crucis affixionibus nostræ causa salutis incipiebat . . . Hic est enim arcus ille quem olim Pater repromisit dicens: Ponam arcum meum in nubibus cœli.[1]

A bow consists of a piece of wood or horn, and a string, which is a worthy representation of our Lord and Redeemer. The string may be taken to mean his most holy body which in the various dire tribulations (of his Passion) was wondrously spanned and stretched. By the wood or the horn his invincible divinity is meant which in a

[1] *Liber de Benedictione Jacob* (PL CLXXIV 1150).

manner of speaking remained rigid and unbending for the bearing of the sum of human miseries. Until the noble bowstring, his holy body, began to be drawn in mockery, spanned with insults and stretched to the *affixiones* [notches of the bow, nails of the Cross] for our salvation. This is the bow which the Father promised when he said: I do set my bow in the cloud. (Genesis ix 13)

The 'lesson of the bow' as we have it here accords well with that of the harp, perhaps too well. As for the final invocation of the rainbow, that is, as an image, more remote than the bow. I should not have wished to give this passage all this space had it not been necessary to show that later writers who think of the bow then they meditate on the Crucifixion are not indebted to this 'lesson' or anything like it. The bow is an image which seems to have suggested itself to the later poets more directly, perhaps with the help of the words of the hymn: *tensa laxa viscera*. The bow, though in its traditional form only vaguely suggested by such words, is apt as a simile. When the bow was displaced by the crossbow the likeness was frightening. Our main difficulty is to know when the word 'bow' came to be associated primarily with the cross-bow.

Here now is the evidence. It is, as I said sparse, but clear. The first passage is taken from a long poetical work of about 1320, *Von Gottes Zukunft*, by Heinrich of Neustadt, a Viennese physician. It incorporates practically the whole argument of Alain of Lille's *Anticlaudianus*, followed, remarkably enough, by a Life of Mary based on the *Vita Rhythmica Salvatoris*. The following lines describe the Crucifixion, necessarily, in view of the source, *jacente cruce*:

> Man legte in uf das cruce nider:
> Da worden sine reinen glider
> Und sin geeder uf gezogen
> Als die senewe uf den bogen.[1]

He was laid down on the Cross. Then his pure limbs and his (sinews and) veins were drawn up like the string on a bow.

One may wonder what kind of a bow this author had in mind, spanned as it lay flat on the ground. Does *uf gezogen* mean 'drawn up', as the sinew of the old bow might be drawn up, or is this already the

---

[1] ed. DTM vii, lines 2791 ff.

'winding' of the crossbow? If the Lateran Council of 1137 had forbidden the use of the terrible *arcubalista* against anyone not an infidel, it
was well established by 1320. Was it old enough to serve as a symbol?
Or shall we surmise that by 1320 symbols and realia were losing and
acquiring patina at about the same rate? Or was the crossbow here
indeed being used against the infidel? Sooner or later the more telling
likeness, particularly when the crossbow was wound to present a Y (the
drawn string and the bolt), was bound to prevail. In fact the crossbow
*being* drawn provided the real likeness with the pulling with ropes,
sometimes with levers.[1] There was no need and no time to seek
authority for the recognition of such likenesses, though anyone so
minded would have claimed to find Isidore not unhelpful.[2] By the
fourteenth to the fifteenth century such support from the authorities
would scarcely be sought. And so we come to the text of the *Mystère
de la Passion* of Angers (1486). This is an enormously long Passion, but
it is a highly disciplined composition. The dragging of Christ's limbs
with ropes is, as always by this date, justified by reference to the 'holes
bored too far apart':

> troys dois de destaunce a
> de la paulme jusqu'aux pertuys . . .
> il s'en fault plus de demy aulne

Then comes the comparison, first with the crossbow, then with the
bowstring, leading immediately to the citation of Psalm xxi: 'they
counted all my bones', as follows:

> oncques arbaleste bendee
> ne tendit de telle facon . . .

> onques corde d'arc ne tira
> mieux que ses ners foibles et fors,
> car on nombreroit par son corps
> ung a ung les os qui y sont.[3]

---

[1] The *Holkham Bible Picture Book* is of roughly the same date as *Von Gottes
Zukunft*: cf the levers, plate 27c.

[2] *Etym.* XVIII x ii *De Fundis* . . . Balista genus tormenti, ab emittendo iacula
dicta; βαλεῖν enim Græce mittere dicitur. Torquetur enim verbere nervorum, et
magni vi iacit aut hastas aut saxa.

[3] *Mystère* etc., ed. Omer Jodogne (Gembloux, 1957) 27, 266 ff and –98 ff.

It is three spans from the palm of the hand – more than half an ell – to the holes.

... never did spanned crossbow so stretch (its string) ... never did a bow-string pull as hard as did his sinews which were both weak and strong, for one might count his bones there, the whole length of his body, one by one.

If I may also quickly add, with forward reference to a matter to be discussed briefly at a later point, the thieves are stated in this same text to have been crucified *a la vielle facon*, that is to say as in Antiquity, in the Roman fashion.

Here then, in the crossbow image we have surely the source of that Crucifixion iconography which we encounter in its most devastating 'realisation' in the Isenheim Altar of 'Grünewald', the Crucified – *quasi leprosus* – on the crossbow, no longer on the harp of the Cross. The bent cross-beam is thereby accounted for, no matter which of the versions of the panel we take. The Bow-Crucifix is also to be seen at the foot of the gigantic tapestry by Graham Sutherland which covers the 'Eastern' Wall of Coventry Cathedral. This is more probably homage over the centuries to Grünewald than intentional crossbow symbolism.

And now finally: in February 1968 I came across a small object in the Mainfränkisches Museum at Würzburg, which seemed to me to demand a reproduction in this book, even if only as an image. It is at this point in our narrative that we may most usefully look at it, plate 30b.

I am grateful to Dr Muth (Oberkonservator of the Museum) for supplying me with the information required as a rubric to the plate and the following details: The badge (a silver cast showing traces of the original gilt) is an exact replica of a cross-bow, complete with cordage, drawing-stirrup, seating for the insertion of the cranequin or rack (beside the feet of the crucifix). An escutcheon on the reverse side has not been identified. On the evidence of the form of the crossbow the date of the badge will be first half of the sixteenth century, provenance possibly Dillingen, say South Germany. The observation I would add is that without a well-established tradition of reference from Cross to crossbow, a badge fashioned in this image would, even in South Germany in the sixteenth century, have seemed a dubiously reverent exercise in 'accommodation'. At any time, however, the badge will seem striking, and the conceit is bold.

We come, therefore, at the end of this long chapter to the somewhat remarkable conclusion that Christian Crucifixion iconography has two main sources, Psalms xxi and lvi, the Psalm for Good Friday and the Psalm for Easter. The 'changes in religious feeling' to which we have been able to make only passing reference in this study are *inter alia* responsible for the fact that it has proved so laborious a task to rediscover those sources.

Here we must simply break off. I regret that I cannot conclude with either a summary of this chapter or any other summing up than I offered in the last paragraph. The chapter itself is a summary. I could have offered a much fuller documentation of my thesis without a great deal of extra labour. At a later stage I hope to work out a general account of the development of Christian narrative tradition from the Apocryphal New Testament down to quite modern times. The problems of organisation presented by such an undertaking will be reduced if the general thesis of this chapter is held to be proved.

# V

## THE ART HISTORIAN'S SOURCE BOOKS[1]

THE Source Books compiled by the art historian contain a good deal of material that is or could be of interest in literary studies. We are wrong to neglect them. The long excerpts in one of them from Albrecht von Scharfenberg (his description of the Grail Temple in the *Jüngerer Titurel*), from Hartmann von Aue (Eneite's saddle in the *Erec*) and from the Middle High German poem *Die Erlösung* (a description of God's Throne)[2] are naturally enough not the characteristic content of such reference works. These passages are 'sources' for the art historian mainly in the sense that they show him what impression Gothic architecture, art, and the crafts generally made on contemporaries. They also show, however, that the poets idealised or otherwise improved on the works of art which they claimed merely to describe. It is in this way that a poem of Theodulf of Orleans (*c*. 760–820) has to be read.[3] It purports to describe 'a certain picture' of the seven Liberal Arts, and indeed offers a wealth of iconographical detail; but one may still ask whether the poet has not completely idealised his pictorial source in re-creating it in words.[4]

Rather strangely, we would think, the art historian has hitherto neglected some major works in the vernacular treating Old and New Testament story. He has considered these simply to be 'the Bible'. There is some justification in this, in that vernacular adaptations can never have served as immediate sources for the artists; they had no authority. But indirectly they have, surely, *evidential* value. Without

---

[1] In the remaining sections of this book I am less generous with translations. Discreet guidance is provided before or after any untranslated passage.
[2] Maurer's edition, see p. 259 n. 1, 393 ff.
[3] *MGH: Poetæ* I 544, Latin and German in Horst Kusch, *Einführung in das lateinische Mittelalter* (Berlin, 1957) I 54.
[4] On the 'picture poem' as a literary genre, see the works listed by Hellmut Rosenfeld in his article 'Bilderbogen' in the *Reallexikon zur deutschen Literaturgeschichte*, 2nd ed. I 174. (This is more recent than his monograph, *Das deutsche Bildgedicht*, Palästra, CXCIX (1935).)

the models of ecclesiastical art, Otfrid's treatment of the Annunciation, for instance, would have been less pictorial. In the case of the *Heliand* one cannot be sure. It is suggested below[1] that the poet may not have been familiar with the Deposition (Descent from the Cross) as a picture. But before making up our minds whether the art historian should admit our poets as indirect witnesses of contemporary artistic tradition, let us look for a moment at the kind of materials which he has to consider as possibly direct evidence of real pictures. That is, texts which claim to be about pictures. We have just mentioned Theodulf of Orleans on the subject of 'a certain picture'. That was a long *poem*. Most of the evidence consists of short and pithy 'titulus' verses so numerous as to constitute a minor literary genre. They contain, as a rule, little enough to excite the literary historian. Their reliability as evidence of real pictures is also often quite uncertain. Therein lies their fascination: that they cannot be neglected. That tends to leave open the question who is to read and interpret them.

According to Franz Fr. Leitschuh's History of Carolingian Painting[2] the *Carmina Sangallensia* in a ninth-century manuscript include 'notable *Uersus de euangelio ad picturam*', giving 'a detailed account of the pictorial decoration of a church'.[3] 'If the cycle of pictures was in fact executed, as I do not doubt,' he continues, 'it was second among the important monuments of Carolingian art of which we have evidence. . . . The right wall of the choir was given up to the following pictures' etc.[4] I reproduce the first dozen lines from the poem which has about eighty in all, and ask the reader to count the pictures. Up to the dream of the Three Wise Men before their return, I recognise perhaps eight pictures, allowing that some may include more than one episode.

> Angelus ecce seni promittit munera nati,
> Quem populus trepidans foris expectabat et orans.
> Concipit en verbo prolem castissima virgo,
> Angelus hic sponsam Joseph commendat alendam.
> Hic genetrix domini meat Elisabethque salutat,

---

[1] Cf pp. 339 f.
[2] *Geschichte der karolingischen Malerei, ihr Bilderkreis und seine Quellen* (Berlin, 1894).
[3] Ibid. p. 65. I treat the 'poem' which is to follow as a series of *tituli*.
[4] Ibid. p. 68.

Utque deo exultet Johannem spiritus implet.
Zacharias suboli nomen posuere propinqui,
Sed mage Johannes certant vocitare parentes.
Nunciat angelicus Christum pastoribus ymnus:
In stabulo dominum celebrant en omnia parvum.
Ecce magi solio præsentant munera vero,
In somnis moniti faciem fugere tyranni.

That these lines were written with reference to real pictures, I myself believe too. First of all because the poet seems concerned merely to identify the various images, adding only the most conventional glosses. But have the art historians exploited these verses, short as they are, as they merit? What does the first picture represent? – 'Behold the angel promises the *old* man that he shall have a son'. And whence the crowd of people: *foris trepidans et orans*? This is not the Nativity according to Luke, but most of the Annunciation and Nativity sequence according to the *Pseudo-Matthew*[1] of which the poet is reminded by the picture cycle. How may it have represented this first scene? The words in Pseudo-Matthew are: 'I see two peoples before me, the one weeping, the other rejoicing.' On the use of the Apocryphal New Testament in art and in literature during the Middle Ages there is more below.

The source books have, in fact, relatively few texts to put forward as direct evidence of actual pictures. More important than the verses in the *Carmina Sangallensia* are the *tituli* for a picture-cycle in the imperial palace at Ingelheim. It appears to have shown episodes from world history, probably following Orosius.[2] This cycle is the 'most important' monument of Carolingian art alluded to in the previous quotation from Leitschuh, above. There was also, on similar evidence, a pictorial composition representing Christian story in the Palatine Chapel at Aachen. For the rest, as we approach our next examples we may observe that in the same measure as 'picture poems' become more interesting to us as poems, they lose in evidential value for the art historian; for as soon as a poet offers more than the merest 'titles' and begins to speak *ad picturam*, he directs his attention from pictures to their *themes*. If his subject is a comprehensive cycle of pictures, he has not the time or the space for more than the briefest formulations. He does not, of course, attempt anything resembling a technical description with 'top left' and the like. He does not comment on the style or even

---

[1] Chapters 11 and 15.          [2] Leitschuh, pp. 60 ff.

on the colours. He expresses himself in his own *writer's* terms – on the themes. Before we exploit his words for any purpose, however, we must recall both points and not forget them: that he has a *picture* before him (or in mind), and that he uses formulations which belong mainly to *literary* tradition. But there are other considerations. The picture itself is static, it presents (presumably) only one moment of sacred story, or it illustrates one point of dogma. The poet's reflections on the other hand are not absolutely restricted to what the picture represents. Here are two examples.

(a) Leitschuh says that in his *titulus* verses Rabanus Maurus seems generally to treat pictures of the crucified Saviour, or of his Resurrection.[1] He then quotes the two-line *titulus* bearing itself the title *Versus in tabula inter seraphin posita*:

> Hic deus est Christus dominus qui regnat ubique,
> Et cruce confixus noxia vincla rupit.

One cannot be absolutely certain that when Leitschuh wrote 'crucified Saviour *or* ... Resurrection' he was referring to this *titulus* and no others. But if we assume that he was, and ourselves try to determine what kind of picture may have given rise to these lines, we too shall have to admit alternatives. I should say that the picture will have been of the Crucified, *or* it will have been a *Majestas Domini* rather than a Resurrection. I argue roughly thus: Either (i) the verses refer to a picture of the Crucified, crowned with regal crown and ruling from the Cross. In this case the second line is not addressed strictly *ad picturam* but to the mysterious events which this image masks, and I should translate 'even while crucified (as he is here represented) he broke free from the injurious bonds' (to harry Hell and save mankind). Or (ii) the picture was a *Majestas Domini*, Christ supported by the four symbols representing each an Evangelist or an *operatio* of Christ.[2] Again only the first line refers to this image. The second recalls the victory over death and the *exsurrectio* from the *vincula* of the Cross (metaphorically the fetters, 'historically' the nails).[3] In short, there seems to be no single image to which *both* lines of the *titulus* would at once apply. Modest in scope as a *titulus* may be, it is a miniature literary work, prompted by a picture.

[1] Ibid. p. 63.  [2] Cf. pp. 127 ff.
[3] Cf pp. 70 and 300 on 'fetters' as metaphor for 'nails'.

(b) My second example is taken from one of the source books of Julius von Schlosser, his volume devoted to medieval art.[1] It is a long poem describing a picture cycle in the Cathedral of Mainz, written by Ekkehard IV of St Gall for Bishop Aribo of Mainz, before 1031: *Uersus ad picturas Domus domini Mogontine*. The roughly nine hundred hexametres deal *seriatim* with a compendious, even stupendous pictorial programme covering Christian history from the Work of the Six Days to the Day of Judgment. On the programme as such, i.e. whether ever executed or not, we are therefore reasonably reliably informed. What can be said of the iconography of the individual pictures? In the majority of cases, probably nothing of any note. The formulations are so brief that they only rarely permit comparison with other common-place statements concerning the biblical scenes or incidents named. I single out the four lines in which Ekkehard refers to the creation and animation of Adam. This is a subject which I have already investigated elsewhere with reference to some pictorial representations and to the 'Genesis' tradition in literature.[2] A point to be noted almost before we begin to read is that for any cleric of the tenth and later centuries, the works of the Six Days were carried out not by God alone, but by the Trinity (*Trinitas creator* is a standard topic). The lines run:

> Uiuit homo primus anima de complice limus
> Quem pater et natus creat et ui compare flatus.
> Personis trinus, deitate perenniter unus,
> Arbitrio simile sibi plasmat et ratione.

The philologist will immediately note certain complications here. First of all there is the singular verb *creat* for the activity of Father and Son: Father and Son 'creates'. This reminds us perhaps of the compound noun *sunufatarungo* ('father and son') in the Old High German *Hilde-brandslied*, or *gisunfader* ('father and his sons') in the Old Saxon *Heliand*, but we see no further connection and dismiss the passing thought (these nouns take a plural verb). Next: in *whose* likeness is it said that man was created? Evidently 'its own', that is the Trinity's; and Latin grammar is able to deal with this problem of congruence and orthodoxy at the same time: 'the first man, clay, lives through the intermingled

---

[1] *Quellenbuch zur Kunstgeschichte des abendländischen Mittelalters* (Vienna, 1896) pp. 158 ff.
[2] See pp. 34 f.

spirit, [man] whom the Father-and-the-Son, and with equal power the Spirit, creates, forms, in the likeness of itself in *arbitrium* and in *ratio*, [itself] three as to the persons, in its divinity ever one'. One might read these lines without particular attention, did one not know that in the Early Middle High German verse paraphrase of Genesis the text at this point says (not *ad picturam*, but in its own narrative context): 'The *Son as the Wisdom of the Father* created in the presence of the Holy Spirit. . . .'

About the *picture* devoted to this scene in the Millstatt manuscript of the German *Genesis* – which shows *three*, not four figures in all – I have myself come to some firm conclusions. See plate 16a. The picture shows Adam and *two* other figures, one being a youthful Creator with only a wisp of beard following the line of his chin. This I take to be, in the light of the text just referred to, 'Christ as the Wisdom of the Father'. The other figure is winged, clad in ornate high-priestly robes, and holds a sceptre with trefoil. This figure represents, I have argued, the Holy Spirit, at the actual moment of the animation of Adam, when Adam receives the *spiritaculum vitæ* according to Genesis ii 7. I consider it therefore at least possible that in the Mainz picture of 1030 there were *three* figures in all to represent *pater et natus, flatus, primus homo*. Even if one thinks that such an enormous schedule of pictures can never have been executed, one has at any rate to ask how Ekkehard visualised such a scene, and be careful neither to impute to him or his pictures an iconography which in 1030 had not yet been evolved,[1] nor a *devotional* image in a 'historical' scene.[2]

We began the discussion under the present sub-heading with a philologist's observations. It is only right that we should conclude with the remark that an *n*-stroke would of course make *creat* and *plasmat* into plurals. The problem is, however, not one of merely grammatical numbers where the persons of the Trinity are concerned.

---

[1] Namely the 'Throne of Grace'.

[2] See p. 227. This argument is not invalidated by the existence of Trinity iconographies consisting of three identical figures in the art of the same and later centuries. The three-figure Trinities are all *devotional* images. They stand or sit, and watch or preside. Cf plate 16b, the *Trinitas creator* of the *Hortus Deliciarum*. The texts in the scrolls: *Sancta Trinitas/post angli casum/fit de homine consilium/trinus et unus dominus/trinus in personis/unus in substantia/hoc una facies tri/um personarum demon/strat//faciamus hominem ad imaginem et similitudinem nostram et præsit cunctis animantibus terræ.* Dr. Adelheid Heimann's article *Trinitas creator mundi* in *JWI* ii (1938–9) is still basic and is well illustrated.

We now carry out an experiment with the source books. Let us assume that we are reading Otfrid of Weissenburg's passage on the Annunciation, *Missus est Gabrihel angelus*,[1] not in the light of Schönbach's 'Otfrid-Studien', or in a standard edition with notes written by the older 'Germanisten', but with what help we can get from Leitschuh's work on the pictorial repertory of the Carolingian and Ottonian artists. From a previous contribution of my own[2] I intercalate one note on the subject of Mary's 'hand-work'. The text runs as follows:

Since then there had gone by half a year, as it might be thrice two months. Then there came a messenger from God, an angel from Heaven. He brought precious tidings to this world. He flew the sun's path, the street of the stars, the welkin way, to that royal *itis*, a Lady of noble lineage, *Sancta Maria* herself. Her forebears were kings to a man. He entered her palace. He found her [with bended head] sorrowing, with a Psalter in her hand. She [had] finished reading her Psalter and taken up her work: she was fashioning a work of fair stuffs and costly threads. [Note: In a Life of Mary based on *Pseudo-Matthew*, the 'work' is the curtain of the Temple, made of purple wools; in a *Gospel Book* one must, after the reference to Mary's reading of the Psalms and her anticipatory sorrowing, think rather of the *tunica inconsutilis* of developing tradition.] That was always her favourite work. Then the messenger declared in a clear voice, as a good messenger should who addresses the Mother of the Lord: [*Ave Maria* etc.].

And now Leitschuh. Clearly we shall not expect to find anything in his work to help us to interpret the style of Otfrid's poetry, or the technical devices used in this passage, 'repetition with variation' or the triad of metaphors ('kennings') for 'the sky', etc.

Let us first look up 'Maria' (as I in fact did, page 151). Here one finds a good deal that seems to have little if any bearing on the Annunciation in Otfrid. 'Representations of Mary . . . are extremely rare in Carolingian art.' That is somewhat surprising, surely; it was evidently a consequence of the 'iconoclast controversy'. The Eastern Church had sought to suppress the veneration of images and forbidden the pictorial representation of sacred persons. There is evidence of attempts to re-designate pictures of Mary as the Sacred Wisdom – *sophia sacra* (*sancta sophia*), that is to allegorise them. One may learn in Leitschuh about the

---

[1] *Evangelienbuch*, I 5.   [2] 'Christlicher Erzählstoff', 262–6.

so-called Caroline Books (*Libri Carolini*), and the decision (let us say) of Charles the Great, despite objections of the Pope to continue to allow sacred subjects to be treated in art in the Kingdom of the Franks. Unexpectedly one comes upon details, still under 'Maria', of a D-initial in a Carolingian manuscript, where there *is* something to attract our attention. We do not need the information at the moment – for the Annunciation proper – but knowing what lies immediately ahead in Otfrid, we note it now. We will make this digression first, and then come back to the Annunciation scene.

Leitschuh fortunately offers a simple sketch of this initial D, see our plate 32b. It occurs in the so-called *Sacramentary of Drogo*. Who is Drogo? We look him up (on p. 80). From this passage on him, which I translate for convenience, I put a few things into italics:

A codex of the Bibliothèque Nationale, No. 9428, which was handed over (*ausgefolgt*) as recently as 1802, the *Sacramentarium* of Drogo (a natural son of Charles the Great, who died in 855 as Bishop of Metz) contains a large number of coloured initials decorated with foliage motifs and with gold-leaf. In this work, the most brilliant creation of the *scriptorium of Metz*, Carolingian art emerges in a new mastery of the art of *narrative representation*, which in its generous scope includes the *stories of the Old and New Testaments*, legends of the saints, and a wealth of skilfully drawn vegetation. The minute pictures enliven the spaces enclosed by the large initials etc.

Reading this passage, the student of Old High German literature resolves, I think, to keep a look-out for reproductions from Drogo's *Sacramentary*. It will probably turn out that he has in fact seen some of them without becoming fully aware of Drogo. There is a D-initial (not the one now under discussion) showing the three Marys at the Tomb which has been reproduced in many places.[1] Returning now to our first D-initial:[2]

The Sacramentary of Drogo shows in a D-initial: the Virgin with nimbus. She wears a tunic and cloak and has the Infant Christ (also with nimbus) on her knee. Filling the vertical band of the D are the two

[1] For instance in Albert Boeckler, *Deutsche Buchmalerei vorgotischer Zeit*, Die Blauen Bücher (1959) illus. 17; Émile Van Moé, *Illuminated Initials* (Engl. ed. London, 1950) under 'D'. See also Beckwith, illus. 53 (initial C) and 54.
[2] Leitschuh, p. 151.

servants of the Virgin. One is spreading the swaddling clothes for the divine child, while the second is pouring water into a bowl. In the curved band of the D we see Joseph seated, his head supported on his right hand, his left rests on his knee.

That is practically everything that Leitschuh has to say about this initial. He knows *of* our poet Otfrid, and he knows the important illustrations in the Viennese manuscript of Otfrid's Gospel Book.[1] He clearly does *not* know or does not recall the account of the Annunciation in Otfrid, which would have interested him. The literary historian will admire the skill displayed in the composition of this historiated initial, but he will notice things which Leitschuh did not mention. In the enclosed space are Mary and the Christ-child – each with a nimbus. That is a tiny *devotional* image, 'Sancta Maria', not a picture of Mary as she sat in the cave or stable. Not even the two animals are present. Mary is seated on a simple throne. From the broad bands of the upright and the curved stroke of the D the two servants and Joseph look in upon this image. They venerate it, as did any faithful observer of the initial. They are, however, not part of the principal image, neither Saint Joseph (seen as an old man) nor the two midwives. These are characters taken not from Luke but from the Apocryphal New Testament. We already knew[2] that Otfrid draws on *Pseudo-Matthew* for Mary's psalter-reading and handwork. We now have contemporary evidence for the annotation of his line in the Nativity scene: 'Mary did not know where she should bath her child.'[3] Otfrid's apparent uncertainty about both the site and the setting of the Nativity may well reflect uncertainty about the use of the Apocrypha. He seems to avoid Pseudo-Matthew's *cave*. For the 'inn' in which there was, according to Luke, 'no room' he uses *gastwissi*, evidently his attempt to deal with the word in Luke.[4] Adding these fragmentary indications together we may deduce that, despite the capitularies of Charles the Great forbidding the use of the Apocrypha, not every monk (Otfrid) or every bishop (Drogo) could be weaned from them.

[1] We meet these too in Schwietering, illus. 4–6.
[2] See p. 314, also below.
[3] I 11, 3.
[4] Luke's 'inn' is in the Vulgate a *diversorium*. This was inferred to be a kind of lean-to or roofed shelter beside a house (as it appears in countless pictures of the Adoration of the Magi in Christian art), or at a street junction, see Isidore, *Etym.* xv iii. 10.

It was therefore apparently not under 'Mary' that we were (if anywhere) to find more about Mary's psalter-reading, her handwork, her sorrowing, and her palace (*palinza*); but our enquiry yielded something. Now we try Leitschuh under 'Annunciation'.[1] After two brief references to other works Leitschuh describes the Annunciation scene in an Evangeliary from Soissons. It is evidently another famous illustrated manuscript, another reminder of the drabness of the image which our Old High German readers present; but this time we will not be seduced by the gold leaf. (In square brackets I insert comments relative to our Otfrid passage.)

... an Annunciation to Mary, an architectural motif representing Bethlehem [in Otfrid there is no reference to Bethlehem or any 'town']. *Left:* beside an arch stands the nimbed angel in white robes, his right arm extended, his finger raised [is there any indication of the sun' spath, the street of the stars' etc., which the angel has flown?].[2] In his left hand he holds a Cross-staff [purely a pictorial device?]. On the *right* of the arch Mary sits on an upholstered throne with a footstool before it [a 'palace' after all; is this Otfrid's 'Lady of noble lineage' or an enthroned 'Sancta Maria'?]. She extends her right hand [no psalter, no handwork?]. Bethlehem is indicated by walls and towers enclosing a few houses.

Somewhat disappointing. But reading on:

... a second drawing in the same manuscript, minute enough to suggest a design for a gem, shows an Annunciation: Mary with her distaff. In front of her the angel with billowing drapery.

At last we have the evidence we needed that Otfrid's account of Mary occupied with her handwork is *not* isolated, and that this scene was to be found in pictorial art north of the Alps by his day.[3] I had not known of any example outside Rome (Santa Maria Maggiore, in a mosaic requiring scaffolding for its inspection). It is moreover interesting that *one* illustrated manuscript may contain *two different* treatments

[1] Ibid. p. 144.
[2] Cf p. 311. The writer contemplating an image recalls antecedent events.
[3] Leitschuh does not (I think) provide evidence for the Psalter reading. I dealt with this in 'Christlicher Erzählstoff' (the motif is present in *Pseudo-Matthew*). Victor H. Elbern, 'Vier karolingische Elfenbeinkästen', in *Zeitschrift des deutschen Vereins für Kunstwissenschaft*, XX (1966) 1–16: fig. 4(d) is a perfectly clear example, contemporary with Otfrid, see plate 15c. Cf for distaff plate 15b (Byzantine).

of the same subject, one hieratic (devotional) the other historical (narrative). Perhaps significantly the historical picture is minute and 'drawn in bare outline' ('gemmenartig . . . in knappen Umrissen').

And now briefly back to Otfrid's Annunciation. What I had difficulty in demonstrating some years ago before I had read Leitschuh, now seems to be confirmed. Namely that Otfrid's passage combines the characteristics of a devotional image with others that are 'historical'. He shows 'Sancta Maria' in an ideal setting, a palace. There is no reference to Bethlehem; Joseph is excluded from the narrative, there is no reference to Mary's betrothal. The Psalter reading and the handwork however are 'historical' details from *Pseudo-Matthew* which *seem* to be no more than attributes. In the context of a prologue to New Testament story and a Life of Christ (as opposed to a Life of Mary after *Pseudo-Matthew*) they allude to the coming Passion and the Sorrows.

And now a final, more general and perhaps somewhat subversive suggestion concerning the use we may make of the art historian's source books, the latter offering, as they do, a more or less complete *conspectus* of medieval pictorial repertories. (We must of course also find the matching illustrations.) We can surely not derive anything but benefit from a fairly thorough revision of the images we have each, largely subconsciously, assembled in the course of our philological and literary training based on texts, the study of words. We must obviously continue always to give the *words* of our texts first attention and ponder on them in the light of verbal and literary tradition. But should we not also ensure that we know the *images*, or the kinds of image which may in fact have conditioned the imagination of the poets and writers we study? Rather than refer this imagination to the often idiosyncratic and haphazard products of our lexical or etymological broodings over words, their meanings and their 'roots'. Without such a corrective from contemporary art we run the risk, I think, of continuing like our predecessors to see the Carolingian and post-Carolingian worlds in a Merovingian or Wagnerian gloom, peopled by impossibly archaic figures. If in the course of such image revision we also, periodically, remind ourselves that medieval pictures were in their own day modern art, and that by their strangeness they prompted associative thinking, that will be useful too, for there is the important corollary that older, pre-Christian traditions, narrative and other, had never been 'fixed' in any visual, representational art. I think we may have underestimated the power of the new images, evolved in the early days of a true representational art, to draw older narrative traditions towards themselves. I am not thinking here of such evident cases as the delayed discovery of a home for Siegfried in Xanten (where artists had in the meantime sculpted a St Victor, dragon-slayer), but of more complicated associations of old traditions with only recently familiar images.

It is in this context that I have long regretted both the solemn nonsense still talked about Valkyries (or shades of them) in the so-called First Merseburg Charm, and the brusqueness with which any attempt to draw attention to associable Christian (stories and) *images* has been rejected. Why do we persist in a hopelessly archaic interpretation of an innocent charm, which comes down to us in an identifiable Old High German dialect, and resist any reference to a better known story and a familiar, revered image? If we had twenty such charms to work on, there would be half the fuss. And so, to ensure that the custodians of our pagan inheritance are kept on their toes, I add that I myself see a not too distant Christian parallel even to the Second Merseburg Charm dealing with Phol and Wodan.

Certainly it would be a temerity – in fact non-sensical – to postulate a Christian *origin* for either of these Old High German charms. But surely the characters and the events of the *second* charm must have seemed, to anyone who heard them in the early ninth century, and to the antiquarian who wrote the charm down, a strangely debased form or a confused reminiscence of something far better known. To see Apollo in the mysterious 'Phol' has always seemed impossible, incongruous: what has Apollo to do with Wodan and the rest of the group of characters, all evidently from a heathen past? Meanwhile the reader of this book has become better acquainted with the Christian Apollo and the tree with his stretched limbs upon it, and his *exsurrexio* from the *vincula crucis*. All this lore was in the ninth century recent, exciting, not yet fully assimilated in Germany and elsewhere north of the Alps. It may have become crossed with ancient lore. *Phol ende Vuodan uuorun zi holza . . . bluotrenki, benrenki, lidirenki* etc. But 'we know that *zi holze varan* means something quite different', it will be objected. Do we know? How? Does the fact that an idiomatic turn of phrase is of frequent occurrence tell us anything about its meaning in a given instance? In the course of a chapter on the semantics of word and image we refreshed our minds on some of the processes of associative thinking to which words and images are subject. There have also been passing references in this book to Veronica (and her sudary) and to Mary (with her headcloth) on the Way of the Cross. 'But this is not really contemporary with our *Zauberspruch*, it belongs to a different genre and has a different ambit of associations!' All that I urge is that these characters, scenes, events which I have just mentioned were all more recently familiar in the ninth century than Wodan, Sinthgunt, Frija, Sunna and Volla (if these beings ever existed in their own right), and it will have been with inevitable reference to the more familiar story that the strange events of the charm were apprehended.

To come back now to the first charm (First Merseburg Charm). Have the winged '*idisi*' nothing to do with angels, or the angel, or the Three Marys at the Tomb? Can we think of nothing but either Valkyries (or bees!) when we have seen the Three Marys at the Tomb as they were drawn or carved in ivory in Carolingian times? The last reminder we were given of such obvious parallels was rejected almost out of hand as 'verwerfliche Überkritik', I know, but I would still ask whether the cleric who wrote *insprinc haptbandun, inuar uigandun*, will not have been reminded of the Easter Psalm which he knew by heart (and repeated once a week if he was a monk) rather than of the Valkyries? If that is a 'far-fetched' suggestion I should enquire what the unit of measurement is, by which we measure near and distant parallels in this area, namely popular charms. Perhaps by the distance of 'Jordan' in the Strassburg Charm from the river Jordan? The Jordan that 'went a-shooting with Genzan' is, I think, the river-God who appears in the Christian artist's *image* of the Baptism of Christ.

*Mare vidit et fugit: Jordanis conversus est retrorsum*, one reads in Psalm cxiii 3. Medieval representations of Christ's Baptism quite generally show the waters of the Jordan raised in an arc. Below, on the river bed, often with his back turned to the Saviour, is Jordan, the river god. His role in a blood charm is not simply to be invoked. He is there by right. He stopped, turned back. His example is quoted 'to stop this bleeding'. *Genzan* might then be a more or less complete corruption of Johannes (Baptista), but in traditions of this sort we know not to expect a nice logic or scrupulous attention to names. To *omit* reference to the river-god Jordan, merely because he is not familiar in our studies, is reprehensible. It is here, I think, not sufficient to refer to New Testament and Old Testament *texts* and incidents: we need to invoke the medieval image. Measured by 'Jordan' standards of relevance, one would have to say that the Merseburg Charms present no problems. Clearly no one will want to go as far as that.

Here, finally, is the place for a brief reference to the image of 'Odin on the gallows' in stanzas 138–41 of the Old Norse *Hávamál*. After my chapter on the Christian Crucifixion, and the references it contains to the Cross as gallows (*patibulum crucis*), it is obvious that there is only one interpretation which I can support. It was last presented by Konstantin Reichardt. The image is a strangely wayward Northern variant of the Christian image of the Crucifixion.[1]

---

[1] Konstantin Reichardt, 'Odin am Galgen', in *Festschrift Weigand* (Yale, Connecticut, 1957) pp. 15 ff. Cf Wolfgang Lange's *Christliche Skaldendichtung*, Vandenhoeck & Ruprecht (Göttingen, 1958) and his *Studien zur christlichen Dichtung der Nordgermanen* (Göttingen, 1958).

# VI

## A GUIDE TO MEDIEVAL ART FOR
## STUDENTS OF LITERATURE

### (a) ART HISTORY

THIS is not a short history of medieval art, but a guide for literary historians. Keeping roughly to the chronology of art history I mention under various headings a number of books which I have myself found useful as introductions, as reference works or simply as 'eye-openers'. Of some I ought to say that I should have used them in this way had I learnt of them sooner, for instance the *Larousse Encyclopædia of Byzantine and Medieval Art*.[1] For some readers this will seem too 'tabloid', but it is the product of scholarly team-work with well over 1000 illustrations, 36 full-page in colour: on the medieval art of Western Europe, the Middle and the Far East.[2]

In the *Atlas of the Early Christian World* by F. van der Meer and Christine Mohrmann[3] one finds many excellent reproductions of works of late Classical and early Christian art, all discussed with reference to Christian textual tradition; also wonderful maps illustrating the history of the medieval Church. Students of modern languages who want to become medievalists could not have a better introduction than this. (The Middle Ages do not begin with *Beowulf*, the 'Serments de Strasbourg' or the *Hildebrandslied*.)

There is a superfluity of **art histories** and 'art books'. Each European country seems since the War to have produced, or to have taken in hand a multi-volumed History of Art, handsomely appointed, each volume the work of an eminent specialist, and very expensive. Whether these works are organised according to countries or 'ages' (or both), and

---

[1] ed. René Huyghe (Librairie Larousse, 1958; English edition, Paul Hamlyn, London, 1965).

[2] Some of the facsimiles and art histories to be mentioned here appeared in a Dutch, English, French or German first edition. There are slight differences in the texts, but none in the pictorial matter of the various editions. I am grateful for information supplied by the Phaidon Press (London) and the Urs Graf Verlag (Olten, Lausanne). (I have generally not given the names of translators.)

[3] Elsevier-Amsterdam, and Nelson, London, 1958.

whether they put art history first, or technical excellence in their reproductions, they are all relatively weak on what concerns the student of literature most – iconography. There is a great temptation to buy out-of-date works, and to lay the foundations of a private collection of cut-outs, arranged according to themes and subjects (the temptation should on the whole be resisted, at any rate until the paperback disintegrates). J. Beckwith, *Early Medieval Art*,[1] appeared when the German edition of this book was in page-proof: I have not been able to refer to it systematically, even in this revision. A German edition of Beckwith has meantime appeared. It offers an excellent introduction.

Museums and Art Galleries collect and arrange their pictures mainly on art-historical lines, which means that their catalogues may be among the most useful reference works for studies of the kind pursued in this book.[2] What they offer in addition is a constant reminder of how narrow is the area in which anyone *not* a specialist in art history can operate; he must generally be content to be told the rest. The more technical information (on processes) is always a salutary warning to keep off things we do not understand. Among more recent guides, Ernst Kitzinger's *Early Medieval Art in the British Museum*, with a hundred pages of introduction and 48 illustrations, offers much more than many a fat volume.

The catalogues of **special exhibitions** have often more to offer than a single visit. Let us take as an example *Les Manuscrits à peintures en France du vii<sup>e</sup> au xii<sup>e</sup> siècle*: 5 coloured plates, 32 illustrations and scholarly introductions to the various periods, pre-Carolingian, Carolingian etc., and descriptions of 340 manuscripts, some detailed.[3] It is no hardship to read a catalogue of this kind from end to end. It is in fact a far more reassuring experience (apart from being genuinely informative) than reading a volume of art history. One is able to revise what one knew (or half knew), and learn more, an item at a time, and so build up a picture from details; it is quite probably a picture which the compiler is not aware that he is drawing for the individual reader. Here are some of the things which I noted on reading this catalogue (many of them will appear notable to anyone who has read what I have had to say so far). First some of the illustrations. Plate XVI is a twelfth-century Crucifix:

[1] Thames & Hudson 1964, 206 illustrations.

[2] It is one thing to mention the older *B.M. Guide to Medieval Antiquities* (1924), another to say where a copy can be obtained.

[3] Bibl. Nat. (Paris, 1954), unfortunately virtually unprocurable, but I have not for that reason deleted this section.

Christ is dead on the Cross, 'they numbered all my bones' (as often, I remark, in *enamels: dinumerata omnia ossa mea* must have been a welcome formula to workers in *cloisonné*: the ribs of the torso are a challenge to the master of this technique). Plate xxv is another Crucifix, eleventh century: Christ is crowned, his eyes are still open;[1] 'all my bones'; four nails, serpent at the foot of the cross, Mary and John; symbols of the Evangelists; Sun and Moon. 'Typical eleventh century.' But the *footrest* is surely strange! Why the seven bosses (or nail heads?) on the front edge of the footrest, and of *what shape* is the footrest? We have only the reproduction in front of us, but to me it looks as though the Crucified is standing on a harp. Is that conceivable? At that we must leave the picture, or do something about it. I continue, without committing anyone.

The text now, and some further illustrations. On p. 13 there is a general review of Carolingian painting, where I think I read for the first time that the names of the various 'schools' (Ada-School, *etc.*) go back to a classification of 1889 by Janitschek, and they now seem to me to be 'working hypotheses'.[2] On reflection it seems that I must have read about Janitschek before, probably on several occasions. Time and again one reads in this catalogue that *dedication* pictures and pictures of the *four Evangelists* are to be found on the opening pages of illustrated books: they are often the only illustrations. Not that this is so surprising, considering what books a monastery or cathedral had to have, namely service books; but this prompts a reflection. Why does Otfrid not preface his Gospel Book with a chapter on each of the Evangelists (the Evangeliaries of his monastery presumably had pictures of them), or, like the *Heliand* poet, on all four of them in one combined statement. Has this something to do with the fact that the *Heliand* poet was following Tatian's Gospel Harmony? Or had he a *majestas domini* in mind? – the pictorial counterpart, in a way, of the *Diatesseron*, of which he prepared a verse paraphrase. Or did he 'harmonise' the Evangelists in this opening passage without such pictorial encouragement? I have no answer; I ask merely. Entry 52 concerns a *Psalter of Charles the Bald*, written, says the catalogue, by one Liuthard.[3] What I read about the ivory plaques of the contemporary book-cover

---

[1] Compare the poem of Rabanus Maurus, p. 311.

[2] See p. 51.

[3] Liuthard; there is also a Liuthar, a century later; there are groups of manuscripts called after each of them, see pp. 130, 337.

startles me to attention here. On an upper plaque is represented: 'David, ayant derrière lui Bethsabé, reçoit les reproches de Nathan; Urias est étendu à leur pieds'. David, the adulterer, also guilty of manslaughter, is represented on the outer cover of the King's hymn book! On a lower plaque 'l'âme de David protégé par Dieu'. (The book covers are not reproduced in the catalogue, see our plate 19a.) It seems on this evidence that we were right in saying that a King could always be reminded by his spiritual advisers, and for that matter by his court poets and artists, of David, the prototypical royal *sinner* and penitent-saint.[1] Charles the Great was called David – for other reasons than this, perhaps, or for this and other reasons. Otfrid of Weissenburg was apparently 'in the tradition' when he alluded at such length to the 'trials and tribulations' of the most Christian Louis,[2] and the strange pairing of images (Caesar and David) in the 'mirror' for Otto III[3] is not completely isolated. Charles the Bald will no doubt have pondered, as he was expected to, on the image of David the Sinner, before the service began; and he will have derived comfort just as certainly from the other image when he knelt to hear the benediction: 'l'âme de David protégé par Dieu.'[4]

As item 75 we meet again the *Sacramentary of Drogo* (Charles the Great's natural son).[5] The catalogue refers to eighteen of the scenes in the historiated initials. Plate XI is a C-initial with Christ's Ascension.[6]

Mary is represented, as often in Byzantine art, amid the Apostles; Christ bearing the Cross of the Resurrection mounts a hill and takes God's proffered hand – a more satisfactory image in every way (I have always thought) than the vertical ascent and those tiresome footprints which pilgrims had seen. This is the volume of which Leitschuh wrote that it was 'handed over as recently as 1802'; here we read the same thing: 'Le volume a été envoyé de Metz . . . 1802.' Item 81 is a Bible

---

[1] Cf p. 105.　　　　[2] Cf p. 104.　　　　[3] Cf p. 129 f.

[4] These two ivories are well known to art historians for being patterned on drawings in the Utrecht Psalter, see Beckwith, *Early Med. Art*, plates 34–40 and text p. 44 ff. The Psalms involved are Psalm l (Beckwith, pl. 37), the subject of which is David's prayer to God for forgiveness of his offence against Nathan, and his crime of manslaughter, and Psalm lvi. Is the latter the *Easter* Psalm in *this* context? Presumably *not*. It is the same Psalm historically understood, in which David prays to be delivered from his enemies and assailants. For reproductions of both plaques see: Adolf Goldschmidt, *Elfenbein-Skulpturen*, vol. I 19, pp. 23–5; the manuscript is Paris, Bibl. Nat., cod lat. 1152, about 860–70 (i.e. contemporary with Otfrid's *Gospel Book*).

[5] See pp. 315 f.　　　　[6] Beckwith, illus. 53.

once belonging to Theodulf of Orléans whom we met in another connection.[1]

Items 93 and 94 are Evangeliaries from Brittany of the ninth and tenth centuries. The portraits of the Evangelists show, instead of human heads, the animal-heads of the *symbols* of the Evangelists. I did not know this convention when I first read this catalogue; perhaps I should have known. I have come across examples since then in medieval Spanish art,[2] and meantime I see that Dr H. M. Taylor interprets the curiously contorted head of Christ in the Anglo-Saxon Crucifixion statue at Wormington, Glos., as in fact a Lamb's head; and he cites as the nearest parallel to this 'remarkable feature' the 'figures of the evangelists on certain Anglo-Saxon cross-shafts'.[3] Dr Taylor may be correct in his interpretation of Wormington, but in saying so I would class this iconography (the crucified lamb-headed Christ) as being so wayward as scarcely to merit credence. It remains outside the canon of Christian art. Item 103 is an illuminated copy of Martianus Capella's *De Nuptiis Mercurii et Philologiae*, a work which we in German studies notice because Notker III of St Gall translated it (to the amazement of the late F. J. E. Raby). In the same volume, works of Terence, Horace, Lucan, Juvenal.

*Das erste Jahrtausend, Kultur und Kunst im werdenden Abendland an Rhein und Ruhr.*[4] This is the monograph following on an exhibition held a few years ago at the Villa Hügel. There is a volume of plates (450 good reproductions, with a descriptive index), and two volumes of commentary are separately available. I have referred to it here on a number of occasions. In the German edition I referred readers to the useful juxtaposition of drawings from the Utrecht Psalter and Carolingian ivories; but Beckwith[5] is equally good on this. I also drew attention to plates 334–5 where one can check in a Cologne register that Anno was indeed 34th bishop, and see his bishop's staff – both of interest to readers of the old German *Annolied*.[6]

A further illustrated exhibition catalogue is *Bayerns Kirche im Mittelalter (Handschriften und Urkunden aus Bayerischem Staatsbesitz)*,[7] with 8 colour plates and 64 full-page illustrations. This came to my

---

[1] Cf pp. 308 f.

[2] Cf Pedro de Palol, Max Hirmer, *Spanien, Kunst des frühen Mittelalters*, etc. (Hirmer, Munich, 1965), illus. 63 and plate xlviii.

[3] Cf *Antiquity*, XXXIX (1965) 55.

[4] Düsseldorf, 1962–.

[5] Illus. 34–40 and adjacent text.

[6] Stanza XXXII, 11, see p. 173.

[7] Hirmer, Munich, 1960.

notice too late to be used in the planning of this chapter, but I mention it, both to recommend it and to suggest that it is not an irrevocable loss to have missed an important exhibition. One can obtain the catalogue and enliven it by seeing a similar exhibition. Catalogues become source books for further study. Take for instance the Charlemagne Exhibition in Aachen, in 1965. The catalogue of this: *Karl der Grosse, Werk und Wirkung*, also available in French,[1] 568 pp. and 158 Plates, has been followed by four massive volumes, *Karl der Grosse, Lebenswerk und Nachleben*, which most ordinary mortals will have to take as read; the Catalogue is in itself a useful reference work.

A further remark may be interpolated at this point. How can the non-specialist in art history organise the records of all kinds which he fairly quickly accumulates? How can he be sure he knows what pictures he has, even in books in his possession? In this chapter so far I have referred, in passing, to over two thousand illustrations contained in a mere half-dozen of volumes, all but one of which I own, without being a real collector. In them are, however, several reproductions of *each* of certain important medieval pictures. The amount of information which the various works give about them differs, and in a number of cases there are clashes. How is one to collate all this? My experience is that there is no practical solution of this problem of organisation if one is not a compulsive card-indexer; and of course any *system* of indexing is bound to fragment what was in its time an important unit of some kind, perhaps a *school* of painters, or an iconographical *tradition*; more tangibly the *library* of a given monastery, or a *volume* prepared for a specific purpose. Of all these the volume has always seemed to me to be the unit which one should never allow to be finally dispersed in the art books. This leads me to the further point that the only unambiguous specification of an individual miniature is by the pressmark of the volume and the folio number of the page. There are of course dozens of famous manuscripts (*Book of Kells*, etc.) which may be referred to by name, but our 2000-odd illustrations occur in manuscripts which can only be identified by their present-day pressmarks.

An art historian would probably make an entirely different selection of points from his reading of the catalogues and handbooks we have considered so far, and he may find mine somewhat strange, but I hope interesting. To take up the thread again: One has to know, even as a non-specialist, something about the 'roots' of **Western European art.**

[1] Schwann Verlag, Düsseldorf–Aachen, 1965.

This part of the art-historical story is, however, fairly familiar: late Classical art, the art of the Eastern Mediterranean and of Alexandria, of the Celtic north-west and perhaps of the North generally. In the following sketch I shall work in some remarks on our own account.

In referring to the *Larousse Encyclopædia* and to the *Atlas of the Early Christian World* (van der Meer – Mohrmann) I had meant to absolve us on the first score, namely the share of the **art of late Antiquity** in the inheritance of our Germanic forebears. For all that I have to ask whether medieval Europe learnt more than techniques and certain conventions of representation from the late Roman art. As for the *subject matter* of early Christian art (in which the techniques and conventions were applied), surely little of that is still to be seen in Carolingian and later ages. Here are a few points as they have occurred to me. The monuments of Late Roman Christian art, particularly carved sarcophagi, are almost exclusively devoted to Christian belief in the immortality of the soul and an afterlife. The recurrent 'historical' image seems to be Jonah, first being cast from the belly of the whale, then sitting on the dry land, or lying asleep beneath his gourd. Similarly there is the Chi-Rho monogram, which, in days when Christ was generally represented in the image of the Good Shepherd,[1] was laden with weighty significance. It was the principal symbol of Christ crucified. By the Carolingian age it could no longer claim to be that. Then there are the anchor and fish symbols. Are these of any importance (or comparable importance) in later art? I myself feel that in the course of our introduction to Christian tradition generally ('the story of the catacombs') we are told too much rather than too little about this early Christian symbolism; or perhaps I should say that we seem to assume an equal familiarity with this lore among the faithful of the Middle Ages. Sarcophagi in Gaul and Merovingian France still use the symbols, but what evidence have we from medieval literature that they were still held in awe or even noticed? The real inheritance from Late Antiquity is the art of realistic (illusionistic) representation.

Next there is the influence of **Syrian–Palestinian art** on the West. This is usually brought home to us in the statement that there was a 'new image' of Christ, dark and bearded, which became part of the tradition we call Byzantine. I have only one point to raise here. It is possibly of little interest to art historians. When do we in German

[1] Cf p. 78.

studies mention Syria at all? There is one context – of some importance. We are first introduced to Old High German literature by way of 'the Tatian translation'. (I first became aware that this translation is of more general concern when, some thirty years ago, a New Testament scholar borrowed my edition (Sievers) and stated it was of considerable interest for 'Tatian studies'.) Otherwise the most we learn is that 'Tatian was a Syrian monk of the second century whose *Diatessaron* (etc.)'. This may now be a reason for our taking a more direct interest in Syrian art; a second is our Old German *Genesis* which is linked through its two illustrated manuscripts with a tradition in art leading back to the art historian's *Vienna Genesis* which is also Syrian.[1]

First of all Tatian. Rabanus Maurus tells us, in his voluminous writings, exactly nothing about the translation of Tatian's Gospel Harmony into Old High German, a translation which 'Germanists' tend to look upon as Raban's main claim to be remembered. The question has still not been solved how the monastery of Fulda hit upon the idea of translating Tatian at all. His 'mosaic' of the four Gospels was not a service book; in the Western Church pericopal readings only were used. According to Professor Ingeborg Schröbler, the *Diatessaron* was 'from the outset rather a private, popular or missionary work'.[2] In correspondence with Prof. Schröbler I have suggested that one might look on the Old High German version as the record of a well organised practical seminar, the work of members of a team. For such purposes (i.e. the translation of 'Scripture' into the vernacular), and as the basic text for a poetic paraphrase as we have it in the Old Saxon *Heliand* (now thought by many scholars to have been written at Fulda, rather than Werden or Corvey), the *Diatessaron* was 'available', as the canonical New Testament was not. We saw above[3] that at a time when the Apocryphal New Testament (at any rate in Latin) was officially pro-scribed (i.e. not available), a vernacular adaptation could be illustrated, possibly by ecclesiastical artists. The parallel is only loose, but it is worth consideration. I do not expect these suggestions to be taken any more seriously by my colleagues than my reminder that Raban's Latin works fill six volumes of Migne's *Patrologia Latina*, which I would interpret as evidence that the Tatian translation was, in the abbot's eyes,

---

[1] Cf p. 34 n. 3.
[2] 'Fulda und die althochdeutsche Literatur', in *Jahrbuch der Görres-Gesellschaft*, NS pp. 1–26, =*Fuldaer Geschichtsblätter*, XXXVIII (1962) 141 ff.
[3] Cf pp. 32 f.

a useful but not an important undertaking which he could entrust to a subordinate; and that he meantime kept to his own researches, the compilation of a whole library of reference works, and the composition of his figural poem (*De laudibus sanctæ crucis*), virtually the only work for which he is famous.

However that may be, in the so-called *Rabbula Gospels* we have a Middle Eastern, Syriac manuscript in which for the first time the Tatian harmony is *not* used.[1] Rabbula was the bishop of Edessa (411–435) who introduced the division of the Gospels into *Canones*. Rabbula is also the name of the scribe and illustrator who completed his work of illustration in 586 in the monastery of St John in Zagba (not identified: Mesopotamia). His pictorial sources may, it is thought, have been mosaics in Palestine. The picture of the Crucifixion on folio 13r of this manuscript has already been reproduced countless times in histories of art; but we need it here, and soon again, see plate 25. It is the first known 'realistic' treatment of the subject in Christian art, with Mary and John, 'Loginos' and Stephaton, the dice-throwing soldiers and the three Marys. (On the mode of the Crucifixion, see pp. 340 f.) On folio 4r there is an *Annunciation*, showing Mary with basket and wools, as in the mosaic in S. Maria Maggiore.[2] It is important to note that when the art historians call the style of the Rabbula Gospels 'Byzantine' they are referring here to *monastic* art, which offers pictorial narrative; this is very different from the official style.

**Byzantine Art, the Byzantine World**. As an introduction to the Byzantine world for students of literature I recommend Ernst Benz, *Geist und Leben der Ostkirche*.[3] This is a short work, scholarly and thorough. It takes us into a Byzantine church, straight to the icon screen (*iconostasis*), which it interprets with reference to the orthodox faith and, by stages, the Byzantine world as it was in the Middle Ages and now is. Then there is H. W. Haussig, *Kulturgeschichte von Byzanz*.[4] This offers pictures, chronological tables, a plan of Constantinople, and something about everything: economics, military organisation, politics, ceremonials, the church, monasticism, liturgy, art, literature, scholarship – with bibliographies to every chapter. But here as in so many

[1] The *Rabbula Gospels, Facsimile edition of the Syriac Ms. Plut. I 56 of the Medicean Laurentian Library*, with notes, by Cecchelli, Furlani, Salmi (Urs Graf, Olten-Lausanne, 1959).
[2] Cf *Atlas of the Early Christian World*, illus. 384, 385, 477, 541.
[3] Rowohlts deutsche Enzyklopädie (Hamburg, 1957).
[4] Kröners Taschenausgaben 211 (Stuttgart, 1959).

places one must be prepared for the basic assumption of all Byzantinists: that everything of any note began in the Byzantine world and was later imitated and in some way spoilt by the West. N. H. Baynes and H. St. L. B. Moss, *Byzantium, An Introduction to East Roman Civilisation*,[1] uses roughly the same headings and covers the same ground much more briefly, occasionally with a touch of humour, particularly in the treatment of the age of the 'galloping bishops'.[2]

For Byzantine art one should see the wonderful photographs of Max Hirmer in David Talbot Rice, *The Art of Byzantium*, with 44 colour plates and 196 illustrations.[3] By the same author, and with roughly the same selection of pictures, *Art of the Byzantine Era*.[4] (The larger volume is now out of print.) There is a limit to the number of accounts of Byzantine art one can read; John Beckwith, *The Art of Constantinople*,[5] with excellent illustrations, happens to be my choice.

**The Celtic World, Celtic Art.** An introduction is essential. Nora K. Chadwick, *Celtic Britain*, 67 plates, 27 drawings, is an obvious starting point.[6] I think that narrow-gauge medievalists like myself, who have never learnt a Celtic language, have to be humble. With the help of Mrs Chadwick's chapters 6 and 8 on the poetry, art and church-life of the island Celts one begins to appreciate what a civilisation was swamped by our Germanic forebears. There is a reflection of this in Old and Middle English poetry, in the Anglo-Saxon elegies, the *Dream of the Rood* and in *Sir Gawain*. Continental Germanic poetry is interesting and can be exciting, but is devoid of mystery and totally lacking in atmosphere by comparison. Many readers will find Mrs Chadwick's urbane scholarship too exacting for them, and prefer the enthusiasm of Ludwig Bieler in *Ireland, Harbinger of the Middle Ages*.[7] Any student interested in Celtic loan-words in Germanic (*Glocke, Geisel, Amt*), Irish missionaries, '*libri scottice scripti*' on the Continent, 'Schottenklöster' in S. Germany – would do well to study both the text and the illustrations here. The Celtic 'bell' (*Glocke*), for instance, is here for him to see as an object. Excellent as Bieler's reproductions may be, one will not want to forego scrutiny of the facsimile editions of the *Book of Durrow*, the *Book*

---

[1] Oxford, 1948; Paperbacks, no. 16, 1961.
[2] Chapter on 'The Byzantine Church', p. 92.
[3] Kastner & Callwey, Munich (London, 1959).
[4] World of Art Paperback (London, 1963).
[5] Phaidon, London, 1961.
[6] Ancient Peoples and Places, xxxiv (London, 1963).
[7] O.U.P. 1963; German edition, Urs Graf, Olten and Lausanne, 1961.

*of Kells* and the *Lindisfarne Gospels.*[1] As is well known, Celtic and Northumbrian art does not represent the real world realistically. It has other aims.

This chapter must not become a series of jottings on famous illuminated manuscripts. Anticipating a good deal of what is to be said in the next few pages, I should like to insert a note here on David Diringer, *The Illuminated Book, its History and Production.*[2] This work of 524 pages is already the fourth in a series dedicated to the history of the book which the author *intends* to write. To me this one volume is a masterpiece of organisation, the like of which I have not encountered before. It is, however, a work of sheer compilation, alarming in its naïve objectivity. (It was the subject of a fairly crushing review by the Director of the Warburg Institute, but I think it is found useful there.) So that one may have a conception of the scale and the style of this work, I mention that on the subject of the Manesse manuscript of our Minnesänger he writes fourteen lines,[3] two-and-a-half of which run: 'There are one hundred and thirty-seven full-page miniatures, including hunting scenes and similar outdoor amusements, which are useful as studies of costume, but otherwise of little interest.' He offers four *aide-mémoire* pictures as plate III, 36 where III refers to chapter III, 'Hiberno-Saxon, Carolingian and Ottonian Illumination', while 36 is the thirty-sixth plate devoted to this chapter. More human, readable and, by contrast, cricitical is J. A. Herbert, *Illuminated Manuscripts.*[4] In any monograph on illuminated manuscripts one will encounter something approaching the 'hundred best books'. It is fortuitous that my own notes on the so-called *Codex Rossanensis* (sixth or seventh cent.? Byzantine) were made from this book. I have reminded myself in them that 'anyone interested in Hartmann von Aue's treatment of the Parable of the Good Samaritan in his Prologue to *Gregorius* must take into account the representation in early Byzantine art'.

The Good Samaritan is represented by Christ himself, three distinct phases of the story [in] one undivided miniature. Christ, assisted by an

[1] *Book of Durrow* (Codex Durmachensis, Trinity College Dublin, 2 vols, 1960); *Book of Kells* (Codex Cenannensis, ibid. 3 vols, 1950–1); *Lindisfarne Gospels* (B.M. Cotton, Nero D IV, 2 vols, 1956–60) – all published by the Urs Graf Verlag, Olten, Lausanne, Freiburg.
[2] London 1958, (quoted above) second edition, London, 1967.
[3] p. 191.
[4] Connoisseur's Library (London, 1911).

angel, tends the wounded man. . . . The second and third scenes are combined in the 'continuous' method, our Lord being depicted at the same time leading a mule, on which the wounded man is seated, and giving money to the innkeeper.[1]

For anyone wanting to know other than Western European and Byzantine styles, the first advice is to keep to familiar subject matter. It is fascinating to see medieval Christian art in its 'Egyptian' or **Coptic** translation. I recommend the illustrated catalogue of an exhibition held 3 May to 15 August, 1963, again in the Villa Hügel: *Koptische Kunst, Christentum am Nil*,[2] 452 pages of text (history of the Church, of art and of civilisation generally in Egypt), 16 coloured plates, plan of Alexandria and entries concerning 625 exhibits (arranged: Hellenistic, Coptic Egypt; Nubia, Ethiopia). **Armenia**: The treatment of Christian subjects in Armenian art in Diringer;[3] of secular subjects in Fréderic Macler, *L'enluminure arménienne profane*,[4] 59 plates, 309 illustrations: there are illustrations from four Alexander romances. We made one passing reference to **Mithraic art**;[5] see the chapter on Mithraic art in Franz Cumont, *The Mysteries of Mithra*.[6]

The art of the **Continental Germanic** peoples. Here I single out the difficult problems of Germanic *ornamental design* and *figure drawing*. At the level of art history they seem soluble; as evidence of cultural history they remain to tempt us into all kinds of fanciful guess-work. The difficulty is to know what meanings are to be attached to things purchased, taken as booty, copied. The owner in each case no doubt ascribed meanings to whatever he recognised. Let us begin with the **Goths** who until recently were thought to be the only Germanic people with art forms of any notable æsthetic value.

From *Roman art* was derived the motif of the eagle with spread wings . . . which in a purely two-dimensional heraldic stylisation is the basic pattern of a definable group of Gothic brooches. For the bird of prey [on the other] hand with its hooked beak we have to look much

[1] Herbert, op cit. p. 25; facsimile edition: *Il codice purpureo di Rossano*, ed. Antonio Muñoz (Rome, 1907), plate xii.

[2] Kuratorium des Villa Hügel e.V., Essen–Bredeney. An alternative work: Klaus Wesel, *Koptische Kunst, die Spätantike in Ägypten* (1963).

[3] Op. cit. plate ii 33 ff.

[4] Paris, 1928.

[5] p. 78.

[6] English translation of the 2nd French edition (Dover Books, 1956) pp. 209–20.

*further to the East*. It begins to settle towards the end of the fourth century as a marginal decoration on the head and base-plates of Gothic brooches. These bird heads are importations from the *neo-Scythian art of Siberia*, and may have come with the Huns to South Russia. The same may be said of some decorative formulæ which are really *Far Eastern* in origin: the Locust motif and the S-shaped brooch from Chinese art of the Han dynasty.

This quotation is from Wilhelm von Jenny's chapter on Germanic Archæology in *Germanische Altertumskunde*, edited by Hermann Schneider.[1] With this objective statement of art-historical facts contrast: 'archæology has never yet attempted to arrive at a systematic interpretation of so-called zoomorphic ornamentation (*Tierornamentik*), nor to infer its magical significance from a study of ornamental forms.' It is in this strain that Joachim Werner writes in an essay entitled 'Tiergestaltige Heilsbilder und germanische Personennamen'.[2] It seems to me to be a highly questionable undertaking to correlate *name-giving* as we find it in Germanic heroic poetry and a 'magical' interpretation of *animal forms* (on ornaments worn by Germanic thanes), on an assumption that both were intended to hedge their bearers against the consequences of their heroics. Similarly I can see no real connection between decorative animal motifs on finery and useful objects, and pre-Christian beliefs as these are inferred (not this time from name-giving but) from burial rites and funerary offerings. This is what one finds in Édouard Salin's *La civilisation mérovingienne d'après les sépultures, les textes et le laboratoire*.[3] Can speculations on such lines ever yield useful results? Scarcely any, I should have thought, which could interest us as literary historians, perhaps as folk-lorists.

What do the art historians say of *interlace* ornament? It is 'not an invention of the Germanic peoples, but is to be seen in association with a stock of motifs centering in the art of the South-East Mediterranean area, particularly Egypt'.[4] Further: 'despite the rich efflorescence of interlace ornament in Ireland, this cannot be looked upon as the antecedent of Continental Frankish interlace which in the mass is considerably earlier'.[5] This seems, whether Egypt (Alexandria) or

---

[1] Munich, 1939 (reprint 1951) pp. 463 ff. (My translation and italics.)
[2] *DVJSchr.* xxxvii (1963) 377 ff.
[3] 4 vols (Paris, 1950–59), particularly vol iv, ch. 29.
[4] Wilh. Holmquist, *Kunstprobleme der Merowingerzeit* (Stockholm, 1939) p. 295.
[5] Ibid. p. 296.

Syria is put forward as the home of interlace, to be the verdict of the art historians. The origins of the decorative motifs which we perhaps tend to associate instinctively with Irish manuscripts, are to be sought in the Eastern Mediterranean: both the models and the 'inspiration'. This is an idea which we find it difficult to assimilate, I think. (Perhaps the story of the Irish missions, which comes so near the beginning of things as we encounter them in literary studies, has suggested a wrong chronology.) This seems now to be further confirmed by the Sutton Hoo treasure,[1] which is characterised as a last flourishing of pre-Christian (Anglo-) Saxon art in the middle of the seventh century. Interlace decorations and animal motifs appear here in a perfection of design and workmanship which owe nothing to (are earlier than) the famous Irish or Northumbrian illuminated manuscripts.[2]

This makes it all the more painful, now that we have masterpieces of West Germanic art (Sutton Hoo) to set beside the brooches of the Goths, to read the verdict of the art historians on such drawings of the human figure as there are on Germanic monuments. The human figure is represented 'with a simple realism which shows something of the naïve powers of observation of children's drawings, and delight in depicting scenes of everyday life'.[3] The hope expressed some time ago[4] that we might recognise something rather more sophisticated than children's drawings, comes to nothing. Turning back to the drawings that Andreas Heusler reproduced in his splendid volume *Altgermanische Dichtung*,[5] one returns to first impressions. These are drawings by people who could not yet draw, not mysteriously remote and deeply symbolical images fashioned by artists who (like the Celts) did not want to represent the human figure. Even the best works, the *Franks Casket* and later work on runic stones,[6] show that Charles the Great was right. For the pictorial representation of Christian subjects, for Old and New Testament scenes and for hieratic images he imported artists from the Mediterranean area, often Greeks. There was work for

---

[1] *The Sutton Hoo Ship Burial, A Provisional Guide* (B.M. Trustees, 1947), 22 plates, 18 maps and, drawings, and *Handbook* (1968) superseding the *Guide*.
[2] Cf Margaret Rickert, *Painting in Britain: The Middle Ages*, Pelican History of Art, vol. Z.5 (London, 1954) 12 ff.
[3] R. Hamann-Maclean, *Frühe Kunst im westfränkischen Reich* (*Merowingische Kunst, karolingische Kunst, romanische Kunst* (Leipzig, 1939) p. 5.
[4] Cf p. 89.
[5] Illus. 35, 59.
[6] Cf Sven B. Jansson, *The Runes of Sweden* (Stockholm, 1962); Engl. transl. by P. G. Foote (London, 1962).

them to do in the kingdom of the Franks. **Pre-Carolingian Art**. I think this is best left to the specialists.[1]

**Carolingian Art**. Leitschuh's[2] is – in theory – far and away the best work for our purposes, but very few libraries have it. He considers the pictorial repertory of Carolingian and Ottonian art, with many cross-references to contemporary authors. What one misses is good reproductions; we have come to expect them. The volume of plates in *Das erste Jahrtausend*[3] is the handiest work to have at hand to supplement Leitschuh, while Beckwith's volume (above) is self-contained. Roger Hinks' *Carolingian Art, a study of early medieval painting and sculpture in Western Europe*,[4] is useful. It is a relatively short book, making few concessions, however, in respect of art history; it devotes a good deal of space to problems of Carolingian style and conventions of representation, both of the real world and of an idealised reality. Hinks interprets the relationship of 'Caesar' and 'David' pictures at some length, in a sense just about the opposite of what I said myself.[5] He considers the most important 'Davids' of Carolingian art to be imperial portraits, and treats them under the heading 'effigy', and speaks of 'disguises'. He invokes no texts in support of his contentions, beyond the nickname 'David' used by Charles the Great. This is, I think, inadequate. In David pictures he also sees Frankish crowns and regalia.[6] In other matters than these I find myself in agreement. Hinks too believes that the fish symbol (but also the lamb and the peacock, the latter a symbol of immortality) were never as popular in the West as in the East: 'the comparatively straightforward, rationalistic, and practical minds of the Frankish theologians had less use for these mystical fetishes than their Byzantine brethren'.[7] One sees, however, only slight traces of familiarity with Frankish theologians in this book. The sections devoted to the æsthetic of Carolingian art are valuable.

**Ottonian Art**. Reluctantly I decided that it would be hazardous in a book of this modest scope, and lead to confusion, if I were to refer to some of the more famous manuscripts by their conventional names.

---

[1] Cf *Vorkarolinigsche Miniaturen*, ed. by E. Heinrich Zimmermann (Verein für Kunstwissenschaft), 4 large portfolios (Berlin, 1916).

[2] See pp. 309 ff, title and an indication of the contents of this manual.

[3] See p. 326.

[4] Michigan, 1935; Ann Arbor Paperback, 1962.

[5] pp. 102 ff and 129–.

[6] Steger in *David Rex et Propheta* (see p. 125), does not.

[7] Op. cit., p. 155.

They are often resounding and memorable names, but it is my experience that they become seriously confused, and one finds oneself
asking whether Henry II's *Book of Pericopes* is the same as his *Gospel
Book* (and his *Sacramentary*).[1] From an *Evangeliary of Otto III* (cod. lat.
monac. 4453) one might cite a 'portrait of the Emperor with personifications of Rome, Gallia, Germania and Slavonia' that would seem for
all the world to be the picture reproduced by Schwietering in his
illus. 14. It is not. The two can be seen together in illustrations 84 (our
plate 14a) and 85 in Beckwith, in a useful 'compare and contrast'
juxtaposition. The three main centres of Ottonian art are traditionally
specified as **Reichenau** (Lake Constance), **Regensburg** and **Salzburg**.
The designation 'Reichenau School' will be found both in scholarly
monographs and in works prepared for a wider public, for instance in
Albert Boeckler's *Deutsche Buchmalerei vorgotischer Zeit*.[2] It is now
doubted by some scholars whether 'Reichenau School' is a valid
designation. Rather than state the grounds for hesitation, I quote from
a German scholar seeking to 'place' specific works in the present
situation of insecure co-ordinates. In *Ottonische Buchmalerei*,[3] an
extremely handsome, slim volume which it is a delight to have by one,
Peter Metz introduces the *Evangeliary of Otto III* (codex lat. monac.
4453) and the *Book of Pericopes of Henry II* (clm 4452)[4] as follows:

'The pictorial decoration of these two works is among the best and the
finest of their period, indeed of the whole of the pictorial art of the
Middle Ages. . . . Other works of the period show the same style. The
oldest of the works [belonging to this group] was also produced for an
Emperor Otto, but for Otto II. It is the Evangeliary in the Aachen
Cathedral Treasury which we call after the donor, Monk Liuthar,[5]
after whom this whole 'stylistic' group of manuscripts is also called.
The style was certainly to be found over a wide area. Where it was
originally evolved cannot be established with certainty, probably in the
South-West German-Lothringian area. We have been in the habit of
looking upon the Abbey of Reichenau on Lake Constance as the
original home of this style, and indeed as the place of origin of our two

---

[1] Beckwith's illustrations 89 and 92–97 show pictures from these books plus one
other. It is this *other* manuscript (the Gospel of Abbess Uota of Niedermünster)
which contains the famous Crucifixion group (with *Vita* and *Mors* beside the
Cross); Schwietering's plate II wrongly ascribes this picture to the Sacramentary
of Henry II.

[2] Die Blauen Bücher, 1959.      [3] Hirmer Verlag, Munich, 1959.

[4] See immediately above.      [5] On Liuthard and Liuthar, see p. 324, n. 3.

sumptuously appointed manuscripts. The place [wherever it was] must have been an artistic centre of outstanding importance, such as one would not seek elsewhere than in the West of the Empire.'

The subject 'Reichenau or not?' has recently been critically reviewed by C. R. Dodwell and D. H. Turner.[1] These two works (Otto III's *Evangeliary*, Henry II's *Book of Pericopes*), in date about 998–1012, were dedicated works, in the sense explained in our Introductory Survey.[2] They were dedicated to Bamberg Cathedral. (The dates of the 'Good Bishop Günther' of the *Ezzolied* are 1057–1065.)[3]

In the case of the **Codex Egberti** the question 'Reichenau or not' seems particularly important. I should like to recommend the 'reading' of this manuscript most strongly; it is available in a full-facsimile edition which university libraries should have.[4] 'It offers the first complete, and at the same time the most comprehensive pictorial cycle in German book illustration devoted to the life of Christ. It deserves to be called the most splendid achievement of Ottonian painting', the editor writes.[5] The authorities agree in this verdict on the quality of the paintings. It would therefore seem important to decide whether this volume, written and illuminated, as a dedicatory picture tells us, for Egbert, Archbishop of Trier (977–993), by 'Keraldus (and) Heribertus Augigenses'[6] originated in Trier, in Reichenau or elsewhere.[7] See plate 19b. One distinguished German authority seems to have changed his mind more than once. I said one should *read* this manuscript: why not? The text pages are all there in the facsimile edition, and written in a clear script. And now the pictures: the harmonising of the *picture cycle* and the *pericopal readings* seems to have presented some 'editorial' difficulties, which means that the cycle was not evolved for just this selection of readings. Some of the pictures of this manuscript have often

---

[1] In *Reichenau Reconsidered*, Warburg Trust Survey, II (London, 1965). The present attitude seems to be one of disbelief in the Reichenau itself as the home of the 'Reichenau style'. The famous mural paintings of Oberzell do not warrant this precise localisation and the hypothesis of a 'school'.

[2] Above, p. 26.

[3] See again p. 27, where we discussed the Bishop's interest in art and literature. See Beckwith, illus. 88, 89, 93, 94, 96.

[4] *Codex Egberti der Staatsbibliothek Trier*, 2 vols (a volume of commentary and the facsimile proper), ed. Hubert Schiel (Alkuin Verlag, Basel, 1960).

[5] Op. cit. p. 11. See our plates 20 a, b, 21 a, b, 22 a.

[6] Augigenses = 'of Reichenau', see Beckwith, illus. 82, our plate 19 b.

[7] Beckwith's illus. 80, 82 are from this MS, which he states to be from 'Reichenau or Trier'.

been reproduced in art books and art histories, particularly the 'Descent from the Cross and the Entombment' (in *one* combined illustration). See plate 21b. It is indeed a memorable picture, about which I have a word to add. The editor of the facsimile volume reminds us that according to Künstle,[1] the miniatures are believed to be the first to offer a pictorial representation of the Descent from the Cross, in closest agreement with the words of Holy Scripture'. This *may* be the first representation of this scene in Western art, but far from being in closest agreement with the Gospel text, it appears rather to contradict it. According to John xix *Joseph alone* 'took the body'. Joseph and Nicodemus undertook the burial. What made me first investigate this matter is the unsatisfactory account of the episode in the Old Saxon *Heliand*. The poem is about a hundred and fifty years *earlier* than this picture (said to be the first of its kind). It struck me that the poet could not have written so unsatisfactorily if he had known such a picture, or (even more important) if he had kept to the source he had been using, namely the Gospel Harmony of Tatian. The latter seems to be the source for the iconography in which Joseph *and Nicodemus* remove Christ's body; of that more in a moment. The *Heliand*-poet writes (in Fitte LXVIII; I italicise for clarity):

Then he [Joseph] went to the 'gallows' where he found the Son of God, the body of his Lord. *He took it* from the Cross, freed him from his nails, received him into his arms . . . wrapped him in linen cloths . . . [suddenly Nicodemus who has not been set on his way with his spices is also there, as follows] . . .
*he* carried him there where *they* had with their hands hewn out a burial place; when *they* had buried him according to the custom of the land . . .

What has happened here is that the poet has gone back to his canonical Gospel, and so missed the opportunity which Christian art seized upon, but evidently as yet not in the land of the Franks. The iconography must, I think, in origin be Syrian, like the Tatian Harmony itself. The latter is a *mosaic* of the four gospels (i.e. not a Gospel Harmony as we now understand it, with the four Gospels printed in parallel). In the section dealing with the Deposition, part of the text according to St John is dropped, with the result that *acceperunt* (John xix 40) takes on the

[1] *Ikonographie der christlichen Kunst*, 1 476 ff – see also below, p. 342.

meaning, or can be read as meaning, '*they* received the body' (from the Cross), while *tulit corpus* (John xix 38 = *Joseph* took the body from the Cross) is suppressed. I write the passage out.[1]

Pilatus autem mirabatur, si iam obiisset, et accersito centurione interrogavit eum si iam mortuus esset? Et cum cognovisset, iussit reddi corpus. Venit autem et Nicodemus, qui venerat ad Ihesum nocte primum, ferens mixturam mirrae et aloes quasi libras centum. Acceperunt autem corpus Ihesu et ligaverunt eum linteis cum aromatibus, sicut mos Iudaeis est sepelire (= Mark xv 44–45 + Matth. xxvii 58 + John xix 39–40).

And Pilate marvelled if he were already dead, and calling unto him the centurion, he asked him whether he had been any while dead. And when he knew it of the centurion [so far Mark; — Matthew] he commanded the body to be delivered [i.e. to Joseph]. [John:] And there came also Nicodemus (which at first came to Jesus by night) and brought a mixture of myrrh and aloes about an hundred pound weight. Then took they the body of Jesus and wound it in linen clothes with the spices as the manner of the Jews is to bury.

Looking carefully at this picture in the *Codex Egberti* one will therefore quietly correct Künstle: 'following more closely the mosaic text of the Tatian *Diatessaron* than the Gospel of St John' or 'using a Syriac model' (this latter being, of course, no more than a suggestion).

The *Codex Egberti* offers over fifty pictures, however. We have already had something to say about Peter's Cock perched above the Column of the Flagellation (80 v), and the Peacock as waterspout at the pool of Siloah (*Aqueductus*, 50 r),[2] see plates 20a and 22a. I now single out three further points. (*a*) The pictures form a sequence. We had observed that in the Bearing of the Cross (by Simon, a Cyrene, 83 v) the cross is portable, scarcely more than a processional cross. In the following, otherwise realistic picture one sees Christ crucified on an enormous, monumental cross in gold, and it is this cross one sees in the next pictures (e.g. the Deposition). How was such a break in 'narrative' continuity explained? (*b*) The two thieves are crucified on Tau-crosses, with their arms bent backwards over the horizontal beam,

---

[1] I have here had to follow E. Sievers' Vulgate Latin 'crib' to the Old High German translation of Tatian (Paderborn, 1892). The Old High German translation is more or less contemporary with, and possibly from the same monastery (Fulda) as *Heliand*.

[2] Cf pp. 134 f.

that is to say crucified otherwise than Christ; I would say that they were crucified 'in the Roman fashion' according to Isidore (in the same way as 800 years later the French Passion would say, 'à la vieille façon').[1] Stephaton is offering the bitter drink; Christ is in the posture of an *orans*. After the lance thrust (84 v) Christ hangs dead on the Cross, a clear *serpens* (S). (c) A detail which I should have liked to pursue further: Medieval representations of the shepherds guarding their sheep occasionally show a tower, a *turris gregis*, see our plate 20b. Schwietering offers another example in his fig. 24. It seems in fact to occur fairly often. In his commentary on the *turris* in the Codex Egberti (13 r) the modern editor quotes a passage in the *Onomasticon* of Jerome, under 'Bethlehem': *et mille circiter passus procul* [Bethlehem] *turris Ader, quae interpretatur 'turris gregis'*. We cannot follow up this etymology. The architecture of the tower is interesting, but I gather that the art historians are not inclined to see representations of actual buildings (in Bethlehem, for instance) in medieval miniatures. After these somewhat detailed notes on the *Codex Egberti* we must simply drop the subject. Practically every medieval illustrated manuscript offers some detail that leads one to look for further elucidation.

With further reference to Liuthar, Keraldus, Heribert, see Evardo Aeschlimann's *Dictionnaire des Miniaturistes du Moyen Age et de la Renaissance*,[2] with 132 plates. There are many names of scribes and of artists to be found in medieval manuscripts, the majority belonging however to the Byzantine area, or dating from only the later Middle Ages. In the work just quoted our Middle High German poet Hugo von Trimberg appears as an 'ouvrage', but that is a minor blemish.

Here, as a final remark under this heading, I should like to refer to the selected essays and papers of Paul Lehmann, *Erforschung des Mittelalters*.[3] These are an inexhaustible mine of information on the Middle Ages. I mention merely the essays on the Cathedral Library of Trier, on Judas Iscariot in the literature and art of the Middle Ages, on figural poems, on Hrabanus Maurus.[4]

## (b) ICONOGRAPHY

I. I give here the titles of iconographies of medieval art which I have used myself. (W. Molsdorf, *Christliche Symbolik der mittelalterlichen*

---

[1] Cf p. 306.    [2] Milan, 1940.
[3] 5 vols, Stuttgart, 1959–62.    [4] In order: i 321 ff, ii 229 ff, iii 60 ff, iii 198 ff.

*Kunst,* 2nd ed. (Leipzig, 1926) is one of many works which I myself have had to neglect; it was not easily accessible to me; a reprint is announced).

**Timmers:** J. J. M. Timmers, *Symboliek en Iconographie der christelijke Kunst,* Romen's Compendia (Roermond-Maaseik, 1947) 1125 pp., 137 figs., a bibliography.

**Künstle:** Karl Künstle, *Ikonographie der christlichen Kunst,* 2 vols (Freiburg i. Br., 1928).

**Réau:** *Iconographie de l'art Chrétien,* by Louis Réau, 6 vols: I *Introduction générale,* II *Ancien Testament,* IIb *Nouveau Testament,* III *Les Saints* (A–F, G–O, P–Z)=vol. III, 1, 2, 3 (Paris, 1955–9).

**Van Marle:** R. van Marle, *Iconographie de l'art profane* . . . 2 vols (The Hague, 1931–2).

It will have been noticed that I prefer to quote from Timmers, which is copious, reliable, handy, and reasonable in price. In Réau I have rarely found anything useful for my special purposes. Künstle and Van Marle are out of print.

II. Erwin Panofsky's *Studies in Iconology, Humanistic Themes in the Art of the Renaissance,*[1] contains a wealth of reproductions, an important methodological introduction and a series of model essays in iconological interpretation. In addition there is a certain amount on themes which interest the medievalist: chapter 3 on 'Father Time' (Chronos and Kronos=Saturn) for instance, or chapter 4 on 'Blind Cupid'. Much as I admire Panofsky's interpretation in the individual essays, I cannot get rid of the suspicion that the author looks upon poetry, particularly medieval poetry, as a treasury of quotations, from which the art historian may quote as he pleases. What he says about *Amor,* which he sees purely in the light of Latin and Romance tradition as a male figure, and what he says elsewhere[2] about the Apocrypha, the *Revelations* of St Bridget of Sweden, Three-Nail Crucifixes, the *Pietà* image, is rarely convincing for a literary historian.

III. Important essays written by art historians for the guidance of literary historians (which I do not presume to summarise) are: Wilhelm Messerer, 'Einige Darstellungsprinzipien der Kunst im Mittelalter'[3] (with 11 illustrations), and Wolfram von den Steinen, 'Der Mensch in der ottonischen Weltordnung'[4] with 19 illustrations, some of which I

---

[1] Princeton, 1939; now Harper Torchbooks, 1962.
[2] For instance in *Early Netherlandish Painting,* 2 vols (Cambridge, Mass., 1953).
[3] *DVJSchr.* XXXVI (1962) 157–78.          [4] Ibid. XXXVIII (1964) 1–23.

have referred to in this book. I refer again to Günter Bandmann's monograph, *Melancholia*[1] which contains a good deal about the medieval antecedents of Melancholia.

IV. Of the German translation by Godehard Schäfer of the famous 'Painters' Handbook of Mount Athos'[2] there is now a new edition: *Malerhandbuch des Malermönches Dionysios vom Berge Athos*.[3] 'The work of Dionysios is based in its essentials on the craft of the icon painters of the 18th century; but in many respects it derives from much earlier tradition.' The use of this work should be left to the Byzantinists.

## (c) MISCELLANEOUS NOTES

Here I touch briefly on a number of subjects which were to have been more fully treated in this book, but which in the end were all but excluded. The points covered can be recognised by the use of bold type; no particular logic should be sought in their sequence.

**Artist's Pattern-books.** I recall the remark made in the Introductory Survey: 'It has been observed that the drawings in pattern-books show a freedom of line' etc.[4] For that statement I was summarising the findings of Hans R. Hahnloser in his Introduction to *Das Musterbuch von Wolfenbüttel*.[5] (I translate):

The independence of the medieval artist is shown most clearly in the so-called sketch-book. The very character of the sketches – they are copies of models which are themselves again to serve as models – sets very narrow limits to . . . the artist's invention. Invention is limited to the choice of models, and certain added details in the copies made from these models. In both respects the pattern-book is superior to the finished work of art. The artist producing a work of art has to follow the iconography of his pattern [i.e. once this has been selected by a patron]; in preparing a pattern-book itself the artist makes a freer choice of the features to be included.

The best known example of a sketchbook is from the thirteenth century, the Album of Villard de Honnecourt.[6] We mentioned above his sketch of a Wheel of Fortune. According to Hahnloser the book

---

[1] Cf pp. 113 f, 123.    [2] Trier, 1855.
[3] Slawisches Institut (Munich, 1960); quotation from p. 5.
[4] Cf p. 60.    [5] (Vienna, 1929); quotations from p. 24.
[6] Cf H. Omont, *Album de V. de H., architecte du XIIIe siècle* (Paris, 1906); facsimile ed. by L. Browne, *The Sketch Book of V. de H.* (Bloomington, Indiana, 1959).

'must have passed through the hands of several masters'. Certainly earlier than this *Album* is a **pattern–sheet** on which D. J. A. Ross reported in an article, 'A late twelfth-century artist's pattern-sheet'.[1]

The manuscript *Vaticanus latinus 1976* contains two sheets of 'pictures which are quite unconnected [with the contents of the book]'. They contain drawings of Old Testament figures and Fathers of the Church whom the artist has not yet finally identified by attributes.[2] Ross considers this pattern-sheet to be late Romanesque and German. 'The existence of pattern-books has long been known... The present example is unique in being a pattern-sheet as opposed to a bound book.' Pattern-sheets of this kind will certainly have been the most usual form employed. It is understandable that scarcely any examples have come down to us. Ross gives information on a possibly analogous case of 'typical' pictures in a Syriac manuscript of the Bibliothèque Nationale. A recent publication (not yet including reference to Ross) is R. W. Scheller, *A Survey of Medieval Model Books.*[3]

On *Physiologus*-illustrations (often associated with Genesis-illustrations) and illustrated **Bestiaries** I have said virtually nothing. I recommend the scholarly and extremely lively introduction by T. H. White, *The Bestiary, A Book of Beasts, being a Translation from a Latin Bestiary of the Twelfth Century.*[4] The manuscript involved is Cambridge University Library MS II, 4 26. The edition offers the Bestiary text, more than 120 illustrations, ten pages of bibliography and a genealogical table of illustrated Bestiaries. Highly recommended, instructive and amusing.

I had promised further information on the subject of **Job** in the art and literature of the Middle Ages. It was not until the later Middle Ages that the West learnt of an apocryphal Job story, the *Testamentum Hiob.*[5] It is assumed that this was known to the Greek Christians before the fifth century. It seems to me to be little more than a vulgarisation of the canonical story, taking as its starting point the characterisation of Job as a *citharista* (Job xxx 31 and xxi 12, see p. 109). Job is, in the Old Testament, a munificent host. In the legend he becomes a **patron of musicians.** It is then only natural that in the legend the three comforters and Job's daughters are all turned into musicians (a reversal of the role

[1] *JWCI* xxv (1962) 119 ff.     [2] See above, p. 59.     [3] Haarlem, 1963.
[4] New York, 1954; Capricorn Book, 1960.
[5] Newly edited by Sebastian Brock as *Pseudoepigrapha Veteris Testamenti Graece* if (Leiden, 1966).

of those who 'pass by the way' and make the wretch by the roadside the subject of their song).¹ The most convenient access to this tradition is provided by G. N. Garmonsway and R. M. Raymo in their edition of the Middle English *Metrical Life of Job*.² They give a full summary of the Job legend as this is to be found in the *Testamentum Hiob*³ and edit the 183 lines of the Middle English text, with an introduction and commentary. They also reproduce three pictures treating Job as the patron of musicians in accordance with this tradition; one of them is in the Wallraf-Richartz Museum in Cologne, see our plate 12. A reference in the editorial material leads one to an earlier article by Kathi Meyer on 'Job as a Patron of Music'.⁴ According to this authoress, the four saints who became patrons of music (Job, John the Baptist, St Wilgefortis and St Cecelia) have 'so far as official sources are concerned' nothing to do with music. I myself should regard Job's words *versa est in luctum cithara mea* and the medieval designation (*citharista*) as being extremely official.⁵ More interesting are the hints given by Meyer that there may be a relationship between **Job** as a musician **and dancing**. This might in its turn be a relationship with the **Dance of Death**. Job is apparently represented as a musician on the title pages of manuscripts of the office *De defunctis*. I find this interesting, particularly because the musician in representations of the Dance of Death has hitherto been taken to be simply 'Death', or 'One of the Dead'. Moreover the Dance itself leading from life to the *charnel-house* (not Heaven or Hell) had not hitherto been properly identified. I am myself convinced that we have to distinguish between the Dance of Death and Dances of the Dead (at midnight in the cemetery, over the gravestones) and the Pied Piper legend.

In this book there has been little about the **initials** in illuminated manuscripts. I recommend Hermann Dembowski, *Initium Sancti Evangelii*,⁶ or Emile van Moé, *Illuminated Initials*, etc.⁷ At the very beginning of this book⁸ I referred to 'hybrid' compositions. I had in mind particularly illuminated initials, and a passage in Dembowski which shows that some scholars read more into initials than I would be

¹ Cf p. 109 ff.
² In *Early English and Norse Studies* presented to Hugh Smith (London, 1963) pp. 77 ff.
³ Pope Gelasius is reported to have sought to suppress the legend in 496.
⁴ *Art Bulletin*, XXXVI (1954) 21 ff.          ⁵ Cf p. 109.
⁶ Friedrich Lometsch Verlag, Kassel, 1959 = Die Arche 28.
⁷ London, 1950.          ⁸ Cf p. 3 and n. 1.

prepared to. 'The [medieval] initial spreads and unfolds, . . . it grows, until in the end it encloses a full page. The word becomes an image, a word-image . . . There is nothing of this kind in the art of late Antiquity.' This is common ground, but Dembowski fears that the initials of (say) the *Book of Kells* might remain mute. He quotes passages from a prayer which was written into a Psalter as a gloss, he believes, on a decorated initial: 'My God, whom every creature serves, every power obeys *etc.*' The medieval prayer names the animals which are represented in the decoration of the initial. All I can add to this is that there are initials which would have produced some queer prayers. I am not at all happy at the idea that we have to make initials *talk*. Are we to be reminded by decorative animal and human figures of the commonplaces of Christian verbal tradition? Are we also to *count* knots and intersections in order that we may discover mysterious symbolic references and turn them into orderly statements about the Trinity, the Four Rivers of Paradise and so on? I think not. In so far as counting was done, and numerical significations were asserted in the Middle Ages, these were mystifications and not mysteries, or they were witticisms of the kind we find in the *Joca monachorum*. Interlace was interlace, and if it was anything before that, it was probably basket-work or filigree. Two-dimensional interlace designs are decorative space-fillers, meant to delight, to deceive and bewilder the eye. They have no more meaning than the acanthus leaves, urns, drapes and scrolls that fill the spaces in a modern design. Discursive interpretations of any of these are a random mix that sets with a thin crust. *Animal* motifs may seem to demand an interpretation of some kind, but if we have no idea what it should be, it is better to say so. Human figures and animals associated with them may be a different matter; but again generalisations are not possible. There are, however, cases where figures in initials form a recognisable programme, for instance in the St Albans Psalter. According to C. R. Dodwell[1] the historiated initials in the St Albans Psalter can be related to a specific *monastic* interpretation of the Book of Psalms, that of Smaragdus, *Diadema monachorum*, ninth century.

Having warned against counting elements in a merely decorative or space-filling pattern I feel bound to add a brief statement on '**numerical composition**', belief in which as a principle observed by medieval poets has for some time dominated medieval German studies. Clearly

---

[1] *The St Albans Psalter*, Studies of the Warburg Institute, xxv (London, 1960) 184 ff.

there are important medieval works in 33 and even 3 × 33 sections, and other works in which one may recognise more than mere symmetry – a playing with numbers. But in so many instances I have found that I neither read texts and scan verse, nor count, divide and factorise numbers as others do.[1] Unless a work has numbers, ages, ages of man, or the mystical numbers themselves as its subject, numerical analysis is futile. What medieval writers write about numbers is a contribution to the *subject* numbers. It is a huge subject, but it does not cover everything. The numbers resulting from our own counting (based on our recognition of divisions in subject matter) are not significant as numbers, but are evidence of our recognition of shape, form, proportions. Anything that has a proper shape will yield numbers for those who elect to count, for the simple reason that shapes are tested in the making. I have ceased to believe that even the subdivision of the *Heliand* into numbered *fittes* and the mysterious divisions of *Parzival* into blocks of thirty lines have anything to do with numbers at all. They are more likely to reflect the standard sizes of wax tablets and sheets of parchment (the medieval equivalent of DIN).

This leads me to a final reference to the latest of the art historian's **source–books**, which deals with art in the British Isles, Otto Lehmann-Brockhaus, *Lateinische Schriftquellen zur Kunst in England, Wales und Schottland vom Jahre 901 bis zum Jahre 1307.*[2] Of the (so far) five volumes, volume III is devoted to 'the artist and his craft'. In that volume, chapter 5 assembles 'allegorical interpretations', chapter 6 'the work of the artist as it is described in visions, dreams' *etc.*, chapter 8 'interpretations of architecture'. The literary historian will find very little to interest him, despite these promising headings.

Hans Naumann's *Deutsche Kultur im Zeitalter des Rittertums* and Hermann Gumbel's *Deutsche Kultur vom Zeitalter der Mystik bis zur Gegenreformation*[3] can still be consulted with profit, for their excellent illustrations, and indeed for a good deal of their text and commentary. I mention them because they are in our libraries. As will be known, Hans Naumann wrote some very curious things in the thirties, but it

[1] Starting with the difference between Plenio's and Heusler's scansion, any line may be given the value x *or* x + 1; add that one may count lines *or* couplets, and every number up to 999 is demonstrably 'significant'.

[2] Publications of the Zentralinstitut für Kunstgeschichte, 5 vols (Munich, 1955–).

[3] In the Handbuch der Kulturgeschichte, ed. Heinz Kindermann (Potsdam, 1938 and 1936 respectively) see p. 23 n. 1.

requires no particular effort to recognise and ignore the notorious passages. It is in fact instructive to read even his more outrageous statements, about the Romanesque (which he claimed as the German style), and the Gothic (to which he thinks that France particularly moved with a febrile and unseemly haste).

Only one final note and then I have finished. When I look back and consider what art-historical note used to tease me by its elusiveness, it was something on the *Hortus Deliciarum* – that work which scores so many illustrations in our handbooks, and seems to have a picture for each medieval theme as it crops up. What a storehouse of medieval lore it once was, one can gather from the title-page of an old monograph of 1818 (in fact a very 'thin' work): 'Herrade of Landsberg, Abbess of Hohenburg or St Odilien in Alsace, in the twelfth century; and her work, the *Hortus Deliciarum*, A contribution to the history of sciences, literature, art, costume, arms and customs in the Middle Ages'.[1] During the siege of Strassburg in 1870 the manuscript was destroyed. There are copies and tracings by Comte A. de Bastard and others in the Bibliothèque Nationale. Today one uses and quotes the edition of A. Straub and S. Keller,[2] where some of the original pictures are shown as they were traced by different hands. The *Hortus* contained a good deal more: 'un recueil de morceaux choisis dans toutes les branches des connaissances humaines, tirés de l'Écriture Sainte, des Péres de l'Église ... le tout entremêlé de gracieuses poésies de sa composition, dont quelques-unes en musique, car Herrade était poète et musicienne; le tout illustré de nombreuses miniatures'.[3] At the end of the volume there was a *Rithmus de Monte Hohenburg*, a *De contemptu Mundi* poem and a 'school portrait' showing the sixty sisters. The pictures in the edition of Straub-Keller exercise such a fascination that one all too readily forgets how much was lost to us in the bombardment of Strassburg.

My very last word is one of apology for my lack of system. How else could I have spent scores of hours in the Warburg Institute and not discovered that there is an article by Saxl himself on the *Hortus*, in his *Lectures*, pp. 245–54, as I was, with all possible tact, finally reminded.

[1] Chr. M. Engelhardt, *Herrade von Landsperg, Äbtissin zu Hohenburg*, etc.
[2] Strassburg, 1899, text volume and volume of plates.
[3] Ibid. Introd. p. vi.

# INDEXES

Of the following Indexes only those devoted to Biblical Quotations and Plates are comprehensive. Generally names are excluded from the Index of Names if they occur once only in Appendix B to Chapter III (pp. 211–22) or in Chapter VI (pp. 322–48). A page reference in italics indicates a more important treatment, one in parentheses indicates a relevant passage in which the head-word itself does not occur. *N.B.* Cross-references are frequently made from one index to another.

## BIBLICAL QUOTATIONS[1]

    [1] Excluding the references on p. 143 (Notes on Hildegard of Bingen).
    [2] See in addition p. 267 n.3 (*a*), Isaiah cited as Jeremiah.

## PLATES
(text references)

Frequent reference is made in the text to illustrations in other works, as follows:
Beckwith, *Early Medieval Art*, illus. 25 (103 n.3), 34–40 (325 n.4, 326 n.5), 37 (105 n.1, 325 n.4), 43 (85 n.1), 47 (103 n.3), 47–9 (55 n.2), 53, 54 (315 n.1, 325 n.6), 60, 64 (55 n.2, 103 n.3), 65–7 (45 n.1, 85 n.1), 76 (85 n.1), 80, 82 (338 nn.6, 7), 84 (55 n.5, 102 n.1, 337), 85 (102 n.1, 337), 88, 89, 93, 94, 96 (327 n.1, 338 n.3), 91 (58 n.2), 92 (337 n.1), 97 (337 n.1), 100 (103 n.2), 202 (156 n.6).

Schwietering, *Deutsche Dichtung des Mittelalters*, plates I (103 n.3), II (337 n.1),
IV (160), V (136), VII (156 n.6); illus. 4–6 (316 n.1), 9 (156 n.1), 11 (45 n.1), 14
(55 n.2, 337), 24 (341), 32 (270 n.1), 35 (160), 36 (158 n.1), 38 (60 n.1), 37–9 (60
n.1), 58–62 (99 n.3), 63 (156 n.6), 75–80 (34 n.1), 83–5 (69 n.1), 105 (95 n.1), 130
(284 n.1).
Van der Meer and Mohrmann, *Atlas of the Early Christian World*, 173, 175 (134),
531, 533 (133), 384, 385, 477, 541 (330).
*Das erste Jahrtausend*, 334–5 (326 n.4), 386 (135), 410–11 (132).